The Miracles Of Our Savior

by
William M. Taylor

ISBN 1-58427-072-1

Guardian of Truth Foundation
P.O. Box 9670
Bowling Green, Kentucky 42102

PREFACE.

The generous reception given to my book on the Parables, has encouraged me to issue this companion volume on the Miracles of our Saviour, the rather, as there seemed to be room for a fresh treatment of these suggestive themes. The "Notes" of Trench, like everything which came from their author's hand, are able, thorough, scholarly, and will always hold a very high place in the estimation of students. But the homiletic element in them is meagre, and in these days, when the question how to turn biblical subjects to the best account, in the pulpit, for the meeting of the necessities of our modern life, is attracting so much attention, there is a call for something more direct and practical than the archbishop has supplied. The recent volume of Professor Laidlaw, of Edinburgh, is evidence of that call and will do much to meet it; but before it was issued the manuscript of the following pages had passed out of my hands, and arrangements had been made for their publication. On such a subject, however, there is no competition, but only co-operation between brethren.

My aim throughout has been expository and practical

rather than apologetic. What appeared to be needful in
the latter department I have put into the introductory
chapter, but in the remainder of the book I have given
more prominence to the parabolic teaching of the Miracles
as "signs," than to their reality and evidential value as works
of Divine power. Those who saw them performed might be
most impressed by the latter, but to us now the former has
become their most interesting feature and we have come to
regard them as forming themselves a part of the Revelation
which at first they introduced and endorsed. We do not
fully interpret them, unless we take this part of their significance into account, and therefore it has been my object
to view each as an illustration in the department of nature
of some feature of the Divine operation in the domain of
grace. That which some despise as spiritualizing, is in
truth only a fuller exposition.

I have not attempted any classification of the Saviour's
miracles, because after Westcott, that is quite unnecessary,
and because, taking each just as it comes and putting it in
its own surroundings we get a fuller view of its teaching
than we could otherwise obtain.

Let me only add, that such as it is, I lay the work " at
the feet of Jesus," praying that he may bless it to the edifi-
cation and strengthening of every reader.

                                    WM. M. TAYLOR.

5 WEST 35th STREET, NEW YORK.

CONTENTS.

CHAPTER   PAGE

INTRODUCTORY 1

I. THE BEGINNING OF MIRACLES AT CANA OF GALILEE 28

II. THE HEALING OF THE NOBLEMAN'S SON . 46

III. THE FIRST MIRACULOUS DRAUGHT OF FISHES 60

IV. THE HEALING OF THE DEMONIAC IN THE SYNAGOGUE 73

V. THE HEALING OF SIMON PETER'S MOTHER-IN-LAW. 86

VI. A SUNSET SCENE IN CAPERNAUM 98

VII. THE CLEANSING OF THE LEPER 110

VIII. THE CURE OF THE PARALYTIC. 122

IX. THE IMPOTENT MAN AT THE POOL OF BETHESDA 134

X. THE MAN WITH THE WITHERED HAND. . 148

XI. THE HEALING OF THE CENTURION'S SERVANT. 161

XII. THE RAISING OF THE WIDOW'S SON AT NAIN. 174

XIII. CURES OF THE DEAF AND DUMB 187

XIV. THE STILLING OF THE TEMPEST. . . . 202

XV. THE HEALING OF THE GADARENE DEMO-
NIAC. 212

XVI. THE RAISING OF JAIRUS' DAUGHTER. . . 230

XVII. THE HEALING OF THE WOMAN WHO
TOUCHED THE GARMENT 243

XVIII. TWO MIRACLES ON THE BLIND 256

XIX. THE FEEDING OF THE FIVE THOUSAND . 268

XX. CHRIST WALKING UPON THE WATERS. . 282

XXI. THE SYRO–PHŒNICIAN WOMAN 295

XXII. THE FEEDING OF THE FOUR THOUSAND. 307

XXIII. THE DEMONIAC BOY 319

XXIV. THE COIN FOUND IN THE FISH 331

XXV. THE TEN LEPERS 343

XXVI. THE OPENING OF THE EYES OF A MAN
BORN BLIND 355

XXVII. THE RAISING OF LAZARUS FROM THE
DEAD. 371

XXVIII. SABBATH DAY MIRACLES 387

XXIX. THE OPENING OF THE EYES OF BARTI-
MÆUS 400

XXX. THE WITHERING OF THE FRUITLESS FIG-
TREE. 413

XXXI. THE HEALING OF THE EAR OF MALCHUS. 426

XXXII. THE SECOND MIRACULOUS DRAUGHT OF
FISHES 438

THE MIRACLES OF OUR SAVIOUR.

I.

INTRODUCTORY.

"Ye Men of Israel, hear these words; Jesus of Naz-areth, a man approved of God among you by miracles, and wonders, and signs, which God did by him in the midst of you, as ye yourselves also know."—ACTS ii. 22.

IN entering upon a series of discourses on the records of the miracles of our Lord Jesus Christ which we find in the gospel narratives, some preliminary matters have to be considered.* My object in these discourses will be mainly exegetic and practical, rather than apologetic, yet we cannot, especially in these days, forget that the miracles of the New Testament are, by many, regarded as a serious hindrance to their acceptance of its truth, and so it is not possible to enter upon their study without taking notice of the objections which have been brought against them. But first let us clearly set before you the place which an investigation into the possibility and credibility of the gospel miracles occupies in the order of our exami-nation into the evidences of Christianity. It is often al-leged that the defenders of the faith are guilty of disingen-uousness, inasmuch as at one time they use the inspira-

---

* For a fuller treatment of the whole subject discussed in this lecture, see the author's "The Gospel Miracles in Their Relation to Christ and Christianity." Randolph & Co., New York.

1

tion and authority of Scripture for the purpose of proving the reality of the miracles; while at another, they
employ the reality of the miracles for the purpose of establishing the inspiration and authority of Scripture.
But this is not the case. Here is the order of our enquiry.
Taking up these ancient books, just as we would any
other productions, the first question that faces us is, by
whom were they written? The next, at what date was
each composed? and the next, have they come down to
us as their authors wrote them. Then having settled
these questions, as far as possible, there emerges this
enquiry: are they credible records of actual occurrences?
And it is at this point that the discussion over the miracles
begins. Objectors allege that the very presence of the
records of miracles in the gospel narratives gives a legendary character to them and takes them out of the category of veritable history; and defenders contend that
though miracles be apparently inconsistent with the uniformity of the operation of what are called natural laws, and
with the common and ordinary experience of men, yet
their performance by such an one as Jesus Christ approved
himself to be, is fully in accord with the fitness of things,
and has been so established by the weightiest testimony,
that it does not take away from the general trustworthiness of the narratives in which they are described.

Before we go further, therefore, we have to settle which
of these assertions is correct, that is to say, we have to
determine whether these miracles were real or not. Then,
supposing that we come to the conclusion that they were
real, the next question is: what do these miracles say
regarding the person and mission of Him by whom they
were performed? Thus there is no such vicious circle
followed by us as the assailants of the gospel allege, but
a strictly logical process is carried on, and each subject

of investigation comes naturally in the place which properly and of right belongs to it. But we cannot fairly be called to settle all of these questions when we are dealing with one, and so here I must be allowed to assume as having been already proved, that the four gospels were written by the men whose names they bear, that they were in existence before the close of the first century, and that they are to-day in our hands substantially as they were when they came from those of their authors.

Now with these things held as proved, let us open the New Testament and see if from what it contains we can work our way to the definition of a miracle. In his sermon on the day of Pentecost Peter describes the Lord Jesus to his hearers, as " a man approved of God among them by miracles, and wonders and signs, which God did by him in the midst of you, as ye yourselves also know," or as the revisers have more exactly rendered the words, " a man approved of God unto you, by mighty works," (or as they have it in the margin, powers,) " and wonders and signs which God did by him in the midst of you." Here you observe are three terms descriptive of one and the same kind of effects. The first ($\delta\upsilon\nu\acute{\alpha}\mu\epsilon\iota\varsigma$) signifies powers and looks specifically to the agency by which they were produced, an agency defined exactly in the words " which God did by him in the midst of you." The second ($\tau\acute{\epsilon}\rho\alpha\tau\alpha$) denotes wonders, and has regard to the state of mind produced on the spectator by the sight of them. They were of such a nature, so entirely out of the common course of things, and so thoroughly transcending merely human powers that the beholders of them were astonished at them. The third ($\sigma\eta\mu\acute{\epsilon}\iota\alpha$), signs, has particular reference to their significance as being the seals by which God authenticated him who wrought them ; and as being themselves also a symbolical or parabolical part of the revelation which he brought to men. A fourth term descriptive of the miracles occurs only in the gospel by John and there always on the lips of the Lord Jesus himself. It is (ἔργα) " works," as in the saying, " though ye believe not me, believe the works :" and again "if I had not done among them works which none other man did, they had not had sin." Taken in connection with the emphatic assertion of the deity of Jesus Christ, in the opening section of John's gospel, this description of the miracles is most suggestive, as indicating that what by men were regarded with wonder as indicating mighty power, were in the estimation of the Lord himself simply works requiring no more exertion at his hands than that which was common or ordinary with him as divine.

Now what were these doings of Christ that are thus variously denominated ? They were such as these : the stilling of a tempest by a word, the healing of disease by a touch ; the raising of the dead to life by a command ; the feeding of a multitude by the breaking to them of five loaves and two fishes ; the walking on the lake without any material support, and the like—all of them works which no merely human power could perform, no operation of the laws of nature, so called, can account for, and no legerdemain can either counterfeit or explain. Now in these particulars regarding them coupled with the words used by Peter, "which God did by him in the midst of you," we have the materials for a definition, and so we understand a miracle to be—a work out of the usual sequence of secondary causes and effects, which cannot be accounted for by the ordinary operation of these causes, and which is produced by the agency of God through the instrumentality of one who claims to be his representative, and in attestation of the message which as such he brings. Now let us observe very clearly from this definition, that a miracle is not a violation of what are popularly called the laws of nature. If from the operation of precisely the same secondary causes an effect entirely opposite to that invariably produced by them were to result, that would be a violation of a law of nature. But a miracle is not such an effect. It is a work due to the introduction and operation of a new cause. When a boy throws a stone up into the air there is a counter-action of the force of gravity, so far as the stone for the time is concerned; but there is no violation of the law of gravitation, for the simple explanation is, that another force generated in the will, and exerted by the muscular energy of the boy, has come into operation and performed its work, while the force of gravity is really as operative as it ever was. In like manner a miracle does not violate nature; but is the result of a new force coming in, to produce a new effect.

Neither, again, according to our definition, is a miracle the suspension of a law of nature. For recurring to the illustration which I have just employed, even while the stone thrown by the boy was ascending into the air the force of gravity continued, and the law of gravitation remained the principle on which the relation of bodies to each other in the universe is regulated. The suspension of any law throughout the universe, even for the briefest time, would, unless prevented in some way by Omnipotence, produce the most disastrous results. But a miracle is not such a suspension. It is the production in a single in-stance of a new effect, by the intervention in that instance of a new cause adequate to its production.

But at this point we are met by two very serious ob-jections, which must be answered and removed before we can go farther. It is alleged by many in these days that such an intervention is impossible; and David Hume affirmed, in his day, that even if such a thing as a miracle could be wrought, it would be impossible to prove that it had been performed. Let us look at each of these assertions, and the grounds on which they are made. First it is affirmed that such an intervention of a new cause, as is implied in our definition of a miracle, is impossible, inasmuch as the absolute uniformity of the operation of the laws of nature has been established by the investigations of scientific men. Now, I do not presume to deny the uniformity of the operation of the laws of nature, but I venture to ask two questions, the answers to which may throw a flood of light upon the matter in hand. What in this connection do we mean by "laws"? and what by "nature"? What do we mean here by laws? In his work on "The Reign of Law," the Duke of Argyll has enumerated no fewer than five senses in which the term "law" is used by good and reputable writers. But for our present purpose it will be sufficient to distinguish between the two which are most commonly confounded. In its physical sense a law is a convenient formula for the expression of the fact that certain antecedents are invariably followed by certain consequents. It is thus a human inference from the observation of a certain class of phenomena, and as Sir John Herschel long ago remarked, "the use of the word in this connection has relation to us as understanding, rather than to the universe as obeying certain rules." They are, as Dr. James Martineau calls them, "nothing else than bundles of facts," and so, as every one can see, they have no causal force in them. They do not, they cannot enforce themselves. But laws in the moral sense are ordinances to be obeyed; and so many are led to introduce that principle of obligation which has place in its meaning in the ethical department into its significance in the physical, and thus make the word denote ordinances which nature is bound to obey. But, as we have just seen, this is not the case. The laws of nature are simply the formulated expressions of the methods, so far as men have been able to discover them, in which the forces in nature work. And whence are these forces? If you put the question to science, she can give no answer. But in her doctrine of the conservation of energy, she tells us that the sum of the actual and potential energies in the universe is a constant and unalterable thing, unaffected by the mutual interaction of these forces; and in her doctrine of the correlation of forces, she teaches that one force may be transmuted into another; and so she prepares the way for the acceptance of the doctrine enunciated by Alfred Wallace, that all force is at last resolvable into will force, and that there is behind the operation of all secondary causes a sustaining, controlling, and guiding energy in the will of a supreme intelligence. Now in this view of the matter, what men call the force of gravity, is just the power of God putting itself forth in the regulation, according to certain principles, of the relation of material bodies to each other; and what they call electricity is the power of God exerting itself, on certain other conditions, and in certain other circumstances. The same is true of attraction and cohesion in chemistry, and in general that which in physical things makes a cause to be a cause, the *nexus* which secures that certain consequents shall always follow certain antecedents, is always and everywhere the power of God. Now, that being the case, where is the impossibility of a miracle, as we have defined it? If the uniformity of a law be sustained all the time by God, how can it be impossible for him, in a single instance, and for a purpose worthy of himself, to deviate from that uniformity? Must we believe that by the maintenance of these usually uniform modes of putting forth his power, the Deity has bound himself, in no circumstances and for no purpose whatsoever, to do anything different from what he has been commonly observed by men to do. If law be God's usual action, and miracle God's unusual action in exceptional individual cases, is not the one just as possible as the other?

But let us ask again what precisely we mean by "nature," in the phrase that has become so popular, "the laws of nature"? If it be restricted to merely physical phenomena, then it must be confessed that we have in these, taken by themselves, no experience of any variation in the uniformity of nature. But if within the domain of nature we include human nature, then we can no longer make any such admission. For in that we come into contact with a new sort of power, namely, that of the soul of man, which does continually intervene among the forces of nature, and either by combining some of them with others, or by the exercise of its own direct and immediate agency upon one or other of them, does produce effects out of the usual sequences of physical antecedents and consequents. All the triumphs of mechanics, of science, and of art, have been won through the bending by man of the forces of nature to his service We are constantly reaching results which the forces of nature, left to their own operation, never would have produced, and if we can do that, may not God do the same, in a higher degree and in a wider sphere; so as to produce effects that shall be not merely supernatural but also superhuman? The truth is that if we admit that God exists, and is in any intelligible sense the upholder and sustainer of all things, then there is no ground on which we can consistently say that miracles are impossible. Nature and the supernatural alike depend on the power

of God, and miracles are only manifestations in an unusual way of the same energy by which the common and ordinary processes of nature are maintained. So we see how those who repudiate the supernatural in the form of the miracles, have been driven by the force of inexorable logic, into either the agnosticism, which says it does not know anything about God, or the atheism which denies his existence altogether. But I enter into no argument with the apostles of these negations now. I merely note the fact that the denial of the possibility of miracles is closely connected with the darkness of these dreary voids, and repeat the affirmation that if we admit the existence and personality of God, as the governor of the universe, there is no longer any valid reason for denying that miracles are possible.

It may be said, however, that the doctrine of evolution which has lately found so much favor among scientific men, is conclusive against the possibility of such divine deviations from the usual order of things as we have described miracles to be. That doctrine, as you are aware, is to the effect that all things had their origin in a primordial germ, just as the tree has its origin in the seed, and that what we see and what we are, are the results of a process of development or growth. Now, in the first place, let it be noted that this hypothesis is held by some, who believe as we do in the existence and personality of God. They regard evolution as simply the divine method of creation. They believe that the primordial germ was called into existence, and that its development is superintended by, the divine intelligence. They admit also that the origin of life is to be attributed to the intervention of God. Now these admissions are no more than we require to establish the possibility of miracles, for they concede such a divine interposition as we have defined a miracle to be. But the hypothesis is held by others in an atheistic sense, and they use it for dispensing altogether with the agency of God in the universe. Now, in that form, we must affirm that it is altogether inadequate to account for the phenomena which the universe presents, for while it may be conceded that nature may in its several departments be so explained as to present a gradual development from the lower to the higher in these departments, yet there are gulfs in it which evolution cannot bridge. One of these is that which lies between dead matter and living creatures. Haeckel indeed believes in spontaneous generation as the origin of life; but though it would make much for his favorite hypothesis, Huxley has vigorously asserted that no case of real spontaneous generation has ever been established. But evolution declares that the forces now in operation are precisely the same as those which have been at work in all ages, and so if spontaneous generation does not occur now, there is a presumption amounting almost to certainty that it never occurred. Here then is a break in the chain of evolutionary continuity, requiring for the production of life such an intervention as a miracle is. A similar gulf exists between the highest of the lower animals and man as a self-conscious moral being, and as one has well said, " It is nothing but assumption on the part of science to lay the principle of continuity across these gulfs, and to conclude that this explains all, without the interposition of creative power." So with these gaps in the evolutionary process, as believed in by its adherents, gaps which cannot be filled up save by the interposition of some cause acting upon the chain from without, it is idle for its votaries to allege, as some of them do, that miracles are impossible. The appearance of life is a miracle, so far as evolution is concerned, as really as any of the mighty works of the Lord Jesus were miracles; and so they cannot consistently object to the possibility of their occurrence.

But passing now to the question of the credibility of miracles, we are met by the famous argument of David Hume, wherein he attempts to show that no amount of evidence can establish the truth of a miracle. That argument may be summarized under these two propositions, " It is contrary to experience that a miracle should be true, but it is not contrary to experience that testimony should be false," and the fallacy lurking under it is effectually exposed when we put the questions, *whose* experience? *whose* testimony? Is it my experience as an individual? or the experience of men generally? or the special experience of those who were contemporaries of the Lord Jesus Christ in Galilee and Judea, when he lived upon the earth? If it be my individual experience that is meant, that has no bearing on the case. If it be the experience of men in general, then of course it is contrary to that experience that miracles should be wrought, for if that were not so, miracles would be no miracles, since it is of their very essence that they should be out of the common course of nature as known and observed by men generally. But if it be the experience of the contemporaries of Jesus, *that* is the very matter about which the debate is, and to assert that miracles are contrary to that, is to take for granted the very thing to be proved. Again *whose* testimony, according to experience, is found to be false? Is it the testimony of such men as those who bear witness to the miracles of our Lord? Nay, verily, for the falsehood of such witnesses would be a greater moral miracle than any of the physical miracles of Christ. But that you may not think that I do injustice to this famous argument, let me quote two sentences of the essay in which it is advanced. The first relates to experience and the second to testimony. As to experience Hume says: "A miracle is a violation of the laws of nature, and as a firm and unalterable experience has established these laws, the proof against a miracle, from the very nature of the case, is as entire as any argument from experience can possibly be imagined, and if so, it is an undeniable consequence that it can not be surmounted by any proof whatever from testimony." But we repudiate the definition of a miracle as a violation of the laws of nature, and we beg you to notice how quietly Hume slips in the word "unalterable" before experience, thereby setting out with an assertion which involves in it a mere begging of the question, for if the experience which establishes the uniformity of the laws of nature is unalterable, there is an end of the matter. Moreover, how do we get to know what the general experience of men in respect to the course of nature is? Our own personal experience indeed comes from personal observation, but, as we have just seen, our individual experience has little bearing on the case, and for our knowledge of the experience of men in general we have to depend on human testimony; and so the whole force of the argument amounts to this, that we must investigate the testimony of those who bear witness to the genuineness of the miracles of Jesus as having been performed before their own observation, and see whether that be enough to sustain their allegation that such works were wrought by him. It simply puts testimony against testimony; the testimony of those who affirm that they saw these miracles, against that of those who were not present and who declare that in all their experience they never saw such wonders wrought by any one. To refuse to examine that testimony or to give it the weight which of right belongs to it on any such grounds as Hume has advanced, or indeed on any grounds whatever, is inconsistent with the very first principles of the inductive philosophy which is connected with the name of Bacon, and to the application of which we owe the whole of our modern scientific progress. These principles are, on the one hand, that nothing which claims to rest on facts is to be rejected without examination; and on the other, that everything which is proved to be inconsistent with facts is to be discarded, no matter how ingeniously it may be advanced or how eloquently it may be expounded. "It may be so," said Sir Isaac Newton, when some one brought to his attention a fact which at first-sight seemed to be inconsistent with his theory, "there is no arguing against facts." But the miracles are set forth as facts, and as such it is unscientific and unphilosophical to reject them without investigation.

But the second sentence which I shall quote from the essay of Hume relates to testimony, and is to this effect: "It is nothing strange that men should lie in all ages." Well, there have been untruthful men in all ages; but have such men been at all like those who give their attestation to the genuineness of the miracles of Christ? That is the question; and when we bring it to that point, we have no fear for the issue in the case of a candid and unprejudiced investigator. Thus this famous argument, where it is not a begging of the question, is simply an enforcement of the duty to examine most exactly and minutely the evidence by which the miracles of Christ are supported, that we may see whether or not that is sufficient to establish the assertion that he was "approved of God unto men, by miracles and signs and wonders which God did by him in the midst of them."

Now the first witness whom we call is Jesus Christ him

self. It is undeniable that he himself laid claim to the possession of supernatural power. Thus when the disciples of
John the Baptist came to him in their master's name to
ask, " Art thou he that should come, or do we look for
another ? " He answered : "Go and tell John what
things ye have seen and heard ; how that the blind see,
the lame walk, the lepers are cleansed, the deaf hear, and
the dead are raised." *   Again to the Jews he said: " I
have greater witness than that of John; for the works
which the Father hath given me to finish, the same works
that I do, bear witness of me, that the Father hath sent
me." †   And in the Gospel by John, we have at least three
other declarations to the same effect from his lips.‡   Now
we may fairly ask if such an one, as all through these narratives he is represented to be, would make such a claim,
if it was ill-founded and untrue ?   If it was, then he must
have been either a deceiver or have been himself deceived.
We cannot reject his testimony without impugning either his
moral integrity, or his intellectual soundness.   If he were
a deceiver, then he can no longer be regarded as a pattern of excellence, but rather as one of the basest of men,
since in Him the practice of dishonesty was combined with
the clearest perceptions of the right, the true, and the good.
Nay, more, if he were a deceiver, we have to face the
question, how came the purest morality that the world has
ever seen, from one who was himself dishonest ?   If we
admit that his miracles were genuine, then we have an
entirely homogeneous character in Jesus, and everything
in it is harmonious with all the rest ; but if we affirm
that in claiming to work miracles he knowingly declared
what was untrue, then we have in him a moral anomaly,

* Luke vii. 19-23.
† John v. 36.
‡ John x. 37, 38; xiv. 11; xvi. 24.

which is more inconceivable in the department of humanity, than a miracle is in that of physical nature, and having before proved that a miracle is possible, we may surely now draw the inference, that if such an one as Jesus was did actually declare that he performed miracles, it is far more consistent with right reason to suppose that he was speaking the truth, than it is to believe that he was uttering a deliberate and predetermined falsehood.

But if he was not a deceiver, was he the victim of delusion? Was he a visionary enthusiast, who believed that he possessed a power which he really had not? Now in answer to that I may simply say that no one can peruse these gospels without coming to the conclusion that, speaking of him now only as a man, the mind of Jesus was pre-eminently healthy, and that his intellect was admirably balanced. There is no evidence of the existence in him of a morbid exaggeration of any one faculty to the detriment of the rest. On the contrary there was in him a wonderful harmony of opposites. In point of intellectual ability he must be placed far above all the philosophers of antiquity; and in the matter of practical wisdom, not one of them may be compared with him. He looked all round every question, and saw, with unerring precision and at once, the principle by which it was to be settled. He was never carried away by impulse or moved by caprice, but his emotions rose out of his judgment and were as sound as their source. The proofs of this are to be found on every page of the gospels, to such an extent, that even at the sacrifice of their own consistency, those who refuse to admit his claims, are compelled to acknowledge the truth of all that we have said regarding him. Even Renan has said that "his admirable good sense guided him with marvellous certainty;" that "his leading quality was an infinite delicacy," and that "he laid with rare forethought the foundations of a church destined to endure." * Now we may safely ask, if such a man—judging him by no higher than a human standard—was likely to become the victim of his own hallucinations? Recollect that the narratives which declare that he claimed to work miracles do at the same time make manifest that he possessed what one has called "the most clear, balanced, serene and comprehensive intellect known to history," and then the dilemma appears as before. Either we must receive this description of his intellectual character and along with that acknowledge the truthfulness of his claim to work miracles; or if, on the ground of his suffering from delusion, we refuse to allow that claim, then we must reject the common idea of his intellectual soundness. We can not hold by both. So here again, we have to make our choice between the acceptance of physical miracles, and that of a psychological impossibility, and we do not hesitate a moment in determining which we shall accept. We accept Hume's criterion here and boldly affirm that the testimony of Jesus to his own miracles is of such a kind that its falsehood would be more miraculous than the miracles themselves. Nay, more, we declare that if such testimony is to be set aside, it will be impossible to establish anything by means of human evidence, and all history is utterly discredited.

So much for the testimony of Jesus himself. We proceed now to put the apostles upon the stand. But before asking them what they have to say, there are two preliminary facts which must be taken into account.

The first is, that they had perfect opportunities for investigating the wondrous works to the performance of

* Renan's "Life of Jesus," English People's Edition, pp. 108, 207, 209.

which they gave testimony. The miracles of Jesus were not wrought in secret. These things were " not done in a corner," neither did they require darkness for their performance. But they were wrought in open day, before enemies and friends alike, and the fullest opportunity of investigating them was given to the world. Let any one read the ninth chapter of John's gospel, and he will be able to judge whether it is likely that the men who could use such means as the rulers of the Jews employed in examining into the case of the man who was born blind would leave Christ's other miracles unsifted. Whatever else may be said, therefore about the miracles of Jesus, it cannot with truth be alleged that no proper opportunity of investigating them was enjoyed by his contemporaries, among whom must be reckoned his own chosen followers. Then, in the second place, we must remember that the apostles were competent to pronounce judgment upon the miracles. I grant, indeed, that the majority of the twelve were plain men of little education and with no great social position. I grant also that if the wonderful works of Jesus had been performed on substances with which they were not familiar, or had borne any resemblance to the experiments of the laboratory, or if, in working them, he had used any material agents with whose properties they were not perfectly acquainted, then their testimony, however valuable it might have been in establishing the fact that he did the wonders, would still have been insufficient to prove that these wonders were true miracles. But he employed means which were perfectly within the sphere of their knowledge, and produced effects entirely beyond anything which these means themselves could accomplish. Thus every man knows quite well what a human touch can do and what is beyond its power. It does not require a commission of philosophers to enlighten us on that matter, for in such a case one man knows just as much as another. But Jesus, by a touch cleansed the leper, opened the eyes of the blind, and unstopped the ears of the deaf, and hence when he did so he wrought a miracle, on which every man of ordinary discernment was competent to pronounce an opinion. His wonderful works were all of the same character. They were such that if they were well authenticated as facts, their miraculous character was at once apparent. But to authenticate them as facts did not require more than the average intelligence and common sense of men, and therefore the testimony of the disciples cannot be rejected or discredited on the ground that they were incompetent to examine the miracles and pronounce upon them.

Now that the disciples do give testimony to these miracles as facts is patent to every one who reads their speeches and writings. But can we believe them when they thus speak and write ? If we cannot, then in their case, as in their Master's, they were either the victims of their own credulity, or they were themselves imposing on the credulity of others. In plain Saxon phrase, they were either fools or knaves, if they were not trustworthy witnesses. Were they the victims of their own credulity? Who can rest in such a theory regarding them ? Take Peter for example. Read his letters, and you will be struck with the thoughtfulness of his words and the wisdom of his counsels ; and as you peruse the first portion of the Book of the Acts of the Apostles you will be compelled to admire not only the earnestness and the acuteness of his appeals, but also the skill which he manifested in the management of affairs. Whatever else he may have been, plainly he was no fool. Now he gives no uncertain testimony on the point before us. On the day of

Pentecost he described Jesus of Nazareth to the Jews as " a man approved of God among them by miracles and wonders and signs which God did by him, in the midst of them, as they themselves also knew," and when writing a letter in his old age, he reiterated his assertion, saying, " We have not followed cunningly devised fables, but were eye-witnesses of his majesty." Is it likely that a man of this mould could be so imposed upon, that he should adhere thus pertinaciously to this testimony ? •

What again shall we say of such an one as Thomas ? Here was a man who would accept of no evidence but that of his own senses, and who was determined to sift every matter to the uttermost. Whatever others might be disposed to do, he would not receive anything save on his own personal experience, yet in the case of the greatest of all the miracles, even he was satisfied, and was constrained to say, " My Lord and my God."

There too was Philip, who, as is evident from his interrupting question in the valedictory discourse, " Lord we know not whither thou goest and how can we know the way ? " had much of the disposition of Thomas in him, and was not willing to rest in that which he did not clearly apprehend, and yet he too was satisfied. Then, to mention no more, there was John, the author of the Fourth Gospel, who was far from being intellectually feeble, so far, indeed, that the record which he has given, for all so simple as, at first, it looks, has taxed the greatest minds of every succeeding age to understand and interpret it. No one can attentively read his pages without seeing the stamp of reality in every line of them and he has said, " that which we have seen with our eyes, which we have looked upon, and our hands have handled of the Word of Life, that which we have seen and heard declare we unto you."

We know too little of the intellectual qualities of the other apostles to be able to speak positively concerning them, but taking those whom I have named as a fair specimen of them all, I am surely entitled to affirm that such men as they were cannot be regarded as blindly credulous followers of one by whom they were cunningly deluded.

But if they were not deluded did they delude others? If they were not fools were they knaves? The supposition that they were so is altogether incompatible with the character which they uniformly manifested. Even their enemies gave testimony to the rectitude of their conduct. They stood out from among those by whom they were surrounded as men of truth and purity. They were often enough before rulers or governors indeed, but never for " matters of wrong or wicked lewdness." They were simple in manner, pure in speech, truthful in character, upright in conduct, and there was found even by their adversaries no occasion against them, except it were in the matter of their Lord. The well-known letter of Pliny to the Emperor Trajan gives an account of the mode of life of the early Christians generally at the end of the first and the beginning of the second century, and describes them as having " pledged themselves that they would commit no thefts nor robberies, nor adulteries, nor break their word, nor deny a trust when called upon to deliver it up." But of these excellent ones the apostles were the earliest and the best, and so if they were impostors we are asked to believe that a system which even its enemies have acknowledged to be the purest which the world has ever seen was founded by men who yet were all the while systematically and deliberately propagating falsehood.

Besides, what conceivable motive could they have had

for persevering in this course of deception? From the time of Pentecost forward all their ideas of earthly glory were abandoned, and they became convinced that the Kingdom of God was not of this world; yet from that same date their testimony was of the clearest and most unwavering character. They could not look for riches, or honor, or power of an earthly sort, but only for persecution, reproach, and a violent death. Yet none of these things moved them, but they took joyfully the spoiling of their goods, and counted not their lives dear unto them, that they might be Christ's witnesses wherever they went. Surely a strange phenomenon, if the testimony which they bore to him was false!

Nor is this all. Among such a company of deceivers, if they were deceivers, it might have been expected that at least one of them should turn against the rest and seek his personal safety by exposing their falsehood. Yet that was never done. The nearest approach to anything of that kind was in the case of Judas; but as one has very quaintly put it: "He was so struck with remorse at the thought of giving up his lies and becoming an honest man, that he went and hanged himself."

Such is an outline of the testimony in behalf of the miracles of Christ, and if you want a judicial summing up before you give your verdict, then take it as given by one of the ablest of the Scottish theologians of a former generation. "The history of mankind," says Dr. Hill, in his well-known Lectures in Divinity, "has not preserved a testimony so complete and satisfactory as that which I have now stated. If, in conformity to the exhibitions which these writings give of their character, you suppose their testimony to be true, then you can give the most natural account of every part of their conduct, of their conversion, their steadfastness, their heroism. But if, not withstanding every appearance of truth, you suppose their testimony to be false, inexplicable circumstances of glaring absurdity crowd upon you. You must suppose that twelve men of mean birth, of no education, living in that humble station which placed ambitious views out of their reach and far from their thoughts, without any aid from the state, formed the noblest scheme which ever entered into the mind of man, adopted the most daring means of executing that scheme, and conducted it with such address as to conceal the imposture under the semblance of simplicity and virtue. You must suppose that men guilty of blasphemy and falsehood, united in an attempt the best contrived, and which has in fact proved the most successful, for making the world virtuous; that they formed this singular enterprise without seeking any advantage to themselves, with an avowed contempt of loss and profit, and with the certain expectation of scorn and persecution; that although conscious of one another's villainy, none of them ever thought of providing for his own security by disclosing the fraud, but that amidst sufferings the most grievous to flesh and blood they persevered in their conspiracy to *cheat* the world into *piety, honesty and benevolence.* Truly," adds the Reverend Principal, " they who can swallow such suppositions have no title to object to miracles." *

It is fair to say, before I go farther, that the adversaries of the miracles have sought to weaken the force of these considerations by insisting on certain apparent discrepancies between the narratives of the different evangelists in their accounts of the same miracles, but these will be taken up and dealt with by us when we come to speak of the miracles *seriatim.*

Meanwhile, accepting the proof of the reality of the

---

* Hill's Lectures in Divinity, Vol. I, pp. 47, 48.

miracles as sufficient, let us go on to consider the question, what testimony they themselves give to the position and claims and teachings of Him by whom they were performed. Going back once more to the words of Peter on the day of Pentecost, we learn on his authority that God approved Jesus of Nazareth " by miracles, and signs and wonders," and the author of the Epistle to the Hebrews affirms that the great salvation which at the first began to be spoken by the Lord, was confirmed by them that heard him, " God also bearing them witness, both with signs and wonders, and divers miracles, and gifts of the Holy Ghost." Now from these and other passages to the like effect, which might be quoted, we deduce the conclusion that miracles were the attestations by God of the commission of Him who represented himself as bearing a message from God to men. They were the credentials of the legate of the Most High, and endorsed the statements of the ambassador by whom they were performed. Their testimony thus was not immediately and directly to the doctrine taught by the messenger, but rather to the messenger himself, and through him they stamped his message as from God. It has been often said, indeed, that power cannot in the nature of things confirm truth. But whether it can or not depends entirely on whose power it is. Now in this instance, as we have seen, it is the power of God, and the moral perfection of Deity vouches for the truth of the claims of him at whose word the divine power is put forth, and through that for the truth of the doctrines which he teaches. We concede most frankly that the claims of Jesus and the doctrines which he taught are true, altogether independently of the miracles, just as a man is innocent or guilty, altogether independently of his being proved to be either the one or the other. The effect of evidence is not to make him innocent or guilty, but to make plain which of the two he is. And in like manner the miracles do not make the claims of Jesus or his doctrines true, but they are the attestation of God that his claims are well founded and his teachings divine. The signature at the bottom of a letter does not in itself guarantee the truth of the contents of the epistle. It only tells me who the writer is, and for my estimate of his statements I must fall back upon what I know of his character. In like manner the power of the miracle taken by itself does not assure me either of the truthfulness of the claims put forth, or of the doctrines taught, by him through whose instrumentality they are performed. For that I must fall back on the character of Him whose power really wrought them, and considering that He is God, I may be well assured that He would not affix the seal of His confirmation to anything that is false, or sanction a claim to speak in His name which is not truthfully advanced.

Thus viewed miracles are the outward and visible confirmation given by God to one who claims to possess an inward and spiritual commission from God, a commission, which from the very nature of the case we cannot investigate, since it belongs to a region that is beyond the reach of our observation. The prophet declares that he speaks in God's name the things which God has commanded him to utter. That is to say he affirms that an intellectual and spiritual miracle has been wrought upon him, by virtue of which he communicates God's truth to men. But the reality of that mental miracle, if we may so call it, we have no direct means of testing, and therefore it is attested to us by the performance, at the prophet's word, of another miracle, this time in the department of physical nature, and such as we can investigate for ourselves. So by the genuineness of the visible miracle that of the invisible miracle is confirmed to us. But an illustration will make our meaning perfectly clear. When on the occasion referred to by three of the evangelists (Matt. ix. 1–8; Mark ii. 1–13; Luke v. 18–26) Jesus said to the paralytic, "Son, thy sins are forgiven thee," He made an assertion the verification of which was impossible by his hearers, because forgiveness when it is given is bestowed in that spiritual domain which lies beyond human inspection. Therefore the bystanders said, "Why doth this man speak blasphemies ? Who can forgive sins but God only ? " as if they had exclaimed, " That is a safe statement for you to make, for who can tell whether he is forgiven or not ? and how are we to investigate a matter of that sort ? " But the Lord, fully aware of their objections, said, " Why reason ye these things in your hearts ? Whether is easier to say to the sick of the palsy, thy sins are forgiven, or to say, Arise, take up thy bed and walk ? But that ye may know that the Son of Man hath power (or authority) on earth to forgive sins (he saith to the sick of the palsy) Arise take up thy bed, and go unto thy house. And he arose, and straightway took up the bed, and went forth before them all; insomuch that they were all amazed, and glorified God, saying, we never saw it in this fashion." * Now observe where the evidential power of the miracle came in here. Jesus admits that only God can forgive sins, and the argument which he draws from the healing of the poor diseased man may be thus amplified. " It is true that none can forgive sins but God ; but it is also true that none can heal this disease of the palsy by a word, but God, if therefore I do that latter work here before your eyes, you have a proof that I am entitled to perform that other work—the forgiving of sins—which belongs to a department beyond

* Mark ii. 1–12.

the range of your observation or investigation. The two works, each in its own province, are such as only God can perform, therefore by my performance of the one I give you confirmation of my authority to do the other." But what is true of this one miracle in its relation to the claim made by Jesus, that he had power on earth to forgive sins, is true of the miracles of Jesus as a whole, in their relation to all the claims which he advanced, and all the doctrines which he taught, affixing to them both the official and authoritative seal of God.

But while at the first the miracles were wrought mainly as authentications and confirmations of the commission and teachings of Christ and his apostles, they had another and quite different value, as being themselves parts of the revelation which our Lord made, and parabolical illustrations of the great salvation which he preached. Their evidential function was mainly for the conviction of those who witnessed them at the time when they were wrought; but their spiritual teaching is for all time. They furnish us with illustrations of the deep spiritual necessities of men, which the mission of Christ into the world was designed to meet. They show us from manifold points of view how the great salvation of the gospel is to be received, and how it works in those who do receive it. They give us a wonderful revelation of the heart of God, and alike by the circumstances in connection with which they were wrought, by the manner in which they were performed, and by the consequences which followed on their having been performed they set before us spiritual truths of the deepest importance. In this sense, as Westcott has most aptly said, " they are a treasure rather than a bulwark." And yet when they are thus regarded and interpreted they become evidences of another sort, attesting the love of God, and revealing the nature of his salvation to sinners of every degree and in every age. We have aforetime regarded them apologetically, but now we propose to view them parabolically, and, as we proceed from one to another in our exposition, we shall grow in our appreciation of them as bringing, at one time, God nearer to us, and at another, us nearer to God, and as giving us a clearer insight into some of the deepest spiritual experiences of the human heart. As types in the department of nature, of the Lord's working in that of grace, we shall find them exceedingly suggestive and intensely practical, and my prayer is that He at whose word of power they were performed may keep us from all mere fanciful interpretations, and lead us into their true and full significance.

And now, having reached the close of my introductory argument, let me conclude by making one personal appeal and beseeching you to accept of the great salvation which has been proclaimed by Christ, and confirmed by God, through his miracles. Here is now the alternative set before us, salvation through faith in him who is the divinely attested Son of God, or everlasting destruction from the presence of the Lord and from the glory of his power, as the punishment of rejecting him. Take heed how you decide between these two, for it is your eternal welfare that trembles in the balance. Beware, I beseech you, of the guilt and doom of those concerning whom Jesus himself thus spoke, " If I had not come and spoken unto them, they had not had sin ; but now they have no cloak for their sin. He that hateth me hateth my Father also. If I had not done among them the works that none other man did, they had not had sin, but now they have both seen and hated both me and my Father." *

* John xv. 22-24.

I.

THE BEGINNING OF MIRACLES AT CANA OF GALILEE.

John ii. 1-11.

THE note of time in the first verse of this narrative sends us back to the incidents which are recorded in the immediately preceding context. The "third day," therefore, must be counted from the interview between the Lord Jesus and Nathanael at "Bethany beyond Jordan, where John was baptizing." This, according to the method of reckoning then followed, would give one clear day between the leaving of Jordan by the Lord and his five disciples, John, Andrew, Peter, Philip and Nathanael, and their arrival at Cana of Galilee. We are not told why they went thither. It could not have been, however, because the invitation to the marriage feast had been sent to Jesus and his followers before they left the Jordan, because the fact that disciples had begun to join themselves to Jesus was not then known at Cana, and they were bidden as well as he, and apparently, also, at the same time with him. The probability seems to be, that the Lord and the others accompanied Nathanael to his home, which was at Cana of Galilee, and that on reaching their destination, they found that Mary and the other members of her family—for the brethren of Jesus are mentioned in the twelfth verse in such a way

28

as to suggest that they were of the company—were already in the village at a wedding feast. The peculiarity of the expression, " the mother of Jesus *was* there," as contrasted with that which says, " both Jesus was called and his disciples to the marriage," seems to indicate just such an order of events as I have described, and it is easy to conjecture how it came about. The appearance in a small hamlet of so many men, one of whom was an inhabitant of the place, would soon be known, and when it was discovered that one of them was nearly related to one of the principal guests, that would lead most naturally to the invitation of them all. The presence of Mary and of the brethren of the Lord, if these last were really present, may be accounted for on the supposition that she was either a near relative or an intimate friend of those in whose house this feast was given, and that is confirmed by the position of prominence which she seems to have occupied among the guests, and the respect which was paid to her direction by the servants.

The proximity of Cana to Nazareth is also entirely accordant with this view of the case. It is, no doubt, true that some difference of opinion has emerged as to which of two sites is to be identified with Cana of Galilee, but neither of these is more than a few miles from Nazareth, and frequent communication might easily be maintained between dwellers in it and those in either of them. The traditional site is now called Keffr Kana, and is about four miles northeast of Nazareth, but in 1838 Dr. Edward Robinson found a place called Kana-el-Jelil, which is the very name given in the narrative before us, and which is about nine miles north of Nazareth, and this is now generally favored by Biblical geographers.* Dr. Wm.

* The suggestion of " Reineh "—only a mile and a half from Nazareth, by Lieut. Conder,--lacks confirmation.

M. Thomson, whose authority on a matter of this kind stands deservedly very high, has said that he sees " no reason to question the identification" made by Dr. Robinson. He tells us, moreover, that " there is not now a habitable house " in the place, that "the immediate neighborhood is so wild as to have become a hunting ground," and that a week before his visit to it his guide " had shot a large leopard amongst its ruined houses." * Alas, how changed from the day on which our blessed Lord manifested his glory there by this first of all his miracles!

It was a *marriage* feast, and, therefore, a time of gladness, for among the Jews such occasions were kept with peculiar rejoicings. The parties were usually formally betrothed to each other a considerable time—sometimes as long as twelve months—before the actual ceremony of marriage. On the occasion of the betrothal, the bridegroom gave to the bride a piece of money or a letter, it being expressly stated, in either case, that he thereby espoused her. From that moment in the eye of the law they were reckoned as if they had been actually married, but the bride still remained in her father's house. On the evening appointed for the ceremony proper, the bride was led from the home of her girlhood to that of her husband, with great processional splendor. To borrow the description of Edersheim, " First came the merry sounds of music, then they who distributed among the people wine and oil, and nuts among the children, next the bride, covered with the bridal veil, her long hair flowing, surrounded by her companions, 'the friends of the bridegroom' and 'the children of the bride-chamber.' All around were in festive array; some carried torches or lamps on poles; those nearest had myrtle branches

* "Central Palestine and Phœnicia," by Wm. M. Thomson, D.D., pp. 304-5.

and chaplets of flowers. Every one rose to salute the procession or join it; and it was deemed almost a religious duty to break into praise of the beauty, the modesty or the virtues of the bride. Arrived at her new home, she was led to her husband. Some such formula as, 'Take her according to the Law of Moses and of Israel,' would be spoken, and the bride and bridegroom crowned with garlands. Then a formal legal instrument was signed . . . . . . then, after the prescribed washing of hands and benediction, the marriage supper began, the cup being filled and the solemn prayer of bridal benediction spoken over it." *

In the case before us, all these parts of the usual programme had been carried out, and the feast had been going on for some time before our Lord and his disciples appeared upon the scene. It was no uncommon thing, in those days, for such a festival to last for a whole week; but it is quite impossible to determine either how long this one had been begun before Jesus and his followers joined it, or at what precise stage in its progress the deficiency in the supply of wine became apparent. All that is recorded is that " when the wine failed, the mother of Jesus said unto him, they have no wine." Either from the poverty of the hosts, or because more guests than had been anticipated had arrived, or for some other reason too unimportant to be specified, enough wine had not been provided for the occasion, and the exposure of that would have been a bitter mortification to all concerned.

But why did Mary come to Jesus with such information? Her words were certainly meant as an appeal to him for help out of the difficulty. But surely that which she sought was not, as Bengel has suggested, to give

* Edersheim's " Life and Times of Jesus the Messiah," vol. i. p. 354.

him a hint to take his leave along with his disciples,
and so set an example that would lead to the breaking up
of the party before the deficiency was publicly discov'
ered. Neither was it, as Calvin has imagined, that he
might be led to fill up the time by some interesting discourse, and so take away the attention of the guests from
that which was giving her so much concern. The appeal
in her words, like that which was afterwards sent to
Jesus by the sisters of Bethany when their messenger
said to him, " Lord, he whom thou lovest is sick," was
a simple statement of the need, leaving it to himself to
meet it as he chose. And if it be asked what specially
she herself had in mind at the moment, we may perhaps
come near to the right answer by looking back over her
past experiences and connecting them with the reports
of recent occurrences, which she must have heard from
the disciples, who accompanied her Son. None knew
Jesus as she did. The circumstances attendant on his
birth had long been pondered in her heart. She remembered the homage of the shepherds, and the adoration of
the wise men from the far East. She had not forgotten
the thrill that tingled through her that day when, after
she had found him in the midst of the teachers at Jerusalem, he said to her, " Wist ye not that I must be about
my Father's business ? " She knew by all these tokens,
and by other tokens which could be given only to herself, that he had come into the world on a special mission,
and she had watched his progress all through his youth-
ful career, waiting with an expectancy, all the more eager
that it was silent, for the day when the nature of that
mission should be manifested to the world. And now
she had heard from the disciples, in the intervals of the
feast, of the marvellous things that had taken place within the last few days at the Jordan. The testimony of

John the Baptist to the glory attendant on his baptism, and to the fact that he was the Lamb of God who taketh away the sins of the world; the greeting which he gave to Simon; the call which he addressed to Philip; the evidence which he furnished to Nathanael of his perfect knowledge both of his general character and of his devotional meditation under the fig-tree, together with the strange, and, as yet, largely incomprehensible forecast which he had given of the future of his work, in the words, "thou shalt see heaven opened, and angels ascending and descending on the Son of Man"—all these would be told her by the zealous disciples. What wonder, then, if she began to feel that now at length the time of his showing forth to Israel had come, and that perhaps he might inaugurate it there and then by some work of love and power? We may not say, indeed, that possibly he had already performed some miracles during his life of seclusion at Nazareth, for the assertion of the Evangelist that this was the beginning of miracles with him is altogether inconsistent with such an idea. But Mary was a Jewess, and, like her people generally, she "required a sign." Perhaps, too, she had just such material ideas of the Messiah's Kingdom as were clung to by the Apostles down to the very day of the Ascension; and so there may have been in her application at this time, a desire to hasten on his public revelation of himself, with perhaps a little secret satisfaction at the anticipation of the earthly glory which she thought would come to herself when his royalty should be recognized.

Now, if this were indeed the case, we can easily understand not only why she made this application unto him, but also why he met it as he did. For he said unto her, "Woman, what have I to do with thee? Mine hour is not yet come." The words have to our ears a tone of abruptness, and almost of harshness in them, but, as Farrar has said, " that is the fault partly of our version, and partly of our associations." Thus much at least is certain. There was no lack of respect or affection in the use of the word " woman," for the same term was employed by him as he hung upon the cross, when, with the utmost tenderness and consideration for her, he committed her to the care of the beloved disciple as to that of a son. He did not call her " Mother," indeed, and as perhaps this may have been the first occasion on which he failed to address her by that name, she may have been deeply moved by its absence, but, as we shall immediately see, his very purpose at this time was to tell her that henceforth there could be no human interference, not even that of one who had been so dear to him as she had been, with the ordering and directing of his life. For the phrase, " What have I to do with thee ? " literally, " What is there to thee and to me ? " wherever it occurs, " marks," as Westcott well says, " some divergence between the thoughts and ways of the persons so brought together." Thus far, Jesus had been subject to Mary as a human son to a human mother. But now they had come to the parting of the road which they had so long traversed side by side. Henceforth he is to know no earthly relationship in the sense of being swayed by it or subordinate to it ; but he is to be guided solely by his Messianic intuition as the Son of God. From this time forward the tie of consanguinity which bound him to mother and brothers and kinsmen, was to be swallowed up in that which united him to his people as a whole, and " whosoever would do the will of his Father in heaven, the same should be his brother and sister and mother." No merely personal considerations now were to have force with him. His life was not to be regulated by regard to earthly relatives. He "must work the work of him that sent him." He "must be about his Father's business." However painful it might be to them both, he had còme to the point from which she could not accompany him farther, and he must be free from all suggestions and interference on her part. To quote again from Westcott, " the phrase, What is there to thee and to me ? here serves to show that the actions of the Son of God, now that he has entered on his divine work, are no longer dependent in any way on the sugges- tion of a woman, even though that woman be his mother. Henceforth, all he does springs from within, and will be wrought at its proper season. The time of silent disci- pline and obedience was over."*

The words "mine hour is not yet come" have been taken in different senses by different interpreters, but, however understood, they carry forward the meaning which we have just given to the expression that precedes them. Some take the "hour" here as that so often re- ferred to in the later chapters of this book, namely, the crisis of his death and resurrection, and would make the reference something like this : " I see that you are thinking of the foundation and proclamation of my King- dom, but we are not come to that point yet. Much has to be done and suffered before we reach that goal, and I obtain my throne, and when I do, it will not be at all what you now imagine." But that is far-fetched. Oth- ers think that they can see from references scattered over this fourth gospel traces of the fact that Jesus had fore- planned his life, as it were in two parallel columns—one marking the time and the other designating the work that specially belonged to it. As each hour was thought of by him, the work to be done in it came up before him.

* " Speaker's Commentary," *in loco.*

As each work which he had to perform suggested itself
to him, the hour for its performance was remembered by
him, and so he went on through his public ministry until he had exhausted both columns, and could write at
the bottom of the time one, "Father, the hour is come,"
and at the bottom of that which registered the works, " I
have finished the work which thou gavest me to do."
Many, therefore, would make the expression here mean,
" Have patience, the time has not yet come for me to do
any thing. I will do something by-and-by." This view
I prefer on the whole as being at once the simplest and
the most satisfactory, while, as you may see by comparing the narrative in chapter seventh, verses 8–10, it is
not without a parallel in the history of our Lord. It is
as if he had said, " All in good time. Everything in
its own season, but the time for doing any thing here is
not yet come. Wait till the hour has struck."

Thus, though he felt it needful, very tenderly, yet
very decidedly, to check the spirit which his mother
manifested in her attempt to intrude the claims of her
earthly relationship into the sphere of his Messianic
work, he did not deny her request, but in that " not
yet " there was a promise of a coming blessing, which
she immediately prepared to receive. She did not fully
understand her Son, but whether she understood him or
not, she had learned implicitly to trust him, and her
faith here was akin to that of the alien woman, who out
of a rebuff made a new plea, for in the very terms of that
which was a present postponement she saw an approaching benefit. Therefore, turning to the servants, who
evidently treated her with special deference, she said,
" Whatsoever he saith unto you, do it." How long it
was before he said anything to them does not appear;
but some may feel a little surprise at his performing the

miracle so soon after he had said, "Mine hour is not yet come," and it may be a relief to them to remind them of some things just similar in his career. When his brothers went up without him to the Feast of Tabernacles, as narrated in the seventh chapter of this gospel, he said to them, (verse 8) "Go ye up unto this feast. I go not up yet unto this feast, for my time is not yet come." And then we have the following statement, "When he had said these words unto them he abode still in Galilee. But when his brethren were gone up, then went he also up unto the feast, not openly, but as it were in secret." And, if any be still troubled, I may simply quote the comment of Westcott, to this effect, "There is no inconsistency between this declaration of Christ, that 'his hour was not yet come,' and the fulfilment of the prayer, which followed immediately. A change of moral and spiritual conditions is not measured by length of time." *

Among the necessary furniture of a Jewish house were water-pots for the numerous washings—both of the hands and of vessels—which were required by their law, as it had been supplemented by tradition, and so, at a feast like that of which we are now speaking, we are not surprised to find, in a convenient place, six of these stone jars of great size. They held two or three firkins apiece, "making an aggregate, when the whole six were full, of from sixty to a hundred gallons, according as we reckon the firkin as the common Palestinian bath," or that of Sepphoris. These water-pots were replenished when necessary, not by being taken to the well, but by the emptying into them of other smaller vessels, which had been filled elsewhere. Pointing to them, Jesus said unto the servants, "Fill the water-pots with water," and, in

* "Speaker's Commentary," as before.

the zeal of their obedience, " they filled them up to the brim." Then he asked them to " draw out " from the water-pots so replenished, and " bear " the result " to the governor of the feast." This was an official whose position corresponded somewhat to that of the chairman of a banquet among ourselves, but his duties were considerably more onerous. He was chosen from among the guests, and as it was a point of etiquette that the bride and bridegroom, though in their own house, were to be absolved from all responsibility as hosts, it was the duty of the governor to superintend the feast, to examine and taste everything that came to the table, to take order that every one was served, and to look after the putting of the dishes on the table and their removal from it. He was expected, also, to guide the conversation of the company, and to discourage every thing like intemperance. If he saw any one in danger of becoming excited, he was to watch his opportunity, and mingle water with his wine. It was his, too, to preserve order and decorum, and when any one transgressed the bounds of good behavior, he had a simple remedy by which he was enabled to restore quiet, without being under the necessity of naming any particular person, for he broke a glass before the company, and the moment they heard the noise thereby produced they returned to the observance of propriety. Such was the man to whom the Lord commanded the servants to take what they had drawn from the water-pots ; but, to their surprise, in drawing it they found that it was wine, the good quality of which, when he had tasted it, so impressed the governor, that he jocularly said to the bridegroom, " Every man at the beginning doth set forth good wine, and when men have well drunk, then that which is worse ; but thou hast kept the good wine until now." The word translated "have well drunk," is very strong, and literally means, "have become drunken," but as Godet has said, "it is not necessary to attenuate its meaning, in order to remove from the guests at the marriage feast every suspicion of intemperance. For the saying is used in a proverbial sense, and does not apply to the actual company." *

It has been usual, in commenting on these words, to give them a spiritual application, and to say that the way of the world is to produce its best first, and at the last to bring forth its worst in the form of remorse and anguish of soul, while the way of God is just the reverse, and he brings his people through trials first, reserving for the last the purest spiritual enjoyment, and for the last of all that which is best of all, the pure and perennial blessedness of heaven. But though all that is true, there was nothing of it in the mind of the speaker here, for he was giving only a proverbial saying, which he sportively remarked had been not only falsified but reversed on the present occasion, and it is better in interpreting his words to take literally what was literally meant.

The miracle was performed either while the water was in the jars or while the servants were in the act of drawing it off, and it is absolutely needless to speculate on the manner in which it was wrought. It was a miracle, and therefore it is inexplicable, though there was poetic sublimity in the description given of it by him who wrote "the conscious water saw its God and blushed." But though we can say nothing of the mode in which it was wrought, it is right to take note of the evidence of its reality which is furnished in the narrative. Observe, then, the following particulars. Real water was placed in the pots. The Lord Jesus himself did not touch one of the vessels. The water was poured in and the wine was drawn out by the

* Godet on John, vol. ii. p. 12.

servants. There was no collusion between him and them, and they saw all that there was to be seen. The water was put where it was not usual to put wine, and so nothing in the vessels from which the wine was drawn could give that which was drawn from them the flavor or appearance of wine. The wine was tasted and judged by one who knew neither how it was produced nor whence it came. Now let all these circumstances be put together and judged as we should judge of the evidence in a court of law, and it will be impossible to come to any other conclusion than that this was a real transmutation of water into wine, and that it was effected by the power of God. All mere naturalistic explanations fail to account for it, and so we do not wonder when we read that " his disciples believed on him." They believed on him before. Just as the Samaritans believed on him at first because of the saying of the woman, so they had believed on him on the testimony of John. But now they could say, " Now we believe, not because of John's saying, but we have seen his wonderful works ourselves and know that this is indeed the Christ, the Saviour of the world."

So much for the exposition of the narrative. But now, in concluding, let us look at the spiritual significance of the miracle itself. This is suggested to us in the eleventh verse, "This beginning of miracles did Jesus in Cana of Galilee, and manifested forth his glory," and to have a right conception of what these words suggest, we must read them in connection with those others in the first chapter, which we have elsewhere called the text of the fourth gospel.* " The Word was made flesh and dwelt among us, and we beheld his glory, the glory as of the

* See " The Limitations of Life and Other Sermons," p. 22.

only-begotten of the Father, full of grace and truth." The changing of the water into wine was thus one of the earliest out-flashings of the glory of Godhead, through the incarnation of the Word, which John brings before his readers, in support of the assertion which it is the purpose of his gospel to prove. We have already seen that it was a work which only divine power could produce. But the power is not the only, if it be even the central glory of the miracle, for it clearly symbolizes the change which by his advent into the world the Lord Jesus Christ was to produce upon individuals and upon society. Out of the water-pots of the law he brought that which may well represent the blessings of the gospel. The mission of Moses to Pharaoh was signalized by the changing of water into blood, but the advent of Christ into the world finds its emblem in the changing of water into wine. The one indicated judgment, the other symbolized joy and gladness. That which is already valuable in human society is made by the gospel more valuable than ever, and is increased so as to become the possession of multitudes, who but for the influence of Jesus would never have enjoyed it at all. The water of earthly fellowship is transmuted into the wine of spiritual communion, and in this regard the very magnitude of the quantity of wine produced becomes a most interesting and suggestive thing, indicating, as it does, the great capacity of the gospel for ministering to the highest enjoyment of mankind. As the bread of ordinary food in the miracle of the loaves became, so here the wine of ordinary drink becomes sacramental at the wonder-working touch of Jesus. Both alike are lifted by him into a symbolism that connects them with himself and his relationship to the world which he came to bless. As the one links itself on to the words, " I am the Bread of Life," so the other

is allied to the far-reaching saying, " I am the true Vine."
That is for me the significance of the miracle at Cana.

Add to this the fact that the first appearance of our
Lord after his baptism was at a *feast* and you will see at
once the difference between the gospel and the message
even of such an one as John the Baptist.   John was an
ascetic, keeping to the wilderness.   Jesus came into the
homes of the people even in their merry-makings.   To
heal the leper, he touched him; to elevate feasts, he took
part in them; and thereby left an example for us; for
while as Christians, we are not to be of the world, we
must still be *in* it, and by our remaining in it help to
purify and ennoble it.   The measures of meal are not to
be changed by religiously keeping the leaven from coming into contact with them, but by the hiding of the
leaven in them.   And so we are to cleanse the world by
our contact with it, not only in its business, but at its feasts.
Only remember that to do that we must maintain our
Christian character there, for by that alone we can influence for good those whom we shall meet.

Then, again, as this was a marriage feast, we cannot
forget that in the beautiful words of the marriage service Christ " hallowed and adorned " that divine institution " by his presence and first miracle that he wrought
in Cana of Galilee."   At the very beginning of the Old
Testament we find the primeval law that one man should
be the husband of one wife, and here, at the very outset
of his ministry, we have Christ giving his countenance
to marriage, thereby showing at what a distance he stood
from those who, already in the days of Paul, had begun
to forbid men to marry, and had cast reproach upon the
holiest and most helpful relationship of life.   At all our
feasts, therefore, let us see to have Christ present, and
to be ourselves Christians.   Above all, at our marriage

feasts let us send our first invitation to him, for when marriages among us shall be entered into in that spirit, there will be fewer divorces in the land.

And now let me say a few words as to the bearing of this narrative on the matter of temperance. Here we must be specially on our guard against running into " the falsehood of extremes." On the one hand, those who have adopted the opinion that it is a positive sin to drink wine in any quantity as a beverage, have come to the conclusion that the wine of this miracle was not in any degree intoxicating. Now, I cannot but respect the motives of all who are seeking earnestly to grapple with the terrible evil of our modern intemperance. But few things do greater harm to a good and noble—and I will even call it a holy—cause, than to attempt to sustain it by an untenable argument, because, when the antagonist has exposed the badness of the argument, he supposes that he has found a good reason for opposing the cause ; and just this has been the result in the case before us. The wine here produced was the common wine of the country, or, more specifically, just such wine as was usually furnished at marriage feasts, only much better in quality. Now, no one can read the account of the duties of the governor at such a feast on ordinary occasions, or give a correct interpretation to the words of the governor of the feast here, without coming to the conclusion that the wine was such as, if taken in excess, would have produced intoxication. We must not, we dare not, even in support of a good cause, give any other than the true and honest interpretation of the statements of Scripture, and so we must dismiss the idea that this wine was not in any degree exhilarating, but was only grape syrup, and with that must go the other opinion, that it is a positive sin to drink wine in any, even the smallest, quantity.

But then, on the other hand, we must beware of running into the opposite extreme. There was a difference between this ordinary Palestinian wine and those alcoholic mixtures which are classed in our day under the generic name of wine, and so the presence of Christ at this feast, and his changing of water into the wine common in Palestine in his day, cannot be held as justifying " the ordinary drinking usages of American society to-day, with its bars, its wine-shops, its saloons, its beer-gardens, its fiery wines, and strong liquors, and all their attendant evils."* Nothing, either in Scripture or outside of Scripture, justifies these things, and we must use every proper means to do away with them. The true ground on which to advocate total abstinence in these days is to appeal to the drunkard to abstain for his own deliverance, while we expose the sin of his intemperance, and condemn him, in all love, but yet with all decidedness, as much as the drink. Then, inasmuch as he must not be required to abstain alone, we ought to appeal to Christians to imitate the sacrifice of Christ, and to give up their wine out of love to those to whom it is a stumbling-block, saying, like Paul, "If meat make my brother to stumble, I will eat no flesh for evermore, that I make not my brother to stumble." " It is good not to eat flesh, nor to drink wine, nor to do anything whereby thy brother stumbleth."† That is a ground from which no man can be dislodged. I have never known a Christian who did not feel in some degree the force of such an appeal, and the more he had of the Spirit of Christ, the more ready he was to respond to it.

Then we can and ought to appeal to the young, on the ground of the danger that lurks in their use of alcoholic

* Abbot's Commentary *in loco.*
† I Cor viii. 13; Rom xiv. 21.

drinks. We can say to them, that if there be two possible courses of conduct, one of which is attended with danger and the other with none, prudence dictates that the dangerous course should be avoided and the safe one followed. The only way to turn the edge of that appeal would be to say that there is no danger in the use of these modern drinks. But no one who has the use of his eyes would say that, for the victims of intemperance meet us on every hand. Therefore let every one take the safe course, and so preserve himself from evil, as well as help to deliver the land from that curse which is eating like a cancer into its cities. That is the ground I have always taken in regard to this question, and I see no reason to change it now. Certainly no reason to substitute for it, what I must call an unnatural and incorrect exposition of this miracle. I say nothing now on the legislative department of the subject, for *that* has no place in the exposition of this miracle, and there can be no effective legislation till public opinion is strong enough to sustain and to enforce it.

II.

THE HEALING OF THE NOBLEMAN'S SON.

John iv. 43-54.

BETWEEN the two miracles wrought by our Lord at
Cana of Galilee, some important events in his life occurred. Foremost among these was his visit to Jerusalem, to attend the first Passover of his public ministry.
It was on that occasion that he purged the temple courts
of " those that sold oxen, and sheep, and doves," and
also of " the changers of money." Then, too, he had
his memorable conversation with Nicodemus, who came
to him by night, inquiring into the nature of that teaching which, as he believed, had been so clearly endorsed
as divine by the miracles which he wrought. From
Jerusalem he passed into the rural portion of Judea,
whence, on his route to Galilee, he went through Samaria, and there, at Jacob's Well, met the woman of
Sychar, to whom he revealed himself as the Messiah.
At the urgent entreaty of the men of the city to which
she belonged, he remained among them for two days,
preaching the gospel of the kingdom with marvellous
success, and after that he came again to Cana. At Jerusalem he did some remarkable miracles, which are not
particularly recorded, but which must have produced
most impressive results. This is evident, first, from the

46

reference made to them by Nicodemus, when he said,[*] " Rabbi, we know that thou art a teacher sent from God, for no man can do these miracles that thou doest, except God be with him ; " and, second, from the statement made in the narrative now before us,[†] to the effect that "the Galileans received him, having seen all the things that he did at Jerusalem at the feast." It thus appears that, so far from seeking to make a sensation, by heaping miracle upon miracle in their narratives of the life of Christ, the Evangelists have given only a few of the more important of his wonderful works, having regard in their selection not so much to the supernatural element in them, as to the spiritual lessons which they taught, or to the characters of those on whom and for whom they were performed, or to the discourses to the delivery of which they led, and of which sometimes they formed the texts. This fact is of special value, from its bearing on the mythical and legendary hypotheses, by which some have sought to account for the stories of the miracles which are contained in the gospels, and it has not always received the measure of attention to which it is entitled. Myths and legends are said to be formed by accretion, but here the latest of the four Evangelists has deliberately omitted the records of some miracles to which, yet, he refers as having produced very striking results, a procedure altogether unaccountable if his gospel had been formed after the manner outlined either by Strauss or by Renan.

But how does it come that the Evangelist here gives as a reason for Christ's returning to Galilee at this time the proverb to which he thus refers, in the forty-fourth verse : " For Jesus himself testified that a prophet hath no honor in his own country" ? Would not that have

been a good explanation rather of his staying away from
Galilee, than of his going to it? Why, then, is it particularly specified in this place? The question is not
without difficulty, and different reasons have been assigned for the apparent anomaly. Some would solve the
problem by alleging that "his own country" here must
be understood of Judea. But such a view is utterly untenable in face of the fact that the Lord used the same proverb on another occasion, with direct allusion to his
rejection by the men of Nazareth, "where he had been
brought up." * Others, therefore, going to an opposite
extreme, would take "his own country" as equivalent
to Nazareth alone, and so would regard the verse as giving the reason why, when he returned to Galilee, the
Lord did not go to Nazareth, but to Cana. This, however, is nothing better than a makeshift; and does not
commend itself in any degree to our acceptance. A third
expedient has been resorted to by those who take the word
"for" as equivalent to "although," and tell us that the
meaning is that Jesus returned to Galilee, although he
quite well knew, and had actually testified, "that a prophet hath no honor in his own country." But that violently cuts the knot, and does not in the least unloose it.
Besides, the business of the true expositor is to give the
meaning of the language before him, not to alter its
terms; to explain the passage with which he is dealing,
not to explain it away. We must, therefore, search for
some other principle of interpretation, which shall har-
monize at once with the terminology of the verse, and
with the place in which we find it here. Now, where so
many different explanations have been given, dogmatism
would be out of place, but one may offer his opinion, to
be taken for what it is worth. It is this, Jesus knew

* Luke iv. 24.

that a prophet, or great man, beginning his public career among his own people, in a country district like that of Galilee, is almost invariably disregarded, if not, indeed, despised, by those who have known him from the first; but that if he have left his native district, and gone to the metropolis of the land, and there made for himself a name, then, on his return to those whose province or whose town he has made for the time illustrious, he is likely to be received by them with every demonstration of enthusiasm. Hence, his plan was to commence his public ministry at Jerusalem. There, and not in Galilee, his earliest revelations of the glory of the Word that was in him incarnate were to be made, and after that, when Galilee had become resonant with the reports of his greatness, he would return and manifest his glory to his former school-fellows and neighbors. This may have been in his mind when on the occasion of his first miracle at Cana he said to his mother, "Mine hour is not yet come." In any event, very soon after that miracle, and without following it up by any other Messianic appearances, he went up to Jerusalem, where the works which he did made such a sensation that he could return to Galilee with the certainty of his being enthusiastically welcomed. This is accordant with all that we know of human nature, and is quite in keeping with the statement made in the forty-fifth verse: "Then, when he was come into Galilee, the Galileans received him; having seen all the things that he did at Jerusalem at the feast, for they also went unto the feast." His Galilean reputation had no effect at Jerusalem; but his Jerusalem reputation put all Galilee, for the time, upon his side, with the solitary exception of Nazareth. Such, as it seems to me, is the simple explanation of that which at first sight seems so anomalous.

Among other places in Galilee to which the fame of
his wonderful works had spread was Capernaum, a city
which, whether, with Robinson, we identify it with the
modern Khan Minyeh, or, with Thomson, with Tell Hum,
was situated on the western side of the Lake of Tiberias,
near to or close upon the shore, and not far from its
northern extremity. It was a place of considerable importance, having collectors of customs, and probably also
a custom-house, within its limits, and it was garrisoned by
Roman soldiers. It was not far from Tiberias, where
Herod had a palace, and its distance from Cana must
have been somewhere about twenty miles. In this place,
at this time, there dwelt a certain " nobleman," or, as the
word is rendered in the margin of the revised version,
" king's officer." The original term ($Ba\sigma\iota\lambda\iota\kappa\delta\varsigma$) signifies of or belonging to a king, and it may designate either
an officer about the court, or a man of rank connected
with the court of Herod. He was neither a Roman soldier nor a representative in any way of the Roman
power, and so the probability, almost the certainty, indeed,
is that he was not a Gentile, but a man of Jewish birth.
But however high his rank, he was not on that account
exempted from " the ills that flesh is heir to," for his
son—then, as seems probable from the terms employed
concerning him, a child of tender years—was lying ill of
a fever, and evidently at the point of death. In these
circumstances, having heard of what Christ had done in
Jerusalem, and of his return to Cana, nothing was more
natural than that he should make speedy and urgent
application to him for the healing of his child. What
will not a fond parent do for the life of his son? So he
travelled all the way from Capernaum to Cana, and " besought the Lord that he would come down and heal him."
There was thus far, you observe, no sense of spiritual

need in the man's heart. He went to Jesus, just as to-day friends will bring a beloved relative who is danger-ously ill, from some rural district to a famous city physi-cian or surgeon, in the hope of thereby saving his life. True, he had a belief in the reality of the miracles that had been already wrought by Jesus, and in his power to work another for the healing of his child, but that was all. Still that faith had in it the germ of something higher and better, and so he of whom it was said, " A bruised reed shall he not break, and the smoking flax shall he not quench," took measures for its further development. And, singularly enough, this was accomplished in his case, as in that of the Syrophœnician woman, by what seems at first like a denial of that which was requested. For the Lord said unto him, " except ye see signs and wonders ye will not believe." These words are by some explained in this way : Jesus had just come from Sama-ria, where, though he had done no miracle, the men of Sychar believed on him " because of his own word," and the contrast between them—among whom, to use his own figure, " the fields were white already to the harvest," and there was a great spiritual readiness to receive the truth at his lips—and the people of his own Galilee, who were chiefly interested in him as a miracle worker, was so great that he could not but mark it with what was in the nature of a reproof, or at least was an observation to their disparagement. To get this interpretation out of the words, however, we must put the emphasis on the *ye,* " Except *ye* see," but as the pronoun is not found in the original, I think it preferable, with Edersheim, to put the main stress on the word " see," " Except ye *see,*" and then it will appear that " what the Saviour reproved was not the request for a miracle, but the urgent plea that he should come down to Capernaum," [for the purpose of

performing it] " which the father afterward so earnestly repented. That request argued ignorance of the real character of the Christ, as if he were either merely a rabbi endowed with special power, or else a miracle-monger. What he intended to teach this man was, that he, who had life in himself, could restore life at a distance as easily by the word of his power, as readily as by personal application. A lesson this of the deepest importance as regarded the person of Christ; a lesson, also, of the widest application to us, and for all circumstances, temporal and spiritual. When the ' court-officer ' had learned this lesson, he became ' obedient unto the faith,' and ' went his way,' presently to find his faith both crowned and perfected. And when both ' he and his house ' had learned that lesson, they would never afterward think of the Christ either as the Jews did, who simply witnessed the miracles, or unspiritually. It was the completion of that teaching which had first come to Nathanael, the first believer of Cana. So also is it when we have learned that lesson that we come to know alike the meaning and the blessedness of believing in Jesus." *
But though the words, " Except ye see signs and wonders ye will not believe," have the appearance, and, to a certain degree, the reality of reproof, they yet contain in them an implied promise that a miracle was about to be performed, and so the courtier was not silenced by them. On the contrary, he became all the more urgent, and ex claimed, " Sir, come down ere my child——" or, for the word in the original is the diminutive of endearment— my dear little one " die." He was afraid the Lord would be too late. Not only had he not attained to the faith that Christ could heal his child at a distance by a

---

* Edersheim " Life and Times of Jesus the Messiah," vol. i. pp. 425, 426.

word, but he had not the faintest idea that he could raise him from the dead. He supposed that if the child died, not even Christ could do anything for him, and therefore he was specially urgent that he should set out with him for Capernaum at once.

When it is felt to be a case of life or death with one dear to us, we cannot think of procrastination—nay, at such a time, even the modern methods of communication by telegraph and telephone are all too slow for us, and we can brook no delay. Ah! if we were only as prompt, and earnest, and urgent in the matter of the soul as we are in that of the body, how much better would it be with us all!

To the pleading pathos of this pressing appeal the Lord answered, "Go thy way, thy son liveth," and then, as the nobleman believed what Jesus said, his anxiety, his urgency, his importunity gave way to a profound peace, and he went calmly to his lodging for the night. On the following morning he started on his return to Capernaum, and on the way he was met by his servants, who, in their eager joy to tell him the good news at the earliest possible moment, had come, we know not how far, to say to him, "Thy son liveth." This elicited from him the enquiry when he began to amend, indicating that he had expected only a prolonged convalescence, but when they answered, "yesterday at the seventh hour the fever left him," the absolute perfection of the cure, and the correspondence of the time of its occurrence with that when Jesus said to him, "thy son liveth," put the copestone on his faith, so that himself believed, and his whole house.

Now see the three degrees of faith in this man's history. First, he believed in the truth which he had heard about Christ. Credible witnesses had told him of what they had seen at Jerusalem, and others reported to him that the Lord had come to Cana. He believed them and therefore went to Cana, and made application for the cure of his son. Second, he believed the words of Christ addressed to himself, so that after he heard him say " thy son liveth," he had no further anxiety about the life of his child. Third, he believed in or on Christ himself, as indeed the Christ promised to the fathers and the spiritual redeemer of men. And that is the full development of faith. Henceforth, nothing that any one could say would shake this man's confidence in Christ. He believed in him absolutely and implicitly, and could trust him in all places, in all cases, and at all times, and in this faith his household, having had the same evidence of the absolute trustworthiness of Jesus, as he had enjoyed, joined, so that, we may well believe, the night of his return to his home was one of glad and grateful consecration of all the members of the family to him who had thus manifested his glory to them through the healing of the child.

And now, having taken this passage in detail, we are in a position to see how utterly they mistake, who regard the narrative on which we have been commenting as referring to the same miracle as that recorded in the opening section of the seventh chapter of the gospel by Luke, which we commonly entitle the healing of the Centurion's servant. There is only one point in which the two histories agree, and that is, that in both the cure was wrought at a distance, but in every other respect they differ. In this the suppliant was connected with the court of Herod ; in that he was an officer of the Roman army ; in this the nobleman came directly and personally to Christ ; in that the request of the Centurion was presented on his behalf by the elders of the Jews ;

in this the diseased one was a son; in that he was a servant; in this the disease was fever; in that it was
palsy; in this Jesus was at Cana; in that he was at Capernaum; in this the faith of the applicant was so weak
that he requested Christ to go to the place where the
sick one was and heal him; in that it was so strong that
the applicant could say " Trouble not thyself, for I am
not worthy that thou shouldst enter under my roof,
. . . . but say the word and my servant shall be
healed; in this a faith weak at first was stimulated into
strength; in that a strong faith was rewarded and eulo-
gized.   To insist, therefore, that the two records must
refer to the same persons, and then on the ground of the
discrepancies between them, as so regarded, to declare
that both the narratives are unhistorical and unreliable,
is a method of procedure which must be pronounced to be
disingenuous, dishonest and contemptible, and yet it is
one to which the antagonists of the gospel have not hesitated to stoop.   They first make the difficulty by per-
verting the history, and then they plead the difficulty as
a reason for rejecting the history.

But let this exposure suffice, and now as we approach
the conclusion of our exposition, let us put once more
into prominence before you, the one great lesson which
our Lord designed to teach by the manner in which this
miracle was performed.   The Jews of his day were almost without exception looking for a Messiah, who should
reign among them in splendor, break the power of
their earthly oppressors, and be in the midst of them a
visible and present help in time of need.   They wanted
to *see* signs and wonders, and, most of all, they wanted to
see their Messiah as visibly present with them in all time
of extremity.   They thought that if he was not thus be-

side them and in their sight, he could do nothing for them ; just as this nobleman supposed that Jesus could cure his son only by going down to Capernaum and coming into physical contact with the boy ; and just as some among ourselves to-day suppose that the evils of the world can be arrested, counteracted, and finally overcome, only by his visible and personal reign upon the earth. But he declined to go down to Capernaum that he might teach, primarily this courtier, and, secondly, the Jews of his day, and all the readers of this gospel, that his physical presence is not required for the forth-putting of his might. He would have them know that in his wondrous personality, the Omnipotence and the Omnipresence of Deity, indeed Deity itself, was united to humanity, that by the exercise of his divine will he could work wonders anywhere, and that by virtue of his omnipresence, he was really equally near to any emergency of necessity, and could meet it, though unseen by those around. He was at Capernaum to work this cure, though in his human visibility he never left Cana.

But that is only one hemisphere of the globe of truth in this matter, and we must complete it by adding to it this other, namely, that we need not travel from one place to another in order to make our requests to Christ. He is not here or there, on earth, but everywhere, and we can reach him with our cry for help anywhere. This man travelled a long day's journey to make his case known to Christ, but we need not now do anything of that kind, for just as his divine power was at Capernaum, though his bodily presence was at Cana, so his divine ear is everywhere, though his presence in glorified humanity is in heaven. Nor let us lose sight of the fact, that the craving among so many modern Christians, for our Lord's visible personal return to earth, is just a repetition in another form of this nobleman's prayer when he asked that Jesus would go down to Capernaum to heal his son. We do not need his visible presence to cope with the evils of our times any more than this nobleman needed it at Capernaum for the cure of his boy. He is here already, fulfilling his own promise, "Lo I am with you alway even unto the end of the world," and in that spiritual presence he is really and truly nearer to his people as a whole than he would be were his throne set up in some special locality of earth, where alone he could be seen and applied to by any one for assistance. So it is a weak faith that is continually crying that the Lord may personally come to earth, and we need to learn from this narrative to trust in his own assurance that he is already here, and go our way to do his will in the preaching of his gospel for the conversion of men.

But another thing strikes us in this miracle, especially when we read the record of it in connection with the narratives of other miracles in the gospel narratives, and that is the difference in the Saviour's method of dealing with different persons. He had no one invariable plan which he followed in his treatment of applicants and enquirers. With the Centurion he took one course; with this nobleman he followed another. I think I may risk the statement that no two of his recorded miracles were granted to those who applied for them in precisely the same way; and as to enquirers, you have but to contrast his conversation with Nicodemus, with that which he had with the rich young man, to be convinced that, knowing what was in men, he dealt with each according to his character and disposition. To the Pharisee, who imagined that he was a model in character and life, he said, "Ye must be born again;" and to the youth who was wedded to his possessions, he said, "If thou wilt be perfect, go and sell all that thou hast, and give to the poor, and thou shalt have treasure in heaven." Now from this characteristic feature in the Saviour's treatment of those who came to him two inferences follow.

The first is, that those who undertake to guide enquirers should seek to vary their methods with different classes of men. That which may be effectual with one, may be very wide of the mark with another. Therefore there should be a separate study of each case, with the view of discovering the general character, disposition, past habits, and present condition of each, and measures should be taken with each accordingly. The skilful physician, beginning with a diagnosis, prescribes what he thereby learns is needed; and no one but a spiritual quack would think of dealing with all enquirers in one fashion.

Then, on the other side, this variation in Christ's methods with different individuals, ought to keep timid ones from being discouraged, because their experience does not run parallel to that of somebody else, of whom they have read or heard. Few branches of Christian literature are more helpful than that of Christian biography when properly used; but there is this danger in it, that the reader is apt to think that there must be something abnormal in him because he has not had precisely the same experience as that which is described in the work before him. Now the simple truth is that he is neither the better nor the worse for that in itself. He is only different, and Christ has respected his individuality in his treatment of him. The great thing is that we let Christ do with us as he chooses, and then he will choose to save us. Nay, even his very denials of the things which we ask may be the means which he uses to give us something better than we ask, and so to strengthen our faith in himself. Only let us believe and obey his word and trust in himself—then his salvation will be our continuous possession, and his service will be our constant joy.

There is is a tradition, or opinion, I can hardly tell which, that this nobleman was Chuza, Herod's steward, which may well enough have been the case, and if it was, we can understand how it came that Joanna, his wife, was prominent among those Gallilean women, who, as Luke informs us,* ministered to Christ of their substance. That is conjecture, but this is true : where Christ has been the healer, he is honored as the Lord, and they who have been blessed by him, are devoted to him. We must freely receive from him, before we shall freely give to him. We say much of consecratien to Christ, and that in its own order is all important. But there can be no consecration to Christ until we have received from Christ. Begin then and open your hearts now, that they may be filled with himself.

* Luke viii. 3.

III.

THE FIRST MIRACULOUS DRAUGHT OF FISHES.

Luke v. 1-11.

WE mark three stages in the course of the first disci
ples of the Lord Jesus, from the time when they were
adherents of John the Baptist, till that of their formal
ordination to the Christian apostleship. First, Andrew
and John had Jesus pointed out to them by the Forerunner, as "the Lamb of God that taketh away the sin
of the world," and after spending a night with him, became convinced that he was the Messiah of whom Moses
in the law and the prophets did write. This led to the
introduction of Peter to the Lord, and that was followed,
according to the deeply interesting narrative contained
in the first chapter of the fourth gospel, by the addition
of Philip and Nathanael to the little band of converts.
After that it would appear that these five adherents of the
new prophet, went with him from the Jordan to Galilee,
and then returned to their ordinary occupations.

The second stage is signalized by the call addressed to
them to follow Jesus, and their giving up for his sake
their secular occupation and receiving from him the assurance that he would make them "fishers of men," according to the account contained in Matthew iv. 18-22,
and Mark i. 16-20, supplemented by the narrative of the

60

miraculous draught of fishes, given by Luke in the passage which is to form the subject of exposition this evening.

The third stage was the actual selection and ordination of the twelve, "that they should be with him, and that he might send them forth to preach and to have power to heal sickness and to cast out demons," of which we have an account in Matthew x. 1–15, Mark iii. 13–19, and Luke vi. 12–16. Thus there was no haste in a matter of so much importance, and though the selection was not made according to the maxims of the world, the result has vindicated its wisdom, and shown that " God hath chosen the weak things of the world to confound the things which are mighty." *

From the statement which I have just made, it will be seen that I take the narrative of the miraculous draught of fishes, as given by Luke in the passage before us, to refer to the same occasion, as that described by Matthew in the fourth chapter of his gospel, and by Mark in the first chapter of his. The only commentator of note who insists that this is not the case is Alford, but the reasons which he gives for this preference are not so cogent as those which he usually presents for his opinions in his admirable work, and do not seem to me sufficient to outweigh the considerations which have been advanced by others in support of the opposite conclusion. The order of events from the date of the temptation of Christ, which took place immediately after his baptism by John, up to the point at which this narrative comes in, seems to me to be this; from the scene of John's baptism, on the Jordan, the Lord, accompanied by John, Andrew, Peter, Philip and Nathanael, repaired to Cana of Galilee, where at the marriage feast he turned the water into wine. Thence he

I Cor. i. 27.

went up to Jerusalem to keep the Passover, and while there he drove the traders from the temple and wrought many miracles, the particulars of which are not recorded. It was at this time, also, that he received a visit from Nicodemus by night, and had with him that important interview with which we are all familiar. From Jerusalem he passed into the rural districts of Judea, but learning there that the faithful Baptist had been cast into prison by Herod, he returned to Galilee, taking Samaria on his way, and meeting thus the woman to whom he spoke so faithfully, yet so lovingly, at the well of Jacob. In Galilee, after having healed the nobleman's son by his miraculous word at Cana, he went to Nazareth, where he entered into the synagogue on the Sabbath, and expounded one of Isaiah's predictions as fulfilled that day in himself. But the effect produced by his words, on those among whom he had been brought up, was such that they were filled with rage against him and went so far as to attempt to put him to death, so that he removed to Capernaum, where for the time he fixed his residence, and it was during the first weeks of his sojourn there that the incidents occurred which are recorded by Luke in the passage before us.

But while Jesus himself had thus gone from Cana to Nazareth, and from Nazareth to Capernaum, the two pairs of brothers, who were his earliest disciples, had returned to their occupation as fishermen, and are found by us here, in their boats and with their nets. It was not that having put their hands to the plough they were looking back, but rather that they had not yet been called to anything higher than discipleship, and would not run before they had been sent. Yet though *they* were not exerting themselves, so far as appears, to disseminate the truth which they had learned from him, the Lord himself was not idle.

No matter where he was, "he could not be hid," and in
Capernaum he had already begun to teach the people;
nay, such was the attraction of his discourses, that
wherever he went, a multitude thronged him, eager to listen
to his words. See how they crowd around him now! He
has but just made his appearance, coming either from his
mountain closet or his home in the city, yet as he moves
along the shore of the Lake of Tiberias, a constantly increasing multitude follows him, until the pressure becomes inconveniently great, and then, that he may the
more easily and effectually address the people, he entered
into Simon's boat, and getting him to "put out a little from
the land, he sat down and taught the people out of the
boat." Some parable from the scene that was before
him, some tender appeal, some solemn warning, or some
far-reaching and impressive enforcement of a spiritual
principle, we are not told what, was the burden of his
discourse. But whatever it was, we are sure it would
gather in upon him the eager attention of his listeners,
while the fishermen by his side, forgetting their nets for
the time, would drink in his words with delight, "for the
common people" always "heard him gladly."

But now the sermon is ended, and the Lord, turning to
Simon, says to him, "Put out into the deep and let down
your nets for a draught." The fisherman is astonished,
and replies, not in unbelief, but in amazement, "Master,
we have toiled all night and taken nothing, nevertheless
at thy word I will let down the net." He did not mean
to say that he feared it would be useless, because the
night was always the most favorable time for fishing, and
because, having been unsuccessful then there was no
probability that they would get anything now. But his
answer was a confession of failure, and an expression of
faith triumphant in failure; as if he had said, "I should

not have thought of casting forth the net at this time, especially after our experience throughout the night; but if thou sayest it, I will let down the net and look yet for success." For Peter knew something of him who gave him this command. He had heard his instructions at the Jordan, and had seen some of his miracles elsewhere, so that the promptitude of his obedience here, sprung from no mere vague expectation of something unusual, but from his actual acquaintance with former sayings and do-ings of the Lord. It was the fruit not of superstition but of faith, and of a faith that rested on a rational foundation. And his faith was graciously rewarded, for he took such a multitude of fishes, that the net began to break, and it was only by the assistance of his partners, James and John, who were in a boat hard by, that Simon secured his haul, which was so great as to fill well nigh to sinking both of their boats.

Now, here was a clear miracle, though it may not be possible for us to say in what precisely the miracle con-sisted. Some have supposed that the Saviour, by virtue of his lordship over the inferior creation, actually brought the fish to that particular spot at that particular time. This seems to be the view of Trench, who says that here " we are to contemplate Christ as the Lord of nature, able by the secret yet mighty magic of his will to wield and guide the unconscious creatures and make them subserve to the higher interests of his kingdom." * Others have supposed that by his omniscience he knew that the fish were actually there at the moment, and so, have seen in the result of Peter's casting of the net an evidence of the actual deity of our Lord. Perhaps it is easier for us to accept this latter explanation, but it is idle for us to speculate on the subject. The main fact to

* " Notes on the Miracles," p. 131.

be observed is that it was a real miracle, attested by one
who as a fisherman was well qualified to judge in such a
case, and who was himself the human instrument in
bringing it to light.

And the effect on him was electric. With that quick-
ness of insight, and that promptitude in yielding to the
impulse of the moment, which were characteristic of him
from first to last, Peter saw the glory of Messiah's Godhead streaming through the miracle, and fell at his knees,
saying, "Depart from me, for I am a sinful man, O
Lord." It is common for men to recognize God's hand
in their afflictions and misfortunes. But they do not so
frequently see his agency in their prosperity and suc-
cesses. Yet Peter saw God here in the unusual blessing
that had come to him. Thereby he showed himself to
be different from other men, and we may almost say that
he whose first impulse in success is to ascribe it all to
God, is on the way to a Christian apostleship. No
doubt, the son of Jonas at the moment besought the Lord
"to depart from him," but here, as later on the Mount of
Transfiguration, we might almost affirm that he knew
not what he said. In the tumult of his emotions his
words did not truly interpret his heart. He saw God in
Christ, and in the consciousness of his own guilt and unworthiness, which was consequent thereon, there was a
shuddering dread lest he should be stricken down by the
outflashing glory of the divine holiness. That feeling,
for the moment, swallowed up all others in him, and he
cried, "Depart from me ; " but most certainly, this petition of his was entirely different from that of the Gadarenes when they besought Jesus to depart out of their
coasts. In their case, their concern was for their property ; but in this, Peter's anxiety was for his soul. The
sight of the divine glory revealed him to himself, and

this petition was his own impulsive, and perhaps slightly inconsiderate way of saying what Job more wisely expressed in these words, " I have heard of thee by the hearing of the ear, but now mine eye seeth thee. Wherefore I abhor myself and repent in dust and ashes," * or what Isaiah exclaimed when he cried out, " Woe is me, for I am undone, for I am a man of unclean lips, and I dwell in the midst of a people of unclean lips, for mine eyes have seen the King, the Lord of hosts." † And so, answering his real thought rather than his hasty words, the Lord said to him, " Fear not ; from henceforth thou shalt catch men ; " and to the others who were beside him, " Follow me, and I will make you fishers of men." Nor did they hesitate as to the course which they should pursue, for when they had brought their boats to land, "they forsook all and followed him."

Now in looking for the spiritual significance of this miracle, we shall find it in these words of effectual calling to Peter and his partners; but before going minutely into them, let me direct your attention to one or two other matters which are too important to be overlooked.

We may learn then, in the first place, that discipleship should come before apostleship. Peter had been, for at least some months, an adherent of the Lord Jesus, before he was called here to forsake all and follow him, so as to be trained for an apostle. They who would teach others about Christ must first be acquainted with him themselves. This is fundamental, and ought never to be forgotten by those of us, who as preachers, missionaries, Sunday-school teachers, or the like, are striving to commend Christ to others. Do we know him ourselves? One may be like a light-ship, useful for guiding others

* Job xlii. 51.   † Isaiah vi. 5.

into the harbor, and yet so anchored as not to be able to enter it himself. What a fearful possibility! Let us see to it that it be not realized in us.

Again, we may learn from this narrative that a knowledge of one's self, obtained through the revelation to us of God in Christ, is one of the main elements of power in those who would labor for the good of others. It is not a little remarkable that when God called some of his greatest servants to signal usefulness, he began by giving them a thorough revelation of themselves, through the unveiling to them of himself. Thus when he appeared to Moses at the bush, the first effect was that "Moses trembled and durst not behold;"* and the ultimate issue was that, with a deep sense of his own unworthiness and inefficiency, he shrank from the undertaking that was set before him. Forty years before he had been ready enough to trust in himself, and stand forth as the deliverer of his people. But that very self-confidence betokened his unfitness for the work which he had assumed, and his self-abasement, albeit he let it go too far, was an indication of his preparation for the enterprise which Jehovah set before him. So, again, when Gideon was visited at his threshing-floor by the angel of the Lord, who summoned him to go forth and deliver his people from the hand of the Midianites, the exclamation of his heart was, "O my Lord, wherewith shall I save Israel? behold, my family is poor in Manasseh, and I am the least in my father's house."† We see the same thing in Isaiah, when he beheld God's glory in the temple,‡ and in Jeremiah, when he was called to the prophetic office,§ and now again we have it here in Peter. And it is not difficult to understand how this comes to be of use

---

* Acts vii. 32. † Judges vi. 15.
‡ Isaiah vi. 1–8. § Jeremiah i. 6.

to him who would be a winner of souls. For a knowledge of his own heart enables him to unlock the hearts of others, and enter into them and turn out their hidden things, so that in a measure they feel regarding him as the woman at the well did, when she said of Jesus, "He told me all things that ever I did."

But mere self-knowledge is not enough. It must be combined with, nay, consequent upon, the knowledge of the Lord. Oh! how far Peter was permitted to see into the heart of Christ through that "Fear not!" It showed him that bad as he had found out that he was, the Lord was willing to receive him, and to use him, and so it gave him the assurance that he was as able to save others as he was to save him. Doubtless, therefore, the remembrance of this "Fear not" was one of the factors of his power on the day of Pentecost, when even to "Jerusalem sinners" he could say, "Repent and be converted, that your sins may be blotted out." It has been the same with men of eminent usefulness in every age of the church. Augustine, Luther, Bunyan, Newton, and many more, never doubted the possibility of the salvation of any man, after Christ had saved them. Each of them could say, like Paul, "This is a faithful saying and worthy of all acceptation, that Christ Jesus came into the world to save sinners, of whom I am chief." * If, therefore, you desire to bring men to Christ, read yourself thoroughly in the light of the manifestation to you of the glory of Christ. Go to your work in self-abasement and in self-distrust, but with confidence in his love, and especially in his mightiness to save, and to you, O teacher, missionary, evangelist, pastor, Christ will say, as to Peter, "Fear not, from henceforth thou shalt catch men."

* I Timothy i. 15.

Thus the special and peculiar teaching of this miracle as a spiritual sign, is to be found in the words, "Fear not, from henceforth thou shalt catch men. Follow me, and I will make you fishers of men." The Lord speaks of the unknown in terms of the known. He uses their intimate acquaintance with their daily occupation to unfold to them the nature of the work to which he was calling them. They were to catch men, not as the huntsman catches his prey, by driving it away before him, and striking it down in death, but as the fisherman does his, by drawing it to him, and taking it alive. And the experience which they had in the homely toil, from which he was about to withdraw them, was to give them wisdom in the nobler work in which they were henceforth to be engaged. "Fishers of men"! what a light did our Lord cast for Peter, over his new occupation, by that phrase! Let us look at it well, for it has lessons for all Christian workers.

Thus it tells us, for one thing, that if we would catch men, we must use the right kind of net. It is to be feared, in these days, that many preachers use no net at all. They do not seek to catch anything but applause for their own efforts. Their desire is to gratify itching ears, by novelty, or wit, or humor, or originality, or the like, but the thought of catching any one, that he may be brought to salvation, or may be made useful in the service of God, or of "his generation by the will of God," does not appear to enter their minds. It is as if one should amuse himself by casting a line into the lake and call that fishing.

Then there are others who use nets with meshes so wide as to let every thing through. They refer to the gospel as if it were something far away from their hearers; a system to be curiously studied, instead of a message to be promptly and universally believed. They speak of sins as abstractions, instead of describing those which are common among their hearers, and so no conscience is aroused, no anxiety is awakened, no man is caught. " When I hear Dr. —— preach," said one, " he makes me think a great deal of him ; but when I listen to Dr. ——, he sends me away with a very poor opinion of myself." Depend upon it, the latter of these two had a net with narrow meshes that would let no one through ! It is useless to denounce sins that are not committed by those to whom they are denounced, but the true fisher of men takes Nathan's plan and says virtually, in one form or another, " Thou art the man." You may admire the skill and dexterity of a man who sets up a target and shoots his arrow at that, and when he hits it in the white, you may give him a cheer as a fine archer. But when another comes, and makes you his target, sending an arrow whizzing into your heart, that is a different affair. Now in all our pulpits I fear there is too much aiming at targets and too little aiming at hearts. When here, and there, and everywhere, in the audience, individuals are saying within themselves as the preacher speaks, " That means me," then he is working with a proper net, but when there is nothing but admiration of him, then either he has no net at all, or the meshes of that which he has are so wide as to catch no one.

But, for a third thing, these phrases tell us that we must follow men to their haunts, if we would catch them for Christ. The fisherman studies the habits and haunts of the fish. He goes where he knows from experience, or from personal observation at the time, that they are to be found. I lived one summer on the shore of a beautiful bay on Long Island Sound. It was a quiet inlet, visited by no steamboat, and traversed only by little cat-boats or tiny yachts. But one morning a great number of boats came in and made an unusual stir upon the waters; for their crews began at once to cast and haul their nets. Why did they come then? Not for the two months during which I had lived in that neighborhood had they been there before? What brought them now? They were following the fish! They had seen a shoal pass in before them, and they came to take them, and went away with a great haul. So we must go where the sinners are to be found if we would win them for Christ. As Archbishop Leighton said, "We must follow sinners to their houses, aye, even to their alehouses." If they will not come into our churches, we must go out of our churches after them. The question has been often asked, "How can we reach the masses with the gospel?" But there is only one answer, we must go after them with the gospel. That is the only way to reach them. And when the church is willing and ready to go after them, through its members, as well as through its ministers, they will be caught for Christ, not sooner and not otherwise. If they will not come to our churches, let us go to their theatres, and speak to them there of Christ. Let us follow them, if possible, into their homes; let us be willing not to patronize them, but to speak to them, to touch them, to regard them as souls that are precious in Christ's sight, and then we shall be a long way on the road toward the solution of that problem which is facing the churches in all our large cities to-day.

And now, there may be some who are eagerly asking, How can I become skilful as a catcher of men for Christ? The reply is easy. It is this, Obey the Master's command. He said, "Follow me and I will make you fishers of men." Follow Him. Keep close to him. The closer the better. You cannot be too near to him, and this very nearness to him will give you success. The magnetism is not in you, but in the Christ whom you are following. Keep near to him, therefore, and whether you preach by word in the pulpit and the Sabbath School, or by life, in the home, the store, and the workshop, men will be caught by you for him.

IV.

THE HEALING OF THE DEMONIAC IN THE SYNAGOGUE.

Mark i. 21-28.

DURING his residence in Capernaum our Lord maintained the custom of attending the services of the synagogue on the Sabbath day which he had followed in Nazareth, and it was most probably in connection with these that he made a formal beginning of his public work in that city. At any rate, it would appear that on the first Sabbath, or at least on an early Sabbath after he took up his abode there, he taught the people at one of their regular meetings for worship, and those who are in any degree acquainted with the manner in which the services of the synagogue were conducted, will understand how naturally he came to take part in them. It has been disputed whether or not synagogues existed among the Jews before the time of the captivity, but there is no doubt that subsequently to that epoch they were to be found, wherever among the Gentiles any considerable number of Hebrews resided, and in every town and village of Judea and Galilee. Connected with each, were a council of elders, with a president, who was called the ruler of the synagogue, two alms-collectors, three or more distributers of alms, the delegate of the congregation, who offered prayer and read the Scriptures, and the

73

minister, who got the building ready for service and taught the school connected with the synagogue. Three members of the council, along with the other officers just mentioned, constituted the so-called " men of leisure " who made up a congregation or quorum, ten being the minimum number required for that purpose, and who were expected always to be " on hand " at the appointed hour " so that there might be no delay in beginning the service at the proper hour, and that no single worshipper might go away disappointed." When the congregation was seated, the delegate of the synagogue ascended the pulpit and offered up the public prayers, the people rising from their seats and standing in a posture of devotion. The prayers were nineteen in number, and were closed by reading some sentences from the books of Deuteronomy * and Numbers.† Then came the repetition of their phylacteries, and, after that, the reading of the lessons for the day, one from the law, and one from the prophets, which were translated by an interpreter from the Hebrew into the Syro-Chaldaic dialect which was spoken by the people. This was followed by the exposition of the Scriptures, and an address by one of the office-bearers, or, at the request of one or more of them, by some distinguished person who happened to be present. Then the services were reverently concluded by a brief prayer or benediction.‡ From this outline of the routine of service in the synagogue, it will be seen how Paul was called upon in the synagogue of Antioch in Pisidia to address the congregation,§ and it is every way likely that it was in this way that our Saviour was invited to speak to the people on the occasion before us.

* Deut. vi. 4-9; xi. 13-21.   † Num. xv. 37-41.
‡ See Schaff's " Bible Dictionary," art. Synagogue.
§ Acts xiii. 15.

We have no report of what he said; but we may perhaps conjecture that he set before his hearers some of the truths, which he afterwards dwelt upon in his sermon on the mount. In any case, the effect produced by his discourse in the synagogue of Capernaum was the same as that which followed the sermon to which we have just referred, for we read that all they who heard it were "astonished at his doctrine, for he taught them as one that had authority, and not as the Scribes."

The term doctrine here means not merely the truth which he presented, but also, and perhaps especially, the manner in which it was presented by him, and, thus viewed, there might be many things fitted to awaken the astonishment of his hearers. For not only was the Lord Jesus utterly removed from the conventionality of his times, but he was also remarkable for the originality of his instructions. He came to earth to make men acquainted with truths of which they had been till then entirely ignorant, as well as to show them the depth and importance of those which they professed to have received. He set before them the nature and attributes of God; and the duty of worshipping him in spirit and in truth. He gave a wide and far-reaching interpretation of the law to which they were so fond of alluding, and which they were so far from keeping. He unfolded to them the love of God as Father, and exhorted them first and before all things else to look to the condition of their hearts before him. He exposed the hollowness of mere outward service, and warned them against the hypocrisy of offering their prayers, or doing their righteousness to be seen of men. He exalted character above reputation; religion above ritual; substance above form, and reality above appearance. He emphasized the long-forgotten doctrine that " God requireth truth in the inward parts," and taught that only the pure in heart could see God, so that " except a man were born again he could not enter into the kingdom of heaven." And if these things were amazing even to Nicodemus, we cannot wonder that they filled the men of Capernaum with astonishment.

Furthermore, his discourses were peculiarly illustrative. The lilies of the field, and the sparrows on the house-top ; the fig-tree and the vine ; the sower going forth to sow and the fisherman casting his net ; the housewife kneading her dough, or seeking for her lost piece of money ; the shepherd tending his flock, and the husbandman reaping his harvest ; the children playing in the market-place, and the virgins waiting till midnight for the bridegroom's coming—all these familiar things were woven by him into the fabric of his discourses, and that with such singular beauty and fitness that his speech was not vulgarized thereby, but only made more luminous and glorious. It is not surprising therefore that "the common people heard him gladly" or that the officers sent to apprehend him returned without doing their errand, and exclaimed, "Never man spake like this man."

Still further, his addresses were characterized by wonderful adaptation to his hearers. He "knew what was in men," and while he repeated his words on some occasions, he commonly varied the character of his discourses so as to make them suitable to that of his audiences. His words were always "in season" and "fitly spoken." He said the right thing, at the right time, to the right people. He spoke to the Pharisees in one way, to the Sadducees in another, and to the common people in yet another. While in and with all these qualities there was a loving gentleness, which would not "break the bruised reed," or "quench the smoking flax," and a pervasive earnestness, which showed that he was not playing with a subject for the amusement of his hearers, but rather pleading with them to " seek first the kingdom of God and its righteousness," and to choose that " one thing " which was "needful," in all places, and in all cases. His preaching was neither an " effort" put forth by him to elicit human applause, nor an intellectual wrestle with some great subject for a display of himself, but it was a grappling with the conscience and a pleading with the heart, an interblending of faithfulness and pathos that is without a parallel in the history of the race.

But the special attribute of his teaching which called forth the amazement of the worshippers in the synagogue of Capernaum was its authority, and the difference by which in this respect it was distinguished from that of the Scribes. These last were the expounders as well as the conservators and guardians of the old Testament Script- ures, but in their explanations of the sacred books they were careful never to put forth an opinion of their own, and contented themselves with repeating the aphorisms of the learned rabbis who had spoken or written on the subjects with which they were dealing. A favorite for- mula with them was "our learned doctors or wise rabbis say," our " ancient doctors thought," and very frequently they gave the names of their authorities in full, as is often done now by scholars in the notes to their prelections. Dr. Kitto tells us that the great doc- tors whose names were most commonly on their lips, in the Saviour's time, were Hillel among the Pharisees, and Shammai among the Sadducees. He adds that the rab- binical writers have recorded a tradition regarding Hillel himself, which curiously illustrates their mode of teach- ing, and shows how even he was obliged to conform to the customary method ; it is to the following effect, " The great Hillel taught truly, and according to the traditions, respecting a certain matter, but though he discoursed of that matter all day long, they received not his doctrine until he at last said—'So I heard from Shemaia and Abtalim.'" * Now the most cursory perusal of the sermon on the mount will show how far removed our Lord was from such a mode of teaching. He spoke on his own authority, saying on one occasion to Nicodemus, "We speak that we do know, and testify that we have seen . . . and no man hath ascended up to heaven but he that came down from heaven, even the Son of Man who is in heaven," and claiming, as he did in his great inaugural discourse, to stand on a higher pinnacle than Moses himself. He set aside all false interpretations of the ancient law, and laid down new principles of obligation with the formula, " Ye have heard that it hath been said by them of old time, but I say unto you." And in all this there was no unwarrantable assumption, for there was that about him which showed that the claim was well founded. His words were living and powerful. They "pierced even to the dividing asunder of soul and spirit, and of the joints and marrow," and discerned the thoughts and intents of the heart; the very effects produced by them witnessed to the rightfulness of his claim to utter them, so that the difference between him and the Scribes was not one of degree, but of kind, not one between a man and other men, but rather one between men and God. His, " I say unto you, " was equivalent to the old prophetic expression " Thus saith the Lord," and as men heard it, they could not but acknowledge that a greater than any of the prophets was addressing them.

But besides this testimony to his claims, in the hearts of his hearers, there was another attestation of them, in the miracle which on this occasion he performed. It was

---

* "Daily Bible Readings," vol. vii. p. 284

on a man with an unclean spirit, who, as it would seem, interrupted the Saviour's discourse with the cry, " Let us alone; what have we to do with thee, thou Jesus of Naz- areth ? Art thou come to destroy us ? I know thee who thou art, the Holy One of God." Now here we are con- fronted with the difficult subject of demoniacal possession, but leaving the full discussion of that, until we come to the history of the miracle that was wrought on the fierce Gergesene, where it comes before us in its most aggra- vated form, I content myself for the present with saying that it was a real usurpation of authority over the spirit of a man by a demon, amounting in many cases to a double personality in the victim ; that it was a constraint exercised by an intruder into the man, over his bodily organs, so that he was convulsed,and driven hither and thither, not only involuntarily, but against his will, and by a power within him other than himself; that while it might be and often was accompanied by or grafted upon some forms of bodily disease, such as blindness, dumbness, epi- lepsy, and insanity, it was yet distinct from all these; and that it is not possible, in my judgment, to believe that our Lord and the evangelists were truthful men if we do not hold that they meant to describe, and he meant to deal with, such an intrusion into, and usurpation over, a man, by an evil spirit as that which I have now indicated.

In the case before us, though the physical utterance was that of the man's vocal organs, the speaker was not the man, but the spirit by whom he was possessed. That usurper is here called "unclean," indicating the moral impurity by which he was characterized, and so we are not surprised to find that he violently recoiled from the unsullied holiness which dwelt in Christ. With the higher intuition of the spirit nature, he recognized the presence of that holiness, and was unable to endure it, so that he cried out for fear. Nay, more, he knew, we cannot tell how, but he evidently did know, that Jesus of Nazareth was the Holy One of God. Yet though his testimony was true, it was immediately silenced by him to whom it was borne. The Lord knew that no good could result even from the telling of the truth by an evil spirit, because it was told not to honor him, but rather with the view of bringing reproach upon him. On a subsequent occasion his enemies founded on a similar testimony to him from a demon, the allegation that he was himself in league with the prince of the demons, and we believe that it was because he was determined to have nothing of that sort on this occasion, that he said to the evil spirit here : " Hold thy peace, and come out of him." He had been till then the strong one in the man, but now one stronger than he was in the field against him, and so, constrained by the superior might of him who came to " destroy the works of the devil," the evil spirit obeyed, but in obeying showed the wanton cruelty by which he was actuated, for he threw the man in whom he had dwelt into a violent paroxysm. He did all the mischief that he could, because he knew that it was his last opportunity. When an evil-disposed tenant is compelled to leave the house in which he has dwelt, he frequently shows his spite by doing damage to the premises, and so in this case, and in that of the demoniac boy at the foot of the Mountain of Transfiguration, the demon tore the victim from whom he was ejected. But, as we learn from the parallel passage in Luke, he did him no permanent hurt, and after the paroxysm was over the poor man was conclusively delivered from his cruel oppressor.

This miracle produced a remarkable effect upon those who witnessed it in the synagogue, and through them upon the whole community of Capernaum. In the immediate spectators it caused amazement, and it was by them at once connected with the discourse to which they had listened, and the authority with which Christ spoke, for they exclaimed, " What is this ? A new teaching ? With authority he commandeth even the unclean spirits and they obey him." As Nicodemus had declared that the miracles of Jesus proved that he was a messenger of God, so these witnesses of this miracle of healing at once associated it with a new teaching. Not for mere purposes of display are such signs shown and such wonders performed. It is not God's wont to manifest his power in this unusual manner except for some unusual and worthy purpose; there must, therefore, so they rightly reasoned, be some new teaching to be given, or some new revelation to be made. To borrow John Foster's striking illustration, they recognized in the miracle the ringing of the great bell of the universe, and so now they stood expectant and waiting for the sermon that was to follow. Here, as if they had said, is a new prophet with a new message to us from our covenant God—else why this wondrous work ? He must bring to us some teaching—nay, some new teaching to illuminate our darkness, for " with authority he commandeth unclean spirits, and they obey him." But not alone upon those who were in the synagogue at the time was such an effect produced. These spectators could not help rehearsing what they had seen wherever they went, and so " the report went straightway everywhere, into all the region round about Galilee." There were in those times no daily newspapers, or rapid postal service, or regular means for the conveyance of intelligence from one place to another, except, perhaps, on the main roads of the Empire; but yet the story of the miracle in the synagogue of Capernaum flew from lip to lip until it filled Galilee. There is some-

thing very remarkable in the manner in which a report
of such a thing as this was, travels. Some unlooked-for
occurrence comes to pass in the central part of a city, and
before an hour has elapsed, it will be known in all the
suburbs. It travels nobody can well tell how. More
rapidly by far than one messenger could carry it, the report is conveyed by one to another, and passed on so
that as we say "it flies," as if on wings, from place to
place. You cannot trace its course, only you find it
there. And in the case before us, as no enmity had yet
developed itself in Galilee against the Lord, the wide-
spread report of this miracle prepared the way for the
ministry of the Saviour in that part of the land, and
made all classes of the people eager to see and hear him.

I have time now for only one or two practical lessons
from this whole subject. The first is that holiness and
sin are mutually repellant. "God is of purer eyes than
to behold iniquity." He cannot even "look upon sin."
And here we see that the evil spirits cannot endure the
presence of the Holy One of God, but cry out, saying,
What have we to do with thee? Now the bearing of all
this on us is tremendous in its force. If we are ever to
be with God, and happy in his presence, we must get rid
of sin. The vision of God would be a source of intoler-
able anguish to an unholy man; and therefore, if we are
to enter heaven and to enjoy its felicity, we must be made
meet for it, by regeneration and sanctification. Behold
how Adam, when he had lost his innocence, shrank from
the presence of Jehovah. Listen how the Israelites beseech Moses to stand between them and God, lest if he
spoke to them they should die. See with what quiver-
ing fear Manoah was affected when he saw the Lord!
Hear how Isaiah bemoans himself when he sees the vision
of God's glory in the temple. What means that strange

request of Peter, when through the glory of the miracle he recognized the deity of Jesus? Yea, how shall we explain the crouching terror which impelled the demon in the poor possessed one to cry out, "What have I to do with thee, thou Holy One of God? art thou come to torment us before the time?" Do not all these cases prove that holiness and sin are mutually repellant? Do they not all declare that like as the magnet attracts one substance and repels another, according to the nature of each, so God by his holiness attracts those who are partakers of that holiness, and repels the unrenewed sinner from his presence? and what must be the force of that dread recoil as, fleeing from him at last, they cry to the mountains and rocks to fall on them and hide them from his face? Now I fear that there are many who have no relish or meetness for the vision of God and the happiness of heaven. Rather than enter into the presence of Jehovah, they would live eternally on earth, but since that is impossible, they would prefer heaven to hell ; that is to say, they would have heaven merely because it is not hell. I earnestly beseech all such to lay to heart the truth which I am now seeking to enforce. With feelings like these, if you could be admitted to heaven, it would be no place of happiness to you. You would be out of your element. You would not be able to endure the constant presence of him who is "glorious in holiness," and would cry to be anywhere, anywhere, if you could only be removed from that region of transcendent majesty and ineffable purity. It is only the pure in heart that can see God and have joy in him. Behold what point all this gives to the assertion of the Saviour, "Ye must be born again." That is fundamental, and to that we must give our earliest care, for without that we cannot endure, far less enjoy the happiness of heaven.

But, as another lesson here, let us learn that when Satan is losing his hold on a sinner, he does him all the harm he can. As the demon was departing from this poor man, he threw him down and tore him with terrible convulsions. When the Israelites were seeking emancipation from Egypt, Pharaoh increased their burdens. Every thing went well with them, until they began to speak about going into the wilderness to hold a feast to their God, but after that their bondage was embittered by more terrible exactions. So as long as one is careless, unconcerned, in a manner almost unconscious of his sin and danger, Satan leaves him in peace; but when he begins to seek salvation, when he is just in the act, as it were, of yielding himself up to Christ, then the devil tears him, and throws him down. He terrifies him perhaps with the thought that his relatives will cast him out. He exaggerates the sacrifices that will need to be made by him. He keeps carefully out of view all mention of the grace that is promised to those who will go after Christ, and does every thing in his power to harass and distress him. That is his way. We must not think it strange, therefore, if he should act after. this fashion with us; and his acting thus ought to make us only the more resolutely determined to break away from his service. Let those among us who as they are thinking of deciding for Christ are torn by fears, or perplexed with doubts, or tormented with all manner of insidious suggestions, know that all these are from Satan, and are the tokens that he feels he is losing his prey. They are but the bloodhounds sent by the great enemy after those who are running away from his degrading slavery.

Finally, let us learn to have no parley with Satan or any of his agents. It is noteworthy that when Christ was tempted in the wilderness, he would not allow Satan to discuss with him, but met him simply with a text of Scripture. It is no less remarkable that when the demons called him the Son of God, he invariably commanded them to hold their peace. If we parley with him, as our first parents did, Satan will be sure to outwit us. Our only safety is in having nothing whatever to do with him. Take no favors from Satan or his agents. The Trojan said, " I dread the Greeks even when they offer gifts," and the deceit practised by them in the gift of the wooden horse, the interior of which was filled with armed men, proved the wisdom of his words. So Satan is most to be feared when he is apparently speaking truth, and is never so dangerous as when he disguises himself as " an angel of light." The most insidious of the temptations presented to our Lord was that in connection with which Satan quoted one of the most delightful promises which the book of Psalms contains, and here the demon seeks to compromise the Saviour by bearing witness to his holiness. But it would not do. The Lord repelled him in the wilderness with another text, and here he bade the demon be silent. So let us shut our ears against all his suggestions, and take no testimonial from his hand. He is never so dangerous as when he is seeking to speak us fair, and giving commendation to our character. Herein lies the principle that is beneath the words, " Woe unto you when all men speak well of you." And when the underlings of the devil begin to give testimony to our worth, the only thing to do is to bid them hold their peace.

V.

THE HEALING OF SIMON PETER'S MOTHER-IN-LAW.

Matt. viii. 14-15; Mark i. 29-31;
Luke iv. 38-39.

THE place where this miracle was performed was the house of Simon and Andrew, in the city of Capernaum. The time was on the Sabbath day, immediately after the synagogue service, in connection with which the Lord had cast out a demon from one of the worshippers who is described by Mark as "a man with an unclean spirit." In the history of our Lord that Sabbath is put by Mark immediately after the call of the fishermen apostles, and by Luke after the rejection of Christ by the men of his own city, Nazareth. The record of it is very brief, but, brief as it is, there are in it some interesting points that are worthy of special mention. Thus it comes out here incidentally that Peter was a married man, so that here again the Roman Catholics are singularly unfortunate in setting up the son of Jonas as the prototype of their priesthood and the first Pope. It is not a little ridiculous to have a claim to infallibility founded on successorship to one whose impulsive nature was constantly leading him into mistakes of rashness, both in speech and conduct, and who was once reproved by his Master in such terms as these, "Get thee behind me, Satan, for thou savorest

86

not the things that be of God, but those that be of men."
And it is no less so here to find a wife and her mother in
the home of him who is regarded as the Rock whereon
is founded that church which enjoins celibacy on all its
clergy.

Another point of interest is in the fact that Luke char-
acterizes the disease of Peter's relative as a "great
fever," in contradistinction to that which is called by
Galen a "small fever," and the fact that this is so clearly
marked by the third evangelist is one instance out of
many that may be found in his gospel and in the book
of the Acts of the Apostles, which corrobate the statement make by Paul, that Luke was a physician.

Notice, also, that the cure was thorough and immedi
ate. Usually when one has been so prostrated by fever
as to be quite helpless, there is a long convalescence
after the fever has been subdued, and many days, and
often weeks, are needed for the full recovery of former
strength, but here the sick one rose from her couch and
was able at once to minister to her benefactor, and,
probably, also, to a houseful of guests that were with
him.

But on these details I do not purpose now to dwell.
Let me rather proceed, according to my design throughout this series of discourses, to unfold the spiritual significance of this mighty work when taken with its environment in the narrative as a sign or acted parable for the
enforcing upon us of important truths connected with the
gospel of Christ.

I. Notice then, in the first place, that the people of
God have no exemption from physical disease any more
than others. Peter was one of the most ardent and devoted followers of the Lord; yet serious illness came

upon a venerable and beloved member of his household. And instances of a similar sort are so numerous that we may call them common. Job, the man who "feared God with all his heart, and eschewed evil," was afflicted in the most sudden, severe and protracted manner. The good King Hezekiah was prostrated by dangerous illness. The cottage home of Bethany, where Jesus himself was a frequent and beloved guest, was not proof against disease and death. The good works of Dorcas did not purchase for her immunity from sickness, and the tears of those whose wants she had relieved could not prevail to prevent her death. We remember, too, how Paul, in a certain place, speaks of " our troubles which came unto us in Asia, that we were pressed out of measure, above strength, insomuch that we despaired even of life." * Nor can we forget how he refers to Epaphroditus as having been " sick nigh unto death," † and how in the last letter that he wrote he mentions that he had left Trophimus " at Miletum sick." ‡ Here, then, were men and women of most excellent character, who were engaged in God's service, whose health and whose lives appeared to be of great importance for the carrying forward of God's work in the world, and yet they were laid aside by illness. We must not, therefore, too hastily conclude that when men suffer sickness they are suffering because of some special sin, far less that sickness is itself a sin. It is true that there is a connection between sin and suffering, yet that is not such as warrants us to infer that those who have been prostrated by some sudden and malignant malady are sinners above all others because they suffer such things ; for the righteous are seen to be the victims of such evils as well as the wicked.

This, however, is only a particular case under the gen-

* II Cor. 1–8.   † Phil. ii. 27.   ‡ II Tim. iv. 20.

eral question, Why do the people of God suffer such
things at all ? and that is a question as old as the days
of Job,—although under the Christian dispensation it as-
sumes a form of even greater difficulty than it had in
those ancient times. For if, as we read, Christ " took
our infirmities and bore our sicknesses," if he came by
his death to remove sin and all its consequences, why
should his people also be required to bear any of these ?
Why are they still subject to disease and death just as
others ?   And to that, so far as disease is concerned, there
is but one answer, to wit, that given to the sisters of
Bethany in the case of Lazarus by the Saviour himself:
"This sickness is for the glory of God, that the Son of
God may be glorified thereby." *   We cannot solve the
problem thoroughly, yet we can see some of the ways in
which the glory of God may be advanced, through the
sufferings even of those who are really and truly his.
For such dispensations may be refining in their influence
upon the sufferers themselves, according as Peter has said,
" that the trial of your faith, being much more precious
than of gold that perisheth, though it be tried by fire,
might be found unto praise and honor and glory, at the
appearing of Jesus Christ."†   Or they may be educa-
tional in their character, as designed to work out in
those who are subjected to them special fitness for the
performance of some duty that is before them.   Even of
the Lord Jesus it is said that he was " made perfect
through suffering; "‡ perfect, that is, not in respect of his
own personal character, but of his qualification for his official work as the Captain of our salvation in bringing
many sons unto glory.   It was in this way that " the
Lord God gave unto " him " the tongue of the learned, that
he should know to speak a word in season to him that is

* John xi. 4.   † I Peter i. 7.   ‡ Heb. ii. 10.

weary," * and the author of the Epistle to the Hebrews is careful to note that because Christ himself suffered, being tried, " he is able also to succor them that are tried." †
Now it is sufficient for the disciple that he be as his Lord, and there have been instances almost innumerable in the history of the church, of men who have graduated through suffering to their special and peculiar usefulness. Or yet again such afflictions may be meant to furnish an opportunity for the manifestation of the sufficiency of God's grace to sustain the believer even under the severest ordeal. The strength of the vessel can be demonstrated only by the hurricane, and the power of the gospel can be fully shown only when the Christian is subjected to some fiery trial. If God would make manifest the fact that " he giveth songs in the night," ‡ he must first make it night. But for the subjection of the great apostle to his thorn in the flesh, we could not have known how much is implied in the assurance, " My grace is sufficient for thee ; my strength is made perfect in weakness." § Thus the good man may be afflicted, simply to show the sustaining power in him of the grace of God, and so the sufferer becomes for the time a living sermon, preaching to every spectator the preciousness of Christ and his salvation. In this way the mystery of suffering in the Christian is nearly akin to the mystery of the cross in Christ. I admit, nay I contend, that no suffering of any mere man can ever be vicarious in precisely the same sense as that of Christ ; yet in a very real sense, the child, whose illness or death results in the conversion of his parent, has suffered for that parent, and in any case, when we find that he who was " holy, harmless, undefiled, and separate from sinners," was also pre-eminently, " a man of sorrows and acquainted with grief,"

* Isaiah l. 4. † Heb. ii. 18. ‡ Job xxxv. 10. § II. Cor. xii. 9.

we are warned against the sweeping conclusion that affliction is either itself a sin or a proof of personal wickedness, and we are reconciled to the thought that even the
people of God have no absolute exemption from affliction.

II. But notice, in the second place, as an inference
from this narrative, that we should seek the cure even of
physical disease at the hand of the Lord Jesus.   When
the Saviour entered the house of Simon, they told him of
the sick woman's case, and he "touched her hand," and
" rebuked the fever, and it left her." Now, of course,
there was miracle here, and we are not warranted to reason
in every respect from the supernatural to the natural, but
still we must never forget that, as Bushnell has admirably
put it, these two together "constitute the one system of God." His agency is the causative element in
both. The natural is usual, the supernatural is unusual,
divine operation. In the natural God's power is exerted
through the working of certain subsidiary causes whose
force, however, depends entirely upon himself; in the
supernatural he puts forth his energy directly and immediately, without the intervention, so far as we can see, of
any intermediate or subordinate agent. In the natural
he works through physical agencies, just as when I lift
a book I do so through bringing my muscles to bear upon it to raise it up; in the supernatural he works upon
physical agencies, just as, to compare great things with
small, my spiritual will operates directly and immediately
upon my muscular system when I determine to move my
arm. But just as in both the illustrations which I have
used, the seat of causation is in my will; so in both the
natural and the supernatural the source of energy is
God; and we shall sink into practical atheism, if we allow the operation of what we call secondary causes to

hide from us the pervading power and providence of him who is the great First Cause.

In ordinary cases the cure of disease may come, does come, through a more circuitous channel than it did in that of this afflicted woman, but yet in every case it comes as really from God, and so when sickness invades our household, or pestilence stalks through our city, we should apply to God for relief. I know, indeed, that in urging the offering of prayer in such circumstances, I am adopting language which in these days will be decried by many as unscientific, and derided by many as superstitious. But "*I believe in God the Father Almighty,*" and if there be a God at all, and that God is an Almighty Father, then it is impossible to conceive that he is unable to hear and answer the cry of his children without working a miracle for the purpose; for if he cannot do that, then,—with reverence be it spoken,—he is a poorer Father than I am myself, since within human limits I can use the ordinary operations of nature for the granting of my child's request. But if, with my poor knowledge and my limited power, I can do that, who dares to say that the omnipotent and omniscient God may not employ the usual forces of nature to an extent that is as much beyond human reckoning, as its mode is above human comprehension, in answering the prayers of his people for relief under affliction? So, in spite of all the objections which have been raised in these recent times, against the offering of prayer for physical blessings, I urge the duty, yea the privilege, of bringing the sick to Jesus and asking their cure from him.

But in earnestly insisting upon that I am as far as possible from accepting the view which some have adopted that nothing else than prayer is necessary for the cure of disease. When we pray, " Give us this day our daily bread," we are not such fools as to expect that God will feed us without the use of means by ourselves. He has indeed, on extraordinary occasions, as in the case of the Israelites in the wilderness, and in that of the multitude on the mountain-side, supernaturally provided bread for men; just as in the instance of my text he gave a cure by miracle to this afflicted woman. But no one expects to be fed by prayer, or even by faith, while he dispenses with the use of the means by which he is to earn his bread. The Christian apostle has laid down the law here, that " if any will not work, neither should he eat," and the principle that is beneath these words holds equally in the case of disease. It is something very much the reverse of piety, therefore, for a man to ignore the use of means which God has put in his own power, or to neglect those measures for the preservation of health, or for the cure of sickness which men have discovered for themselves, by their investigation of his ordinary laws, and then pretend to trust in prayer alone for safety or deliverance. We have learned by the study of our own nature that there are certain principles the contravention of which sooner or later generates disease, and therefore to set these at defiance and have recourse to prayer, as if that alone would ward away all evil, is not faith, but presumption. The laws of health, or whatever you may choose to call them, are just as really the commandments of God, as are the precepts of the decalogue, and you may as well thrust your fingers into the flame and expect that God will keep them, while you pray, from being burned, as dwell in filth, or breathe the foul atmosphere of a badly drained house, and expect that, as the result of prayer, you will be preserved from disease. Such conduct in the matter of health is completely parallel to that in the matter of holiness, which Paul ex-

posed when he said, " What shall we say then ? shall we
continue in sin that grace may abound ? " It is anti-
nomianism in the physical sphere, as the other is in the
spiritual, a pretending to honor God, by trusting in him
and praying to him, while the man is really dishonoring
God by disobeying him. And just as Paul has conclusively proved that he who has intelligently accepted forgiveness will also strive actively after holiness, so we may
allege that he who rightly understands what prayer for
the warding off of disease means, will be diligent in the
removal of all its causes.

But the same principles hold in the matter of cure as
in that of prevention. We have discovered certain med-
icines which are valuable for the healing of certain
diseases; and there are among us men who have given
themselves to the study of the human frame, and the
sicknesses to which it is liable, with the view of finding
out what that mode of treatment is by which they may
be alleviated or removed. So just as although the husbandman prays, " Give us this day our daily bread," he
takes good care to plough his fields and sow his seed, the
sick man who prays that Christ may make him whole,
will send for the physician and faithfully apply the remedies which he prescribes, and he will look for an answer
to his prayer through the Lord's blessing on these remedies,
or through the providential suggestion to the mind of the
medical man of other remedies which may be efficacious.
To take another course and trust in prayer alone is, to
follow a course which in its own way is as dishonoring
to God as is the blackest unbelief. Effort without
prayer is an ignoring of God; but prayer without effort
is a mockery of God. The true believer is he who com-
bines both prayer and effort. He does not trust in the
means alone any more than he does in the prayer alone,

but his confidence is in God's blessing with and on the means. He looks for the answer to his prayer through the ordinary channels of that providence whereof Isaac Taylor has so truly said, " This is in fact the great miracle of Providence, that no miracles are needed to accomplish its purposes." Nor will his faith be staggered if the answer should come in the form of death, in spite of the use of all means, and the offering of his earnest supplication, for he has so learned to say " Our Father," that it is not difficult for him to add, " Thy will be done," and that is the essence of all true prayer.

III. But now, leaving these matters on which I have dwelt so long because so much that seems pious, but is really impious, has been recently advanced among us concerning them, I ask you to notice, in the last place, as an inference from the narrative in my text, that when we have received healing from Christ, we should show our gratitude by ministering to Christ. How beautiful and touching is the statement, " and immediately she arose and ministered unto them. " Now here, as I have already hinted, is a striking though incidental proof that this woman was healed by miracle. We know the extreme weakness to which fever reduces a patient; and not seldom long weeks are required for recovery after the fever has disappeared. But, in a moment this woman has her wonted strength. Truly " this is the Lord's doing, it is marvellous in our eyes. " Yet it is not to the manner in which she regained her strength, so much as to the use which she made of it, when it was regained, that I would now turn your attention. Her first act was one of grateful ministration to him who healed her. Doubtless there is spiritual truth taught here; and we may learn that when Jesus has cured our souls, we should spend our whole lives in his service. But I do not dwell now especially upon that, for I am afraid that in insisting upon gratitude for the great blessing of our soul's salvation, we sometimes forget to incite you to thankfulness for the mercies of God's daily providence. I am anxious, therefore, to remind you, that we ought to show gratitude for common mercies, and, especially among these, for recovery from illness, and even more particularly for the blessing of continued health. And if you ask me how you are to render such thanks, I answer, " By ministering to Christ." " Yes," you reply, " but where shall I find him ? If he were here in person, I might do as this woman did, and as Martha and Mary did when they entertained him in their home, and if I know my own heart I would make him welcome to the best I have ; but he is not here, and how can I minister unto him?" To which I answer that you can do so through loving attendance on those who are suffering. You remember how he said to Saul, who, so far as we know, had never seen him in the flesh, " Why persecutest thou me, " intimating thereby that he had stricken him through his followers, and you cannot have forgotten that sublime saying, " Inasmuch as ye did it unto one of the least of these my brethren, ye did it unto me. " When, therefore, you ask me, Where shall I find Christ, that I may minister to him ? I point you at this time to those who are stricken with disease, or disabled by accident, and say, Go minister to them, and seek to heal them, and that will be ministering to him. And if you feel that you have no such resources as would enable you to deal with all cases of that sort that are needing succor, then I invite you to join with others in the maintenance of such institutions as exist among us for relieving the necessities of the diseased.* These institutions owe their very origin to this Christian

* This discourse was preached on Hospital Sunday.

motive—and by it also are they to be liberally supported.
It is true, indeed, that this is a way of dispensing char-
ity in which you may have almost absolute certainty
that you are not giving aid to imposition and deceit. It
is true, also, that the facilities afforded by hospitals for
the study of diseases, and the best modes of treating
them, have largely contributed to the progress of medical science, and the training of intelligent and efficient
nurses of the sick, so that ultimately every home in the
city comes to reap a benefit from their existence. But
to do our best work we must draw our motive from the
highest source, and even as Paul, in pleading for a contribution for the poor saints at Jerusalem, put it thus,
" For ye know the grace of our Lord Jesus Christ, that
though he was rich, for your sakes he became poor, that
ye through his poverty might be rich "—so our motive for
the relief of the diseased must be one of gratitude to
Christ, for the blessings, both temporal and spiritual,
which we have received from him. Have you ever
thanked God for your health ? If you have not, then do
it at once, and if you would give your gratitude the most
appropriate practical form, let it take that of a contribution to a Christian Hospital. Have you ever made a
thank-offering for your recovery from that serious illness
which threatened to be mortal ? If you have not, then
make that offering for the securing of medical attendance,
skilled nursing, and comfortable couches for those who in
their sickness have no such advantages ; and be sure
that he who has promised, that " whosoever shall give a
cup of cold water to a disciple in the name of a disciple
shall in no wise lose his reward," will not forget your gift.

VI.

A SUNSET SCENE IN CAPERNAUM.

Matt. viii. 16, 17 ; Mark i. 32, 33 ; Luke iv. 40, 41.

I HAVE always regarded the scene which these verses describe as one of the most beautiful in the life of our Lord Jesus Christ upon the earth. It was the end of the Sabbath in the city of Capernaum. The sun had just gone down behind the mountains, and its afterglow was lingering yet upon the summits of the hills on the eastern shore of the lake of Tiberius, whose waters lay dark and motionless, as if preparing themselves to mirror the earliest of the stars. The Master and his disciples were still in the home of Peter, where he had gladdened all their hearts, by healing the mother-in-law of his apostle of the fever which was burning in her veins. But on the outside a multitude so great that it might be said to comprise all the inhabitants of the place, was gathered together. Unlike other crowds, this was divided into groups, and in the centre of each of these, an object of intense solicitude to all its members, was some poor afflicted relative, who was suffering from one or other of the diseases that flesh is heir to, and whom they had brought for healing to the Great Physician. There were those who were possessed with demons, and those who were blind, and deaf, and lame. The chronic

98

invalid, and he who had just been seized with some acute malady, were there, and when the Lord came forth " he laid his hands on every one of them, and healed them." What glad gratitude would fill all their hearts at such a result of their application to him, and who may attempt to describe the feelings of each group, as its members separated through the deepening darkness to their homes, or the emotions of those who were healed, as they felt the vigor of health once more giving elasticity to their steps and buoyancy to their spirits ? And yet the whole story is told here most artlessly, without any attempt at amplification, far less of exaggeration, as if it had been the most natural thing in the world ! What a striking, although incidental, proof, we have in this of the inspiration of the evangelists ! Other writers would have tried to make the most of such a constellation of miracles, but they do not stop in their narratives to remark upon it at all ; they let it shine with its own light in the firmament of that life in which what seemed to men to be natural was really supernatural, and what appeared to mere human view to be supernatural, was most truly natural, because it is the life of him who was and is incarnate God.

Have we not here also an impressive illustration of the compassion of Christ ? He never saw a multitude without feeling for all that were in it, and no sufferer ever made application for relief to him in vain. So here " he laid his hands on every one of them and healed them." Each had his own form of disease, but that touch of power was enough to convey health, no matter what the particular malady might be. And in all this, viewed as a sign, or acted parable of gospel truth, we have the assurance that the Saviour is able and willing to remove from us every form of sin, and to work in us that holi-

ness without which we cannot see the Lord. You
remember that suggestive phrase in Solomon's prayer at
the dedication of the Temple, " What prayer and supplication so ever be made by any man, or by all thy
people Israel, which shall know every man the plague of
his own heart, and spread forth his hands toward this
house, then hear thou in heaven thy dwelling-place." *
" Which shall know every man the plague of his own
heart." Ah ! yes, there is a plague in every heart, different in each, yet incurable in all by merely human
power. It is a great thing, often a terrible thing, when
a man comes to the knowledge of what his plague really
is. But whatever it be, he is welcome to take it to the
Lord Jesus Christ, in the full assurance that he will cure
it. There is balm in Gilead, there is a physician there.
That remedy is sovereign for every form of malady of
heart, and there are no hopeless cases in that physician's
practice. The only incurables are those who persist-
ently refuse to make application unto him. So as I think
out the full significance of this sunset scene in the gospel
story, the vision widens from Capernaum to the world,
and still I see the blessed Redeemer exercising his
divine and chosen vocation as the Spiritual Healer of
humanity. From " every clime and coast " the sin-sick
sons of Adam, " every man that knoweth the plague of
his own heart," come to him—the guilty, the backslid-
ing, the burdened, the forlorn, the tempted, the victims
of evil habits, and the worn-out votaries of pleasure, and
"he lays his hand on every one of them and healeth
them." My hearers, at whose hearts a plague is aching,
why should not you join the throng ? With some of you
the sun may be setting, in some of you the malady may
be of the most violent sort, but no one of you yet is beyond

* I Kings viii. 38, 39.

his help. Go then to him, and his touch of power will make you whole.

But, leaving this line of remark, I wish more especially to-night to direct your attention to the bearing of this narrative on one of the most interesting and successful methods of Christian effort both at home and abroad. A few weeks ago, at a conference held in Chickering Hall, on the religious condition of this city, I was at once greatly surprised and deeply pained to hear one of the speakers make what I must call an unjustifiable attack on medical missions, and lest the sentiments which he expressed should spread among the church members of the city I have determined to devote the remainder of my present discourse to an explanation and defence of this form of Christian aggressiveness, founded more especially on the passage which we have just been considering. The speaker to whom I have referred was alluding to the folly of bribing people to come to the house of God, by giving them food, and said a few strong and sensible things in reference to that to which I could heartily say, Amen. But when he put medical missions into the same category, he seemed to me to be very wide of the mark, and when he used these words : " Medical missions, and flower missions, and soup kitchens and such things, in the wake of the church of Christ, are all right, but pushing them ahead and making them a bait, or an introduction to the human heart, I believe does not meet with the divine sanction," * and again, " I believe that as ministers of Christ we are making a mistake in thinking that anything can be even a temporary substitute for the gospel of Christ," he seemed to me to arraign the wisdom

* See "Report of the Proceedings of the Chickering Hall Conference."

of the Lord Jesus Christ himself, and to be speaking in
ignorance of the nature and purpose of the work which
he so emphatically condemned. For, in the first place,
what medical missionary ever thought of substituting his
work among the sick for the gospel of Christ? On the
contrary, the great design which he has in view is to secure an opportunity of presenting the gospel of Christ to
those who otherwise would never come to hear it, and
while some other methods of attempting to obtain such an
opportunity may be open to question, may even be worthy
of condemnation,—the plan adopted by the medical missionary is a direct following of the example of the Lord
Jesus as given in the narrative which has been to-night
before us. For, in a very real sense, the open space before the door of Simon's house on that occasion was a
great dispensary, in which the Saviour went through
among the patients, and healed them all, thereby directing their attention to himself, accrediting his mission to
them as divine, and disposing them to receive him as
their Saviour from the deeper malady of sin.

Moreover, did not the Lord himself, when commission-
ing his twelve apostles, say to them, "As ye go, preach,
saying, The kingdom of heaven is at hand. Heal the
sick, cleanse the lepers, raise the dead, cast out devils;
freely ye have received, freely give." * True, he gave to
these apostles the miraculous gift of healing, and that has
now disappeared from the church, but in the healing art,
as presently practised among us, we have a modern equivalent to miracles. For as Dr. Post of Beyrout said in
his most eloquent address at the late London Conference,
the cures effected by the surgeon are " miracles of science,
and science is a miracle of Christianity." † When,

---

* Matt. x. 7–8.

† "Report of the Missionary Conference, London, 1888." Vol. I.
p. 385.

therefore, with the means which we have at our hands, we heal all manner of diseases, and combine with that the proclamation of the gospel, are we not following as closely as our limitations will allow, the example of our Lord and obeying the precept which he gave to his apostles ? To say that such a course does not meet with the divine sanction, is most unwarranted, is entirely inconsistent with the gospel record of the ministry of our Lord himself, and is positively contradicted by the history of missionary enterprise during the last forty years.

But that we may proceed intelligently, let me put before you what a medical mission is. The missionary is a fully qualified medical man, whose heart is full of love to Christ, and consecration to his cause. He is accompanied by an evangelist, and a staff of assistants likeminded and similar in spirit to himself. He opens, in some suitable place, a dispensary, which has in connection with it a hall of dimensions ample enough to contain all the patients who may come to him for healing, and with a private room adjoining in which each of them may be dealt with in turn. The labors of the day begin with a religious service in the hall, conducted by the doctor himself, a hymn of praise is sung, a portion of Scripture is read, and, founded on that, an earnest evangelical address is delivered. After that the medical man retires to the consulting room, and each of the patients in turn goes into him, is examined, and is prescribed for. In the meantime, while others are waiting to be examined and those who have seen the doctor are lingering to get the medicine which has been prescribed, the evangelist takes the desk, and speaks to them all of Jesus and his love, holding the uplifted Christ before their eyes, and exhorting them in his name to be reconciled to God, or goes through among them to speak to each one separately of

Christ and his salvation. After a while the success of
the dispensary leads up to the erection of an hospital into
which patients are received, and in which they remain
necessarily for a longer time than they could in a dispensary. During their stay there, they are always open to
receive the visits of the medical man and his assistants,
and the result is that not a few of them leave the institution spiritually blessed, healed in soul as well as in body.
Then, in association with these two forms of work, there
is often, especially in foreign lands, a system of itineracy.
The doctor goes out, accompanied by the best of his assistants, to some outlying district, in which he receives dispensary patients and treats them, and to which he returns at
intervals, looking after those whom he has formerly seen,
and carefully inquiring into the results of his seed sowing
in the past. In this way the door is opened for the entrance
of other missionaries, the confidence of the people is secured, and much direct good is effected. Now where, I
ask, is the dishonor done to the gospel in all this? where
is the disloyalty to Christ? where is the putting forth of
anything as a substitute for the cross?

But let us descend now from generals to particulars.
I have given you a description of what a medical mission
is; let me tell you something of what it accomplishes. I
wish that I could reproduce to you the speech of Dr.
Post in London, to which I have just referred. It was
one of the most remarkable that were delivered in that
great conference, and thrilled every one who was privileged to hear it, but let me give you one item, taken almost at random from it. He was describing a Christmas
festival in the hospital at Beyrout, and here is his graphic
sketch of one of those who were present: " Just behind
him sits an old man with a venerable presence, a long
white beard, a turban, a girdle about his loins, and a loose

flowing robe. Whom do you suppose that man to be ?
Why, he is a lineal descendant of the great Saladin. He
is proud of his lineage. But here he is, in an hospital, a
Mohammedan. A month ago, if I had gone to his house,
he would have driven me away as a Christian dog.
But now, as he comes into this room, he seizes my hand,
covers it all over with kisses, and bows himself to my
very feet. What led him to bow down to that Christian
dog ? That dog gave him the use of his two eyes. He
came there blind, and now he sees, and here he sits . .
with his eyes opened and his ears ready to receive the
message of the gospel." * Take another example in the
experience of Dr. Colin Valentine, who went out to India
in 1861, as a medical missionary from the United Presbyterian Church of Scotland, with which I was connected
at that time. I cannot go into details. These may be
found in the numbers of the "Medical Missionary Record,"
for November, December and January, and I give the
following summary from the speech of Dr. Lowe at the
Missionary Conference. " Dr. Valentine settled first at
Beawr. God had laid his hand heavily upon him; he
was very ill, and recommended to go to the Himalayas
for change of air and rest. On his way thither, having
to pass through Jeypore, he was brought into contact with
the Maharajah, who told him that his wife, the Maharanee,
was very ill, and that the native physicians had given
her up. Dr. Valentine said that he would be glad to see
her, and do what he could for her. The way was opened
up. The Maharajah was pleased, and arranged that—difficult as it is to gain access to the women there—Dr.
Valentine should visit the Ranee. The result was
that through God's blessing upon Dr. Valentine's treatment, she was restored to health. The Maharajah said,

---

* Report of Missionary Conference as before, vol. i. p. 383.

'What can I do for you?' He said, 'Let me preach the gospel here.' The Maharajah said, 'If you stay here and be my private physician, I shall be glad.' But Dr. Valentine replied, 'I am a missionary of the gospel.' Now no missionary had previously been allowed to settle in Jeypore, that great stronghold of idolatry, perhaps one of the greatest in northern India. The Maharajah said, 'You will be my private physician, will you not?' The doctor answered, 'Yes, but only on one condition, that you will allow me to preach the gospel from one end of the province to the other without let or hindrance.' The Maharajah agreed, and Dr. Valentine remained at Jeypore for fourteen years, and now the United Presbyterian Church has a large and prosperous mission there." *

A similar story might be told of the late Dr. Mackenzie and the Ladi Li in China, and, in the face of facts like these, it is idle to talk of medical missions as putting the gospel in a subordinate place, or as being entirely without the divine sanction. The facts are that the door is open to the medical man when it is closed to all others, and that his entrance has been the means of securing a welcome to all Christian missionaries for his sake.

If time allowed, I might speak of the opening up of the Zenanas in India to female medical missionaries, and of the good results which have flowed therefrom; but I have said enough to prove that the combination of the healing of the sick with the preaching of the gospel has been under God pre-eminently blessed in the opening up of regions to the truth which else had been hermetically sealed against the preacher. I must add, however, one or two testimonies to the direct results of the prosecution of this work. For it is useful not only as preparing the way for the entrance of the gospel, but also as a

* Ibid p. 390.

missionary agency in itself. Dr. Lowe, in his excellent
work entitled "Medical Missions, Their Place and
Power," tells us,* that "during 1883, in the Swatow
Hospital, in China, upwards of one hundred and forty
patients, men and women, gave in their names as candi-
dates for church fellowship. For such, special services
are held more or less regularly during the week, and on
Sunday afternoons they assemble for examination on the
subjects taught. Of this large number of applicants
only a few were baptized previous to their leaving the
hospital, the missionaries, as a rule, requiring that, before receiving baptism, they should go home and show the
sincerity of their profession by conducting themselves
as Christians among their relatives and neighbors." The
same writer gives us the following : † At a meeting held
lately in the Medical Mission House, Edinburgh, the Rev.
Mr. MacGregor of Amoy gave a most interesting account of medical mission work in China, and among other
gratifying results he told of a man, from an unevangel-
ized district of country, who came, nearly seventeen years
ago, to the hospital at Amoy, where he was cured of his
disease and received daily Christian instruction. When
quite recovered, he returned home and told his friends
and neighbors of the kind treatment he had received,
and of the gospel of God's love which he had heard.
The hearts of a few were opened, and they believed ; the
numbers increased, persecution arose, at one time so
fierce, that they had to flee the village. At length they
communicated with the missionaries and begged for a
teacher ; one was sent, and a congregation of about a
hundred was gathered. Many came from a considerable
distance, and a new community had to be founded further inland. The work has gone on increasing, and " to-

* P. 129.　　　　　† Pp. 132, 133.

day," said Dr. MacGregor, " there are seven congrega-
gations, each numbering from thirty to upwards of a hundred persons, all the outcome of God's blessing on the
good seed sown in that one patient's heart, while in the
mission hospital." A fact like that prepares us to believe the statement of Dr. J. L. Maxwell in his paper
before the London Conference to this effect. " The congregation in an hospital chapel is unique in its com-
prehensiveness. It is not merely one or two hundred souls, it is one or two hundred souls gathered
probably out of fifty towns and villages. And what
does that mean ? It means, of necessity, the diffusion of a fair measure of gospel truth in all these different
directions. As many as twelve hundred to fourteen
hundred towns and villages have been represented in a
single year among the in patients of a single hospital.
Does not this speak of rare and glorious possibilities ?"
and his paper closes with these words: " I say it with
an absolute conviction that I speak the truth, that, in
heathen and Mohammedan lands, there is no class of
men to whom the Lord has entrusted more choice and
blessed opportunities of sowing the seed of the Word in
the hearts of men, than those which are enjoyed by medical missionaries and I am satisfied that a right appreciation of the methods and opportunities and results of
medical missionary work ought to constrain the Church
of Christ to enter with a far more confident and liberal
heart upon a ministry which is so nearly after the Lord's
own pattern."*

Surely statements like these are enough to refute
the assertion that medical missions put healing in
the place of the gospel and are without the divine
sanction. And when the speaker on that occasion as-

* Report of London Conference, vol. ii. pp 123, 124, 125.

serted that Mr. J. Hudson Taylor was of his way of thinking, he must have spoken in ignorance of what that noble man affirmed at the London Conference of which he was one of the most interesting and distinguished members. It is true, indeed, that, by way of caution, Mr. Taylor said that even " medical work must be a means of bringing souls under the influence of the gospel, and not a substitute for it." But in running away with the second part of that statement, and leaving out the first, the objector grievously misrepresented Mr. Taylor, and made him appear as the antagonist of a form of work which he has warmly endorsed. Thus in the very paper from which I have made the above quotation he has said, speaking of itinerant work, " Missionaries who have some knowledge of medicine may do much good and win golden opinions while on journeys, and will be successors of the apostles who were commissioned to preach and to heal."

I have dwelt, perhaps, at too great length on this matter, but I own that I have scarcely yet recovered from the shock of surprise with which I heard the attack to which I have referred, and because, even for the evangelization of our own city, there are few agencies likely to be more successful than that of medical missions—a kind of agency the efficacy of which has been tried and proved abundantly elsewhere, not alone in Syria, India, and China, but also in London, Liverpool, and Edinburgh. Why should we not make more use of it in New York, and why should we allow an institution like Dr. Dowkonth's to languish for lack of funds ? I propose, therefore, that this evening we make a contribution for this meritorious society, as by far the best answer we can give to the foolish aspersions that were cast upon medical missions by the orator of Chickering Hall.

VII.

THE CLEANSING OF THE LEPER.

Matt. viii. 2-4. Mark i. 40-45. Luke v. 12-15.

WE have no data from which we can conclusively identify the place where this miracle was performed, but Mark enables us to fix its date, at least approximately. For he tells us that immediately after the ever-memorable sunset scene in the city of Capernaum, our Lord, rising up a great while before day, went out and departed to a solitary place and there prayed. Thither in the morning he was followed by Simon Peter, and them that were with him; and they told him that all men were seeking for him. Yet he did not at once return with them, but said unto them, " Let us go into the next town, that I may preach there also ; for therefore came I forth," and in accordance with that determination he preached in the synagogues throughout all Galilee, and cast out devils. It was, therefore, at some point in this Galilean journey, undertaken for the preaching of the gospel and the healing of the sick, that the miracle which is this evening to be the subject of discourse was wrought, and it was probably nearer the close of his journey than its beginning, and in the neighborhood of one of the towns in Galilee.

It is every way likely, therefore, that this poor

man accosted the Saviour from a distance, while he
was moving on from one village or town to another,
there to deliver his message of mercy to mankind,
and the miracle which he wrought was itself a figura-
tive presentation of the gospel which he preached,
for the disease which in this instance he cured was
specially and peculiarly selected in the law of Moses to
be the physical analogue of the moral malady of sin. All
disease, indeed, is the fruit of sin, and every form of it
might have been regarded and treated under the law of
Moses as an emblem of evil. But that would not have
taught so striking a lesson to the people, as was given
to them by the choice of one special malady, and would
besides have been intolerably burdensome ; therefore, a
selection was made, and leprosy was well calculated, from
its ghastly nature and revolting accompaniments, to serve
the purpose. It is minutely described in the book of
Leviticus, and seems to have had its origin among the
Israelites, while they were laboring among the dust and
heat of the brick-kilns of Egypt. It makes its appearance first upon the skin, in the shape of certain spots,
small at the outset and of a reddish color, but gradually
increasing in size, and presenting by and by a white,
scaly, shining aspect. After a time the spots spread over
the whole body, " the hair falls from the head and eye-
brows ; the nails loosen, decay and drop off ; joint after
joint of the fingers and toes shrink up and slowly fall
away. The gums are absorbed, and the teeth disappear.
The nose, the eyes, the tongue, the palate are slowly
consumed, and finally, the wretched victim sinks into the
earth and disappears, while medicine has no power to
stay the ravages of this fell disease or even to mitigate
sensibly its tortures."* It was thus in point of fact

* " The Land and the Book," English edition, pp. 653, 654,

a living death. After the priest had pronounced that a man was really afflicted with it, he was rigidly cut off from all fellowship with his fellows, and was compelled to put on the marks of mourning which were usually worn for the dead. He had his clothes rent, his head bare and his lips covered, and whenever he saw any one approaching he had to give them warning of his proximity by calling out " Unclean! unclean!" These precautions were taken not merely for sanitary reasons, or to guard against contagion, for it is not certain that leprosy was contagious, but, in order that the people might be taught through the parable of leprosy, what a fearful and loathsome thing sin is in the sight of God. As I have already said, no medicine could effect either its mitigtaion or its cure. The leper might perhaps recover, but he was not cured, for, as Dr. Thomson has said, " Leprosy has ever been regarded as a direct punishment from God, and absolutely incurable, except by the same divine power that sent it. " Hence the King of Israel, when the King of Syria sent Naaman to him, that he might recover him of his leprosy said, " Am I God, to kill and to make alive, that this man doth send unto me to recover a man of his leprosy ?"

When the leper recovered, and was declared by the priest to be clean, there were two stages in his purification. He was restored first to his position as a citizen, and readmitted to the fellowship of men, and it was in connection with this stage that the priest observed the ordinance of the two birds* which bore a striking resemblance to that of the two goats on the great day of atonement. The second stage was the re-establishment of the right to participate in the sacred privileges of the clean, and, in connection with that, the leper brought a trespass offer-

---

* Leviticus xiv. 4-7.

ing, a sin offering, a burnt offering and a meat offering:
and there was a consecration service very similar, though
of course with well marked differences, to that observed at the setting apart of Aaron and his sons to the
office of the priesthood.* Thus leprosy set before the
minds of the Hebrews the insidious beginning, gradual
increase, and final prevalence of sin; it illustrated its incurable nature, save by the gracious intervention of
God, its loathsome character, and its dire results; while,
on the other hand, the services connected with the
cleansing of the leper remind us that the blood of Christ
applied to the conscience and the renewing and sancti-
fying grace of the Holy Spirit are the only revealed,
as they are the only effectual, means of purification from
the defilement and death of sin; and that those who have
been thus delivered ought in deepest gratitude to present their bodies living sacrifices to God, which is their
reasonable service.

These details concerning leprosy will enable us, in
some degree, to understand the peculiar form in which
this poor man in the narrative before us made his request
to the Saviour. Matthew says, " He came and worshipped him ; " and Mark puts it thus, " There came a
leper to him, beseeching him, and kneeling down to him,"
thus manifesting both his earnestness and reverence, and
saying, " If thou wilt, thou canst make me clean." He
had, therefore, no doubt of the ability of Christ to heal
him, and that, considering the incurable nature of
leprosy, was an indication of great faith. How he came
to have such faith in the power of Christ we are not informed. But he must have heard of his miracles of
healing elsewhere, and though this is the first recorded
instance of the cure of a leper by the Lord, it is possible

* Leviticus xiv. 10-32.

that there might be cases of leprosy among the diseases which he had healed. But whether there were or not, there was in this man's heart an unwavering assurance that the Lord could make him clean, if he would. There might be the ability without the will, or the will without the ability, but his hope was that in Christ there would be the combination of both, and all that was needed for that, in his estimation, was the will. He was sure of the ability. After all that he had heard, he could not doubt that, and so it all hinged on this "if thou wilt." But he needed not have doubted that either. For the Lord was never unwilling to bless those who were willing to receive blessing at his hands. So we are told by Mark that, "moved with compassion, he put forth his hand and touched him, and saith unto him, I will, be thou clean." He touched the leper! What a thrill of joy would vibrate in the man's heart at that unwonted experience? The miracle altogether apart, that was the first touch of love he had felt from human hand since first he was isolated from men by his uncleanness; and it was the touch of One who was the holiest that ever wore our mortal frame! "Here is one," he might say within himself, "and he the purest of them all, who is not afraid to touch me, outcast, loathsome, scaly as I am, and so, whatever comes of it, I bless him for that touch, for there is love, and sympathy and tenderness in it. But there was healing, too, for his flesh came to him again, as the flesh of a little child, and from that moment he was clean. If others had touched him, they would have been defiled thereby; but when the pure One put his hand upon him, he communicated thereby his own purity to him, and the disease retired from before his hand of power.

After this act of healing, our Lord straightly charged

the man to say nothing to any one, but to go at once to
the priest, that he might be examined and pronounced to
be clean by the legal authority in the case, and that he
might offer for his cleansing those things which Moses had
commanded. The Lord came "not to destroy the law,
but to fulfil" it, and so he sent the man to obey the particular precept which was appropriate to his circumstances, while at the same time he secured that the genuineness of the miracle would be attested by the official
who had been designated by the law for the particular
purpose of determining whether or not in a given
instance the leprosy had disappeared. The charge to
tell no man might be given, lest by the premature publication of his wondrous works matters might be preci-
pated to a crisis before the time; or lest the Lord
himself might be hindered in his work by the crowds
which would be attracted to him by the publication of the
miracle; or lest the man might be injured spiritually by
making a boast of his cure, looking at it and speaking of
it as a manifestation of special divine favor to himself.
But the charge was disregarded, for he "began to pub-
lish it much, and to blaze abroad the matter," and the
result so seriously retarded the work of Christ that
"he could enter no more openly into the city; but was
without in desert places; and they came to him from
every quarter."

But leaving now the exposition of the narrative, let
us pause a few moments more to lift out of it and carry
with us one or two lessons of practical importance. And,
in the first place, let us note that he who could cure the
leprosy which was the type of sin, can cure sin itself.
The very purpose for which he came into the world was
"to take away sin by the sacrifice of himself," and his

resurrection from the dead and ascension into glory have proclaimed that he succeeded in that which he undertook. The second in the ever-blessed Trinity, he took our nature upon him, and bore our sins, nailing them with his own body to the tree, so that now the most aggravated sinner amongst us, believing in him, may be freely and righteously forgiven for his sake. Not only so, by the gift of his Holy Spirit, secured by him on his ascension, he provides that the soul which believes in him is regenerated; so that it loves what it formerly hated, and hates what it formerly loved. The man, while preserving his identity, is a new man; just as the leper, though the same man, was set free from the corruption and loathsomeness that formerly characterized him, and virtually received what was to all intents and purposes a new body, freed from the taint of that rotting putrefaction which was eating into his very vitals. In like manner the " old man " of the believer is crucified with Christ, and he is renewed in the spirit of his mind, in knowledge, righteousness and holiness. Christ can do all this for the sinner. He is able to save, thus, " to the uttermost, all who come unto God by him," and he has done it in cases innumerable. Even in our own days he has done it for multitudes, who are living evidences of his saving power. There are, probably, some such cases here now. You will see many of them to-night, if you care to look for them in the mission-rooms and churches of the city, men and women who have been lifted by him out of a life as loathsome and repulsive as was the body of this leper, and are now walking in light, and purity, and peace. They have now no relish for their old iniquities, but are seeking evermore closer conformity to Christ's image, and are habitually following that holiness without which no man can see the Lord.

They are now no more enslaved by their former evil habits, but have been emancipated from their bondage and are walking in the glorious liberty of the children of God. They "are washed, they are sanctified, they are justified in the name of the Lord Jesus, and by the Spirit of our God." We can no more doubt of his ability to save sinners, than the spectators of this great miracle could doubt of his power to cleanse the leper. And we are as sure of his willinghood as we are of his ability. Has he not said, " Come unto me, all ye that labor and are heavy laden, and I will give you rest"? Are not these also his words, " Him that cometh unto me I will in no wise cast out"? And who can forget this gracious declaration, " God so loved the world that he gave his only-begotten Son, that whosoever believeth in him should not perish but have everlasting life"? Where is the exception here? What can be more universal than " all "? What more inclusive than " Him that cometh unto me "? What more comprehensive than that grand word " whosoever "? If any one is excluded here, he must exclude himself. Come, then, all ye who feel the guilt, the degradation, the foulness, and the corruption of sin, no matter how numerous, or how aggravated your iniquities may have been, come unto him and he will make you clean. Though you be as loathsome in your own sight as this leper was to himself, come unto Christ and cry for salvation, and it shall come to pass that " before you call, he will answer, and while you are yet speaking he will hear." If, after all this, you are still unsaved, it will not be because he cannot or will not save you, but because you " will not come unto him that you may have life." Ah! that will of yours, the trouble is all there. Why should you be unwilling to be blessed ? That is the only thing that stands now between you and salvation. Do not let it so stand a moment longer, but take the gift he freely offers, and give yourselves back to him enriched thereby for his service in the world.

But, in the second place, let us learn that if we wish to benefit those who are distressed, or to elevate those who are degraded, we must somehow put ourselves into sympathy with them. We must, if I may so express it, put ourselves for the time on a level with them, and make ourselves one with them. The Lord Jesus, as we see from this narrative "touched" the leper. He thereby put himself for the time on a level with him, became, if the law had been insisted on, unclean along with him, manifested his compassion for him and interest in him, and so touched the man's heart as well as his body. Now this was just a particular instance of the same great law which underlies the incarnation itself. When God wished to save men he touched humanity, by taking human nature upon himself. He became flesh and dwelt among men, that thereby he might raise them to be sons of God. He took upon himself the likeness of sinful flesh, but without the sin, that for sin he might condemn sin in the flesh. And so if we would save the degraded, we must put ourselves on a level with them, while yet we are not partakers of their sins, in order that by our sympathy with them we may lift them up to the platform from which we have stooped. You remember that very suggestive scene in "Uncle Tom's Cabin," when Miss Ophelia was compelled to revise all her theories about the training of Topsy, by overhearing the dark little woolly head saying to some of the other slaves, "La! Miss Pheely would no more touch me than she would a toad." She felt that the child had spoken the truth, though she did not know how in the world she had come to discover it, but the revelation of it to herself let her see the great mistake she had been making in the education of her *protégé*, and told her how it was to be remedied. Now here, as it seems to me, is the very mistake which not a few earnest Christians of Miss Ophelia's stamp are making in these days. They are seeking to save the lost without touching them, and their efforts are powerless, because those on whom they are exerted feel that all the while they are making them from a mere sense of duty, and not out of any compassion for them, or sympathy with them. They are afraid of coming into contact with them. They feel almost as if touching them were like touching pitch, and would defile them, and so, however well meant, their efforts are but failures after all. I have somewhere read of a hardened criminal who was condemned to die and waiting for execution. Christian people were deeply interested in him and wished for his salvation. Pastors of different churches visited him and talked with him and prayed with him. But all they did and said seemed only to harden him the more, for they never got near him. They were afraid of him. They never touched him. At length they bethought themselves of a member of the community, known of all men for his holiness and tenderness and wisdom in the winning of souls, and they got him to visit him. When he entered the condemned cell, he sat down beside the prisoner, by whom also he was well known, and told him the simple story of the cross, and when he had finished it, he laid his hand upon the criminal's shoulder and said to him with a look of inexpressible emotion : " Now wasn't it a great sacrifice for the Son of God to lay down his life for guilty sinners like me and you ? " In a moment the fountains of the great deep were broken up. The heart of the man was touched. The big tears ran down his cheeks, and the bursting sobs seemed to convulse his frame. From that time he was a different man, and listened with interest to all that was said to him, while ever and anon he would exclaim, " To think of such a good and holy man, as I know him to be, putting himself on a level with me, and saying ' Sinners like me and you'!" If, therefore, we want to do good, we must go about it in conformity with this great law. We must not give our money and our efforts merely, but our sympathy as well. The lines of the Christian hymnist are as true of effort as of words :

> " Thy soul must overflow if thou
> Another's soul would'st reach,
> It needs the overflow of heart
> To give the lips full speech."

So if we seek to labor successfully in raising the fallen, and reclaiming the wanderer, our efforts will be powerless without this " overflow of heart " into them; for with that alone can we " touch " the objects of our solicitude.

But, in the third place, let us learn that obedience is better than zeal. This man blazed abroad the miracle, after Christ had straightly charged him to tell it to no man, until at least he had showed himself to the priest. It was, perhaps, natural for him to do as he did, and probably he thought that no harm could come of it. But still it was disobedience. It was arrogating to himself greater wisdom than that of Christ. It was virtually saying that he knew what to do better than Jesus knew what to command him, and it led to inconvenience, and perhaps also did injury to himself. It is not always wise to encourage young converts to tell the story of their conversion, and from the fact that in some cases the Saviour forbade and in others encouraged those whom he had healed, to tell how he had blessed them, it seems probable that he had respect in each case to the subject-ive effect on the individuals themselves. Some would not be harmed by it at all, because all they told, they told for his glory, while others would be greatly injured by it, because they put themselves in the forefront. Therefore in our dealings with young converts, we should not have one unvarying rule for all, but should study the idiosyncra-sies of each and act accordingly. There is surely some-where a good middle ground between the absolute reti-cence on the sacred matters of personal experience which some practice, and the irreverent and flippant familiarity with which others delight to parade the magnitude of their sins and the manner of their conversion, as if a special honor were due to them because they had fur-nished such an opportunity to Christ for the manifesta-tion of his ability to save. But in any case when Christ bids us be silent, we have nothing to do but to obey him. He who has healed us has the best claim upon our obedi-ence, and if we love him, we will keep his command-ments, *all* of them, without selection or exception. We can lay down no rigid rule that will cover all cases, re-garding the obligation under which the young convert lies in the matter of bearing testimony to Jesus, but if he does give such testimony, let him give it humbly, rever-ently, lovingly, keeping himself in the background and with the view simply of glorifying Christ, and encourag-ing others to apply to him. Then no evil can ensue, but much good may be accomplished.

VIII.

THE CURE OF THE PARALYTIC.

Matt. ix. 2-8. Mark ii. 1-12. Luke v. 18-26.

THE miracle which we are this evening to consider was performed by our Saviour in Capernaum, to which, as " his own city," he had returned after that tour " throughout all Galilee," to which reference was made in our last discourse. His own house was there, and either in that, or in the abode of Peter, a great multitude had collected because " it was noised " that he was " at home " ; and because they were eagerly anxious to hear his word of wisdom, or to see his works of power. The crowd was so great that there was no room to receive the people, and even the door was blocked by the pressure of those who vainly sought to find an entrance. Nor was the multitude entirely local in its character, for Luke tells us that there were present " Pharisees and doctors of the law, which were come out of every town of Galilee and Judea and Jerusalem." What *they* came for we can only conjecture. It may be that they were sent to observe, and to report to those of their class in their own districts what they should see or hear. It is not impossible, indeed, that we have in their presence on this occasion the first manifestation of that malicious antagonism to the Lord which ultimately culminated in his crucifixion on

122

Calvary, and the colloquy between him and them which almost immediately ensued lends some probability to this view of the case. But whatever was the motive that brought *them* there, he did not alter his message on their account, for we read that " he preached the word unto them." He neither feared their frown, nor courted their favor, and the gospel which they heard from his lips was the same as that which the common people listened to so gladly.

But as he was proceeding with his discourse, he was interrupted in a very singular fashion. Mark tells the story with his usual graphic minuteness: "And they came unto him, bringing one sick of the palsy, which was borne of four. And when they could not come nigh unto him for the press, they uncovered the roof where he was, and when they had broken it up, they let down the bed whereon the sick of the palsy lay." Now to understand how this was done, it is necessary that we have some clear idea of the difference between an oriental and a western dwelling-house. This is admirably described, and the whole difficulty connected with the narrative removed, in the following sentences which I extract from Dr. Thomson's well-known work, " The Land and the Book." The houses " of Capernaum, as is evident from the ruins, were like those of modern villages in the same region, low, very low, with flat roofs, reached by a stairway from the yard or court. Jesus probably stood in the open lewan," (or reception-room) " and the crowd were around and in front of him. Those who carried the paralytic, not being able to come at him for the press, ascended to the roof, removed so much of it as was necessary, and let down their patient through the aperture. Examine one of these houses, and you will see at once that the thing is natural and easy to be accomplished.

The roof is only a few feet high, and by stooping down, and holding the corners of the couch—merely a thickly padded quilt, as at present, in this region—they could lay down the sick man without any apparatus of ropes or cords to assist them. And thus, I suppose, they did. The whole affair was the extemporaneous device of plain peasants, accustomed to open their roofs and let down grain, straw, and other articles, as they still do in this country. The only difficulty in this explanation is to understand how they could break up the roof without sending down such a shower of dust as to incommode our Lord and those around him. I have often seen it done, and have done it myself, to houses in Lebanon, but there is always more dust than is agreeable. The materials now employed are beams about three feet apart, across which short sticks are arranged close together, and covered with the thickly matted thorn-bush called *bellan.* Over this is spread a coat of stiff mortar, and then comes the thick marl or earth which makes the roof. Now it is easy to remove any part of this without injuring the rest. No objection, therefore, would be made on this score by the owners of the house. They had merely to scrape back the earth from a portion of the roof over the *lewan,* take up the thorns and the short sticks, and let down the couch between the beams at the very feet of Jesus. The end achieved, they could speedily restore the roof as it was before. I have the impression, however, that the covering at least of the *lewan* was not made of earth, but of materials more easily taken up. It may have been of coarse matting, like the walls and roofs of Turkman huts, or it may have been of boards, or even stone slabs, (and such I have seen) that could be quickly removed. All that is necessary, however, for us to know is that the roof was flat, easily reached, and easily opened, so as to let down the couch of the sick man; and all these points are rendered intelligible by an acquaintance with modern houses in the villages of Palestine." *

In some such way, then, as is here described by one who was long a resident in Syria, this helpless paralytic was let down immediately in front of Jesus, by his kind and sympathetic bearers, and before he had time to utter a word, the compassionate Redeemer said to him, with a divine insight, as I cannot but think, into the burden which was pressing on his conscience, and which was troubling him even more than the disease with which he was afflicted, " Son, thy sins are or have been forgiven thee," for such, and not " thy sins be forgiven thee," is the true reading of the words. The discipline through which this man's malady had brought him, had led him to discover his guilt before God—and *that* was at the moment his sorest trouble—so, addressing that, the Lord said, " Thy sins are forgiven thee," while the word *Son* may perhaps point to his youth, and is certainly an indication of the tenderness of Jesus towards him. It was not, therefore, because he wished to provoke a discussion with the Scribes and doctors of the law that were sitting by, or because all diseases are the results, in one way or another, of sin, and the removal of the cause would ensure that of the effect, that Jesus spoke to him in this fashion. On the contrary, perceiving the faith of the man, and knowing how his sins were weighing on his conscience, the Lord wished to give him true spiritual relief, and the discussion with the Scribes and doctors was only incidentally occasioned thereby. For, so soon as the words were uttered, these cavillers began to reason within themselves, " Why doth this man thus speak ? He blasphemeth. Who can forgive sins but one, *even* God ? " They did not

* " The Land and the Book," English edition, pp. 358-359.

give articulate expression to their thoughts, but that did
not prevent the Lord Jesus from being fully acquainted
with them, for " he perceived immediately in his Spirit,"
that is, by his divine nature, that they so reasoned within
themselves, and he sought at once to convince them of
their error.

But let us take precise note of what that error was.
They started with a right principle, but they made a
wrong application of it, and drew a wrong inference from
it.   They were correct in thinking that no one can forgive sins but God : but, it did not follow from that premise that the Lord Jesus, in announcing that the sins of
this man had been forgiven, was guilty of blaspheming
God, in the sense of arrogating to himself that authority
to forgive which is the prerogative of God alone.   For
there were two other possibilities in the case of which
they failed to take account.   It might be that Jesus was
a divinely accredited messenger, commissioned by God
to make this declaration in his name, and if that were so,
he was no more guilty of blasphemy in making it, than
Nathan was when on a memorable occasion he said to
David, " the Lord also hath put away thy sin" ; or again
he might be, as indeed he was, Incarnate God himself ;
and in that case, he had in himself the full prerogative
which here he claimed to exercise.   Thus their error
here was precisely the same as that of those described
in the fifth chapter of John's gospel, who sought to
kill Jesus, " because he said that God was his Father,
making himself equal with God."   This was their error.
Now let us observe how the Lord met it.   He did not
deny that no one could forgive sins but God, neither did
he affirm that the man who presumed on his own authority to forgive sin would not be guilty of blasphemy ; on
the contrary, he tacitly admitted, that, if without author-

ity or right, he had claimed to forgive this man's sins, he would be a blasphemer. He virtually accepted their way of putting the case, but then he claimed for himself, on proper and personal grounds,—as himself being God,— authority to forgive sins, and proceeded at once to establish that : for he said, " Whether is it easier, to say to the sick of the palsy, Thy sins are forgiven thee, or to say, Arise, take up thy bed and walk ? But that ye may know that the Son of Man hath authority on earth to forgive sins, he saith to the sick of the palsy, I say unto thee, Arise, and take up thy bed, and go thy way into thine house." The appeal here, you perceive, is from the unseen, to the seen. From the nature of the case, the forgiveness of sins is a divine act, in the spiritual sphere, the reality of which cannot be tested by any merely human observation. One may declare to another that his sins are pardoned, and no earthly investigation can determine whether or not he is speaking the truth, for the transaction lies in a department which is beyond the possibility of human investigation. Forgiveness is the act of God on the conscience of the sinner, a spiritual exercise in a purely spiritual sphere. But the healing of a man sick of the palsy by a word is a matter which can easily be tested, for that is within the sphere of human observation, and men can mark whether or not such a cure is genuine and permanent. It is, besides, a divine act, just as really as the declaration of forgiveness is. It is just as true that no one save God can heal paralysis with a word of power, as it is that no one can forgive sin save God only. " If, therefore," says the Saviour, " I by my word heal this palsy-stricken man, you may thereby be assured, that, as the Son of Man, I have authority on earth to forgive sins. Thus he pivoted his whole claim to the possession of inherent authority to forgive sin on the reality of this miracle ? He said, in effect, to his objectors, " You think it a safe thing for me to claim that I possess the authority to forgive sin, inasmuch as no one can test whether, when I say to this man, ' Thy sins are forgiven thee,' they are forgiven or not. Let us therefore put it to the test. It requires divine power to say to this man, ' Arise, and walk,' so that he shall at once be cured of his paralysis, just as really as it requires divine prerogative to say, ' Thy sins have been forgiven thee,' so that he shall have the full assurance that God has forgiven him. If therefore, when I say, Arise, take up thy bed and walk to thine house, a physical cure of his palsy follows, you may know assuredly that when I say to him, Thy sins are forgiven thee, his forgiveness is a reality." *That* is the proposal. It was much like Elijah's act on Mount Carmel, when he said to the assembled throng, " The God who answereth by fire, let him be the God." He would not ask them to believe without evidence, but he gave the evidence, that their faith might have a rational ground on which to rest. So, looking tenderly to the afflicted man, he said to him, " Arise, take up thy bed, and go thy way into thine house," and, to the amazement of all the onlookers, the paralytic " Arose, took up his bed, and went forth before them all." There was room enough made for him now, and he who had been carried in helplessness by his friends, went forth calm and strong, while the multitude glorified God, saying, " We never saw it on this fashion. We have seen strange things to-day." What an experience for this poor man! two cures wrought on him by one act ! Often and often, as he recalled the minutest incidents of this ever-memorable hour in his history, he would hear again these two voices," Son, thy sins have been forgiven thee," and, " Arise, take up thy bed and

go unto thine house," and his heart would thrill with
gratitude, but, while both were dear to him, he would
dwell with fondest rapture on the first, as the more gra‹
cious and the more precious of the two: " Thy sins have
been forgiven thee."

But let us see now what lessons we may take with us
for our guidance from the study of this interesting narrative. And, first of all, we may learn that though we
cannot become the saviours of our friends, we yet may
be serviceable in bringing them to Jesus, who alone can
save them. All honor to those four bearers, by whom
this paralytic was lovingly and tenderly carried to the
house in which the Lord was preaching, and by whose
ingenuity and care he was let down through the roof
and laid directly before the Saviour. Their faith was
as remarkable as was that of the sick man himself, and
was made manifest also by their works, so that, although
there is no mention made of such a thing in the history,
we cannot doubt that they were spiritually blessed as
well as he. Now we may be able to do something analogous to their act, in helping to bring loved ones to
Jesus, that they may be saved by Him. True, no such
physical bearing of a friend is needed now to bring him
into contact with the Lord. But yet we may be useful
spiritually to him, and that in one or other of many ways.

We may bring him to Christ, for example, by our prayers on his behalf. That is the first, and perhaps the
greatest thing we can do for him. For who can trace
the history of a prayer? You may see the flight of an
arrow through the air, or mark the effect of a bullet
from a rifle, but the course of a prayer transcends our
power of observation. We know only that it enters into
the ear of God; that in his heart, and by his wisdom,

the answer is shaped; and that the answer comes down through the ordinary channels of his providence, violating no natural laws, and bringing blessing with it as real ,and as rich as its course has been inscrutable. Which among us, who have prayed at all for unconverted friends, cannot tell of instances of such answers ? Think of Monica, the mother of Augustine, and her constant prayers for his conversion! Think, also, that at the very moment, when by his going to Italy, in violation of his sacred promise to her, he seemed to be putting himself beyond the possibility of his being influenced for good, he was brought thereby into contact with Ambrose of Milan, and by him was led to Christ, and let a history like that encourage you to bear your unbelieving friends to Jesus in your arms of prayer.

You may bring them to Jesus also, by your conversations with them on the gospels, and your taking of stumbling-blocks out of the way of their faith. Or you may accomplish the same thing by the method of indirectness, through the report made by you of a discourse which you have just heard ; or you may carry your loved friends to Jesus, by the very exaltation of your Christian character before them, and so win them to him, without a word. Or you may bring them with you to the sanctuary, where Christ may be so preached that they cannot choose but listen, and turn to him. But, the manner of your doing it, is not material— that you should do it, is the main thing, and if you do not attempt it, then the reason must be that you lack either the faith, or the love, or both, that animated these four bearers, when they laid their helpless friend at the feet of Jesus.

But, in the second place, we may learn—that Christ often confers blessing on a man by commanding

him to do that which, according to human logic, pre-
supposes that he has already the blessing which is to be
bestowed. He said to this poor man, " Arise, take up thy
bed, and go into thine house." Now, if this sufferer had
been destitute of faith he might have said, " Have they
brought me hither, at all this cost of trouble, to be
mocked for my misery ? Do you not see that it is my
very malady, that I cannot do what you have said ?
Surely I have been misinformed regarding you, else why
this bitter and unfeeling insult ? " But no ! he had
heard the gracious words, " Thy sins have been forgiven
thee," and he did trust the Lord. So he made the attempt to do as he was commanded, and in the making of
that attempt the strength came, so that " he arose, took
up his bed, and went forth before them all." Now, see
the bearing of all this on the sinner and his salvation.
When he is commanded to repent and believe in Jesus
Christ, that he may be saved, he is prone to make reply,
" You bid me exercise faith toward the Lord Jesus
Christ and repentance toward God. You tell me at the
same time that these two things, faith and repentance,
are the gifts of God, and that I cannot exercise either,
without the help of the Holy Spirit. Very well. I will
wait till I get that help, and then I will believe and repent." He imagines that this divine work in him is to
be a matter of distinct and separate consciousness, of
such sort that he will at once recognize it as a gift from
above, and so he will tarry until he receives that. But
he forgets that God works in a man by working through
him; or, in other words, that the supernatural runs along
the line of the natural, and that the two so interpenetrate
each other as to make it impossible by any analysis to
detect the one apart from the other. If this poor man
had waited until he felt Christ's strength in him as a

thing separate from his own, he never would have been cured of his paralysis. But he made the volition to arise, and in the making of that he received strength to carry it through. If, therefore, there should be any one here to-night who is caught and detained in this eddying whirlpool of " waiting for the Spirit," let him see from the parable of this miracle how foolish he is. His simple duty is to obey the divine command, and as he attempts to do that, he will receive the strength to do it. Indeed in the very determination to do that, God is already working in him, and, as he goes on, God will continue to work in him to do, just as he wrought in him to will, but he will not be conscious of God's operations as distinct from those of his own spirit. The sum of it all, then, is, obey the command, that is your part, and be sure that as you attempt to do that, the Spirit of God will do his, and the result will be salvation.

Finally, let us learn that when a man claims the right or authority to forgive sin, he should be required to prove the genuineness of his claim by working a miracle as real as this of the healing of the paralytic was. It is just as true now as it was when Jesus was on the earth, that God alone can forgive sin. Yet there are priests among us who aver that they may hear confessions, and, by divine authority, grant absolution. Now it is easy to meet and rebut that claim, by showing from the New Testament that Jesus Christ is the only high priest of his people, and that all believers are in him equally near to God, no one of them being on a different plain from the rest, and all alike needing to be forgiven by him. But in the light of this portion of the gospel narrative, perhaps a shorter and easier way to meet this pretension is to say, " Well, when the Lord's claim was challenged, he wrought a miracle to prove its genuineness. Go you and do likewise, and then we will rest in your absolution as divine; but until then, your absolution is of no value to us, for it is God's forgiveness we need, and you cannot give us that." As one has admirably put it, "No angel in heaven, no man upon earth, no church in council, no minister of any denomination, can take away from the sinner's conscience the load of guilt and give him peace with God. They may point to the fountain open for all sin. They may declare with authority whose sins God is willing to forgive. But they cannot absolve by their own authority. They cannot put away transgressions. This is the peculiar prerogative of God,* and he exercises that prerogative for the sake of Jesus Christ his Son. If you desire forgiveness, therefore, go and make confession of your guilt to God, and ask him to pardon you. Take with you this prayer from the liturgy of the Psalter, "For thy name's sake, O Lord, pardon mine iniquity, for it is great," and he will answer you through the lips of Jesus Christ his Son, " Thy sins are forgiven thee, go into peace."

* Ryle's "Expository Thoughts on Mark," pp. 29, 30.

IX.

THE IMPOTENT MAN AT THE POOL OF BETHESDA

John v. 1-17.

IN entering upon the exposition of this portion of the word of God, we are at once confronted with three questions of some little importance. The first respects the particular feast to which reference is made in the opening verse of the chapter. On general principles, indeed, it would not matter much which of the Jewish feasts is meant when the Evangelist says, " After these things there was a feast of the Jews," but special importance belongs to the settlement of that question here, because of the bearing which it has on the duration of our Lord's public ministry. For if here the Passover is meant, then John makes mention altogether of four passovers between the baptism and the ascension of the Saviour, and that would fix the length of his ministry as about three years and a half, while if any other of the three great feasts be here referred to, then we must hold that his public life lasted only two years and a half. A great amount of learned investigation has been given to this matter, the result being that opinion may be said now to be divided between two hypotheses ; one, that the feast here mentioned was the Passover, and another that it **was** Purim, which was instituted by the Jews in Persia

to commemorate the deliverance of the chosen people
from the destruction which had been planned for them
by Haman the Agagite in the days of Esther and Mor-
decai. But this feast could hardly have been Purim, for
that was a social and family festival, and did not require
that those who observed it should go up to Jerusalem for
the purpose. Then the very indefiniteness of the expression seems to imply that the oldest and greatest of
the annual festivals is meant, and not a feast of which
we have no mention in Scripture, like that of the
" Wood-offering," which Edersheim, alone, so far as I
know, among expositors, has fixed upon as that which is
referred to here. In a case like this it seems to be a
safe principle that the more general the language is, the
more surely does it point to the most important of the
feasts, and that if a minor festival had been intended, it
would have been especially named. Therefore, although
there is still diversity of opinion on the subject among
biblical scholars, and although such men as Tholuck and
Alford have said that it is impossible to decide with certainty what the feast was, I incline to the view of those
who believe that it was the Passover.

The second question which we have here to face has
respect to the site of the pool of Bethesda, with its five
porches. Up to the time of the publication of Robinson's
" Biblical Researches," the pool of Bethesda was generally
considered to be the modern Birket Israel, which is a
deep reservoir or trench on the north side of the area of
the great Mosque, in Jerusalem, having at its southwest
corner two long vaults which were supposed to be two of
the five porches. This identification depended mainly,
however, on the proximity of Birket Israel to St.
Stephen's gate, which was erroneously regarded as occupying the site of the Sheep-gate, to which and not to the

sheep-market, John here alludes, therefore it cannot be
substantiated, and when I mention that the reservoir is
three hundred and sixty feet long, one hundred and
thirty feet broad, and eighty feet deep, you will see how
utterly improbable it is that a sick man should plunge
into such a depth of water, and thereby incur the risk of
being drowned while in pursuit of health. Since Dr.
Robinson's time, however, opinion has drifted toward the
identification of the Fountain of the Virgin with the pool
of Bethesda. This fountain, so-called, was situated on the
west side of the valley of Jehosaphat, about twelve hundred feet northward from the rocky point at the mouth
of the Tyropœan, and connected by a subterranean passage with the pool of Siloam. Dr. Robinson found that
the water in this fountain rose and fell at intervals,
giving it an intermittent character, corresponding somewhat to the irregular troubling of the waters spoken of
by the impotent man. He says, "As we were preparing
to measure the basin of the upper fountain and explore
the passage leading from it, my companion was standing
on the lower step near the water, with one foot on the
step and the other on a loose stone lying in the basin.
All at once he perceived the water coming into his shoe,
and supposing the stone had rolled, he withdrew his
foot to the step, which, however, was also now covered
with water. This instantly excited our curiosity, and
we now perceived the water rapidly bubbling up from
under the lower step. In less than five minutes it had
risen in the basin nearly or quite a foot, and we could
hear it gurgling off through the interior passage. In ten
minutes more it had ceased to flow, and the water in the
basin was again reduced to its former level. Thrusting my
staff in under the lower step whence the waters appeared
to come, I found that there was here a large hollow space,

but a further examination could not be made without removing the steps." * Robinson does not himself speak
with assurance as if the Fountain of the Virgin were beyond doubt the pool of Bethesda, but many regarded
his statements as establishing the probability of their
identity. Now, however, through the labors of the Palestine Exploration Society, taken in connection with
collateral evidence running down through many centuries,
the veritable site has been discovered, and proves to be
neither the Birket Israel, nor the Fountain of the Virgin,
but a locality lying in the northeast angle of Jerusalem,
just inside the East wall, but about one hundred and
fifty feet north of the Via Dolorosa, and almost hidden
up to a comparatively recent period by the Church of St.
Anne. The full particulars were given by Prof. Paine,
in a carefully written article contributed to " The Independent," of date August 16, 1888, from which I tran-
scribe the following paragraphs: "About thirty years
ago the Church of St. Anne was given to the Emperor
Napoleon III., as a special favor by the Sultan, and immediately the restoration of the monument was ordered
by the French government. The architect upon whom
this commission fell, Monsieur Mauss, on attempting to
clear the surrounding area, discovered numerous evidences of resort here in ancient times, as to a bath, held
in high estimation for curative effects—mainly inscrip-
tions and fragments of statues. Among them was one
of great significance—a native white marble foot, bearing
a dedication in Greek characters, showing it to be the
offering of a thankful Roman woman named Pompeia,
healed at the pool of Bethesda !

" Naturally this led to the discovery of a portion of
the veritable pool, whereupon M. Mauss acquired the en-

* "Biblical Researches," vol. i. pp. 241–242.

tire area for his government, and carried forward the task of emptying the buried bathing place. At the depth of twenty-five feet he came upon a very old fresco on one of the walls, representing a human or divine figure, but too nearly destroyed for determination. For some reason, however, the search was not then carried beyond the limits of the one reservoir, which was not far enough for complete correspondence with the biblical requirements, because one pool having four sides might have four porches, not five, which number could be provided only by a ' twin pool,' between whose two tanks the fifth porch might lie.

" More recently in this same vicinity the Algerian monks have been carrying on excavations, and have laid bare a large rock-cut reservoir thirty feet deep, fifty-five feet long and about thirteen wide, and provided with a flight of twenty-four steps leading down the eastern scarp into the pool.

"And now the Chairman of the Executive Committee of the Palestine Exploration Fund, Mr. James Glaisher, has received a communication from Herr Conrad Schick at Jerusalem to the effect that he has just discovered the second pool, lying in relation to the first, end to end, sixty feet long and equally wide. Thus the structural conditions of the problem are completely satisfied, which, with the close relation to historical landmarks and the archæology of the spot, appear to render the identification at last absolutely sure." This is only one out of many cases which serve to prove the efficiency of the service of the Palestine Exploration Fund in settling the sites of some of the most interesting scenes in the history of our Lord.

The third question to which our attention is called in this narrative is the state of the original text. You will observe that in the Revised Version, the words "waiting for the moving of the water," in the third verse, and the whole of the fourth verse are omitted, as being in all probability a spurious addition to the narrative as it came originally from the hand of the Evangelist. We cannot go at length into the discussion of such a matter here. But from the form of the expression used in the margin of the Revised Version, "Some ancient authorities read," we are given to understand that in the opinion of those most competent to pronounce a judgment in such a case, the weight of manuscript authority is in favor of the course which they have adopted. The likelihood is that the portion which they have left out as spurious, was an early gloss, or marginal note, designed to explain the words of the paralytic himself in verse seventh, when he speaks of the water being troubled, and that by and by it found its way into the text, and was regarded as a portion of the original narrative. It is met with as such as early as in the Codex Alexandrinus, and in the Latin and early Syriac versions, and may be regarded as the popular interpretation current at the time when the interpretation was made of the phenomena which were observed in the spring, and to which in his answer to the Saviour the impotent man refers. "The bubbling water moving as it were with new life, and in its healing power seeming to convey new energy to blind and halt and lame, was to them as the presence of a living messenger of God. They knew not its constituent elements, and could not trace the law of its action, but they knew the source of all good, who gave intellect to man, and healing influence to matter, effect to the remedy and skill to the physician, and they accepted the gift as direct from him." * So we account for this early explanation of the

* Hawkins on John, *in loco*, Elliott's Commentary.

medical virtue in the waters of the pool, but if it be, as there is now little doubt that it is, an interpolation into the narrative, then the Evangelist is not responsible for its insertion, and we are relieved from all necessity of defending it from the assaults of modern sceptics. The verse takes its place beside that concerning the three heavenly witnesses in the First Epistle of John, and forms no part of the original gospel.

But we must hasten now to the exposition of the narrative itself. It was the Sabbath, and the Lord Jesus, going about, as usual, doing good, made his way to the pool of Bethesda—which has been supposed to mean "house of mercy"—beneath the sheltering porches of which he knew he should find at least one man who sorely needed his help. For these porches were rarely if ever empty; since, as we have already incidentally learned, the spring was both medicinal and intermittent, and as the healing virtue was greatest at the moment of the disturbance caused by the rising of the water, and the intervals between these geyser-like upheavals were irregular, the poor diseased ones waited in patience for the opportunity that might come to them of obtaining relief. Some of them had been carried to and from the fountain daily for a long time; and he who was to be healed, had been helpless for eight and thirty years. Observe, it is not said that he had been at the pool for all these years, but simply that he had been the victim of disease for all that time. His coming to Bethesda was perhaps only the last of a long series of experiments which he had tried, in the hope of being cured; and it may be, too, that like the woman whose case is elsewhere described, he had spent all his living upon physicians, neither could be healed of any. We cannot

tell, but in any case he had been greatly afflicted.
Eight and thirty years an invalid! Think of it; and
then as you contrast your own case with his, you may
learn how ungrateful you have been in accepting your
health as a matter of course, and giving no thanks for it
to God.

But relief was now at hand. For when Jesus saw
him and knew, by his divine omniscience, that he
had been a sufferer so long, he said to him, "Wilt thou
be made whole?" That seems a strange question for the
Lord to ask. The superficial reader might say, He
might have taken that for granted. What was the man
there for, if he did not want to be made whole? But the
Lord designed by his inquiry to awaken, if possible, the
expectation of a cure. He would rouse him first to wonder as to what he could be driving at, and then, through
that wonder, to hope, and, if possible, also to faith. It
was like that "Look on us," addressed by Peter to the
lame man, at the Beautiful Gate of the Temple, and, as in
that case, the first effect was that the cripple "gave heed
to them, expecting to receive something from them," in
the way of an unusual amount of the same sort of alms as
he commonly received; so here the effect of the Lord's
question upon the impotent man was to lead him to expect assistance in the only way in which he imagined
that it could be given to him. Therefore, he told him
how he had no man to help him to reach the pool at
the favorable moment, and how, even as he was creeping
along in his impotence, he was forestalled by some one else.
What pathetic helplessness there is in his words—"I
have no man, when the water is troubled, to put me into
the pool; but while I am coming, another steppeth down
before me." It was a delicate way of asking Jesus if
he would not stay for a little by him, and, when the criti-

cal moment came, assist him to the water. And the answer of Jesus virtually was, "I can do more for you than that. Rise, take up thy bed and walk." He tried to obey, and lo, what new sensations are these that tingle through him? Is it a fancy, or is it a fact? Has he really the power which appears to have been restored to him? Yea, he can rise, for he has done it; he can fold up the pallet, on which he has lain so long, for he has done it. He can walk, for see he has laid his mattress on his shoulders, and so much is he absorbed in his own consciousness of his cure, that, without one word of gratitude to his benefactor, he is off and away, glad to be out of those porches which had become so dreary to him.

But he was not permitted to go far, for "the Jews," that is, as usually in John's gospel, "The Jewish officials," some of those who were in authority either as members of the Sanedryn, or as elders of a synagogue, or the like, meeting him said, "It is the Sabbath day. It is not lawful for thee to carry thy bed." He answered with great promptitude, and with a logic that could not be confuted, "He that made me whole, the same said unto me, Take up thy bed and walk." The miracle of my healing justifies my obedience of him who healed me. That was his argument, and it is invulnerable. He who could of his own power perform such a work is greater than the Sabbath, and what he tells me to do, I must do, whether on the Sabbath or on other days. They felt that they could not reply to such an argument, and so, taking another tack, they ask, "What man is he?" or rather, as the Revisers have it, "Who is the man that said unto thee, Take up thy bed and walk?" Mark the emphasis, "who is the *man*?" It is as if they had said, From what you have replied to us, you seem to put your healer

above men, but you shall not so impose on us. A man
he is, only a man and no more. But he that was healed
could not tell who it was, for the porches were crowded,
and Jesus had gone at once, after he had performed the
cure. So they got nothing further out of him then, and
he went on carrying his bed, such as it was, in spite of
them.

But later in the day, being in the Temple, to which
it is permissible to believe that he went up to give
thanks unto the Lord for his cure, he met Jesus there,
who said to him, " Behold thou art made whole. Sin
no more, lest a worse thing come unto thee." That was
an electric flash, which at once revealed to the man that
Jesus was fully acquainted with his history, and was indeed superhuman. It was to him a moment of experience like that described by the woman of Samaria, when
she said, " He told me all things that ever I did." Though
we are not warranted to say, as a general rule, that special sickness is caused by special sin, this was a case in
which the sickness had been connected with sin, and so
this man is dismissed with a warning. He had had one
experience, and a terrible one it had been, but if he went
back again to sin, a worse thing—(worse than thirty-
eight years of helplessness—ah, me ! what a terrible evil
sin is!)—would come upon him. I dare not judge, and we
are not always safe in arguing from silence. But it is at
least suggestive, that here we have no assurance of pardon, and no utterance of benediction. We miss such an
expression as that to the other paralytic, " Thy sins are
forgiven thee," or that other to the woman at the feast,
" Go into peace," and we cannot but see a contrast between these and this—may I say, somewhat stern expression, " Behold, thou art made whole. Sin no more,
lest a work thing come unto thee." What does it mean ?

Does it indicate that this man's cure was only of the body, and not of the soul also? and that his protracted illness, and miraculous deliverance, had not been so sanctified to him as to turn him from his sin? I cannot tell; I only suggest the questions, that they may in their turn suggest other questions to ourselves.

So soon as the man knew by whom he had been made whole, he returned to the officials and told them. This I cannot think he did with any evil intent. He simply wished, as I believe, to honor the Lord. For the antagonism of the Jewish officials to Jesus was only beginning, and there is little probability that the sick man knew anything about it, while it is wholly unnatural to suppose that he was moved by so diabolical a purpose as that of betraying his benefactor into the hands of his enemies. But, in any case, he unwittingly by his information, stirred up the anger of the Jews, who persecuted Jesus and sought to slay him, because he had done these things on the Sabbath day. Thus, in their view, it was unlawful to make a man whole on the Sabbath, but perfectly lawful to concoct mischief against another, and persecute him, and seek to slay him, on the Sabbath. Alas! alas! how prone men are, ourselves included, to "strain out a gnat, and swallow a camel." But the Lord was ready with his answer, for he said, "My father worketh hitherto and I work." Enigmatic words they seem to be to the unthinking reader, but malice quickens the perception and makes it more clear sometimes, even than love does, for the Jews saw into his meaning, which I take to have been something like this: "We are living now in the seventh day of the creation week. This is the time of God's rest. There is now no work of creation being done. God has rested from that. But though he is in this sense resting now; yet he is continuously at work in upholding all that he has made, and he has put forth special efforts for the restoration of man to the state in which he was formed at first, but from which he has fallen by his own sin. If, therefore, during the Sabbath of creation's week, and while God is resting, he can yet work for the redemption and education of men, I am only following in the same line, when on the Sabbath of an ordinary week, and while I am resting from ordinary labor, I put forth my energy for the restoration of this impotent man to health. 'My father worketh hitherto and I work.'" Now, perceiving that, or something like that, to be implied in the Saviour's words, his adversaries immediately changed their base, and instead of accusing him merely of Sabbath-breaking, they cried out against him for blasphemy, "because he said that God was his Father, making himself equal with God." A good premise, but a bad conclusion. He did make himself equal with God, but he was not therefore guilty of blasphemy, for he was God. And, indeed, there is no alternative even now but these : Either Jesus Christ is God, equal with the Father, or he was a blasphemer. The idea that he was merely a model man is, in the face of these gospels, absurd. If the perfection of his deity is denied, his moral character as a man is destroyed ; if his moral character as a man is to be regarded as a model, his deity must be accepted.

But we must not attempt to go at this time into the consideration of the long and important discourse delivered by our Lord in connection with the attack made upon him here by the Jews. The exposition of that belongs rather to a series on the entire gospel by John, or on the discourses of our Lord, than to one on his miracles. We may only say that in this address the Saviour speaks of himself as working with the Father, as having all judgment committed to him by the Father, and as worthy of equal honor with the Father ; that he describes himself as the giver of life, by whom the resurrection of the dead is to be accomplished, and that he supports these claims by the testimony of John regarding him; by the endorsement of the Father through his works, and by the statements in their own Scriptures, particularly in the writings of Moses, that refer to him. Thus Christ follows here very much the same line which the Evangelist himself has taken in the prologue of his gospel, and makes it impossible for any one accepting these statements as his consistently to believe in his truthfulness and honesty as a man, without also believing that he is God Incarnate.

But, returning to the miracle which has been under consideration by us this evening, let me conclude my discourse by contrasting the healing qualities of the fountain opened for sin and for uncleanness, by the death of Christ, with those which were possessed by the pool of Bethesda. In the medical spring around which these porches were reared, the healing virtue was only intermittent. It was due in some occult manner to the troubling of the water, and only at that particular moment could the applicant receive benefit. But the efficacy of the blood of Christ is continuous. No one needs to wait a single moment for a cure from the Lord Jesus. He may have it at once, if he will only apply, believingly, for it. Turn then, O sinner, from your evil way : and repair to him. He will deliver you from your guilt. He will wash away your sin. He will give you salvation in the fullest significance of that word. "He is able to save to the uttermost all that come unto God by him, seeing he ever liveth to make intercession for them."

Then, again, it is not with the fountain of salvation

which Christ has opened, as it was with Bethesda, at which only one was healed at intervals, but those who apply to him may all be cured at once. I cannot forestall you, nor you me; but if we go to Christ now, in earnest faith and true repentance, we shall both receive the blessing of his forgiveness and regeneration. Then, having received these, let us go and serve him, "without fear, in holiness and righteousness before him, all the days of our lives." In days gone by, when cripples went to a so-called sacred spring, for healing, and received a cure, they hung up over the fountain the staff on which they had leaned, or the crutches by which they had supported themselves in the time of their weakness, and the visitor to Holywell in Wales may see, even in these days, many such things there. But the true trophy of Christ's healing power, and the best votive offering we can make for having received the cure of sin at his hands, is a holy life. So let those of us who profess to be saved by him, manifest at once the genuineness of our cure, and the fervor of our gratitude, by "perfecting holiness in the fear of the Lord." Let us go and sin no more, and thereby we shall show forth the praises of him who hath quickened us from the death of sin unto the life of righteousness.

X.

THE MAN WITH THE WITHERED HAND.

Matt. xii. 9-13. Mark iii. 1-6. Luke vi. 6-11.

PUTTING together the three narratives of this miracle
given by the Evangelists, we get the following result:
That on a certain Sabbath of unknown date, Jesus entered into a synagogue, in a place which is not mentioned,
and taught; that there was a man there who had a withered hand; that the Scribes and Pharisees, perceiving
him, watched to see whether the Lord would heal him,
and so give them an opportunity of bringing an accusation against him, which might end in his being condemned to death; that they first put the question to him,
" Is it lawful to heal on the Sabbath day ? " that he,
divining their purpose, replied with another question, " Is
it lawful to do good on the Sabbath day or to do evil ? to
save life or to kill ? " that to this question they could
make no reply; that then he looked round upon them
with anger, being grieved at the hardness of their hearts,
and answered his own question by this *argumentum ad
hominem :* " What man shall there be among you that
shall have one sheep, and if it fall into a pit on the Sabbath day, will he not lay hold of it and lift it out ? How
much then is a man better than a sheep ? Wherefore it
is lawful to do well on the Sabbath day ; " and finally that

148

he healed the withered hand, not by doing anything, but simply by a word, and so furnished no shadow of a ground for any charge against him.

It thus appears that the account of this miracle is introduced by all the three Evangelists to illustrate the position taken by the Saviour in reference to the keeping of the Sabbath, and if any doubt regarding that should remain on the mind of any reader of the record when taken by itself, a reference to the immediately preceding context will be sufficient to dispel it. For in each of the three gospels the account of the healing of the man with the withered hand directly follows that of the disciples plucking the ears of corn on the Sabbath day, and of their vindication by their Master for so doing. Therefore the best introduction to the consideration of the miracle will be an exposition of the narrative in connection with which the rehearsal of it is introduced.

One Sabbath morning—called by Luke the second-first, supposed by some to mean the second Sabbath after the beginning of the Passover—the Master and his disciples, on their way probably to the synagogue, passed through the fields of grain. They did not, as I judge, go through the wheat, trampling it under foot, but went along a stile path similar to those which are still common in agricultural districts, with the ripe stalks waving their golden obeisance to them on either side as they passed. The disciples were hungry, and, as they went, they plucked the ears, rubbed out the grain from them with their hands, and ate it, to still the cravings of their appetite. But the Pharisees who were in the company, or mixed multitude, which by this time seemed always to follow the Lord, were scandalized by their procedure, and said, " Why do they on the Sabbath day that which is not lawful ? " They did not accuse them of theft for taking that which was not their own, for the Mosaic law gave its sanction to what they did in these words, " When thou comest into the standing corn of thy neighbor, then thou mayest pluck the ears with thine hand, but thou shalt not move a sickle into thy neighbor's standing corn." * That which they objected to was their plucking the ears and rubbing them with their hands, which they regarded as a kind of reaping and threshing, and therefore as forbidden on the Sabbath. This was a very narrow and enslaving view of what was required by that Sabbath law, which, as laid down by Moses, was evidently designed to make the seventh day one of rest and happiness, and it becomes an interesting question how the Pharisees came to hedge the day round with restrictions which were so oppressive.

Now, in investigating this question, we find two explanations, which, taken together, go far to account for the hold which these opinions had upon the Pharisees. The one is historical, and the other spiritual or philosophical. The historical is to be found in the fact that as one great reason for the captivity of the Jews in Babylon was their guilt in the profanation of the Sabbath, it was followed by a reaction into what may be called an opposite extreme. During their exile, they were very rigid in their observance of the Sabbath, because, as they were then situated, that was almost the only way in which they could give outward and visible expression to their religion. The festivals of the Mosaic law being all local in their character, and requiring attendance at Jerusalem, could not then be observed, and so they put more stress on the Sabbath keeping which could be maintained, going so far as to lay down a great many restrictions, of which their written law knew nothing. One of their

* Deut. xxiii. 25.

books enumerates thirty-nine acts, with many subdi-
visions, which were to be considered unlawful; and
the Talmud gives the most minute specifications of
the distance which might be lawfully passed over even
in the greatest emergency, as, for example, in that of
fire.* Thus traditionally the Pharisees were prone to
take the narrowest possible view of the keeping of the
Sabbath.

Then the philosophical explanation is connected with
the fact that in religion, as well as in other departments,
the rejection of a matter of essential moment revenges
itself by the reception of much that is positively false.
Thus the sceptic who disbelieves the Scriptures is in
some other matters the most credulous of men, going so
far, as some modern instances have shown, as to believe
in spiritualism, with its mediums, and the like. In like
manner, where there is little or no religion of the
heart and life, there is often an extremely punctilious
attention to form and ritual. Hence the Pharisees
who could devour widows' houses, could also for a
pretence make long prayers; and, neglecting judgment,
mercy and faith, they paid tithes of mint, and anise
and rue. As Matthew Henry has expressed it, "They
had corrupted many of the commandments by interpreting them more loosely than they were intended;
but concerning the fourth commandment they had erred
in the other extreme, and interpreted it too strictly. It
is common for men of corrupt minds, by their zeal in
rituals and the external services of religion to think to
atone for the looseness of their morals ; but they are
cursed who add to, as well as they who take from, the
words of this book."

* See on this whole subject Appendix xvii. in Edersheim's "Life
and Times of Jesus the Messiah," vol. ii. p. 774.

But, however we may explain the position of the Pharisees on this subject, there is no doubt as to the nature of the position itself, and the Lord met it by five different arguments.

The first is taken from a familiar incident in the life of David. Coming on a Sabbath day to the Tabernacle at Nob, weary and faint, he asked for food, but none was to be had save the sacred shew-bread which had just been taken from the sanctuary to make way for the fresh loaves that had to be put in the presence of the Lord on that day, and which it was lawful for the priests only to eat. In his emergency, that was given to him and to his men, the high-priest rightly judging that it was better to relieve the wants of hungry men than to keep the letter of the law and perpetuate their sufferings. The principle here is that when two obligations seem to conflict, the higher suspends the lower. Children are to obey their parents, but when their doing so involves their disobeying God, they are absolved from their obedience to their parents and must do what God requires. In like manner the obligation to rest on the Sabbath is suspended, when the higher law of love to God or love to man requires us to labor. When it is absolutely necessary that something should be done, in the way of mercy to a fellow-man, or of duty to God, then we not only may, but must do that, even on the Sabbath.

The second argument used here by our Lord is taken from the case of the priests. He affirms regarding them that they profane the Sabbath and are blameless. The duties of the priestly office had to be performed on the Sabbath as on other days, because it would have been a greater evil that no sacrifice should be offered, than that the priests should work in order to offer it.

They were engaged in the service of God, and they were thereby justified in performing their usual work. If, therefore, argues the Saviour, they were blameless in ministering in the Temple, which was after all only a type, how much more are these my followers in satisfying their hunger by plucking and eating of the ears of corn, while they are in the service of him who is greater than the Temple—nay, is himself the true Temple, inasmuch as deity abides within the Tabernacle of his flesh ?

The third argument is derived from that passage in Hosea which the Lord quoted on another occasion in reference to the charge that had been brought against him of eating with publicans and sinners : * " I will have mercy and not sacrifice." Mercy there stands for the spirit of the law, and sacrifice for its letter. Wherever, therefore, the carrying out of the law in its letter would amount to a violation of its spirit, there the letter must give way to the spirit. Now the spirit of the Sabbath law is the promotion of the physical, intellectual, and moral well-being of man, and so whenever obedience to its letter would interfere with that, the letter is to be disregarded, that the spirit may be kept.

The fourth argument is but the formulation into an epigrammatic aphorism of the principle which I have just announced, and lays down clearly the design for which the Sabbath was instituted. " For the Sabbath was made for man, not man for the Sabbath." It was intended to promote the highest and best interests of man. The keeping of the Sabbath was not the end for which man was made, but the Sabbath was ordained to be kept by him, in order that he might the better attain to the higher end of glorifying God and enjoying him forever. The Pharisees, however, made that into an end which

* Matt. ix. 10-13.

God meant only for a means, and thereby they turned into an oppression that which was originally intended to be a blessing. Thus they clearly evinced that there was something radically wrong with their manner of keeping the Sabbath.

The last argument is drawn from the relation of the Son of Man to the Sabbath. By the phrase "the Son of Man," here, as everywhere else in the gospels, the Messiah is designated, and it is as if the Saviour had said, My disciples cannot be wrong in what they do, for they are serving him, who, as the Representative Man, having in charge everything that concerns the welfare of humanity, is Lord of the Sabbath—Lord of it, not to abrogate it, but to explain it and defend it, alike from those who would altogether destroy it and those who would turn its liberty into bondage. The connection between the phrase "the Sabbath was made for man" and the statement that "the Son of Man is Lord also of the Sabbath," is very close. The latter is in fact an inference from the former, introduced by the word "therefore," and the force of that particle has been by no one more clearly brought out than by Dr. James Morison in his comment on the passage,* to the following effect: "Since it is the case that the Sabbath is an institution that finds the reason of its existence in man, the law that enjoins the details of its observance is something altogether different from those eternal and immutable principles which are identical with the moral perfections of the Divine Being. It is elastic in its application to the circumstances of men. It is susceptible of modification by the super-induction of higher laws into the sphere of its operation. And hence he who is emphatically "the Son of Man," and who has in charge all the higher interests

* "Commentary on Mark," p. 64.

of man, has full authority to regulate, as he may see cause, the amount and modes of that rest from worldly work which is needful for the highest weal of men. The regulation is safe in his hands, though it would not be safe in the hands of every man."

These principles, thus clearly and succinctly laid down by the Lord, are of permanent importance and abiding force. They apply to the biblical Sabbath itself, and therefore they condemn most emphatically the rabinnical Sabbath, which the Jewish doctors had so spun over with their cobwebs of restriction as to make it well-nigh impossible for others to recognize the beneficent design of the institution through their oppressive enactments concerning its observance.

Now the enunciation of these principles by the Lord is followed in all the three synoptic gospels by an illustrative application of them to the case of the man with the withered hand. On the Sabbath immediately following that on which the conversation which we have just been considering was held, our Lord, as his custom was, went into the synagogue where he saw a man whose right hand was "withered." You will observe it was the hand, not the arm, that was diseased, so that the statement often made, that Christ commanded him to stretch forth his arm, knowing that he was helpless to do so, but gave him the power through his making of the effort,— however true it may be as an analogy to the case of the sinner who is commanded to believe and repent, is not true to fact. It was not the arm but the hand that was powerless. The vital force in it was dried up. It was atrophied, and the man could do nothing with it. Naturally, the attention of the Saviour was drawn to him; and the Pharisees, rightly divining that the Lord meant to cure him, asked, "Is it lawful to heal on the Sabbath

day ? " Upon this he called the man to stand forth in
the midst before them all, that the entire congregation
might see and commiserate his state, and he kept him
standing there until he had silenced his assailants. First
he begins with an *argumentum ad hominem:* " What man
shall there be among you that shall have one sheep, and
if it fall into a pit on the Sabbath day, will he not lay
hold of it and lift it out ?   How much therefore is a man
better than a sheep ? "   If it be right on the Sabbath to
care for the welfare of a sheep, how much more is it so
to minister to the health and comfort of a man ?   Therefore you need not condemn me for healing this man.
But taking up more directly the question which they had
asked, he in turn proposes a question, " Is it lawful to do
good on the Sabbath day, or to do evil ? to save life or
to kill ? "   As if he had said, The question is not, as you
seem to think, one between working or not working on
the Sabbath ; but one between doing good or doing evil,
between saving or destroying life—a very stinging and
severe reproof, inasmuch as at the very moment they
were seeking occasion for the taking away of his life.
But note where the pertinence of his question lies.   He
does not mean to say, that if he did not heal this man,
there and then, he would be guilty of destroying his life.
But he puts an extreme case in order to show the better
the absurdity of their position.   He takes their principle
and carries it out to its legitimate consequences, in order
to show them to what cruelty it would lead.   For if in
no possible case it is allowable to work on the Sabbath,
then, in a case in which the neglect to work involves the
loss of a human life, the keeping of the Sabbath, instead of being a blessing to men, would be a curse.
Wherefore, reasons the Master, it is lawful to do good on
the Sabbath day.   Then the Evangelist Mark, to whom

principally we are beholden for descriptions of our Lord's feelings, gestures, and looks, adds this graphic touch: " He looked round upon them with anger, being grieved for the hardness of their hearts." The meek and lowly One was angry, righteously indignant, yet see the singular inter-blending of emotions! His anger was accompanied with grief, for he knew their sin, and the awful consequences which it would bring upon them. Here is at once an illustration of obedience to Paul's command, " Be ye angry and sin not," and an unfolding of the means whereby we may be enabled to obey it. We may be angry at the sin, with all safety, so long as we cherish grief for the sinner, but when we lose the latter, the former becomes dangerous.

Then the Lord said to the man, "Stretch forth thine hand, and it was at once restored whole as the other." But the sight of all this only made the enmity of the Pharisees more fierce, and forthwith, Sabbath as it was, they went out and took counsel with the Herodians to destroy him, while he withdrew, as Luke tells us, into the mountain, and continued all night in prayer to God.

So much for the exposition of this section of the gospel history. Now let us pause for a very few minutes while we gather up two or three lessons for our daily lives. And first let us see the advantage of attendance on the public observance of God's worship. Jesus was regularly in the synagogue, wherever he might happen to be. This was not only a benefit to himself as a man, but also an example to us. And his presence was a blessing to every devout worshipper in the assembly. But he has promised to be with his people now wherever two or three are gathered in his name, and we not only fail in duty, but miss a privilege when we causelessly absent ourselves from the sanctuary. What a loss it would have been to this poor man if he had not been in the synagogue that day ? The mere sight of him there moved the Saviour to heal him, by restoring power to his right hand. But if he had not been there, at that time, humanly speaking, he might never have received such a boon. Now, of course, there are no such physical advantages to be derived from Church attendance now, but there are spiritual blessings richer and better far than any cure of bodily disease, to be obtained in the house of God, and if by negligence or carelessness we absent ourselves from the sanctuary, we may miss much that would have been salutary to our souls. Value then the privileges of public worship. Think of the sanctuary as a fountain of blessing, for there God maketh the valley of Baca into a place of springs, and where Christ is there is always healing to the sick and burdened soul.

Learn, in the second place, that works of necessity and mercy are lawful on the Sabbath. We are still under obligation to rest one day in seven, although the Son of Man, as Lord of the Sabbath, has sanctioned through the example of his Apostles the change in the time of the observance of this periodic rest from the seventh day of the week to the first. We are set free, too, from the ceremonial and judicial restrictions which Moses laid down regarding the seventh day ; yet we are not thereby absolved from the duty of resting on the first day of the week. But in the keeping of that day, we must beware of falling into the mistake committed by the Pharisees, and turning this beneficent institution into a means of oppression. There are obligations of a higher sort than that of the observance of the Lord's day, and when the absolute necessities of men, or calls for works of love and mercy come in, we must not allow ourselves to be withheld from meeting the one or responding to the other, because they come on the Lord's day. I find no exception made, however, in favor of mere amusement. But just because we feel restrained by the law of God from seeking amusement on the day of rest, we ought to hold ourselves all the more ready for the performance of works of necessity and mercy. Of course the most urgent claims will be first attended to, and if it be but a sheep that is in peril, we will seek to deliver it; while, recognizing that a man is incalculably more valuable than a sheep, we will not condemn the doctor for attending to cases of danger or urgency on the first day of the week; and as God gives us opportunity, we will seek to advance the spiritual welfare of our fellowmen during its sacred hours as on other days, for it *is* lawful to do good on the Sabbath day. But, indeed, the special danger of our times is not in the direction of over-rigidness in the observance of the Lord's day. We need now to be far more on our guard against losing it altogether. And I would warn those who are advocating the giving up of a large portion of it to amusement of the sure result of such a movement. Mammon is stronger than pleasure, and if the day should ever come to be devoted to amusement, it will soon be claimed by labor. Those who are now urging the giving up of its hours to recreation, call themselves the friends of the workingmen, and I have no doubt that they think themselves to be so, but even such a man as Bradlaugh in England sees clearly what the result will be, and so he stands out against them, not for any religious reason, but simply to preserve one day of rest in seven. If, therefore, you do not desire to be robbed of a day of periodic rest altogether, do not allow any part of it to be claimed for mere amusement. The religious character of the day must be maintained, if we would preserve it from becoming at last an ordinary working day, and if it ever comes to that, the working-man will be the greatest sufferer.

Learn, in the third place, what bitter antagonism to holiness there is in the unholy heart. When the Pharisees heard what Jesus said, and saw what he did, they took counsel with the Herodians to slay him. Alas! what inconsistency !—so anxious to keep the Sabbath, yet themselves breaking it, by plotting on it to destroy a life! So devoted to the Jewish nationality, and yet consorting with the Herodians, who were the pronounced upholders of the Roman domination over the Jews. The proverb says, that " When thieves cast out, honest men get their own ; " but it is equally true that when antagonists are leagued together, some one is sure to be crucified. It is the old, old story ; for since the days of Abel, he that is born after the flesh persecutes him that is born after the spirit. The only argument against holiness which the world can use is violence. Intolerance is the world's testimonial to the genuineness of the saintly character. Let us see to it, therefore, that when we suffer, we suffer for well doing ; then, as the cross was the ladder up which Christ climbed to his throne, so we, suffering with him, shall also reign with him.

XI.

THE HEALING OF THE CENTURION'S SERVANT.

Matt. viii. 5-13. Luke vii. 1-10.

THE narrative which is now to be considered has by some been regarded as descriptive of the same incidents as those which are recorded in the concluding section of the fourth chapter of the Gospel by John. In other words, they would identify the healing of the centurion's slave at Capernaum, with the cure of the nobleman's son. But, as we saw in our exposition of the latter, there are no valid grounds for such an opinion; and it is to be feared that those who have advanced it, have done so rather with the view of disparaging the gospel narratives than with that of interpreting them. Because the two accounts agree in representing Christ as performing a cure from a distance and in the absence of the sick man, by a word, they argue that they must refer to the same miracle; and then, they go on to reason that because they refer to the same miracle, but differ from each other in many important particulars, therefore the narratives are entirely unreliable. Thus they first insist, in spite of all the differences between the two accounts, that they describe the same thing; and then they set forth these discrepancies to prove that no miracle whatever was performed. That is a fair specimen of the manner in which

161

some rationalistic writers deal with the sacred records, and, as such, it may serve to show how little weight is due to their objections.

But while we expose this manufacture of discrepancies where none exists, we must not shut our eyes to such as really appear in the case before us between Matthew and Luke. The first Evangelist tells us that the centurion came to Jesus himself; while the third affirms that he sent elders of the Jews to plead with Jesus on his behalf. But, no serious difficulty is thereby created, except to those who are such slaves to the letter as to be unable to perceive the harmony of spirit existing between the two writers. If the narratives had been *verbatim et literatim* identical, it would have been said that the one was taken from the other. But such a difference as we find between them establishes the independence of both; while the substantial agreement of the two is at once apparent when we remember the old Latin saying, " *Qui facit per alium, facit per se.* " As Dr. James Morison has said, " Matthew is not aiming at giving scientific descriptions of unessential details. He is giving us a succession of vivid tableaux, in which Jesus is represented as at work. And to his eye, while engaged in painting the tableau of the scene before us, the centurion was really present with the Lord, by means of his deputies. The presence of the deputies, is shaded off for the moment by a particular fold of the drapery of the painting." * At any rate, such differences in representing one and the same application are common in all historical writings, and both ways of putting the case are substantially true; while perhaps even in Matthew there is an indication of the presence of the Jewish elders, in

* Commentary on Matthew, p. 118.

the warning which, founded on the centurion's faith, the Saviour addresses to the Jews "that followed him."

But, leaving this microscopic matter, let us proceed to the exposition of the two narratives themselves. They tell us of the application made by an officer of the Roman garrison then stationed at Capernaum, in behalf of his slave, who was " dear unto him and ready to die." The Roman army, as it then was, would hardly be considered a promising school for the education of men into preparation for the reception of Christ, and yet it is not a little remarkable that all the centurions mentioned in the New Testament were, in a very real sense, " not far from the Kingdom of God." In addition to the officer referred to in this narrative, there were the centurion at the crucifixion, who said concerning Jesus, "Truly this was a righteous man, truly this was the son of God ; " Cornelius, who is described by Luke as " a devout man, and one that feared God with all his house, who gave much alms to the people, and prayed to God alway ;" and Julius, who at Sidon, " courteously entreated Paul and gave him liberty to go unto his friends and refresh himself," and who at the time of the shipwreck exerted himself, for Paul's sake, to prevent the prisoners from being put to death. Perhaps the most interesting of them all was he with whom we have now especially to do, and the better we become acquainted with him, the more are we drawn toward him. We are impressed in his favor at the very first by the fact that through the Jewish elders he makes application to Jesus on behalf of his *slave*, " who was dear unto him." It was not common for the Romans to care much for their slaves. Rather they were proverbial for their cruelty to those whom they thus held in bondage, and instances were frequent in which the slave was put to death by his master, without any judicial investigation being made, or indeed any imputation of crime having been committed. It was therefore equally creditable to the slave and to the master when the one was " dear unto the other." The servant must have been kind, loving, faithful, attentive, else he would not have been so dear to the master; and the master must have been considerate, affectionate, and largely indifferent to public opinion, else he would not have been so anxious for the welfare of the slave. As Bishop Hall has said, " Great variety of suitors resorted to Christ. One comes to him for a son, another for a daughter, a third for himself. I see none come for his servant, but this one centurion. Neither was he a better man than a master. His servant is sick, he doth not drive him out of doors, but lays him at home; neither doth he stand gazing at his bed-side, but seeks forth, and he seeks forth not to witches or charmers, but to Christ. . . . . Had the master been sick, the faithfulest servant could have done no more. He is unworthy to be well served that will not sometimes wait upon his followers."

Our appreciation of this soldier grows, when we hear what the Jewish elders say concerning him. For he did not come to Christ in person. He had heard such things regarding Jesus as convinced him that he was more than man; and with a true modesty, he shrank from drawing near to him. This was not simply because he was a Gentile, and Jesus was a Jew, though that may have had some influence in keeping him back, knowing as he did how particular the Jews were, in general, in the matter of their intercourse with Gentiles; but it was principally and especially because of his consciousness of the spiritual distance at which he stood from Jesus. He considered that it would be taking too great a liberty to go to the Saviour himself, and therefore he sent elders of the Jews

to beseech him that he would come and heal his servant.
And when they came to do his errand, they bore this
testimony concerning him : " He is worthy for whom thou
shouldst do this. For he loveth our nation, and himself
built us a synagogue." Now that was a very striking
certificate which these elders gave to this soldier. It
would have been a great thing for a Jew to receive such
a testimonial from Jews. But that one belonging to the
army of their oppressors should have earned from official
Jews such a commendation as that which here they gave,
was something altogether unprecedented, and showed that
he to whom it was given was a man of more than ordinary worth. He had not only lived down the prejudice,
with which Romans were regarded by the Jews, but he
had also gained the confidence, and, indeed, the affection
of the community.

Then, again, this was the testimonial of neighbors.
They had enjoyed the best opportunities for forming a
correct judgment regarding him. They had seen him,
not merely on review days and on great occasions, but
also when he was in undress and off his guard. They
were not so likely, therefore, to be imposed upon by appearances as those would have been who had met him
simply on formal or routine business. Moreover, they
saw him in a position which invested him with large authority, and there is no test of character so severe and
searching as is the possession of power. Hazael was not
the only man who has had his head turned and his
heart hardened by exaltation to a place of authority.
The great dramatist was right when he exclaimed :

> " How oft the sight of means to do ill deeds
> Makes ill deeds done. "

But this man's rank did not affect his intercourse with

his neighbors. He performed, so we must believe, painful duties with delicacy ; manifested the strictest justice
in all public affairs, and showed a kindliness of disposition in all ordinary matters, so that the people of Capernaum almost forgot that he was a Roman officer, because he was so good a man.

Then, over and above all this, his residence among the
Jewish people had made him acquainted with their religion. He had become a student of the Old Testament
Scriptures, and though he had not connected himself
formally with the Jewish Church as a proselyte, he had
broken with his old polytheism, and become a believer
in Jehovah as the only true God. This drew him still
more closely to the people, gave him a deeper interest in
their nation, and a more active participation in their
worship, which he showed in rearing for them a synagogue at his own expense. Thus, if I have read his history correctly, this act of his on which the elders dwelt
with such loving gratitude, was not a mere matter of
policy, done to secure the favor of the people ; but rather
an honest tribute to the truth which he had found in the
Old Testament and a grateful offering to the Lord whom
he had discovered therein.

On hearing these things regarding him, the Saviour
set out for his abode. But, when he had nearly reached
the house, he was met by friends of the centurion, whom
he had commissioned to say to him, " Lord, trouble not
thyself, for I am not worthy that thou shouldst enter
under my roof, wherefore neither thought I myself
worthy to come unto thee, but say the word, and my
servant shall be healed. For I also am a man set under
authority, having under me soldiers, and I say unto one
go, and he goeth, and to another come, and he cometh ;
and to my servant, do this, and he doeth it." His mean-

ing was, that just as he himself belonged to a great organization, in which the word of the emperor was supreme, and each in his own rank had to obey the command of those who were above him, all being under one individual head, so he recognized that the universe was under law to the Lord. Diseases had to do his bidding just as he had to obey his superior officer, and his soldiers or his servant had to obey him ; and so for the cure of his servant it was not necessary that the Lord should go into the house, or indeed do anything save speak the word that should order away the malady by which he was affected. When the Saviour heard his message, he exclaimed, "I say unto you, I have not found so great faith, no, not in Israel." And no wonder he gave such commendation, for, if our explanation of his words be correct, the centurion placed the Saviour on the throne of the universe. He regarded him as the ruler of the world, having all its resources at his command. He saw not only that he was the Messiah, but also that he was God Incarnate, and therein lay the superiority of his faith to that of any Israelite. Not any one of the apostles, as yet, had reached the lofty altitude on which this Gentile soldier stood. Not even the eagle-eyed John had thus far perceived all that the words of this centurion had implied, and so he was placed above them all. Matthew adds in his account this admonition, addressed to those "that followed"—"I say unto you that many shall come from the east, and west, and shall sit down with Abraham, and Isaac, and Jacob in the kingdom of heaven. But the children of the kingdom shall be cast into outer darkness ; there shall be weeping and gnashing of teeth." The kingdom of heaven here is not the state of glory after death, but that spiritual system which Christ came to found in the hearts and lives of

men, and which, beginning in time, stretches into eternity.
And so this passage takes its place among the numerous
warnings, given in parable and in direct discourse, to the
effect that if the Jews—the chosen people of God, the
legitimate children of the kingdom—should despise their
opportunity and reject Christ, the privileges of the
kingdom would be taken from them and given to the
Gentiles. Even at this early date in the Saviour's ministry, as the spirit manifested by the Scribes and doctors of the law on the occasion of the healing of the paralytic showed, there were symptoms of that antagonism
toward him which came to a head on Calvary, and so
this warning voice was addressed to the people, if haply
they might yet be prevented from pursuing a course
which would inevitably end in the destruction of their
city, the desolation of their nation, and the introduction
of the Gentiles into that place of privilege which the
Jews so long had held. After this the friends of the
centurion went to his house, and there they found the
slave who had been sick completely restored to health.

But now let us glean a few lessons from the field in
which to-night we have been reaping. And, in the first
place, let us learn not to judge too hastily of a man from
the occupation in which we find him, or the profession to
which he belongs. Unless a man's business be, in and
of itself, sinful—as pandering to the vices and demoraliz-
ing to the characters of his fellows—he may serve God
in any trade or profession. The soldier is apt to be anything but spiritually minded. His temptations are great,
and his environment is often far from wholesome. His
occupation is apt to have a hardening influence, and yet
the records of the Christian Commission during the Civil
War abound in instances of devoted piety alike among

officers and men. The sailor is proverbially rough and regardless, and yet among seamen have been found some of the bravest and most earnest Christians of our times. The mining population is commonly considered somewhat wild, and yet when a dreadful explosion has occurred, and some of the workmen have been almost buried alive for days together, we have read such accounts of their devotions, as have convinced us that those who conducted them were genuine disciples of the Lord. It must be admitted, indeed, that there are not a few who might make the confession of the actor-poet who thus writes :

> " Thence comes it that my name receives a brand,
> And almost thence my nature is subdued
> To that it works in like the dyer's hand."

Yet, though character may take some of its coloring from circumstances, it may be also largely independent of cir- cumstances, for it is the choice of that personal will by which a man is enabled to contend against his environ- ment and to make it subservient to his one great life purpose. Let us test a man, therefore, by what he is, rather than by the place of his residence, or the nature of his occupation. Let not the evil character of the quarter in which he dwells, or the bad repute of the pro- fession to which he belongs keep us from being just to him or from recognizing the image of Christ in him, if it be really there. The determining question is whether he is serving Christ or not, and if he is, let the difficul- ties with which in his situation he has to contend only awaken our consideration for him, and commend him the more strongly to our confidence and assistance.

But let us learn, still farther, that the best men are

those who have the lowliest estimate of themselves. When the centurion said, "I am not worthy that thou shouldst enter under my roof," he was not feigning humility. There was no hypocrisy in his protestation. With the conception which, as we have seen, he had of the nature and dignity of Christ, the very last thing which he would have thought of doing with *him* would be to attempt to appear before him as other than he really was. His was a genuine humility, like that which in a greater or smaller degree is characteristic of every truly good man. He who thinks himself good is not nearly so good as he thinks he is, while he who is most conscious of his imperfections is often a great deal nearer perfection than he supposes. Humility is a constituent element of holiness, and, therefore, the more holy a man is, the more he is disposed to say, " I am but an unprofitable servant." Hence we would be much more ready to believe in the perfect holiness of those who, in our modern days, are so eager to declare that they possess it, if they said less about it, and were more ready to acknowledge their imperfection. For as when the skin of Moses' face shone, he wist not that such was really the case, so the holier a man is, the less is he conscious of his holiness.

Now it becomes an interesting question why it is that the good man's estimate of himself should thus fall below that formed of him by his neighbors. And in answer to that we may remind you of the undoubted fact, that he knows more about himself than any other man can possibly do. There is not one of us who would not shrink from letting others into the innermost secrets of his heart. We feel that if even those to whom we are dearest should know the thoughts that flit across our minds, the imaginations that fill our souls in moments of interval between serious things, the struggles which we have with meanness, or covetousness, or evil desire, or envy, or ambition, the defeats which we suffer in our encounters with self, the trail of sin which is over our very devotions, and the like, they would spurn us from their embrace, and the consciousness of that keeps us humble. How true to our experience in this regard are the lines of Trench:

> " Best friends might loathe us, if what things perverse
> We know of our own selves they also knew.
> Lord ! Holy One ! if thou who knowest worse
> Shouldst loathe us too !"

Then again, as a man rises in holiness, his standard of holiness rises with him. The better a man is, the loftier does his ideal become. We see this illustrated intellectually in the department of knowledge. The more a man learns, the more he learns of his own ignorance. We are accustomed to say of the conceited youth, who talks as if what he did not know was not worth knowing, that when he is twenty years older he will not know so much, and Paul spoke truth when he said, " If any man thinketh that he knoweth anything, he knoweth nothing yet as he ought to know." The wiser a man becomes, he is always the more humble and the more modest, and naturally so, for the more he knows, he comes at just so many more points into contact with the unknown. Every new acquisition reveals to him some new defect. Every new answer to a question starts up some new inquiries, and thus an increase of knowledge is not only an increase of light, but is also, if I may so express it, a discovery of new darkness, according to the mathematical formula which Chalmers was so fond of using in this very connection, " the wider the diameter of light, the greater is the circumference of darkness."

But it is quite similar with holiness. The higher one

grows in holiness, the loftier holiness seems to him to become. Or, exchanging the abstract for the concrete, the liker I become to Christ, the more I see in Christ that I have yet to acquire. That which is highest in me, is my appreciation of, and longing after, that which is still higher. Then from the other side that which is holiest in me is my consciousness of even the least impurity in me, so that, as I grow in grace, I perceive the evil of things in me which in the beginning of my spiritual life hardly seemed to be sins at all. The deepest conviction of sin is not that of the newly awakened sinner, but that of the most advanced saint, for to his cleansed eye and purged heart sin is a far more hideous and repulsive thing than it can possibly be to one who has just found out that he is guilty before God. Hence we may lay it down as a general law, without any exceptions, that when a man congratulates himself on his personal worthiness, he is really unworthy. Here he who is satisfied has never really eaten, or, in the words of the hymn:

> " Whoever says, I want no more,
> Confesses he has none."

Satisfaction with ourselves is a clear indication that God has no complacency in us. Humility and holiness go hand in hand.

Finally, let us learn that we may be instrumental in introducing others to Christ, without repairing to him for ourselves. These Jewish elders very probably were among those who finally rejected Christ. We cannot certainly say so, yet the warning given by Christ, to the effect that while many should come from the east and from the west, and sit down with Abraham in the Kingdom of Heaven, the children of the Kingdom should be cast out, seems to imply so much. In any case, there is a fearful possibility that some who have introduced others to Christ may be themselves at last unsaved. Many years ago I read a tract entitled " Noah's Carpenters," which dwelt upon the thought that the very men whose hands had built the ark were themselves drowned in the flood. It made a deep impression on my mind, and has often since led me to earnest searching of heart, lest "having preached to others I myself should be a castaway." Let every one of us who are engaged—whether as parents, or Sabbath-school teachers or ministers of the gospel—in instructing others, lay this warning to heart, and make sure that we are in Christ ourselves, for who may describe the agony of those who shall have to say at last when they are shut out of the Kingdom, " Have we not prophesied in thy name ? " and he will reply, " I never knew you, depart from me, ye that work iniquity."

XII.

THE RAISING OF THE WIDOW'S SON AT NAIN.

Luke vii. 11-16.

IF we accept the common reading of the first verse of this narrative, the miracle which is to be our theme at this time was performed on "the day after" the healing of the centurion's slave at Capernaum; now, although Nain was twenty-five miles from that city, the Lord might easily make the journey between the two places in a single day. For, as Farrar has said, "Starting, as Orientals always do, early in the cool morning hours, Jesus in all probability sailed to the southern end of the lake, and then passed down the Jordan valley, to the spot where the wadies of the Esdraelon slope down to it; from which point, leaving Mount Tabor on the right hand, and Endor on the left, he might easily have arrived at the little village soon after noon." *

But if, with the Revisers, we adopt another reading, which in their judgment is better supported than the common one, and which differs from it only in one letter, we are under no necessity whatever to account for the rapidity of the Saviour's movement from the one place to the other, since the statement then becomes, " It came to pass soon after." It matters little how we decide the question, since in either case the raising of the widow's

* Farrar's " Life of Christ," vol. i. p. 285.

son finds its proper place in immediate connection with the story of the centurion's faith, and the cure of his servant on the intercession of the Jewish elders.

The place at which this miracle—one of the greatest recorded in the gospels—was wrought, was in the immediate vicinity of the gate of a city called Nain. This, one of the *certain* sites in Palestine, has been identified with the modern "Nein," which lies on the northwestern edge of the little Hermon, as the ground falls into the plain of Esdraelon. Its present condition and environment have been thus described by Canon Tristram : "We were now on the highway from Tiberias to Nain, and following the path along the northern edge of Jebel Dûhy, [the little Hermon] in about an hour or more we reached that spot of hallowed memory. The foreground was singularly uninteresting, but the distant landscape on the way was of striking beauty. Hermon, clad in spotless snow, was now clear of Tabor, and the two thus stood forth side by side ; Tabor with its bright green foreground, dotted all over with grey trees, contrasted finely with the dazzling white of the former. Somewhere near this the sacred poet may have passed, when he exclaimed, ' Tabor and Hermon shall rejoice in thy name.' They are eminently the two mountain features of Galilee.

" To the east of Nain, by the roadside, about ten minutes' walk from the village, lies the ancient burying ground, still used by Moslems, and probably on this very path our Lord met that sorrowing procession. A few oblong piles of stones, and one or two small built graves with whitened plaster, are all that mark the unfenced spot. Nain must have been a ' city,' the ruined heaps and traces of walls prove that it was of considerable extent, and that it was a *walled* town, and therefore with gates,

according to the gospel narrative ; but it has now shrunk
into a miserable Moslem village, *i. e.*, à few houses of
mud and stones, with flat earth roofs, and doors three
feet high, sprinkled here and there, without order or system, among the *débris* of former and better days." *

As the Saviour, attended by his disciples and a great
multitude, approached this place, a funeral procession
emerged from the gate, on its way to the graveyard,
which, as was usual among the Jews, was outside of the
limits of the city. It was a striking coincidence, and
yet something more than a mere coincidence, that just
at the moment of the coming forth of this sad company
from the city, it should be met by the Lord Jesus Christ.
A coincidence, we have called it, because it happened in
the ordinary course of things, without miraculous intervention of any kind, yet more than a mere coincidence,
because it was in the plan of Providence, and so brought
about by God working in and through natural laws, for
"this is the great miracle of Providence, that no miracles are needed for the accomplishment of its purposes."†
Had the Saviour been some time earlier in his arrival,
the funeral would not have been begun ; had he been
much later, it would have been over ; and it is idle to
conjecture what then would have followed ; but as it was,
the two processions met each other, and that concurrence
led to the miracle. It is a great mystery how such
things should be both natural happenings and supernatural arrangements ; but no day passes over our heads
without instances of a similar sort occurring in our own
experience, and if we could explain them,

> " What they are, and all in all,
> We should know what God and man is."

With a little effort of the imagination, we may bring

* " Land of Israel," by H. B. Tristram, M. A., pp. 125, 126.
† Isaac Taylor.

the scene before us. First, came the women making loud lamentations, then followed what in this narrative is called " the bier," which was not an enclosed coffin, as with us, but a board with narrow sides attached to it, or sometimes a kind of basket made of wicker-work, and on this was laid the corpse, wrapped in linen cloth, but having the face exposed. After the bier, which was borne by friends, who relieved each other at frequent intervals, came the chief mourners and their friends, and after them, the sympathizing multitude. In the present instance there was but one mourner, a sad, lonely woman, doubly stricken, for he whose remains lay upon the bier was " the only son of his mother, and she was a widow." What a concentration of sorrow there is in these few words: " Behold, there was a dead man carried out, the only son of his mother, and she was a widow." It was a funeral, a common sight, but never a commonplace one, for it reminds us of the sin which brought death into the world and all our woes, and it bids us remember that ere long, others shall do for our remains what those friends are doing for those of the departed. It was the funeral of a young man cut off in the beginning of his days, all his plans upset, all his hopes disappointed, all his earthly helpfulness to those dependent on him at an end. It is not so hard to see the aged pass away, for, if they have improved their opportunities,

> " like ripe fruit,
> They fall into their mother's lap, or are
> With ease gathered, not harshly plucked
> For death mature."

But no age is sure of immunity from death. No period of life, no station in society, no peculiarity of circumstance insures a man against the attack of the last enemy. We know not what a day may bring forth, and we cannot calculate upon an hour. The old must die, but it is equally true that the young may ; and when they do, their very youth adds an element of bitterness to the cup which their surviving relatives are made to drink. But this funeral was also that of an only son. Scripture dwells plaintively and frequently on the bitterness of those who bewail the death of their first born, and the grief of those who mourn for an only son, and those of us who have been in similar circumstances can well understand and appreciate such allusions. When one is taken out of a large family, the sadness is great, but in such a case duty to the living that remain comes to mitigate our sorrow for the one who has been removed, and the mourners help to bear each other up, but when an only son is taken, the house is desolate, and its very silence is a trial. The music of the beloved footstep is heard no more, the snatches of song, that used so often to fall upon the ear, as he came and went, are now only things of memory. At the table, there is a constant blank, and as the sad reality grows upon the parents, there comes forth the irrepressible sigh

> " For the touch of a vanished hand,
> And the sound of a voice that is still. "

But, saddest of all, this was the only son of a widow. The husband of her youth had been taken from her, and she was left with an only son to breast the hardships of life. At first her child had been a part of her burden. There was comfort, no doubt, in his company, but he had to be provided ·for, and educated, and she had to work for the securing of these blessings. But now he had grown up to work for her. He had became her staff, her

support, her protector, and it seemed that in her case
the words were to be true, " at evening time it shall be
light "—when she was again bereaved. The new wound
made the old one bleed afresh ; and now, heart-broken
and desolate, she was in the utter isolation of a solitude
so dreary, that

> " God himself
> Scarce seemed there to be."

But he was nearer than she thought, for " when Jesus
saw her, he had compassion on her and said unto her,
Weep not. And he came nigh and touched the bier, and
the bearers stood still. And he said, Young man, I say
unto thee, Arise. And he that was dead sat up and began to speak, and he gave him to his mother."

Here let it be noted that the source of this miraculous
relief was in the spontaneous intervention of the Redeemer. On other occasions he was applied to by the
diseased one himself, or by some one in his stead ; but
here the sorrowing widow spoke no word. It is doubtful whether she even knew him, and there is no mention whatever of the exercise by her of any faith in
him. She was absorbed in her own sadness, and the
interposition of the Lord on her behalf was entirely
unsolicited. He had taken in the whole circumstances
at a glance, and they pleaded, silently, yet most eloquently, on her behalf. Just as, without any request
of man for his assistance, he came to earth for human
salvation, and " though he was rich, for our sakes he
became poor, that we, through his poverty, might be
rich," so here, though unasked, he brought to this bereaved one the greatest relief, by giving her back her
son. The command is, "Ask and ye shall receive," but
oh, how many things we are constantly receiving without

any asking of our own, and out of the spontaneous prompting of the Lord's compassion.

Nor let us forget to notice the tenderness of the Lord's expression of his sympathy with this afflicted widow. He said unto her, " Weep not," not seeking thereby to chide her sorrow, but rather to relieve it. He sought to stay her grief just as a mother seeks to comfort a sobbing child. Nay, more, his words were the prophecy of the miracle that was so soon to follow. *Our* sympathy is largely passive, but his is active, and when he bids us not to weep, he gives us that which will enable us to wipe away our tears. He dries the stream by draining the fountain. The poor widow did not know this at the time, but ere long she discovered it all, and meanwhile the gentleness of his tone kept her from misinterpreting the expression of his sympathy or regarding it as an intrusion into the sacredness of her sorrow.

Remark, again, that without any regard for the ceremonial uncleanness which another would have contracted by coming into contact with the dead, "he came and touched the bier." Just as formerly he touched the leper without being thereby defiled, so here again he who is himself "the life" takes no pollution from the dead, for there was that about him which could not be defiled with sin, which is the cause, and, therefore, he could not be polluted with death, which is the consequence, of sin. Observe also, how, when he touched the bier, they who bore it stood still, without the utterance of any request to that effect from him. There was such a look of compassionate purpose in his countenance, that they paused expectant of something extraordinary. The intervention of another might have aroused opposition, but his created only silent anticipation. They could not tell what was coming, but they stood still to see, especially as they had clearly perceived the deep sincerity of the sympathetic " weep not," with which he had sought to stay the widow's tears.

Nor can we fail to take note of the potent brevity of the words by which in this, as in other recorded instances, he recalled the dead to life, " Young man, I say unto thee, Arise." That was all, and the saying takes its place, with " Maid, arise," on the occasion when he restored the daughter of Jairus to her parents, and " Lazarus, come forth," with which he brought back the loved Lazarus to his sisters. Truly this is he " who raiseth up the dead and quickeneth them," and " calleth those things that be not as though they were." For the effect was immediate. " He that was dead sat up and began to speak." What a surprise to the bearers, to the multitude, and to the young man himself! Above all, what a turning back of the tide of feeling in the mother's heart! Now she can obey the " weep not " which before he had addressed to her, or, if she weep at all, her tears will be those of grateful gladness and not of despairing sorrow.

And with what ease all this was done! When Elijah raised the child of the widow of Zarephath, it was on this fashion : " He said unto her, Give me thy son. And he took him out of her bosom, and carried him up into the chamber where he abode, and laid him upon his own bed. And he cried unto the Lord and said, O Lord my God, hast thou also brought evil upon the widow with whom I sojourn by slaying her son ? And he stretched himself upon the child three times, and cried unto the Lord, and said, O Lord my God, I pray thee let the child's soul come into him again. And the Lord hearkened unto the voice of Elijah, and the child's soul came unto him again and he revived." * When Elisha

* I King's xvii. 19-22

raised the child of the great woman of Shunem, it was on this wise: "And when Elisha was come unto the house, behold the child was dead and laid upon the bed. He went in, therefore, and shut the door upon them twain and prayed unto the Lord. And he went up and lay upon the child, and put his mouth upon his mouth, and his eyes upon his eyes, and his hands upon his hands, and he stretched himself upon him, and the flesh of the child waxed warm. Then he returned and walked in the house once to and fro, and went up and stretched himself upon him, and the child sneezed seven times and the child opened his eyes."* Now with these narratives, contrast that before us, " And he said, Young man, I say unto thee, Arise, and he that was dead sat up and began to speak ; " and does it not clearly appear that these prophets wrought with a power not their own, but bestowed on them in answer to prayer, while Jesus wrought with his own power—this " *I* say unto thee," being as emphatic as that so frequently recurring in the Sermon on the Mount, and betokening here as great a superiority to Elijah and Elisha, as there to Moses? What these prophets, with an agony of effort strained after, and could, as it were, barely touch with the tips of their fingers, was easily within the reach of Jesus, who is thereby proved to be the God-man.

This young man "began to speak." But there is no record of what he said, and it is idle to conjecture. One thing we do know ; he uttered no word concerning the state from which he had been recalled. It was not his to bring " life and immortality to light." That was reserved for him whose own resurrection was itself a revelation, and was so because it was essentially different from this. This was a resuscitation, a bringing of the young man

* II Kings iv. 32-35.

back to the old life, a restoration of him to his mother,
whereas the resurrection of Christ was a going forward
to a higher life, indicated by this as by other things connected with it, that he did not give himself back to his
mother, as here he gave her son to the widow of Nain;
and hereby we explain and account for the fact which
so few have noticed, but which was so clearly significant, that in all the interviews which he had with his
disciples after his resurrection, we do not read of any
meeting between our Lord and his mother.

Now let us take note of what followed this wonderful
work. The motive of it all was compassion for the
widow, and so the climax was that he gave him back to
his mother; and who may attempt to describe the joy that
filled her heart as once again she folded him in her embrace? When the Greek painter portrayed a scene that
evoked indescribable emotion, he put a veil over the face
of her who was so deeply moved; so the Evangelist here,
guided by a higher inspiration, simply notes the incident and passes on, leaving it to speak for itself, and
where he is silent we may be well content to be the same.
But the spectators were moved with awe, as having
been brought into immediate contact with one who
had been in Hades, and as having been brought face to
face with one who had the keys of death at his girdle,
and could roll back the door which for thousands of
years had opened only inwards. So they said, probably
with the miracles of Elijah and Elisha in their minds,
" A great prophet is risen up among us, and God hath
visited his people." And they spake the truth, for this
was indeed that prophet of whom Moses spake, saying,
" A prophet shall the Lord your God raise up unto you,
of your brethren, like unto me. Him shall ye hear in all
things, whatsoever he shall say unto you." Nor was

this all. The report of such a wonderful work, which had been seen by so many witnesses, went out and out over all Galilee, and overflowed into Judea, until at length it penetrated even the castle of Machaerus, where John the Baptist was imprisoned by the cruel Herod, and moved him to send to Jesus the memorable deputation that asked, " Art thou he that should come or do we look for another ? "

One is curious to know what became of this young man in after days. We would have liked to have been informed in what fashion he ministered to his mother after his restoration to her from the grave, and especially, how he lived as before God, after the unique experience through which he had been brought. Surely, we say to ourselves, he would not spend his life in sinful excess, in self-indulgence, or in godlessness. There may be no truth—we do not believe that there is any—in the legendary story which affirms that after his resurrection, Lazarus was never seen to smile, but the story is the mythical and exaggerated expression of the expectation that after such an experience a man should live a more earnest and godly life. Whether this young man did so or not, we cannot tell. But a similar obligation rests as really, though not perhaps to the same degree, upon us all, for God has given us our lives at first, and he has preserved them until now; therefore we owe it to him that we should make them sacrifices unto him, by denying ungodliness and worldly lusts, and living soberly, righteously, and godly in this present evil world. Young men, I make my appeal especially to you. How are you spending your lives ? What is the object which you have set before you ? What is that which to you would be the greatest success ? and what is that which in your view would be the greatest failure in life? Are you seeking only the means for self-indulgence? Are you working only for the riches, or the honor, or the favor of this world? If that be so, then you are dead, spiritually indeed, but as really as was this youth whom they were carrying to his grave. The better, the higher, the nobler part of your nature is still dormant within you. It is there, but it is as good as dead, and to-night the Lord Jesus has come to you and has said, " Young man, Arise." Begin to live indeed. Heretofore you have been only existing, but mere existence is not life for a man. Life for a man is to hear and obey the voice of God. Arise then to that, and in the measure in which you obey that call you will glorify God, benefit society, bless the world, and secure that kind of success which alone is worthy to be the highest object of the ambition of an immortal man. O may the Lord Jesus raise you from the death of sin unto the life of holiness, that from this hour you may serve him with your whole hearts by doing everything in his name and for his glory.

And you that are in circumstances of sadness, whether as bereaved parents, or broken-hearted mourners over departed friends dear to you as a son is to his mother. Behold, here, how tender and true is the compassion of the Redeemer for you. He is the same Jesus now that he was that day at the gate of Nain, and though he may not show his sympathy and help to you in the same way as he did to this widow, he will help you just as truly as he helped her. Trust him, therefore, for in him is everlasting strength. If he so marvellously blessed this woman who did not ask for his assistance, will he not much more comfort and sustain you who cry to him so plaintively, " out of the depths"? I know not what your trial may be, but he knows it all, and for him to know it is to sympathize with you under it—while again for him to sympathize with you is to help you according to your need. Hear, therefore, O stricken one, this " weep not " of his to-night, and let that be to you the prophecy that deliverance is at hand.

XIII.

CURES OF THE DEAF AND DUMB.

Mark vii. 31-37. Matt. ix. 32-33. Matt. xii. 22-30.

WE have grouped these narratives together because
to take each one of them separately would necessitate
the repetition in each case of much the same line of remark; while by adopting the method which we have
chosen, we may have some thoughts suggested to us
which we might otherwise have overlooked. One thing,
however, must be clearly understood. We do not mean
to imply that the order in which we have arranged them,
is that of their chronological sequence in the life of our
Lord, but we have adopted this method simply because
it seems to us to be that which is best suited for bringing
out before you both most naturally and most cogently the
lessons which they teach. If we were treating the life
of Christ as a whole, we should feel it necessary to follow the order of events, as far as that can be determined;
but as our special business at this time is with his miracles, we consider ourselves at liberty to take them in
such groups as shall best bring out their distinctive features as illustrations of his method of dealing with sinners
in the matter of their salvation.

The incident recorded by Mark, (in chap. vii. 31–37),
belongs to that journey taken by our Lord into the

borders of the Gentile cities of Tyre and Sidon, which
was specially signalized by his healing of the daughter
of the Syro-Phœnician woman. After the performance
of that miracle, the Saviour on his return towards the
Lake of Galilee passed through Sidon (see Revised
Version) and went through the midst of the borders of
Decapolis. He was therefore somewhere in that region,
lying for the most part to the east of the Jordan, and to
the east and southeast of the Lake of Galilee, which, because of the number of cities which it contained, was
called Decapolis, or the district of the ten cities. We
have no means, however, of more closely identifying the
locality. Let it suffice to say, that somewhere in that
neighborhood, and not long before the feeding of the four
thousand, interested friends brought to him " one that
was deaf, and had an impediment in his speech," and
besought him to lay his hand upon him.

The malady in this case was deafness, accompanied by
some defect in utterance. Literally rendered, the phrase
would be "a deaf stammerer." It is difficult to say which
of the two privations, blindness or deafness, is the greater ;
but if we may judge from the fact that it is rare to find a
deaf person lively and cheerful ; while the happiness of
the blind is matter of constant observation, we may agree
with Bishop Horsley in his remark that " of all natural
imperfections deafness seems the most deplorable, as it is
that which most excludes the unhappy sufferer from society." The blind man, indeed, is cut off from all perception of the external appearance of things ; but it is
easy to communicate with him ; and in whatsoever company he finds himself, he can hear the conversation that
is going on, and take an intelligent part in it. But
though the deaf man has the use of his eyes, he is altogether isolated in company, and the very fact that he sees

the effect of the words of a speaker, in the laughter which they evoke, or the tears which they cause to flow in those around him, makes him the more impatient and discontented, so that he courts solitude, and is apt to become suspicious. In these modern days, indeed, a language of signs addressed to the eye has been invented, which has been an untold blessing to the deaf and many have been taught so to read the lips as to be able thereby to make out what one is saying to them, but before these mitigations of their condition were devised, their solitude must have been most dreary, and their misery most profound. The case of this man, however, was not one of the saddest, for he had not been born deaf. So much is evident from the statement that he had " an impediment in his speech." Had he been born deaf, he would not have been able to speak at all. He must, therefore, at one time have heard with more or less distinctness. How he lost his hearing is not stated, but disease, either of the ears, or of the throat, or some accident that affected his ears, may have been the cause of his sad privation. Those who are acquainted with the life of John Kitto, the famous biblical illustrator, whose deafness was caused, when he was twelve years old, by a fall from a ladder up which he was carrying a load of slates upon his head, will remember that it was not till his twentieth year that he attempted to speak, and that even then his voice was harsh and not very distinct. In my first parish there was a young man who had lost his hearing, while a boy at school, and though he continued to speak, he was always most reluctant to do so, because his voice was hoarse, and unnatural, and his articulation indistinct. Now cases of that sort, occurring among ourselves, will help us to understand that described by Mark in the narrative before us, and the plaintive wail in which Kitto laments his deaf-

ness will enable us in some degree to appreciate the misery of his case. " To me the whole world is dumb, since
I am deaf to it. No more, the music of the human voice
shall charm. All around, below, and above me is solitary silence ; ever-during silence, stillness unbroken." *
Alas ! for the deaf. Let them have your sympathy, and
do your utmost to make up to them in some degree for
the loneliness of their condition.

But, bad as that condition is, we have in it only a
faint illustration of the sinner's spiritual state, for he hears
without hearing: that is to say, though the physical
sense may be acute, the spiritual ear is stopped. Swift
to hear everything that concerns his worldly interest, he
is deaf to the voice of God, and that deafness is not so
much his misfortune as his fault. For, as the well-
known adage has expressed it, " there are none so deaf
as those who will not hear " ; and that is just his case.
He will not listen to the Word of God, and to open his
ear to that there needs first to be an opening of his heart,
as there was in the instance of Lydia at Philippi. O,
may he who so often on earth unstopped the ears of the
deaf, open the hearts of those who hear the word, that
they may attend to the things that are spoken " in his
name !"

This deaf man was brought to Jesus by friends who, in
their application on his behalf, specified the mode in
which he was to be healed. But the Lord would not
be dictated to, and perhaps as much to assert his own
sovereignty as to meet the peculiar personal experience
of the deaf man, he dealt with him in quite another fashion than they asked. First, as in the case of the blind
man at Bethsaida, " he took him aside from the multitude," either that he might rebuke the disposition of

* " Life of John Kitto, D.D.," by John Eadie, D.D., LL.D., p. 97.

those in the crowd who were constantly seeking after a sign, and who allowed the external miracle to eclipse the better and more glorious miracle of grace which it was the chief glory and happiness of Christ to perform; or that he might awaken in the man himself a more confident hope, yea, if it might be, a most assured faith, that he was to be healed. Then he " put his fingers into his ears, and touched his tongue" with saliva, " and looking up to heaven he sighed, and saith unto him Eph-phatha, that is, be opened." The purpose of all this is hidden from us, but perhaps we shall not err if we suppose that these different actions of Christ were designed to strengthen the faith of the deaf man. He could not hear, therefore if he were to be encouraged at all, it had to be by touch; and so the Saviour touched alike his ears and his tongue, and then, for the sake of the little group of friends that stood by, just as in the parallel case, at the grave of Lazarus, he lifted up his eyes to heaven, and sighed,—perhaps in sorrow, over the vast multitude of human sufferers who would have to suffer on without having him present to relieve them; or perhaps in supplication to his father, for, as one has profoundly remarked here, * " the deepest sympathy with man springs out of the loftiest communion with God,—and said, " Eph-phatha, be opened."

Observe, here, in passing, one of Mark's peculiarities. He describes the Saviour's emotion, and gives us the very word in the Aramaic vernacular which he used. This is characteristic of the second Evangelist, and taken with other interesting features of his style, stamps his narrative with independent individuality, and helps to refute the foolish theory of those who imagine that the second gospel is little better than an abridgment of the first.

* Morison or " Mark," p. 203.

But now, let us note the perfection of the miracle. The
man from that moment heard distinctly and spoke plainly.
The word that was spoken, was spoken by Christ, and
therefore it was a word of power, the finger which
touched was the finger of Christ, and therefore there
was healing in the thrill of its contact with the stammerer's tongue. Just as the bringing of wire into touch with
wire completes the circuit and transmits the electric influence to its goal, where it is made to do its work, so
the union between the applicant and the Saviour, whereof the touch was the symbol, conveyed the healing
energy from the God-man to the deaf and dumb, and all
who saw the result were beyond measure astonished,
saying, " He hath done all things well. He maketh both
the deaf to hear and the dumb to speak." But though
the man who was healed, and those who were beside him
were thus affected toward Christ and his work, they were
not so deeply impressed as to obey implicitly the command that they should tell no man, for "the more he
charged them, the more a great deal they published it."
Thus far the narrative in Mark.

The miracle recorded in Matthew ix. 32–34, like that
which we have just been considering, is a cure effected
on a dumb man; but its distinctive peculiarity is that
the dumbness was the effect of demoniacal possession, so
that when the demon was cast out, the dumb spake. It
was not the result of any local physical injury or disease,
neither was it congenital, but the man was dumb because
he was possessed by a demon. This statement is to us
conclusive as a proof that demoniacal possession was not
an ordinary physical disease. There was that in this
man's case which showed that it was not due to func-
tional or organic disorder ; and which was recognized by
onlookers as possession by a demon. Dumbness was

not connected here, so far as we know, with any malady
of the ear, or any imperfection of the organs of articulation ; but there was that about it, which differentiated it
as a case of demoniacal possession, and no minute diagnosis was needed to find out that such was indeed the fact,
for it was patent both to the multitudes and to the Lord.
The conclusion therefore is that demoniacal possession
must be distinguishable from a mere physical disease.

But mark now how different was the effect produced
upon the spectators by this miracle from that which followed the healing of the deaf man in Decapolis. In that
case, the onlookers were all of one mind and said, "He
hath done all things well." But in this, while some said,
"It was never so seen in Israel," others, and these belonging to the Pharisees, regarded the miracle with ab-
horrence and exclaimed, "By the prince of the demons
casteth he out demons."

Now observe that in this outcry of the Pharisees, we
have the point of contact between this narrative in Matthew ix. 32–34, and that in Matthew xii. 22–32, to
which I proceed to call your attention. The poor afflicted
one in this last case was blind and dumb. Nothing is
said about his being deaf, and therein he differed from
the man in Decapolis, although Kitto seems to think
that he must have been deaf also. Again, this poor man
was blind, and so, if Kitto's supposition regarding his
deafness, is correct, his privation must have been as great
as that of Laura Bridgman, whose earthly life has so
recently ceased. But the blindness is here the peculiar
feature, for, as in the instance of the man referred to in
Matthew ix. 32, the physical privations here are traced
to demoniacal possession as their cause, and with the
casting out of the demon, the sense of sight and the
power of speech were restored.

Still farther, in this last instance, as in the former re-corded by Matthew, the effect of the miracle on the spec-tators was twofold; for while some were amazed and said, " Is this the Son of David ? " the Pharisees said, " This man doth not cast out demons, but by Beelzebub, the prince of the demons." That is to say, he is in league with Beelzebub ; he is, as the word literally means, *in* Beelze-bub, and Beelzebub is in him. Beelzebul was the name given by the Ekronites to one of their gods. The term literally means the god of flies, and probably commem-orates some deliverance from a plague of flies which in their ignorance they traced to this idol; but, in their scorn of idolatry, the Hebrews changed the name into Beelzebub, the god of filth, which they came afterwards to use as a name for Satan himself, and " as thus applied," to use the words of Dr. Morison, " it is really, when the idea of literary sport is excluded, not a bad name " for him. Now, it is curious, to say the least of it, that this charge should have been brought against Jesus in connection mostly with the cure of the dumb, and perhaps Dr. Kitto has given the explanation of that which is at first sight so remarkable. He says,* " It strikes one with some surprise to see this charge specially associated with this form of miracle. In the former case the man was dumb ; in this, dumb and blind. Pondering on this, it occurs to us that, as is usually the case, the persons were not only dumb but deaf. As therefore the person could not physically hear with his own ears the words of ejection addressed to the possessing demon, who used and acted through his organs, this was considered as the most difficult and incurable species of possession, beyond the reach or pretension of the popular exorcists, who therefore declared dispossession to be in such cases

* Daily Bible Illustrations, vol. vi. pp. 359, 360.

impossible, save through some diabolical compact or influence. This interpretation of the matter is confirmed by the fact that the disciples, during our Lord's absence upon the Mount of Transfiguration, attempted in vain to cast out a spirit possessing a lad who had been deaf and dumb from a child. And when they asked him the cause of their failure, he said, primarily, because of their unbelief; but he added, ' Howbeit, *this* kind goeth not out but by prayer and fasting.' It was probably their preconceived sense of the difficulty of the case which prevented them from exercising the faith requisite to effect the miracle."

The charge of the Pharisees was thoroughly met and answered by the Saviour in three sufficient arguments. The first was founded on the antagonistic character of Satan's kingdom to his own, thus : " Every kingdom divided against itself is brought to desolation, and every city or house divided against itself shall not stand, and if Satan cast out Satan, he is divided against himself ; how then shall his kingdom stand ? " There is here, therefore, a recognition of the kingdom of Satan as a unit held together by the opposition of its head and its members to the kingdom of God. As in an earthly kingdom there may be parties opposed to each other, and actuated by selfishness in their conduct towards each other, but these are unified whenever an attack is made on the kingdom as a whole from without; so in the kingdom of Satan there are discords and divisions between its members among themselves; but when it is assailed as a whole kingdom, then its unity is displayed by all its parties coalescing for its defence ; or, if that should not be the case, it falls an easy prey to its adversary. Now the casting out of demons is an attack on Satan's kingdom as a whole, and it is not likely that Satan himself would be a party to such a suicidal policy, for the end of it must be his utter downfall. That is so plain as to be indisputable. Satan is not such a fool as to contribute in that way to his own destruction.

The second argument is of the sort known among logicians as the *argumentum ad hominem*: "And if I by Beelzebub cast out demons, by whom do your own children cast them out?" As if he had said, There are exorcists among youselves, actuated by your principles, and marching under your banners, and they have had the reputation of success; if, therefore, you have never accused them of being in league with Satan, why should you bring that charge against me? As Dr. Addison Alexander has said: "It is certain, both from the Scriptures and Josephus, that exorcism was a common practice among the Jews. See Acts xix. 13, where itinerant exorcists are found at Ephesus, the seven sons of a high priest, which may throw some light upon the term ' sons ' (or children) in the passage before us. It is of little moment whether they really exercised this power or not. If they professed, and were believed to do so, this is all that is required to give force to the argument *ad hominem*." *

But, the Saviour proceeds;—there are only two kingdoms in the spiritual domain, and, therefore, if I am not in league with Satan, there is but one alternative, and so "if I cast out demons by the Spirit of God, then the Kingdom of God is come unto you." Either be consistent and charge your own children with being in union with Beelzebub, or else withdraw your accusation from me, and admit that the kingdom of God is among you.

The third argument is one from the reason of the case. " Or else,"—that is, as if he had said, " or to make the

* Alexander on " Matthew," *in loco.*

case yet plainer,"—" how can one enter into a strong man's house and spoil his goods, except he first bind the strong man ? and then he will spoil his house." As much as to say—" When you see one with spoils that had belonged to a strong man, you infer that he has bound the strong man, and then taken his goods; so when you see me leading captive the subordinates of Satan, you may conclude that I have bound Satan himself, and may rightfully dispossess his agents." In the wilderness of temptation, the Lord had vanquished and bound the prince of darkness, and thereby acquired the right to cast out demons. So parties were polarized by himself. A man's relation to the kingdoms of light and darkness is determined by his relation to Christ. If he is with Christ, he is in the kingdom of light; if he is against Christ, he is in the kingdom of Satan, there is no middle ground. " He that gathereth not with Christ, scattereth abroad." These are aphorismic utterances, determined by the great truth that a man's relation to the kingdom is fixed by his relation to the king; or, in other words, that Christ himself is the divider of the kingdom of light from that of darkness. We do not get to Christ through the kingdom, but we get to the kingdom through Christ, and in that is the principle of harmony between the statement made by the Saviour here, and that other saying of his, apparently contradictory to it (Luke ix. 50): " He that is not against us is for us," for he to whom that refers was casting out demons in Christ's name, was, therefore, in the great conflict between Christ and Satan, on the side of Christ, and so was gathering with him. The one proverb declares that no neutrality is possible where Christ is in the case; the other affirms that among those who are on the side of Christ, there should be the fullest mutual tolerance in all minor matters and they must not anathematize each other, because they do not both walk together, or follow in each other's fellowship.

Here our exposition might properly stop, but as the warning which the Lord proceeds to give concerning the danger in which those Pharisees stood because they ascribed his miracles of exorcism to his being in league with Satan, contains, or rather consists of, the passage relating to what has been styled the unpardonable sin, we may never have a better opportunity of considering that. I cannot hope to go into it critically, but there is still time for a brief explanation of its meaning. Here are the words: " Wherefore I say unto you, all manner of sin and blasphemy shall be forgiven unto men, but the blasphemy against the Holy Ghost shall not be forgiven unto men, and whosoever speaketh a work against the Son of Man, it shall be forgiven him, but whosoever speaketh against the Holy Ghost, it shall not be forgiven him, neither in this world, neither in the world to come." There is thus a gracious assertion that any sin will be forgiven to the man who penitently and believingly comes to God by Jesus Christ, while there is a distinction drawn between blasphemy against the Son of Man and blasphemy against the Holy Ghost. Now what particularly do these phrases mean ? Blasphemy against the Son of Man is the rejection of Jesus Christ, as he then was, as it were, in disguise before them, and before the revelation of his glory through his resurrection from the dead, his ascension into heaven, and his bestowment of the Holy Spirit—contemptuous treatment of Christ in ignorance of who he was, and what he had come to do for men. Blasphemy against the Holy Ghost again denotes a defiant and persistent rejection of Christ, after the Holy Spirit has approved him, to the conviction of our own intellects as truly divine. The one, therefore, is a sin of ignorance, the other a sin of presumptuous and persistent defiance, not only against knowledge, but also against the conviction produced in the mind of the individual by the Holy Spirit, that Jesus is the Christ, the Son of God. And by using these words at this time, the Lord virtually says to these Pharisees, "Beware how you go further in the course on which you have entered. So long as you reject me in ignorance of my real position, you may be forgiven if you repent, but if you persevere in your rejection after you have come to the actual conviction that I am indeed the Son of God, you may commit that awful sin for which there is no forgiveness."

This explanation is in harmony with the other portions of Scripture which refer to the subject, as well as with the argument of the Saviour in the passage before us. The Lord Jesus, as he was being nailed to the cross, said, " Father, forgive them, for they know not what they do." Peter, in persuading the people to repentance, said in his sermon after the cure of the lame man, "And now, brethren, I wot that in ignorance ye did it, as did also your rulers." Paul also says to Timothy, " but I obtained mercy, because I did it ignorantly in unbelief." While, on the other hand, in his address to Simon Magus, Peter said, " Repent of this thy wickedness and pray God, if *perhaps* the thought of thine heart may be forgiven thee." To a similar effect are the words of the author of the Epistle to the Hebrews in chapter vi. 4–6, and chapter x. 26. From all which it appears that the blasphemy against the Holy Ghost is the persistent refusal of the heart to submit itself to Christ, even although the intellect is convinced that the claims of Jesus to such submission are fully authenticated.

But even so, the impossibility of forgiveness is not grounded in any imperfection of the work of Christ, for

his blood cleanseth from all sin ; but in the perverseness
of the individual which will not allow him to apply in
penitence for forgiveness. Judas might still have been
saved after his treachery, so far as the sufficiency of the
work of Christ in redemption was concerned ; but he
would not, and did not come repentingly to ask forgiveness of his sin, and therefore he went " to his own place " ;
or, borrowing a phrase from the passage in the Epistle to
the Hebrews to which I have just referred, we may say
that the impossibility is in their repentance and not in
any lack of sufficiency in the atonement of Christ.

Your time, however, forbids me to enlarge. I stay
only a moment or two longer, to draw attention to one
inference from this whole subject, namely, that the
effect of a miracle or of the testimony in behalf of a miracle, on a spectator or inquirer, will depend on the creed
or disposition of the spectator or of the student. If the
onlooker already believes in God, the miracle will confirm that belief, and be to him a sign that God is about
to reveal something more to him. But if he does
not believe in God, a miracle will not convince him
of the existence of God. Bacon has truly alleged
that God does not work miracles to convince atheism, because his ordinary works convince it. If a man is
not convinced by the works of creation, or what is loosely
called the world of nature, that there is a God, a miracle
will not convince him, and it is on the same principle
that Abraham said to the rich man in the parable, " If
they believe not Moses and the prophets, neither will
they be persuaded though one went unto them from the
dead." These Pharisees, though they could not deny the
miracles wrought by Jesus, were not led by them to receive Christ, because in their secret hearts they were
determined to oppose him. They would rather ascribe

his wonderful works—no matter how inconsistently—to Satan, than regard them as the seals that witnessed to his claims to be received as one who had come from God, It is sometimes said by those who have not yet submitted themselves to Christ as the Saviour and sovereign of their souls, that if they had lived in his day, and seen his works, they would not have rejected him. But that is all a delusion. If they are rejecting him now, they would have rejected him then ; nay, inasmuch as now the events of eighteen hundred years of history have greatly enriched the proofs of the deity and Messiahship of Jesus, the guilt of rejecting him is greater now than it was in the case of those Pharisees. They who are now rejecting him are therefore nearer to the commission of this blasphemy against the Holy Spirit than those were to whom the warning regarding it was originally addressed. That is an awfully solemn thought, and I leave it to be silently pondered by you in your retirement. Do not trifle with such a danger, and as the best safeguard against it, let me urge you, while it is called to-day, to repent and harden not your hearts.

XIV.

THE STILLING OF THE TEMPEST.

Mark iv. 35-41.

By the phrase, "the same day," Mark fixes the precise time when the miracle, now to be considered by us, was performed by Jesus. It was in the evening, or, more specifically, in our western mode of speech, the latter part of the afternoon, of the day on which the Lord had spoken from the boat of one of his disciples, the parable of the sower and those others which are associated with it, in the thirteenth chapter of Matthew's gospel, that he and his followers set out from the neighborhood of Capernaum to cross the Lake of Galilee to its eastern shore. The other evangelists, Matthew and Luke, connect this episode in the life of our Lord with quite different incidents than those specified by Mark. Thus Matthew places immediately before it,[*] the account of the different treatment given by the Saviour to the three men who came to him eagerly professing their determination to follow him ; and Luke [†] introduces it just after the remarkable words occasioned by the coming of his nearest earthly relatives to see him : "My mother and my brethren are these, which hear the word of God and do it." But there is no real discrepancy, for it is well known that

---

[*] Matthew viii. 19-26.   [†] Luke viii. 20-25.

Matthew and Luke do not relate the incidents of our Lord's life in chronological order, but give them in groups, according to an arrangement of their own, and so when Mark specifies a precise date, he does so, not in opposition to them, but because, for a reason peculiar to himself, he felt it needful to indicate the exact time to which this part of the narrative is to be referred. And what that reason was in this instance it is not difficult to discover. He desired to suggest an explanation of the fact that Jesus fell into such a sound sleep in such singular circumstances. You observe that the proposal to cross the lake emanated from him, and that after they had sent away the multitude, the disciples took him, "even as he was," in the boat. "Even as he was," without making any preparation, and that they might bear him away as speedily as possible from the exciting and fatiguing work in which he had been engaged. We have a parallel to this manner of speech in the statement made by John when he says, "Jesus, being wearied with his journey, sat *thus* on the well." It was not only when a miracle was wrought by him that "virtue went out of him." His strength was exhausted by his teaching and preaching as well, and seeing his exhaustion, his followers made haste to get him away, that he might have a season of repose, and be free from the interruptions and distractions that were inevitable, when the multitude was near. So after the people had been dispersed on the shore, and with only a small following of little boats, whose owners still desired to be near him, they set out at once for the other side; while, that he might obtain the rest he needed, their Master went to the stern of the skiff, and threw himself back upon the cushion which was a usual part of the furnishing of such tiny craft, and fell fast asleep.

But they had not gone far when a fearful storm arose. Every one at all familiar with boating on lakes surrounded by mountains knows how rapidly such squalls will rise on them. Some years ago, while descending the Brunig Pass in Switzerland to the Lake of Brientz, I had a striking illustration of this. As we came down that splendid road, the day was delightful, the very perfection of summer beauty, and the lake lay without a ripple on its surface at our feet, a perfect mirror of the sky. But within a very few minutes, not more than ten or fifteen, and before we had time to run for shelter into the nearest house, a terrible storm arose. Immediately the waters were churned into foam. Great waves in which no little boat, unless very skilfully managed, could have lived, came tumbling in upon the shore, and the whole aspect of the scene was changed, while overhead the lightning flashed out vividly, and the reverberations of the thunder rolled from peak to peak among the surrounding Alps. But the Lake of Galilee is peculiarly liable to be visited by such sudden storms, for, as Dr. W. M. Thomson says, " We must remember that it lies low—six hundred and eighty feet below the sea ; that the mountainous plateau of the Jaulân rises to a considerable height, spreading backward to the wilds of the Haurân, and upward to snowy Lebanon; that the water-courses have worn or washed out profound ravines and wild gorges, converging to the head of this lake, and that these act like great funnels to draw down the cold winds from the mountains."[*]

The storm in the case before us was so violent that the waves broke over the boat, so that it began to fill, and even the fishermen, skilful as they were in all matters pertaining to the management of their boat, and accustomed as they were to the navigation of the lake, were seri-

[*] "Central Palestine and Phœnicia," p. 351.

ously alarmed. But their Master remained asleep until, in an agony of earnestness, not unmingled with disappointed surprise, they roused him with the cry, "Master, carest thou not that we perish?" Then, with the composure of Deity, "he arose and rebuked the wind, and said unto the sea, Peace, be still. And the wind ceased and thre was a great calm." Now here was a clear miracle. Usually after a storm like that which is described in these verses, the swell on the water remains for a considerable time after the wind has died down, but here the lake became calm at once, or, in the words of the old Scottish metrical version of the one hundred and seventh Psalm we may say :

> "The storm is changed into a calm
> At his command and will ;
> So that the waves which raged before
> Now quiet are and still."

Then, having removed the cause of the alarm of his followers, he began to deal with themselves, and said, "Why are you so afraid? have ye not yet faith?" for so the latter clause is more accurately rendered in the Revised Version. As if he had said, "After all you have seen of me and heard from me, is it possible that you have not yet such faith as to give you the assurance that you are always safe when I am with you." It was only arrogance in the great Roman, when, to calm the fears of the rowers when he was caught in a storm, he said, "You carry Cæsar and his fortunes," for the waves would not go down at his bidding, any more than they would roll back when Canute gave command. But there was no boasting in the words of Jesus here, for he had already stilled the tempest, and besides, he had a right to expect that those who had seen his power over the diseases of men, would have had confidence that he could also rule the elements of Nature, and as the conviction that this was indeed the case grew strong within them, the disciples were filled with reverence and awe, and said, "What manner of man is this that even the wind and the sea obey him ?"

Turning now from the exposition of the verses, let us see what we may learn from the narrative as a whole. And, in the first place, let us take note that we have here an incidental confirmation of the great truth that the Lord Jesus Christ is both really human and truly divine. He was asleep—there is his humanity ; for of God it is said, "Behold, he that keepeth Israel shall neither slumber nor sleep." He commanded the winds into silence, and the waves into peace—there is Deity; for to God alone can it be said, "Thou rulest the raging of the sea ; when the waves thereof arise, thou stillest them." Thus side by side in this narrative we find the manifestation of each of the two natures that are united in his wondrous personality. And it is somewhat remarkable that this is characteristic of the gospel histories as a whole. Wherever in them you have a remarkable evidence of his divinity, you will find not far off as striking a confirmation of his humanity, and *vice versa*. Thus you enter the stable of Bethlehem ; you see a babe slumbering on its mother's lap; you mark her eye beaming with maternal pride, and you say, "this is the child of Mary." Anon, a company of shepherds enter, and they tell that while they were watching over their flocks by night, the glory of the Lord shone round about them, and an angel came to them to tell them of this infant's birth, and scarcely have they finished their description of the anthem sung by a company of the heavenly host, when Magi from the

far East appear, alleging that they had been guided
thither by a star, and worship the child with offer-
ings of gold and frankincense and myrrh, so that in
amazement you ask, what manner of child is this to whose
manger-cradle men thus supernaturally guided have been
led ? You stand on Jordan's bank and mingle with the
thousands who have come to hear the words and submit
to the baptism of John. You behold one go down to the
water to be baptized, but you think little of it, for he
differs apparently in nothing from those by whom he is
surrounded, but lo ! as he comes up from the water, the
heavens are opened unto him, and the Spirit of God de-
scends like a dove and lights upon him, while from the
excellent glory comes a voice, " This is my beloved Son
in whom I am pleased." And again you say in subdued
and solemn awe, what manner of man is this to whom this
divine endorsement has been given ? You accompany him
to the grave of Lazarus ; you see the tears trickle down
his cheeks, and you know he is a man, for neither Deity
nor angel weeps ; but soon you behold Lazarus come
forth from his sepulchre in answer to his word of power,
and once more you ask in wonder, now verging on adoration, " What manner of man is this ? " You follow him
to the cross ; you see his back lacerated with the scourge,
and his brow bleeding from the pressure of the crown of
thorns ; you hear the words, " It is finished " and see
the pale cast of death settle on his countenance, and from
his very death it is manifest that he was a man. But on
the third day after, you meet him in the upper room at
evening, with his followers, risen from the grave, and
like them you fall at his feet and worship him.

Now what shall we make of this wondrous " dualism,"
as I may call it, in the sacred narratives? The question
is akin to that proposed by Christ himself unto his adver-

saries concerning the Messiah, "If David in Spirit call him Lord, how is he his Son ? " We must either reject both presentations or accept both. But we cannot reject both without doing violence to all the laws of evidence whereby the genuineness and authenticity of these gospels are established. We must therefore accept both, and we find the harmonizing element in the great mystery of the incarnation. " The Word," who was God, " became flesh and dwelt among us." How he did so is and ever will be inscrutable to our finite minds. But when we accept that incarnation, it makes all other mysteries of redemption plain. It lightens the law, and illuminates the prophets of the Old Testament. It takes away all difficulty from the question of the miracles of the New Testament, for what is supernatural to us is perfectly natural to God. It shows us how the death of such an one can make atonement for the sins of men. And it is the only sufficient explanation of the fact, that wherever it has been proclaimed and believed, the story of the cross and resurrection of Jesus has revolutionized individual character, domestic life, social morality, and national institutions. So with all these facts before us, we rest in the doctrine which wise men have distilled from the inductive examination of this book, namely, that the Lord Jesus Christ, " being the eternal Son of God, became man, and so was, and continueth to be, God and man in two distinct natures, and one person forever."

But we may learn, as a subordinate lesson from this narrative, that the disciples of Christ are not exempt from trial. They have afflictions, like other men, and besides these they have some that come upon them just because they are followers of Jesus. Of the first sort are sickness, poverty, bereavement, death. These are just as likely, and some of them just as surely, to come on the Christian as on other men, and they may come with all the suddenness of this squall upon the lake, so that almost before he is aware, he may be all but swamped. Of the the other sort are temptations to be unfaithful to the Lord, persecutions for adherence to the Lord, the assaults of evil men, and the like. Now regarding both of these classes of trials, we may say that they do not necessarily imply that the Saviour is not with us. He was here with the disciples in the boat, and he may be just as really with us. We need not, therefore, add to the severity of our trial by upbraiding ourselves with grieving away from us the Saviour to whom we owe our all. We may have done that, but our affliction is not an infallible proof that we have. It is just as possible that the Lord is with us, waiting his own time to interpose for our relief, as he was in the case before us, for although his humanity was asleep, his divinity, as Calvin reminds us, was awake, and we may be sure that he would never have let them go to the bottom.

Now if it be asked why, though he be really with us, he should thus wait before rising to our help in time of storm, we may not be able fully to answer, but we can see plainly two reasons suggested by this narrative ; the first is, that he delays in order that we may apply to him in prayer for deliverance. On the day of his resurrection, when he reached Emmaus, in the company of the two disciples, we are told that "he made as though he would have gone further," apparently just that they might be brought to "constrain him to abide with them." So here he tarried till they came and said to him, "Master, Master, we perish." Then, as another reason for his delay, we find the fact, that this was a part of his training of his disciples for their future life-work. Knowing that

when he had left the earth, and was no more visibly present with them, they would be attacked by manifold storms,
he desired to prepare them for meeting these, by leaving
them to themselves for a time here, and suggesting to
them, that, seen or unseen, he was always in the boat along
with them.   Thereby also he gave them the assurance
that he would bring them at last into the calm and quiet
haven of heaven.   Those who are to do great things for
Christ, are prepared for the doing of them by special and
peculiar training.   Thus they learn that Jesus is not far
from them, though the storm is beating upon them, but
is indeed " a present help," and that he is especially near
to all that call upon him in truth.

Finally, let me remind you, as suggested by this narrative, that Christ never found fault with his disciples for
trusting him, but always for their lack of faith in him,
and their consequent fear.   He loves to be trusted.   You
cannot trust his word too much.   There is indeed such a
thing as presumption, that is, the going beyond what his
word and promises warrant.   But we cannot put too
much confidence in his word and promises.   Our fears
all spring from lack of faith.   Trust him, therefore, for
in him is everlasting strength, and he is faithful who
hath promised.

And O! sinner, when you are in the agony of conviction, with your sins staring you in the face, and calling
for divine and eternal punishment on you, here is a
prayer for you, short, comprehensive, easily remembered
and easily offered: " Lord, save me; I perish."   Cry to
him, trust in him, and he will give you forgiveness.   He
will renew your hearts.   He will say to your storm-
heaved spirits, " Peace, be still," and immediately there
will be a calm, so that you will be constrained to say,
" What a word is this, for with authority he commands

even the heavings of my troubled heart, and they obey
him."

  " O Jesus, once rocked on the breast of the billow,
  Aroused by the shriek of despair from the pillow;
  Now seated in glory, the poor sinner cherish
  Who cries in his anguish, Save, Lord, or we perish.

  " And O, when the whirlwind of passion is raging,
  When sin in our hearts his wild warfare is waging,
  Then send down thy grace thy redeemed to cherish,
  Rebuke the destroyer. Save, Lord, or we perish."

XV.

THE HEALING OF THE GADARENE DEMONIAC.

Matt. viii. 28-34. Mark v. 1-20. Luke viii. 26-39.

AFTER commanding the storm into a calm, as set forth
in our last discourse, our Lord landed with his disciples
on the eastern shore of the Sea of Galilee, in a locality
which is called by Mark and Luke " the country of the
Gadarenes," and by Matthew that of the Gergesenes, or,
as the Revisers have it, Gerasenes. Gadara was a city
of some importance, about six miles southeast of the
Lake of Tiberias, and gave its name to the district in
which it was situated ; but that could not be the place
of the miracle which we are now to consider, because it
is too far from the lake for the herd of swine to run into it
precipitately in one short spurt. The country of the
Gerasenes has been described by Plumtre as the district
around Gerasa, which was a city of Gilead, twenty miles
east of the Jordan, spoken of sometimes as belonging to
Coele-Syria, and sometimes as belonging to Arabia. But
that was even farther from the lake than Gadara. So,
as in all similar cases, men who are eager to find discrepancies in the gospel narratives have made much of
this apparent contradiction. But Dr. Wm. M. Thomson
has cleared up the difficulty; . Here are his words : " On
the south bank " (of the Wady-es-Semak) " and near the

shore of the lake, is the site of a ruined town, in which I
was greatly interested, when first I discovered it, after a
long ride from Banias over the mountainous region east
of the lake. By a steep descent from the lofty plateau
of the Jaulân I came down to the shore at that place, and
my Bedawin guide told me that the name of that prostrate
town was Gersa. . . . It was a small place. . . .
but the walls can be traced all round, and the suburbs
seem to have been considerable. I identify these ruins
with the site of Gergesa, where our Lord healed two
men possessed with devils, and suffered those malignant
spirits to enter into the herd of swine. . . . The
city was close to the shore and there we should find it.
In Gersa we have a position which fulfils the requirements of the narrative, and with a name so near that in
Matthew as to be in itself a strong corroboration of the
identification. The site is within a few rods of the
shore, and a mountain rises directly above it, in which
are ancient tombs, out of some one of which the man
possessed of the devils may have issued to meet Jesus.
The lake is so near the base of the mountain that a herd
of swine feeding above it, seized with a sudden panic,
would rush madly down the declivity, those behind
tumbling over and thrusting forward those before, and
as there is not space to recover on the narrow plain between the base of the mountain and the lake, they would
crowd headlong into the water and perish." * He tells
us, also, that there is no other place on the eastern shore
that would satisfy the conditions of the narrative in these
respects; while, again, Capernaum is in full view, a
little to the north on the opposite shore, and Galilee is
immediately in front, or " over against it," as Luke says
it was. He accounts for the use of the phrase " country

* "Central Palestine and Phœnicia," by Wm. M. Thomson, 353–355.

of the Gadarenes," by Mark and Luke, by saying that
they were strangers to this locality, and probably intended to point out to their distant Greek and Roman
readers the vicinity of the place where the miracle
was wrought ; while Matthew, who, as an inhabitant of
Capernaum, must have known the locality well, gives its
specific name.

Another difficulty in the narrative arises from the fact
that Matthew speaks of the presence of two demoniacs,
whereas Mark and Luke mention only one, just as
Matthew speaks of two blind men at Jericho, while the
other two refer only to Bartimæus. But this is hardly a
contradiction, and the explanation may perhaps be, that
only one of the two came into prominence, and that
therefore the other is not mentioned.

Directly on landing from the boat, the Lord was met
by a man with an unclean spirit, who came to him out of
one of the tombs in the side of the hill ; and as this is,
perhaps, the most remarkable instance of demonaical possession referred to in Scripture, it may be well, once for
all, to devote some little time to the consideration of that
malady. It is not to be concealed that the subject is be-
set with difficultis, and that various opinions have been
expressed regarding it. Some have maintained that the
cases of possession recorded in the gospels are simply and
only symbolical, and are to be understood as representing
the prevalence of evil in the world ; and that the casting
out of the demons by Christ merely means his victory over
that evil by his doctrine and life. But this explanation
gives up entirely the historical character of the narratives,
and cannot, therefore, be entertained by us for a moment.

Others have alleged that the phrase " possessed with
a demon," was only an intensified way of describing
ordinary diseases. They remind us that among the

Jews'physical evil was traced to Satan, that Paul's mysterious malady was called by himself a messenger of Satan,
and the like; and so they conclude that demoniacal
possession is only a synonym for insanity, or epilepsy, or
other form of disease. Now we do not deny that in
most of the cases of possession mentioned in the gospels
there was also physical disease, but such disease was
either the consequence of the possession, or the precursor
of it, and therefore aggravated by it. Moreover, there
are some considerations which seem to me to be fatal to
the view that they were identical. Thus we find that
possession with demons is always carefully distinguished
from other and ordinary forms of disease. In proof of
this I refer you to the very first mention of these cases
in the New Testament (Matthew iv. 23, 24), where we
read that Jesus healed "all manner of diseases among the
people. . . . and they brought unto him all sick
people that were taken with divers diseases and tor-
ments, and those which were possessed with demons, and
those which were lunatic, and those that had the palsy."
It is clear, therefore, that possession with demons was
recognized as something different from ordinary disease.

Again we find the same form of physical disease
spoken of in one instance as ordinary, and in another
as due to the presence of an evil spirit in the man.
Thus (in Matt. ix. 32, 33), we read "as they went out,
behold they brought to him a dumb man possessed with
a demon. And when the demon was cast out, the dumb
spake"; and again (in Matt. xii. 22) : " Then was brought
unto him one possessed with a demon, blind and dumb,
and he healed him, in so much that the blind and dumb
both spake and saw." On the other hand, we find (Mark
vii. 32) that when they brought unto him one that was
deaf and had an impediment in his speech, there is no

mention made of demoniac agency in that case, and when we meet with Bartimæus at the gate of Jericho, his blindness is not traced to the influence of any evil spirit upon him. Thus while some deaf and dumb ones are said to be possessed with demons, it was not so with all, and therefore, though the physical privations were the same in both, there must have been something in the former that was not in the latter.

Once more the Saviour dealt with those who were possessed in a different manner from that which he adopted with those who were not. In the one class of cases, he almost invariably directly addressed the demon; in the other, he contented himself, either with announcing that the man was cured, or with addressing the man himself, or with making some application to the organ affected. Thus the deity and truthfulness of the Lord are involved in the settlement of this question, for if, as some have asserted, he spoke to the demons, not because he believed they were there, but entirely out of regard to the opinion of his times, and indeed knowing well that there were no evil spirits in the case, it is impossible for us any longer to retain our confidence in him as a veracious man, much less as the Son of God. As Alford has said here : " Either our Lord spoke these words, or he did not. If he did not, then we must at once set aside the concurrent testimony of the Evangelists to a plain matter of fact ; in other words establish a principle which will overthrow equally every fact related in the gospels. If he did, it is wholly at variance with any Christian idea of the perfection of truthfulness in him, who was truth itself, to have used such plain and solemn words repeatedly, before his disciples and the Jews, in encouragement of and connivance at a lying superstition." I find it therefore impossible for me to give a fair and honest interpretation of the gospels without recognizing that they imply the reality of demoniacal possession. The Evangelists, to use again the words of Alford, " are distinctly pledged to the truth of such occurrences," and their narratives, taken in their most natural and obvious sense, are decisive in the matter.

But what precisely was this possession? It was not the same as, for example, that of Judas when we read that " Satan entered into him." That implied that the traitor had given himself up to Satan to do his will, that in fact he had become morally an abandoned man. But though the demons are the subordinates of Satan, possession with them had a different effect. Moral depravity, indeed, might precede this possession, but the possession itself was in its nature more an evidence of mischievous maliciousness on the part of the demons, than of immorality on the part of their victim. The man into whom Satan has entered as he did into Judas, is wicked and deserving of punishment; but the demoniac was rather an object of compassion. Some indeed have supposed that wickedness, especially in the form of sensuality, prepared the way for the entrance of a demon into a man; but I question much if that can in all cases be substantiated. At any rate, the peculiarity of this terrible infliction was that there was a double personality in the man. Another was ruling in his soul, and yet he himself was conscious of the usurpation and oppression. He was driven hither and thither by the might and malignity of the demon, but he felt and knew himself to be so driven; therefore, he was utterly miserable, abhorring himself, and inflicting all manner of evil upon himself. At one time the Ego in him was personated by the demon, which, overmastering all the powers of the soul, and the organs of the body, led him captive at his will; at another the

" Ego," was his own proper self, conscious of his degra‑
dation and helplessness, and longing for deliverance.

Now if it be asked, why there should have been so
many cases of this possession while the Lord Jesus was
upon the earth; and why they have disappeared now, I
would answer to the first of these enquiries, that the pres‑
ence of the Son of God in the world, moved his spiritual
adversaries to put forth all their energy, if by any means
they might overcome him.   The period of the first ad‑
vent was in an especial sense " the hour and the power
of darkness," and all hell was stirred to meet the second
Adam, if haply he might be vanquished as the first had
been.   Then, in reply to the second enquiry, it may be
said that it is not quite so certain that there are no in‑
stances of demoniacal possession in our own times.   We
know too little of the influence of spirits, whether good or
evil, on human beings to be able to say assuredly, that
there are or that there are not, such cases now.   But
some medical men of note, have indicated their belief
that there are still demoniacs, and if there are, the infre‑
quency of the occurrence of such cases now as compared
with the days of Christ on the earth may be accounted
for by the fact that when the Lord rose from the dead,
he vanquished Satan and his subordinates.   The head
of the serpent was thereby crushed, and therefore he can‑
not now put forth such strength as he manifested while
the Saviour was on earth, and before he had finished the
work that was given him to do.   For the rest, we must
be content to remain in ignorance, believing that " there
are more things in heaven and earth," and hell, " than
have been dreamed of in philosophy."

It was, then, a demoniac of the most miserable kind,
who, accompanied by another victim of the same posses‑
sion but of a milder type, came to meet Jesus when he

landed at this time, on the eastern shore of the Lake
of Galilee. He was so violent that he had been bound
with chains and put into fetters; but even these could
not restrain him, for " the chains had been plucked
asunder by him, and the fetters broken in pieces; and
always, night and day, he was in the mountains and in
the tombs crying and cutting himself with stones."

And now we come upon a manifestation of that double
personality of which I have spoken. Seeing Jesus and
reading in his face the expression of love and tenderness
which dwelt within him, the man ran to fall at his feet in
worship and ask relief. The Saviour, understanding the
case at a glance, said, " Come out of the man, thou unclean spirit," and then the demon in the man, overpower-
ing him, and holding down his personality, while at the
same time he took possession of all his powers, and spoke
through him, exclaimed to Jesus : " What have I to do
with thee, Jesus, thou Son of God most high ? I adjure
thee by God, that thou torment me not ; " or, as we have
it in Matthew, " Art thou come hither to torment us before the time ? " Here, let me remark, in passing, is another evidence of the reality of the possession, in the fact
that the demon knew Jesus to be the Son of God. And
this is not a solitary instance. We have repeated cases
of the same kind spoken of in the gospels : and this recognition of the divine dignity of Christ cannot be explained as resulting from ordinary disease. It was the
effect of the demon's consciousness of the presence of
perfect holiness in Jesus, and cannot be accounted for
on any principles of human philosophy. But, be that as
it may, by his words here the evil spirit begged to be,
for a season at least, exempt from torment, and we note
here his distinct recognition of the fact, that there is an
appointed time for which the demons are reserved, when

they shall be consigned to their full and final doom. In
the present case they feared, for as we learn there were
more than one demon in the victim, that their expulsion
from the man involved their being sent at once to the dark
abyss (as Luke in the parallel passage has it) in which
they were to be subjected to their endless punishment;
and perhaps the strong word " I adjure thee by God "
may imply that they considered it inconsistent with what
they knew of God's will concerning them that they
should be so soon consigned to torment. But the Lord
took no apparent notice of their appeal. He only said,
addressing the man once more, if haply he might lead
him back to the possession of himself, " What is thy
name ? " But the demon, still retaining his power over
the poor victim, made reply, " My name is Legion, for
we are many." It was thus a case like that of Mary
Magdalene, out of whom were cast seven devils. There
were in this poor man a number of demons, but all under
the power of one will, animated by one purpose, and
united in one mode of operation, just as in the Roman
army a legion moves with compact phalanx to carry out
the orders of its commander, and the victim of their
malice was like a land possessed by a hostile army,
which desolates its fields and lays waste its cities.

But though they had hitherto carried all before them in
the soul of this afflicted man, they felt themselves now to
be in the presence of One who was mightier than themselves, and seeing that they could not hold out against him,
thinking too, perhaps, that they would bring Jesus into
disrepute among the people, they begged that they might
be permitted to enter into a herd of swine that was feeding
near by and he suffered them," and the unclean spirits went
out and entered into the swine : and the herd ran violently
down a steep place into the sea, (they were about two thous-
and); and they were choked in the sea."

Few incidents in the gospel history have been assailed with so much ridicule as this. It has been alleged that the very idea of demons entering into swine is in itself absurd, but to me, there is nothing more mysterious in that than there is in their entering into a human being. In the lower animals there are certain principles or propensities which are closely allied to some which we find in ourselves. Now, for aught we know, it may have been in connection with these, that the demons took possession of men, and if that were so, they might enter through the same principles and propensities into animals. So if we accept the reality of human possession by evil spirits, we need not make a difficulty of their entering into the lower animals, and in choosing to take possession of the swine we may surely say, that they showed their own affinity with the grovelling debasement which is characteristic of the hog. Moreover, we may say farther, that men who give themselves up to the gratification of the lowest sensual principles of their nature, are opening themselves up for the entrance of an evil spirit into them. It is besides worthy of notice that we read in the Scriptures of the powers of darkness entering into only two species of the lower animals: the one was the serpent, and the other the swine; the one the symbol of intellectual cunning, the other of gross uncleanness, and perhaps we shall not go far astray, if we infer that we should be specially on our guard against sinning in either of these directions, lest we should give ourselves over to the full dominion of the evil one.

Another objection is brought here, to the effect that the Lord Jesus was accessory to the destruction of property. In reply to that some have said that as it was unlawful for the Jews to keep swine, the loss of this herd was a deserved punishment on its owner for violating the ordinance of God. But as the district in which the miracle was wrought was about as much Gentile as Jewish, and as the swine might belong to one who was a Gentile, this answer cannot be regarded as perfectly satisfactory. I prefer, therefore, to take another view of the matter, suggested by the Saviour's own query on another occasion, " How much is a man better than a sheep ? " The healing of a man was in the case, and the destruction of the swine seems to have been necessary for the securing of that. How it was thus necessary, we cannot tell, but we may say, with Trench, " if this granting of the evil spirits, request helped in any way the cure of the man, caused them to relax their hold on him more easily, mitigated the paroxysm of their going forth, this would have been motive enough. Or, still more probably, it may have been necessary for the permanent healing of the man, that he should have an outward evidence and testimony that the hellish powers which held him in bondage, had quitted their hold." * These conjectures seem most reasonable, yet, whether we adopt them or not, it was clearly a question as between the deliverance and salvation of the man, and the possession of the swine by the devils, and between these the Saviour could not hesitate. Then, as to the matter of property, the beasts of the field, and the cattle on a thousand hills are Christ's by right of his deity. The men who called this herd their own were only the hands, by which he held them, and he had a right to do what he chose with his own.

Seeing their charge thus frantically run down the hill in such haste, that they could not stop themselves before they rushed into the lake, those who kept them fled into the neighboring city and told all that had

* " Notes on the Miracles," p. 173.

occurred, and in consequence of their report the inhabitants came out in a body to see for themselves
what had been done. When they arrived at the
spot they were amazed at beholding the man who
had been such a terror to the community, " sitting
at the feet of Jesus, clothed and in his right mind."
Observe that word " clothed " in the account given by
Mark. He had not before said that the man was naked.
It is Luke alone who tells us that " he wore no clothes,"
but this term used by Mark implies all that Luke ex-
presses, and so we have here a minute and incidental coincidence between the two narratives which is not without its weight, as a testimony both to the independence
and to the agreement of the two writers.

It might have been supposed that the sight of the
transformation which had been effected on the poor demoniac would have delighted them all. But no, they
could not get over the loss of their swine, and fearing lest
more of their property might be destroyed, they began
to pray Jesus to " depart out of their coasts." When
Peter said, " Depart from me, for I am a sinful man, O
Lord," he did not really and in his inmost heart desire
what he asked, and so Jesus said unto him, " Follow Me."
But these people were in earnest when they besought
Christ to depart. They were wedded to their worldly
possessions and because they supposed these were in
danger, they begged the Saviour to be gone.

And he took them at their word, for going back to the
lakeside he prepared to enter the boat and return to the
western shore. But just as he entered the skiff, there was
a touching scene which must have deeply affected all who
witnessed it. The man out of whom the demons had been
cast came and clung to his deliverer and begged to be
taken with him. Was it that he feared lest his tormentors

might return unless he kept continually beside the Lord?
or did he merely wish to show his gratitude? or was he
longing for instruction? We cannot tell. But the contrast between him and the men of the district was remarkable, and is most suggestive, as showing that while
some for grossly material reasons desire the Saviour to
go from them, those who have been really blessed by him,
do not wish to be separated from him. It was very natural that this man should desire to be always with Christ,
yet the Lord " suffered him not " to accompany him, but
said, " Go home to thy friends, and tell them how great
things the Lord hath done for thee, and hath had compassion on thee." The Saviour was better to the people
than they knew. They asked him to depart, but he left
a representative behind him who would act the part of a
missionary among them, and the result was that as he
went through the region of Decapolis, or the ten cities,
" all men did marvel."

I have dwelt so long on the exposition of this narrative
that I have left myself but little time for the treatment
of the valuable lessons that may be deduced from it,
nevertheless, even at the risk of trespassing on your patience, I must turn your attention very briefly to one or
two of the more important.

And, first of all, we see here very clearly that " the
Son of God was manifested to destroy the works of the
devil." For this demoniacal possession was only one
form of the dominion of Satan over the souls of men, and
the casting out of the demons was only one of the many
ways in which the primal prophecy, " it shall bruise thy
head," was fulfilled by " the seed of the woman." Jesus
came to cast out the prince of this world, and even if it
should be true that now the phenomona of possession as

here described have disappeared (which is doubtful), yet
in other ways and with equal efficacy the Prince of Life
is even now working to cast Satan out of his strongholds.
There is such a thing yet as men being the spiritual
captives of the devil, and yielding themselves up to be
his slaves, and deep as was the degradation of this
demoniac, his was not so deep as that of those who
wallow in the mire of their sensuality and debauch.
Talk of men as sinking themselves to the level of the
brutes ! There are those who are beneath the lower
animals, for the brutes have instinct to guide them, but
when men give up the restraints of reason and religion,
there is no instinct to keep them right, and so they sink
into uttermost debasement, and become helpless in their
devotion to their own appetites and lusts. How many
such there are in this very city ! Go through the streets
and lanes, and see how in their reeling helplessness they
inflict injuries upon themselves, as serious often as those
here described in the phrase "cutting himself with
stones." Enter into the rooms of the tenement houses,
in which they have what they call their homes, get to
know their mode of life, become acquainted with their
habits, and you will be compelled to admit that their
condition is not better than that of this Gadarene. But,
blessed be God, Christ is stronger than Satan, and even
among such as those whom I have described he has
trophies of his might, in whom it has been shown that
the gospel is still the power of God unto salvation to
every one that believeth. Have we not heard and
known, thanks under God to the Christian Home for In-
temperate Men, and other agencies, of some dreadful drunkard, formerly the terror of the street, and the
plague of the neighborhood, saved, by the power of
Christ, from his dreadful appetite, and now a member of

the Church, " sitting at the feet of Jesus, clothed and in his right mind ? " What then ? Seeing the degradation of the lowest of the people through their sin, knowing, also, the power and willingness of Christ to raise them from the fearful pit and from the miry clay of their iniquity, shall we not do our utmost that they may be led to know him and to trust in him ? Brethren, a solemn responsibility rests on us in this matter. Let us see to it that we realize it, and do what in us lies to send the light, and healing, and life of the gospel to those who at our very doors are perishing for lack of it. To do that is to become partakers with the Lord Jesus in his heavenly work, and to secure even for ourselves a brighter inheritance in the celestial home. Let us, therefore, by the preaching of the gospel and the might of the Holy Spirit, carry on this great work of exorcising Satan from the city and from the land, for " they that turn many to righteousness shall shine as the stars for ever and ever."

But, in the second place, we may learn to let Jesus choose for us the sphere in which we can serve him best. Very naturally this man wished to go with his deliverer, but he was not permitted. The Lord required a witness in the region from which the people besought him to depart, and so he was left to tell all things that God had done for him. It used to be a common idea that the Saviour can be best served in the office of the ministry, or on the mission field, or by entering upon some office in his church, and I do not mean to deny that he may be served in these positions very efficiently, but these are not the only spheres in which we may give earnest and effective testimony to him, and this thought is full of comfort to multitudes. Perhaps there are some here, whose present places in the world are very different from those which years ago they had thought that they should fill. They fondly hoped that they might by this time be occupying some prominent pulpit in the land, or that they might be working in some far-off country as missionaries of the cross, but in the providenee of God they have been hindered. The death of a father left special responsibilities on them, in the care of a widowed mother and younger children, or something else altogether beyond their control has come in the way, and so they have not attained their desire. "Jesus suffered them not." But let them be comforted, that is simply the way which he has taken to give to them the commission which he gave to this demoniac, and if they only look aright upon their opportunities of service where they are, they will find them in abundance. If our lives are failures, it will not be because we do not reach the sphere which we had set before our ambition, but because we do not perform the duties of that sphere in which God has kept us. He ordaineth our lot, and to serve him faithfully where he has placed us is life's highest success.

Let us learn, in the third place, that in working for Christ, we should begin at home with those nearest and dearest to us. The Lord said to this man, "Go home to thy friends and tell them what God hath done for thee." And if we study the New Testament attentively, we shall find many beautiful instances in illustration of the wisdom of following this course. Thus Andrew's first work was done with his own brother, Simon. Philip brought his friend Nathanael to Christ, and Barnabas was not content until he had preached the gospel in his native Cyprus. Our sphere is where we are, and when we have filled that, we shall get a larger one. The horizon will widen as we climb the hill; and beginning with our friends in the country of the Gerasenes, we may end as this man did, in filling ten cities with the story of the goodness of the grace of Christ. Let then the husband begin with the wife, and the wife with the husband; the brother with his brother, and the sister with her sister; the friend with his friend, and the neighbor with his neighbor, and then when we have used the little strength we have, and kept Christ's faith and not denied his name among those who are immediately beside us, the Lord will " set before us an open door " into a larger field and ampler opportunities, and no man shall be able to shut it.

Finally, let us beware of sending Christ away from us by our love for our earthly possessions. These Gadarenes were afraid of losing more of their swine, and therefore they besought Christ to leave them. And how many there have been like them in the world! Demetrius and his craftsmen stirred up all Ephesus against Paul because " the hope of their gains was gone." And there are multitudes among ourselves who want nothing to do with Christ, because they feel that if they become Christians, they would have to give up some gainful traffic in which they are engaged. They do not know that wherever Christ comes, he brings the highest gain. He is the pearl of great price, the possession of which fills the heart with joy, even though all else has been given for it. Even temporarily speaking, it is a mistake to imagine that to become a Christian brings pecuniary loss to a man. I could point you to many who never began to prosper until they were converted. Other things being equal, the Christian makes the most of this life. Godliness has the promise of the life that now is, as well as of that which is to come. It would be a poor motive, indeed—an altogether wrong motive—for one to act on if he should come to Christ in order to secure worldly property. But it is not true that adher-

ence to Christ must necessarily cause the loss of money
or of earthly comfort. Sometimes it may. But not
always—nor indeed usually now. A husband and wife
were sitting together one Lord's day morning in their
home, before starting for the house of God. There was
to be a collection in the church that day, and they were
speaking of the amount which they should give. The
wife, who, Martha-like, was careful and troubled about
many things, was concerned that her husband should
think of giving so much as the sum that he had mentioned, and in a querulous tone she said : " It seems to
me that we have lost a great deal by our religion."
" Yes," he replied, " we have lost a great deal. Before
I was converted, we had only one bare room without a
decent chair, and with the bed on the floor, and we have
lost that, for now we have a comfortable and well-fur-
nished home. I had a dreadful evil habit in my slavery,
to which I became more like a beast than a man, and I
used to come and beat you, and now we have lost that,
so that we live in peace and love. I had a suit of rags
which hardly sufficed to cover me, and you were so
thinly clothed that you went shivering in the cold, and
we have lost all that, for now we are as well dressed as
the best. I was in debt all round, and was ashamed to
look men in the face, and we have lost all that, for now
we have money in the savings bank." And he would
have gone on further, had not his wife burst into tears
and cried, " Stop! stop! May God forgive me. I was
so ungrateful to speak as I did." Brethren, the Christian's losses for Christ are in the end all gains, and it is
the greatest madness to allow our love of property,
whether it be in the shape of thousands of dollars, or, as
here, in that of thousands of animals, to keep us from receiving him. May God preserve us from all such folly!

XVI.

THE RAISING OF JAIRUS' DAUGHTER.

Matt. ix. 18-19; 23-26. Mark v. 22-24; 35-43. Luke viii. 41-42; 49-56.

AFTER our Lord had returned to the western shore of the Lake of Tiberius, it would appear, according to Matthew, who seems in this instance to be following the exact order of events, that he went to Capernaum, where he cured the paralytic, called Matthew himself to follow him, and attended the banquet given by the Evangelist to his friends. At the close of that feast, though not necessarily while they were still in the house and at the table, he had that memorable conversation with the disciples of John on the relation of fasting to the new economy, in which he showed that it would be as incongruous for his followers to fast while he was yet with them, as it would be to patch an old garment with a piece of unfulled cloth, or to put new wine into old wine-skins. And it was while he was thus engaged that a " certain ruler " came, and falling at his feet, reverently and earnestly besought him, saying, " My daughter is even now dead, but come and lay thy hand upon her, and she shall live." Mark and Luke give the name of this ruler as Jairus, the Greek form of the Hebrew Jair, and tell us that he was " a ruler of the synagogue." Every synagogue was managed by a board of presbyters or elders, and it may be that Jairus was the president of that consistory or session. At any rate, he was a member of it, and that is a proof of the estimation. in which he was held by the community to which he belonged. He was at this time in great distress, owing to the mortal illness of his only daughter, who seems also from the peculiarity of the expression used by Luke,* to have been his only child. Matthew says that he affirmed that his daughter was just then dead, while Mark and Luke make it evident that at first his statement was, that she was " at the point of death," or lay a dying, and that a messenger came later to inform him that she was dead. But the narrative of Matthew is so condensed, that he gives in one clause, the sum of the information which was conveyed regarding her, at two different times, and emphasizes the fact from the beginning that the miracle was one of raising the dead, and not merely of healing the sick.

When the Lord heard the entreaty of the broken-hearted father, he at once set out, with the tenderness and compassion that were ever characteristic of him, to give the blessing that was sought.

But he was detained on the way, by the great pressure of the crowd that thronged around him, and by the modest yet effectual application to him of the poor diseased woman, which we shall consider, by itself, in our next discourse. During this delay a messenger came from the ruler's house and said to Jairus, " Thy daughter is dead. Why troublest thou the Teacher any further ? " But Jesus, overhearing his words, turned immediately to the afflicted father, and said unto him, " Fear not, only believe." Then, after he had brought the woman from secret faith to open confession, he took with him Peter and

---

* He uses the word μονογενής, only begotten.

James and John, and passed on to the house of Jairus, where he found a motley crowd of neighbors, and hired mourners, making a perfect tumult of noise, according to the custom prevalent among Jews on such occasions.

Matthew tells us that "minstrels" or "flute players" were there making a noise; and Dr. Wm. M. Thomson, in "The Land and the Book," informs us that the hiring of mourners is still customary in Palestine and that there are in every city and community women exceedingly cunning in this business. These are always sent for and kept in readiness, and when a fresh company of sympathizers comes in, they "make haste" to take up a wailing that the newly come may more easily unite their tears with the mourners." *

When the Lord saw the confusion and heard the noise, he said, "Why make ye this ado and weep? The damsel is not dead, but sleepeth." Just as at a later day he said to his followers concerning Lazarus, "our friend sleepeth," so now he said, "the damsel sleepeth," not because she was not really dead, but because in this case, as in that, he was going to raise her at once from the dead. Her lying under the power of death would be of such brief duration that it might well be called asleep. But not understanding the sense in which he used the words, they laughed him to scorn, and so, not wishing to cast his pearls before scorners, he turned them all out. Then taking with him only the father and the mother of the maiden, and the three favored disciples, he went into the chamber where the damsel was lying, and taking her by the hand, "he said unto her, Talitha cumi—Maid, arise, —and straightway she arose and walked, for she was of the age of twelve years." They were all amazed, and he charged them, vainly as it would seem, that no man should

* "The Land and the Book," English edition, p. 103.

know it, and commanded that something should be given
her to eat—not to prove the reality of the miracle, for the
Saviour was not always thinking, as some commentators
would have it, of the establishment of the genuineness of
his mighty works, but simply because after her illness
she needed nourishment, and because in the ecstasy of
their hearts at receiving her back to life, this very commonplace matter might be forgotten even by her parents.

Now before proceeding to bring out the spiritual lessons of this narrative, permit me to draw your attention
to two things that are somewhat interesting in connection with it. The first is the thorough independence of
the testimony borne by the three Evangelists to the main
facts of the story. All agree in connecting this miracle
with that of the healing of the woman with the issue of
blood, but there are shades of difference between their
accounts, which indicate that no one of them was bor-
rowed from another, and make it absolutely certain that
the gospels of Matthew and Mark could not have been
constructed, the one from the other, " by an obscure and
popular elaboration," as Renan affirms. Thus, as we have
seen, Matthew, giving at once the sum total of the information that was communicated at two separate times,
makes Jairus say, " My little daughter is even now dead."
While Mark and Luke agree in affirming that this was
told, if I may so express it, in two different instalments.
So again Luke alone tells us that the dying girl was the
only child of Jairus, and Mark and he agree in informing
us that she was twelve years old, while Matthew is silent
regarding both particulars. Still farther, Mark alone
gives the words in the Aramaic language which Jesus
spoke to the damsel when he took her by the hand and
recalled her to life : " Talitha cumi." This is a peculiarity of the second Evangelist, as may be seen by com-

paring the passage before us with chapter vii. 34, chap. xiv. 36, chap. xv. 34, and it is supposed by some that we may trace in it the influence of Peter, who, as an ear-witness, would remember well the very words employed by Christ on such an occasion. Then again it is Luke who tells us that " her spirit, or her breath," came unto her again; words that are quite appropriate as coming from a medical man. Thus, while agreeing in the main facts, there are minute peculiarities in each of the narratives which serve to show the individuality of the writers, and the independence of their testimony; and in days when so many attempts are made to destroy the credibility of the Evangelists, it is well to note these incidental evidences of the absence of all collusion between them.

The second thing worthy of notice in the narrative of this miracle is the place which this class of wonderful works holds in relation to the others which Jesus did. There is a clear difference between the raising of the dead and every other kind of miracle wrought by our Lord. No doubt each miracle required divine power for its performance, but the evidence of the presence and operation of that power is stronger in the case of the raising of the dead than in all others. For in the others the line of demarcation between the natural and the supernatural is not so clearly and sharply defined, but in this it is distinctly marked; and however a man may stand in doubt at other times, if he admits the fact that the dead were raised, he cannot stop short of the acknowledgment that they were so raised by the agency of God. As Trench has well observed, " the line between health and sickness is not definitely fixed, in like manner storms alternate with calms; and there are other processes of nature closely analogous to some of the wondrous works which Jesus did, but here there is a contrast and no resemblance. Nature never could, never did, raise the dead, and hence it is that miracles of this sort in the New Testament are those which on the one hand do bring most conviction to the candid inquirer, and which, on the other, are most assailed by the sophistry of the sceptic." *

Now, as if to silence all objections that might be brought against them, our Lord repeated this kind of miracle three times, probably more frequently, but we have the record of only three, each time with such circumstantial variation, as to remove doubt from the unbiased mind. In the present instance the little girl was just dead; in the case of the widow's son at Nain, friends were carrying his remains to the tomb; and in that of Lazarus the corpse had been four days in the grave, and corruption had advanced in some degree—all this, that it might be proved to men that " Jesus is the Christ, the Son of God, and that believing they might have life through his name."

The spiritual teaching of this miracle—that is, its significance as a sign—is not far to seek. It lies, indeed, upon the surface. It declares to us that it is Jesus alone who can raise us from the death of sin to the life of righteousness. He quickens those who are " dead in trespasses and sins." And in this view of the matter, two thoughts suggest themselves.

The first is that parents should bring their children to Christ with the prayer that he would quicken them into newness of life. Jairus was very prompt and earnest in applying to Christ for the healing of his daughter. Equally so should every parent be in asking that his children may be renewed, and translated out of the king-

---

* " Notes on the Miracles," p. 187.

dom of darkness into God's marvellous light. They should, as it were, in the language of Paul to the Galatians "travail in birth for them again until Christ be formed " in them.   It is a great thing when a child is born, but it is a greater when it is born again, and to the attainment of that blessed result all the prayers and efforts of a parent in its nurture should be directed.   No doubt the agency of the Holy Spirit is needed for that.   But He works through human instrumentality and the instrumentality which he most delights to employ and bless is the godly example, wise instruction and earnest supplications of parents.

The second thought here suggested is that children should open their ears to Christ.   Do you not hear him now, my dear young people, saying unto you, " Arise"? Rouse yourselves, then, at his bidding, to think of spiritual things.   Give him your hand, that he may lift you up, and lead you on.   Do not grow up in sin ; but before it has woven its web around you, before habits hard to break have been formed by you, begin to serve the Lord.   Listen, he is saying to you again, " Arise."   Oh that you would obey his voice, that he may work in you by his Spirit to will and to do of his good pleasure !   Here is a beautiful poem, written by a dear friend in the old country, recently gone to glory, that may induce you to obey his call.

> " Maiden to my twelfth year come,
>   I had read, in Scripture story,
> Of a damsel cold and dumb,
>   Wakened by the Lord of glory ;
> And it seemed to me he spoke,
>   And his living word thrilled through me,
> Till in me new life awoke,
>   As he said, ' Talitha cumi.'

"I had to my chamber gone,
   Eyes all swollen, and red with weeping,
For my heart felt like a stone,
   And my life a dream in sleeping;
Jesus in my chamber stood,
   Jesus stretched his hands unto me,
Hands all pierced, and dropping blood,
   As he said, 'Talitha cumi.'

" Friends and neighbors gathered in,
   Made no small ado and weeping,
Dead I was, yes, dead in sin,
   Dead, but I was only sleeping ;
For thy will renewed me, Lord,
   Freed from the disease that slew me,
And to pious friends restored,
   Crown'd with thy ' Talitha cumi.'

"Now with lamp I watch and wait
   For my Lord's returning to me ;
Should I slumber when 'tis late,
   Let that word rouse and renew me,
And when long laid in the tomb,
   Long forgot by those who knew me,
Thou wilt not forget to come,
   Come with thy ' Talitha cumi.' " *

These are the main lessons of the miracle as a sign,
but we may not conclude without drawing some practical
inferences from the narrative as a whole.

Let us learn, then, that death has no respect for the
most tender years. This is a truth so very true as to
seem trite, and yet we so frequently forget it, that it is
well to make it sometimes the theme of distinct and definite meditation. If we ask ourselves when is the time
to die, we shall seem prone to muse the answer, which
we have not courage to express, and to say within ourselves, " Not now." Whatever be our age, there will
be some plan unfinished, some project unaccomplished,

* " Life of W. B. Robertson, D.D.," by James Brown, D.D., pp.
174, 175.

some ambition unrealized, and that will dispose us to think it undesirable that we should die now. So ever as the matter comes into our minds we try to put it away from us into the indefinite future. Now if this be the case with those advanced in life, how much more so is it with the young! The world is all before them. Their minds are full of day-dreams as to the future. They cling to the belief that, whoever dies, they are sure to live. It would be unnatural if it were otherwise, and it would not be good for them to be always thinking of death. Indeed few things seem to me to be so " eerie " as to hear from the lips of childhood some strange remark about the grave. Yet if it be an evil, as it surely is, to have all our lives darkened by the thought of death, it is just as bad to have all thought of death banished from our minds. The true safeguard from both of these extremes is to have such faith in Christ, and to live so in his love and service that it will not matter when we die. Let the young before me, therefore, get such faith, for death to those who trust in Jesus and love him, is not a thing to be afraid of, or to weep about, but only a going home to " the Father's house on high." And this is just as important for those of riper years as it is for childhood and youth. None of us knows what a day may bring forth. To be ready for dying will not make our lives shorter, or less happy, or less full of usefulness,—nay, it will make them all the happier, as delivering us absolutely from slavery through the fear of death.

But, secondly, let us learn that we have a sure resource in Jesus, in every sort of trouble. How different were the cases of those who thronged around him for relief on earth? No two of them were precisely like each other. Every one had his own cup of bitterness. The leper, with his scaly loathsomeness; the paralytic in his helplessness; the blind man groping his way with the tip of his staff; the deaf and dumb, looking in mute earnestness the prayer which he could not speak; the poor demoniac in his direful slavery to the invader of his soul; the sick one with the fever galloping in her veins; the timid one touching the hem of his garment for her secret malady; and the widow weeping over her only son lying dead on his bier—all received help and healing from him. No matter at what point in the circumference of human misery they stood, he was at the centre of gracious supply. It was, moreover, easy for them to reach him, and no one appealed to him in vain. And the same is true still, though now he is unseen and on the throne behind the veil. Though now, ascended upon high, he is still " that same Jesus " that he was on earth; and whatever be the cause of our distress, he can and will help all that call upon him. Either he will remove the cause of our trial, or he will sustain us to bear it until it has done its work in us. Let us therefore betake ourselves to him in every emergency, and he will give us relief.

But, lest you should misapprehend his method of dealing with the afflicted, I ask you to notice, in the third place, here, that in coming to our help the Lord may delay until we are in absolute extremity. If he had so chosen, he might have deferred his interview with the woman until after he had gone to the home of Jairus, but in this case, as in that of Lazarus afterward, he deliberately delayed until the circumstances were such as to make all human help impossible. Nor do these two instances stand alone. When Abraham was on Mount Moriah, it was not until the very latest moment that the angel intervened; when Jacob wrestled with the angel, the day was breaking ere the blessing was bestowed; at the marriage feast in Cana, the wine ran dry before the miraculous supply was given; and if you will carefully read through the hundred and seventh psalm, you will see that in all the cases there so graphically described, the sufferers were in extremity before God came to them with help.

Now, by this delay, at least, two purposes were subserved. The Lord thereby tried, and by trying strengthened the faith of the applicants. The prayer of the Syro-Phœnician woman met at first with what seemed a refusal, in order that he might lead her up to such strength of faith as enabled him to say, " O woman, great is thy faith! Be it unto thee even as thou wilt." The cry of Jacob for deliverance from Esau was apparently disregarded, just that he might be led to the discovery of a deeper need, and to offer the prayer, " Tell me, I pray thee, thy name." So it is still, and, therefore, when the answer to our prayer is delayed, let us not imagine that the Lord is disregarding us, but let us wait on him, and be of good courage, for he shall strengthen our hearts. Yes, wait on the Lord. He is worth waiting on, since he never comes empty handed. " Though he tarry, wait for him. He will surely come, he will not tarry."

But another purpose subserved by this delay was that it might be seen that the help, when it did come, was from God himself. The hand of omnipotence, as we have seen, is more clearly recognized in the raising of the dead than in the healing of the sick, and so the more helpless we are, the more distinctly do we see, when we are assisted, that " our help cometh from the Lord, who hath made heaven and earth." Therefore, let us never despair, for " man's extremity is God's opportunity." And while you are waiting thus for God, it will do you good to observe **how kindly** Jesus spake here to Jairus, when his servant came to say to him, "Thy daughter is dead." It was a painful thing for him to hear that announcement. It went like a dagger to his heart, and would have crushed all hope within him. But the Lord, turning to him at that moment said, "Fear not, only believe," and that held him up. It was as if the Saviour had given him his hand to grasp, that he might thereby be steadied and maintained. And so when the Lord delays to answer our cry, he gives us something to support us while we wait. If we must bear the sharp pain of some thorn, either in the flesh or in the spirit, a little longer, he is sure to say to us, "My grace is sufficient for thee ; my strength is made perfect in weakness."

Learn, finally, from this narrative, that Christ will not show his gracious power to scoffers. When he said to those who were making the house of mourning like a Bedlam with their noise, "Why make ye this ado ? The damsel is not dead, but sleepeth," there was a promise, if they had only understood him, of an immediate restoration of the maiden to life. But they laughed him to scorn, and for that they were excluded from the chamber when he wrought the miracle. You remember how the nobleman who leaned upon the hand of the king of Israel sneered at Elisha's prophecy of immediate plenty in Samaria during a time of siege and famine, and how, because he did so, he was trodden to death in the gate, seeing the plenty, but not permitted to partake of it. You remember, also, how to the prejudiced priests and Scribes, the dissolute Herod and the sceptical Pilate, Jesus was silent; while to those who loved and trusted him, he was confidential, as friend is with his friend. That is the principle which he follows in his dealings with men, still. It is written, "The *meek* will he guide in judgment ; the *meek* will he teach his way ; " and again, " the secret of the Lord is with them that fear him, and he will shew them his covenant." But with " the froward he will show himself froward," and the scoffer will be left to the fruit of his own doings. In a certain place we read that Christ did no mighty works because of the people's unbelief; but with believers, the rule of his administration is " according to thy faith, so be it unto thee." Let us beware, therefore, of sitting " in the seat of the scornful," for just as the scoffers were turned out of the house of Jairus, they will be ultimately excluded from the happiness of heaven.

XVII.

THE HEALING OF THE WOMAN WHO TOUCHED THE GARMENT.

Matt. ix. 20-22. Mark v. 25-34. Luke viii. 43-48.

WE have in these narratives an account of what might be called the parenthetic miracle of the gospels. It may be said, indeed, of all the miracles of our Lord, that they were but like alms given by him incidentally to the poor and needy and suffering and sorrowful of mankind, as he journeyed on toward the making of the great gift of himself upon the cross for the sins of the world. In that sense they were all parenthetic; but in a lower and more limited sense this one is especially so, for it was performed by Jesus as he was on his way to the house of Jairus, and the record of it comes in as a long parenthesis between the application of the ruler on behalf of his daughter, and the granting of his request by the Lord.

Among ourselves, the judge on the bench, in clearing the ground for his decision of the main question submitted to him, will sometimes incidentally let fall opinions on other matters not immediately before him. These are often of very great value, and are quoted and referred to as " *Obiter Dicta.*" So this is an *obiter* miracle of Christ; a miracle wrought by him by the way, as he was going forward to the house of Jairus for the special purpose of giving life to his daughter.

We read in Luke that " as he went the multitudes thronged him." The word rendered " thronged " is very strong. It means that they pressed round him so as almost to suffocate him—that the pressure was so great that it was difficult for him even to breathe. The great majority of this moving mass of people were doubtless actuated by mere curiosity. They were convinced that a miracle was about to be performed, and they were eager to see it. But there was one among them with a deep, earnest, hidden purpose in her heart. She was a poor, weak woman, pale, worn and wasted from the draining effect upon her of an inner malady of twelve years' standing, which no physician could cure, though she had " spent all her living " on medical advice. As a last resort, hearing that Jesus was there, she determined to apply to him, but with shrinking modesty she did not wish to reveal the nature of her disease—the rather, perhaps, that it was of a sort that rendered her ceremonially unclean—and so she made her way through the crowd until she came immediately behind him, and, saying within herself, " If I may but touch his garments, I shall be made whole," she put forth her hand and touched the border of his garment. As Dr. James Morison has said, " Her attention was fixed, not on her act of touching, as contradistinguished from some other mode of contact, but on the garments of the Lord as contradistinguished from his person." And the moment she did touch his garment's hem, a strange, electric thrill of new-given life tingled through her frame. She felt that she was cured. She had within her that indescribable sensation which told her that she had been healed of the plague which had so long afflicted her. But the virtue was not in the gar-

ment, or even in the fringe to which so much importance
was attached as a thing required by the law of Moses,
(Numbers xv. 37–40 ; Deut. xxii. 12). It was in Christ
himself. There was, no doubt, something of superstition in the mode of her application, but he who " doth
not break the bruised reed or quench the smoking flax,"
did not reprove her for that. Rather he used it to lead
her up to something higher, for he cured her by an
act of his divine will, and then took means to bring her
to intelligent faith.

What these means were is fully set before us here.
He turned about and asked with apparent abruptness,
"Who touched my clothes ?" A question proposed
by him not in ignorance, but simply with the view
of eliciting publicly, for the benefit not only of the
woman herself, but also of the multitude, the real facts
of the case. It is not to be supposed, therefore, from the
language which he employs, that the influence that
wrought the cure, went from our Lord involuntarily.
On the contrary, he knew perfectly the circumstances of
the woman, and he willed to cure her, but the purpose
of his question was to lead her up to a public confession
of all that he had done for her. Those who cavil at this
mode of procedure should remember how common it is
for men who are themselves well informed as to a particular case to put questions as if with a view to obtain
knowledge regarding it, but really for the purpose of
bringing the whole matter to public notice. Thus, to
take a familiar illustration : in the British House of
Commons there is a certain part of every sitting known
as "question time," during which members, who have
already given notice of their intention, rise in their places
to put questions to the representatives of the government, though they know all about what they ask, and

only desire to bring the truth concerning it to the notice of the nation. Now it was just similar here, but the disciples, who knew nothing of what had occurred, were amazed at the words of their Master, and Peter, their usual spokesman on such occasions, said : "Master, the multitudes press thee and crush thee, and sayest thou, Who touched me ? " But it was no ordinary touch he was inquiring after. He did not ask who had been pushed against him involuntarily by the pressure of the crowd ; but which of them it was who of set purpose and deliberate intention had applied to him by touch for a supernatural blessing, and had, as he knew, received such a blessing from him. " And he looked round to see her that had done this thing." Then, finding that he knew all about it, the poor woman came, fearing and trembling, and fell down before him, and " told him all the truth," or, as Luke has it, " declared in the presence of all the people for what cause she had touched him." This was what he sought, and having obtained that, he said to her, with the deepest tenderness, " Daughter, thy faith hath saved thee, go into peace." Thus she went away with a double cure,— with the fountain of her blood dried up, and with the peace of God in her heart. I call your attention to the words which I have used, " Go *into* peace." As Plumtre has said, the " phrase go in peace," has become so idiomatic that we dare not change it, but it may be well to remember that the true meaning of the Greek is, " go into peace." * It is as if he had said, " take thankfully the cure which you have received for the body, but as you go away, enter into the peace which I came to impart to all those who trust in me."

---

* " New Testament Commentary for English Readers," edited by Bishop Ellicott, Vol. i. p. 202.

Now, taking this miracle as designed to instruct us concerning the nature of sin, the characteristics of Christ's cure of sin, the means of obtaining that cure from him, and the obligation resting on those who have obtained it, let us see what light we may obtain from it on these four things.

In the first place, it sets before us the fearful nature of sin. We need not too curiously inquire into the nature of the malady with which this woman was afflicted. There is enough on the very surface of the narrative to indicate its significance as a symbol of sin. For twelve long years her physical strength was drained away, and she was enfeebled and wasted by it, almost to a shadow. Now it is quite similar with sin. It is a wasting thing. In many of its forms it wastes money. In many others it wastes health ; but, worst of all, in all its forms, it wastes the soul itself. How many, who in their youth gave high promises of mental greatness, are now reduced to the merest drivellers, under the influence of opium or of alcohol ? Then morally, how does sin blight the conscience, eating it out of the man, until he is ready for any iniquity ! How it weakens the will too, so that he who once stood firm as the oak against all storms, now bends like a reed before the most trifling breeze ! In a word, Delilah-like, it shears from a man the locks of his strength, and leaves him a helpless prey to his appetites and passions. But, besides all this, all the efforts which the sinner puts forth to get rid of his sin only make matters worse. This woman had " spent all her living upon physicians, and was nothing bettered, but rather grew worse : " so the sinner, when he becomes conscious of his guilt and depravity, tries many expedients to get rid of them, but these are all miserable failures. At first, perhaps, he thinks he will forget it in a round of pleasure.

He goes to places of amusement, he tries the flowing cup ; he seeks frivolous, or, as the world prefers to phrase it, cheerful society, and for a season all seems to go with him merry as a marriage-bell. By and by, however, he discovers that he has only been acting the part of the ostrich, which buries its head in the sand, thinking to get rid of its pursuers by making them invisible, and at length the sad confession is wrung out of him—I quote the words of one who wrote from experience—

> " Though gay companions round the bowl
> Dispel a while the sense of ill ;
> Though plsasures fill the maddening soul,
> The heart, the heart, is lonely still."

Another of perhaps a more serious turn of mind thinks he will make himself better. He imagines he will effect his cure by the performance of good works. But he has not gone far until he discovers that he has begun at the wrong end. He is trying to heal the tree by working on the fruit, in utter forgetfulness of the precept : " Make the tree good, and its fruit will be good." He finds that he cannot satisfy himself, and so that it is vain for him to dream of satisfying God; or, if he thinks to say, like the young man, concerning the commandments of the law, " all these have I kept from my youth up," there comes some testing acid which reveals him to himself and shows him that he lacks the one thing which is especially needful, the new heart, for the prosecution of the new life. Another perhaps tries formalism in religion. He joins the church. He gives punctilious attention to outward services. He attends the sanctuary, he observes the sacrament and the like. But he also discovers, at length, that he has reversed the proper order of procedure, for these things are really valuable only after the sin is cured, and have no virtue in them to effect its cure. We may and do get to the church through Christ, but we cannot get to Christ through the church. So one hope after another fails the sinner. He has not improved his case, but all the time it has been growing more serious, for all the time his heart has been estranged from God, and everything that issues from it has in it the tincture and the taint of evil.

But now, in the second place, look at the cure of sin which Christ effects as that is symbolized in the case before us. It is, for one thing, *thorough.* It goes to the root of the disease. Other physicians deal with the symptoms, Jesus alone grapples with the evil itself. So far as it is guilt, he removes that by the sacrifice of himself upon the cross. He tells the sinner that he has suffered in his stead. He declares that he has nailed his sins with his own body to the tree, and that now on the ground of the atonement which he has made, God is able and willing righteously to forgive him, and believing that, like the woman in our text, the anxious one " goes into peace." In so far, again, as the disease is depravity, Christ bestows his Spirit on the believer, who is by the agency of that divine person renewed in righteousness and holiness and delivered from the slavery and pollution of sin, as well as from its punishment.

Further, this cure, thus thorough, is *immediate.* The woman in this narrative experienced relief the moment she touched the border of the Saviour's garment. That which for twelve long years she had been seeking in vain, was bestowed on her by Christ at once. So the salvation of the soul from sin comes immediately on faith. Many a man, indeed, has been for a long time anxious, and, therefore, it has come to be supposed by multitudes that before one can be a real convert, he must be for a lengthened period under what is called conviction of sin; but if you look into the matter carefully, you will discover that wherever an inquirer has been a long while in obtaining a cure, it has been because he was unwilling to apply to Christ for it, or to accept it in Christ's way, and that the moment he really did these things he was delivered.

I say not, indeed, that the applicant will be in a moment perfectly emancipated from the dominion of sin and completely sanctified. But he is fully forgiven, and actually renewed. There is bestowed upon him a perfect pardon, and there is implanted in him a new principle of life, which by the grace of the Holy Spirit gradually develops itself, in his character and conduct here, and will be thoroughly perfected in the world to come.

Finally, here this cure is *given freely.* The woman before us had spent all her living on physicians, and at length obtained relief from One who took from her no money, and desired nothing from her but her love. Even so the Saviour does not sell his pardon and regeneration. If we wish to buy these blessings, we cannot obtain them at any price; but if we will accept them freely, we may have them at once. No money, no tears, no sufferings, no good works of ours will ever deserve them, but if we will receive them as free gifts, he will bestow them on us at once. This is, indeed, the great stumbling-block in the way of many a sinner's cure. He *will* purchase it. He does not wish to be beholden altogether to the Saviour for it. But thus alone is it that any man can be saved. "What," say you, "am I to do nothing for my cure?" No, I answer, for you cure nothing; only accept it in humble faith. But, *once cured,* do everything for Christ, and thereby show your gratitude to him who has done so much for you.

But, looking still farther at the spiritual significance of this miracle, let us see what it teaches us as to the means by which we are to obtain salvation from Christ. Luke tells us that the Master said, "Somebody has touched me." So, to be saved by Christ, we must touch him, not, indeed, with the touch of physical contact, for that is now impossible, but with that of the application of our spirit to his. Observe, however, that this touch is neither a work which deserves healing, nor a price that pays for it. It does not furnish a foundation, on the ground of which we can claim salvation as a matter of right. But it is the means through which the healing energy of Christ passes from him into our spirits. Let me illustrate It is a well understood mechanical principle that if we wish to transmit force from one body to another, we must first establish some kind of union between them. In the cotton mill you may have the most admirable machinery ; and in the basement you may have the most powerful engine careering along at full speed in the very wantonness of its strength, but unless you connect the one with the other, every spindle will be motionless, and every loom at rest. If the shaft between the engine and the screw in the steamship be broken, the propeller will immediately stand still. If the wire be snapped asunder the telegram cannot be dispatched. Now, though we cannot in all respects reason from the mechanical to the spiritual, still we have in this law of material force an outward analogy to the great moral principle that if influence is to pass from one spirit to another, a union between them must be first established. If a young man is to be ruined, his tempters well know that in order to effect their purpose they must first obtain his confidence, and so establish a union between him and them ; while, if a bad man is to be reclaimed, the good man who seeks to do so, must begin in a similar way, by gaining his confidence and affection. We are influenced only by those with whom we are connected by some uniting bond, or, in the phraseology of this narrative, whom in some real and spiritual sense we touch. Now it is only another application of this principle when we say that the sinner who is to be saved must in some way be brought into spiritual union with the Lord Jesus Christ. The forgiveness of his sins results from Christ's being connected with him and acting in his stead, and the regeneration of his soul results from his being connected with Christ and being animated by his spirit. Now what is that link that so connects the sinner and Christ? It is, as we have indicated by the illustrations which we have employed, the faith or confidence of the sinner in Christ. We are one with those whom we trust, in so far forth as that for which we trust them is concerned. The touch here, therefore, represents, not bodily contact with Jesus, for that is now impossible; nor the outward profession of confidence in him, for that is but like a being pushed against him by the crowd; but the deliberate and believing application of the soul to him, for that deliverance from the guilt and power of sin which you feel you need. And when you make that application, you will receive pardon and renewal.

I say that without any qualification, for the most superficial reader cannot fail to remark here the sensitiveness of the Saviour to the faintest and humblest appeal to him for cure. Behold how bashfully this woman came to him! Timidly, from behind, she reaches him, and touches softly the border of his robe, and then quicker than the electric spark flashes forth, at the touch of a human hand, the energy of Christ came from him for her cure. Now, just as he responded to this woman's modestly expressed desire, he will bend his ear to your faintest entreaty for salvation, if only it be real. There needs no eloquence to move him. We require no well-rounded form of words to express our request to him. All that is requisite is reality, that we do apply to him. He casts no one out for lack of boldness. Therefore if you go genuinely to him, you may depend upon it that he will respond to your entreaty. The grandees of earth may turn you away repeatedly from their doors, but Jesus will not thus repel you. The men of the world may plead the pressure of engagements as a reason for sending you away from them ; but though the government of the world is upon his shoulders, the Lord Jesus has both the time and the heart to listen to your faintest cry. O thou timid, bashful one, who scarcely darest to speak thy petition, let the desire of thine heart go forth to Jesus now, that he may deliver thee, and even where thou art he will attend to thy request.

But, finally, see what light the spiritual significance of this miracle casts on our obligation to Christ after we have obtained salvation at his hands. He allowed this woman to remain in the background until she had received healing from his power ; but as soon as that had been obtained by her, he called her forward to bear testimony to him before the multitude. So Jesus does not ask any protestations of attachment from those who are as yet unconverted and unsaved ; but after he has saved us, he calls us openly to avow what he has done for us and in us. And by this I mean not simply that he requires us to connect ourselves publicly with his visible church ; though he does require that, and that is of great importance in its own place. He calls us to live for him everywhere ; to confess him wherever we are and whatever we do ; to transact our business for his glory ; to speak on his behalf to our fellowmen ; and to commend him by our declaration of that which he has done for us, to the acceptance of the sinners with whom we are brought into contact. To confess Christ in the church, is a noble thing—if it be accompanied by such a life for Christ—nay, more, if the confession be sincere, it will help us maintain such a life. If therefore you have anything to confess regarding him—let me entreat you to do it, both in the church and out of it. Say not to me that you are afraid, that you may be like the barren tree on which there was " nothing but leaves." That was bad, very bad ; but it is not much better with a fruit tree on which there are no leaves. Visiting a friend one day in the neighborhood of Liverpool, I found that he had just gone out, but was expected back in a few minutes; and I went out into his garden to wait for him there. As I walked about, I saw some gooseberry bushes, from which the caterpillars had eaten all the leaves, and on the branches there were only a few tiny, stunted, withered berries, that had not grown an iota since the leaves had been taken away, and were not worth the gathering. The sight of these bushes set me thinking, and led me ultimately to the conclusion that if it is bad to make a confession of Christ which is simply formal and unreal, if it is bad to make a confession which is " nothing but leaves," it is not good either to have no leaves ; or, in literal phraseology, to make no confession, even if you be really in Christ. Without such a confession you will live a poor stunted life ; your fruit will not ripen, your Christianity will not thrive. Therefore, for your own sakes, as well as for Christ's sake, if you have received salvation at his hands, come forth, and alike in the church and in the world make public expression of your indebtedness to him. "Who touched me?" is the inquiry of Christ as he looks round among you to-night, and if you have touched him and have thereby obtained salvation from him, make an open confession of the fact, for you may rest assured that such a confession will bring new blessings into your heart, as he says to you : "Be of good cheer, thy faith hath saved thee; go into peace."

XVIII.

TWO MIRACLES ON THE BLIND.

Matt. ix. 27-31. Mark viii. 22-26.

WE have brought these two narratives together, not because they refer to the same incidents in the Saviour's life, or because they belong to the same time of his ministry; but because, alike by their resemblances to each other and their differences from each other, we may learn some lessons which neither of them when taken separately might have suggested.

The first, which tells of the cure of two blind men in a house, in an unmentioned locality, is peculiar to Matthew. If we were to judge from the place in which we find it, we should conclude that the miracle which it records was wrought immediately after the raising of the daughter of Jairus to life; but as Matthew has, for the most part, arranged the miracles of our Lord in groups, without regard to their chronological sequence, we cannot reach any certainty either as to its date or its locality from the position in which the account of it is here found.

The second is peculiar to Mark, and the miracle which it describes seems to have been wrought in Bethsaida, not far from the place where the five thousand were fed by the five loaves and two fishes. The Saviour was then on

256

his way to Cæsarea Philippi, and the transfiguration on Mount Hermon occurred only a week or two later, so that we can at least approximately fix its date.

Both miracles belong to the same class. They are both works of healing ; and the disease, in both instances, was blindness. Both of them, however, differ from the case of the man described in the ninth chapter of the fourth gospel, for he was born blind, while they had lost their sight in consequence of disease in the eyes. This was a very common malady in those days in Palestine, as it is still in Syria and Egypt. Its prevalence and severity are easily accounted for, " by the quantities of dust and sand, pulverized by the intense heat of the sun ; by the perpetual glare of the light ; by the contrast between the heat and the cold sea-air on the coast, by the dews at night while the people sleep on the roofs ; by smallpox," * etc.

But, however we may account for the frequent occurrence of cases of blindness among the people, every one can see, that, as a disease, it is a most suggestive symbol of the spiritual effects of sin ; and that especially in three respects. First of all, it is a state of darkness. The eye is the window of the mind, and there is a certain class of objects which can be correctly perceived through it alone. So far, therefore, as all such objects are concerned, the blind man is thrown for his ideas regarding them, on other and lower senses, which give a very defective report about them. In like manner, there is an inner eye of the soul, through which alone spiritual things can be discerned, and sin has blinded that, so that the sinner now is beholden for his conceptions of such objects to those lower faculties of his nature which, never having been designed to serve such a purpose,

* See Smith's Dictionary, article " Blindness."

give most defective and distorted notions concerning them. The inner eye, indeed, is still there, but it is diseased, dormant, and for all practical purposes closed; so that not only has he no correct ideas of those things which can be perceived by it alone, but he has imperfect and therefore false ideas of other things which ought to be viewed in relation to them. The lower principles of his nature, and these alone, are active and alive; nay, just because of the dormancy of the higher, the lower are more largely developed. His appetites, passions, and desires are strong. His intellect, even, may be active and vigorous, but it is exercised only regarding natural things. He knows nothing of those higher realities which are only " spiritually discerned."

The effect of all this is not only that he knows nothing of spiritual things strictly so called, but also that even common things are not seen or known by him in their relation to spiritual things, and so have an exaggerated and disproportionate importance in his regard. The blind man, taking a chair, a table, or a book, feels all over it, and so gets a knowledge of it—such as it is—by itself; but he knows little or nothing of its relation to other things. And so, in a similar way, the sinner's knowledge of such things as he does know, is simply of the senses, and is altogether apart from their relation to things spiritual and divine. Like the blind man, he knows only what, as we may say, he can hold in his hand, or touch with the point of his staff; that is, he knows only things tangible and material. He lacks the inner sight that is essential to the vision of God; and therefore, though he may be an admirable observer of natural objects, and peerless as an investigator of phenomena, through the glass of the microscope, he may yet be blind to spiritual and eternal realities, and utterly unable to understand the author of the Epistle to the Hebrews when he says of Moses that " he endured as seeing him who is invisible," or Paul when he speaks of himself as looking " not at the things which are seen, but at the things which are not seen, for the things which are seen are temporal, but the things which are not seen are eternal."

But, a second point of resemblance between the case of the sinner and that of the blind man is found in the fact that they are both in a measure of danger from their privation. How liable is the blind man to stumble over some obstacle in his path ? or to be run over by some rough rider, or reckless driver ? and how perilous is his condition as he approaches, all unconsciously, the margin of some rugged precipice ? But, are not the same things true, in another department, of the sinner ? His feet stumble on the dark mountains. Ever and anon some emissary of Satan rides over him ; and, without knowing it, he is walking along the edge of a perpendicular cliff over which at any moment he may fall.

And, to mention only one particular more, the blind man is in a condition of helplessness. Set such an one down in the middle of one of our busy streets, or in the heart of one of our great wildernesses, and what could he do to insure his safety or to find his way ? Like Elymas of old, he will cry for some one to lead him by the hand, and if his cry be not responded to, he will sit down in absolute despair. Now this also is an illustration of the sinner's case. He is helpless. He has lost himself. And his cry is for a guide. O! did he but know that Jesus of Nazareth is passing by! and would he but cry in earnestness to him that he might receive his sight!

But we must not press the analogy too far, for the sinner is unconscious of his blindness. He is blind even to his blindness, and that accounts for the fact that he

seems to care very little about it. He is also to blame
for his blindness, for it is the result of his sin. The bit-
terest pang in Samson's dark and desolate condition
would be that he had brought it all upon himself, for had
he not allowed Delilah to worm out of him the secret of
his strength, his enemies had not been able to put out
his eyes. And, if he only knew it, that is equally the
case with the sinner and his inner sight. He has embraced iniquity. By it he has been robbed of his
strength, and set at length to grind in weariful and cease-
less drudgery.

Turning now, however, to another aspect of the subject,
let us observe that all of these three men made application
to Jesus for the cure of their blindness. The two of
whom Matthew tells followed the crowd that was round
him, until he entered a house, and then they pushed
their way in to where he was. They made application
for themselves, saying, "Thou Son of David! have mercy
on us!" But he who is described by Mark was brought
to Christ by friends, who besought the Lord to heal him
by his touch. He must, however, have been himself a
consenting party to the making of their appeal. In fact
there was a plea of the strongest sort in his mere presence, and the patient yet eager expectancy that lighted
up his sightless face, would of itself say, "Have mercy
on me," more eloquently than his tongue could have uttered the words. But why did they appeal to Christ?
It was because they had heard of his wonderful works and
tenderness of heart, and because they believed that what
he had done for others, he would do also for them. The
two who were together, and who seem to have been companions in misery (like those other two at the gate of
Jericho) called on him as the "Son of David," indicating
their belief that he was indeed the Messiah promised to

the fathers, and perhaps also connecting with him as such the prophecy of Isaiah (xxxv. 5): "Then the eyes of the blind shall be opened, and the ears of the deaf shall be unstopped." But, however that may have been, they all applied to him, and in that they gave an example which should be followed by every one who desires spiritual salvation. Let all such repair at once to Jesus. It is a waste of time and energy to go elsewhere. No one can remove the blindness of the soul but he, for "Neither is there salvation in any other, for there is none other name under heaven given among men, whereby ye must be saved." Turn away, therefore, from every other, and apply to Jesus, saying, in words too plain to be misunderstood, and too familiar to be forgotten:

> "Just as I am; poor, wretched, blind,
> Sight, riches, healing of the mind,
> Yea, all I need in thee to find,
> O Lamb of God, I come."

But observe, once more, that while Jesus healed all these three men, he did not heal them all in precisely the same way. He said to the two men of whom Matthew writes : "Believe ye that I am able to do this ?" and when they answered, "Yea, Lord," he simply touched their eyes, and tenderly gave them what they asked, saying unto them, "According to your faith, be it unto you." That was all, and their eyes were opened, so that they saw clearly and at once. It was otherwise, however, with him of whom Mark tells, for the Saviour led him out of the town, and "when he had spit on his eyes, and put his hands upon his eyes, he asked him if he saw aught, and he, looking up, said, I see men, for I behold them as trees walking." After that he put his hands again upon his eyes and made him look up, and he was restored and saw every man clearly.

Both cures were distinctly miraculous. There is nothing in a touch that in or of itself can remove blindness, and though we read that saliva was sometimes, in those days, applied to the eyes for relief in cases of ophthalmia, yet there was in that just as little to produce healing as there was in a touch of the hand. The power that removed the disease and restored the sight was in Christ, and the touch was the symbol of that contact between his Spirit and theirs, through which his power was transmitted into them for their cure. But they were not all dealt with in the same way, and a similar diversity is seen in the Lord's dealings with sinners. The history of his treatment of one soul is not precisely identical with that of his treatment of any other soul whom he saves by grace. We must not seek, therefore, to have the experience of another exactly repeated in ourselves. What we need and ought to cry for is that our souls may be saved, but we must let the Lord take his own way of answering our request. With one he may deal in the great congregation, while he may take another apart and treat him in the solitude of a great affliction. He may, as it were, touch the eyes of one, and those of another he may anoint with clay. From one he may call out a declaration of faith, before he performs the cure, while in another he may work the cure before he requires such a confession. In one the crisis may be sharp and the cure immediate, in another the work may be gradual and the cure marked by stages like those specified in the man of Bethsaida.

He takes his own way with each, and that way may be, I believe really is, determined in a great measure by the individual characteristics of each. No one man is run precisely into the mould of another, and therefore no one man's experience in conversion or spiritual growth is precisely the same as another's. This is a matter of some importance, because many have been greatly retarded in their attainment of joy and peace in Christ, and in their growth in holiness, because they have been looking for an exact reproduction in themselves of experiences which are described in the biography of some good and worthy man that they have been reading. We must not prescribe to the Saviour how he is to treat us. The friends of this man of Bethsaida desired the Lord " to touch him," but before he did that he led him out of the town and spit on his eyes ; and in general, it may be said, that what we set our hearts on having in the way of experience in conversion is what Christ will not give us. Naaman wanted Elisha to " come out to him, and stand and strike his hand over the place, and call upon his God, and recover the leper; " as probably he had heard that he had done in some other case, but the prophet only said, " Go and wash in Jordan seven times, and thy flesh shall come again to thee, and thou shalt be clean." * Let us be instructed, therefore, by such instances, and be content with the having of our eyes opened, no matter whether or not the miracle of grace is attended with the same accessories in us as it has been in others.

But, amid all such variations in spiritual experience as are suggested by these miracles, two things are true of every conversion, and we find them indicated here, one in each of these narratives. The first is that there is no salvation without faith and that the measure of the faith is the measure of the spiritual blessing. Salvation is by faith. It has to be so, if it is not to be of works, for faith

* II Kings v. 1-14.

is not a meritorious work done by the soul, but simply
the receptive act of the soul.   It is the hand held out to
take hold of what God offers in Christ ; the vessel which
we bring to the well, and which determines the quantity
of the water which we carry away from the well.   As
Trench has said, " The words, According to your faith be
it unto you, are very remarkable for the insight which
they give us into the relation of man's faith and God's
gift.   The faith which in itself is nothing is yet the
organ of receiving everything.   It is the conducting link
between man's emptiness and God's fulness ; and herein is all the value which it has.   It is the bucket let down
into the fountain of God's grace without which the man
could not draw up out of that fountain ; the purse which
does not itself make its owner rich, but which yet effectually enriches him by the treasure which it contains." *

The other feature always present in conversion is the
fact that it is a personal matter between the individual
soul and Christ.   That is suggested by the statement
made by Mark to the effect that the Lord led the blind
man out of Bethsaida into the country.   Why he did so
is not expressly declared, but the statement itself reminds
us that in its time of crisis each soul is dealt with apart
by Christ alone.   The Lord said unto Saul of Tarsus,
" Why persecutest thou me ? "   What an eye-opener that
question was ? and how swiftly it brought this inquiry,
" Lord, what wilt thou have me to do ? "   Each man at his
conversion is taken thus apart by Christ.   Why ? thou ?
me ?   What ? thou ? me ?   These are then the pointed
inquiries.   The soul is then confronted with Christ alone,
and compelled to face these questions.   What am I
to thee ?   What wilt thou be to me ? and what wilt thou

* "Notes on the Miracles," p. 197.

that I should do for thee ? The gate into the new life is like a turn-style wicket, through which each must pass alone, and be reckoned with by himself. My hearer, have *you* passed through it yet ?

But now let us note in conclusion that Christ gave to all these three healed men alike the charge to say nothing about their cure to any one. To those of whom Matthew tells, he said, " See that no man know it ; " and to him of Bethsaida he gave this very stringent injunction, " Neither go into the town, nor tell it to any in the town." Now how shall we account for such a prohibition ? Where no reason is given in the record, it is always hazardous to conjecture. Still we may perhaps find the explanation in one or other of the following considerations, or in the combination in some degree of them all. Perhaps the Saviour saw that men were beginning to be more attracted toward himself by the miracles which he wrought than by the spiritual blessings which he bestowed, and he wished to discourage them from putting his miracles above his grace. Or he might not desire to have his movements retarded, and his work hindered, by such crowds as would be collected simply to see his miracles. We know that on other occasions he was both seriously incommoded and deprived of needful rest, by the presence of immense multitudes, and therefore he might not wish to have this evil increased by the spreading abroad of the report of these new works of wonder. Or, perhaps, most probable of all, the prohibition was rooted in his regard for the spiritual welfare of the men whom he had cured. Their constant rehearsal of the kindness of the Lord to them might tend to create and foster in them a spirit of Phariseeism. It might lead them to think that they were better than others because he had done so much for them. They might tell the

story for their own glory, and not for his, and so their
telling of it would become a serious danger to their spiritual life, and he, foreseeing that, forbade them to speak
of it at all. It is not always wise to encourage a new
convert to tell what Christ has done for him. Whether
it is or not depends very largely on the disposition of the
convert himself. It may be safe enough for some, and
yet it may be very dangerous for others. I know, indeed, that great good has frequently resulted from the
giving of personal testimonies by converts in some of our
city missions and elsewhere, but such testimonies ought
not to be indiscriminately stimulated and encouraged,
and the moment any symptom of self-glorification appears, the speaker should be silenced, for if he proceed
in that spirit, he will do no good to others, but great
harm to himself.

We read, to our surprise, concerning the two men in
the narrative of Matthew, that though they were forbidden to say anything about their cure, " They, when they
were departed, spread abroad his fame in all that country." And, still more to our surprise, we find that many
commentators have declared that they did quite right in
thus disregarding the injunction of their benefactor. But
surely these authors have written without sufficient
thought. The motive of the men might seem to them to
be good; but their conduct was neither grateful nor intelligent. It was not grateful, for " to obey is better
than sacrifice, and to hearken than the fat of lambs." It
was not intelligent, for they might and ought to have
known that Christ was wiser than themselves, and knew
far better than they what it was best to do in the circumstances. And in general, this principle may be laid
down: When Christ has given a distinct command, it is
ours to obey it, even although it may seem to us a strange

one. True faith, or true obedience, (for obedience is simply faith in action), does what it is told, asking no questions, and making no objections. But to do what Christ has forbidden because we think we shall honor him more by breaking than by keeping his injunction, is to put ourselves above him, and do him deep dishonor.

XIX.

THE FEEDING OF THE FIVE THOUSAND.

*Matt. xiv. 13-21. Mark vi. 30-44. Luke ix. 10-17.
John vi. 1-14.*

THE expression " after these things " (John vi. 1) is
not definite enough to fix the date of this miracle. But
the mention of the fact that " the Passover, a feast
of the Jews, was nigh," (John vi. 4), while serving also to
account for the presence of such a multitude, fixes the
time as being shortly before the third Passover in our
Lord's ministry. The scene of the miracle was in the
" desert place belonging to Bethsaida." The place was
called desert, not because it was barren, for we find that
there was " much grass " in it, but because it was unin-
habited, and, therefore, suitable for rest and meditation.
It was situated on the northeastern shore of the Sea of
Galilee, and as that was in the district of Ganlonitis,
while the Bethsaida in which Peter and Andrew were
born is elsewhere called " Bethsaida of Galilee,* it has
been conjectured by some that there were two places of
that name, one on each side of the lake, that on the eastern being also called Julia, and having been built by
Philip the tetrarch. But I am disposed to accept the suggestion made by Dr. Wm. M. Thomson, in the first edi-

* John xii. 21.

tion of "The Land and the Book," when he says,* "The *invention* of a second Bethsaida is wholly unnecessary . . . . All admit there was a Bethsaida at the entrance of the Jordan into the lake. . . . Any city built at the mouth of the Jordan would almost necessarily have part of its houses on the west bank of the stream, and this would be literally and geographically within the territory of Galilee. Peter, Andrew and Philip were born there and would be mentioned as Galileans, and further, I think it probable that the whole city on both banks of the river was ordinarily attached to Galilee, and that one object which Philip the tetrarch had in rebuilding the part on the east side, and changing its name, was to detach it from its former relations, and establish his own right over it. I believe, therefore, that there was but one Bethsaida, at the head of the lake, and that it was at the mouth of the Jordan." Now if this opinion be correct, the scene of the miracle must have been somewhere on the plain now called Butaiha, which is a level tract of land, stretching eastward from the mouth of the Jordan along the margin of the lake. This place could be reached by boat, while at the same time, it was not too far away to be easily got at by land from Capernaum and the neighboring cities. It belonged to Bethsaida; it was a solitary place; it was and still is plentifully covered with grass, and there is a mountain close at hand. So all the conditions of the narrative are satisfied by it.

This is the only miracle which is described by all the four Evangelists, and though their narratives agree in all essential matters, there are incidental variations which serve to show that each wrote independently of the others. Three different reasons for our Lord's withdrawal to this place at this time are given by the four witnesses.

---

* English edition, pp. 373-374.

Matthew connects it with his receipt of the intelligence of the murder of John the Baptist by Herod, and so suggests to us that he desired a season of retirement in order that he might prepare himself for the crisis that was coming to himself, and of which the execution of his forerunner gave the warning note. Mark associates it with the return of the Apostles from their preaching tour, when they told their Master "what they had done, and what they had taught," and when he said to them, "Come ye yourselves apart, into a desert place, and rest awhile, for there were many coming and going, and they had no leisure so much as to eat," leaving the impression on our minds that he wished to have with his followers a season of peaceful retreat, during which by fellowship with himself they might be further trained for the work to which he had called them. Luke, again, appends it to the statement that Herod was perplexed at the appearance of Jesus, was asking who is this? and was desiring to see him, and that leads us to suppose that just at this time the Saviour thought it best to go for a season to a place that was beyond the limit of Herod's jurisdiction. John gives no particular reason, and leaves the miracle to stand out in isolated distinctness, because he introduces it here, not so much for its own sake, as for that of the discourse which was founded on it, and by which in his gospel it is followed. But surely there is no incongruity, or incompatibility between these different statements. No one of them is contradictory to, or inconsistent with the others. They might all be true. They were all true, and we may learn that no one of the four Evangelists professes to give all the particulars concerning any one fact in the history of the Lord, but merely those which fixed themselves most deeply in his own memory, and harmonized most thoroughly with his design in writing.

Again, in comparing the four accounts you will find
that by Matthew, Mark and Luke the disciples are said
to have come to Christ and asked him to send the multitude away, that they might have time to go to the villages round about and buy the food which they needed ;
while in John's narrative we are told that Christ himself
took the initiative by saying to Philip, " Whence shall we
buy bread that these may eat ?" But neither is there
here any incongruity, for you perceive that it was while
Jesus was on the mountain with his disciples, and seeing
the arrival of the crowds, that he so spoke to Philip. He
foresaw that the people would linger with him throughout the day, and so before he began his teaching and
miracle working among them, he put this question, leaving it to find its solution, if possible, in the minds of his
followers, and then, as the evening drew on, they came
to him, in hopelessness, and said, " Send the multitudes
away, that they may go into the towns and country
round about, and lodge, and get victuals, for we are here
in a desert place." I do not say that this is the true
solution of what looks like a discrepancy, but it is a very
probable solution, and in reference to all such cases as
this, the words of Alford are characterized by such judicial fairness, that I may quote them for your guidance :
" I repeat the remark so often made in this commentary,
that if we were in possession of the facts as they happened, there is no doubt that the various forms of the
literal narrations would fall into their places, and the
truthfulness of each historian would be apparent ; but as
we cannot at present, reconcile them in this way, the
humble and believing Christian will not be tempted to
handle the word of God deceitfully, but to admire the
gracious condescension which has given us so many independent witnesses whose very difference in detail

makes their accordance in the great central truths so
much the more weighty.   On every point of importance
here, the four sacred historians are entirely and absolutely agreed.   That every minor detail related by them
had its ground in historical fact we fully believe; it is
the tracking it to this ground in each case which is now
beyond our power: and here comes in the simplicity and
reliance of faith; and the justification of those who believe and receive each gospel as they find it written." *

But now, leaving these matters of minor interest, let
us advance to the story of the miracle itself.   As we have
seen, it was on the return of his Apostles from their trial
mission, that the Lord requested them to accompany him
to a retired place described by Luke as " belonging to
Bethsaida."   They went thither by boat, and so their
departure was witnessed by the multitudes whom they
left behind upon the shore.   These, as soon as they could
ascertain from the course taken by the boat, the place for
which they were bound, set out on foot round the upper
end of the lake, and crossing the Jordan at Bethsaida,
made their way to the plain of Butaiha, which we have
already described.   Meanwhile Jesus and the disciples
had ascended the hill in the immediate neighborhood, and
as the Lord saw the crowds who had gone along beyond
them into the plain, all thought of either retirement or
rest was abandoned by him.   So acting on the principle
which he followed with the woman of Samaria, he took
advantage of the opportunity of doing good, which was thus
presented to him, " he received them, and spake unto them
of the Kingdom of God, and healed them that had need
of healing." †   Very suggestive is it to read in Mark that
the source of all this patience under the loss of his much
needed rest, and of this earnest effort for the welfare of

_____

* Alford, Greek Testament, *in loco.*   † Luke ix. 11.

those who thus intruded upon his privacy with his followers, was in the fact that "when he saw much people
he was moved with compassion toward them because they
were as sheep not having a shepherd." Thus, here
again, as in the cases of the widow of Nain, and the impotent man at Bethesda, he did not need to be asked to
do anything, but out of his knowledge of the need and his
pity for the needy, he began to teach them many things,
and gave relief to all that required healing among
them.

While he was engaged in these labors of love, the day
rapidly wore away, and as the evening drew on he re-
sumed the subject, which at an earlier hour he had
suggested for the consideration of his disciples. Turning to Philip, not, probably, because of any unbelief
which he saw in the heart of that Apostle more than in
those of the others, but, simply because he was close at
hand, he asked him, "Whence shall we buy bread that
these may eat ?" He knew himself what he was about
to do, but he wanted to bring out what Philip and the
rest of them thought upon the subject, or perhaps he
spoke in a spirit of playfulness, as if he had said:
"Well, Philip, have you solved that problem yet, whence
are we to get bread for all these people ? You know all
this district well; tell us what we are to do, for we cannot let them go fasting, lest they faint by the way."
But Philip was not prepared with any plan, and he had
no idea that a miracle was forthcoming; so, like one bewildered, he replied, "Two hundred pennyworth,"—that
is, in our currency, thirty-five dollars worth—"of bread
is not sufficient for them that every one of them may
take a little." He did not add what yet we instinctively
feel was in the tone of his words: "and there is no such
amount of money among us; while if there was, it would

be well-nigh impossible to find a place at hand where we could purchase so much bread."

The other apostles, feeling that it would be impossible for them to do what was required, suggested that the multitude should be sent away in time for them to reach the neighboring towns before sunset, and that they should be left to buy food for themselves in them. But he would not have the question evaded after that fashion, and replied, "They need not depart: give ye them to eat." This command made them dumb with astonishment. They knew not what to do, or to say, and accordingly he asked them, " How many loaves have ye?" To this Andrew, who had been inquiring into the resources of the multitude, replied, " There is a lad here which hath five barley loaves and two small fishes, but what are they among so many?" One can fancy the smile that broadened Andrew's face when he contrasted the meagre supply with the multitudinous demand. But still we wonder that he has so soon forgotten the wine at Cana or the miraculous draught of fishes brought to the shore of the lake by his brother and himself. " What are they among so many?" Not much, certainly; but then put them into the hands of Jesus, and they are more than enough for the necessity. Andrew forgot that at the moment, and so we account for the despondency of his question. Small things are not always contemptible. It all depends on the hands in which they are, and if they are in his who is God manifest in the flesh, he will make them suffice for the occasion. It was his purpose to do so at this time. Therefore he said, " Make the men sit down." There were women and children too, as we learn from Matthew, but they sat by themselves promiscuously, while the men were arranged in companies of fifties and of hundreds, reclining on the grass. Mark's description is very graphic.

He uses the plural of the word which signifies a garden plot or bed, and so as Thayer * has paraphrased his expression, he portrays them as reclining in ranks or divisions, so that the several companies resembled separate plots. Probably, as suggested by some, they were ranged in two semicircles of forty fifties and of thirty hundreds; but however they were placed, the fact that the multitudes were divided into companies accounts for the definiteness of the computation which in more than one of the Evangelists gives the aggregate of five thousand men.

But what a magnificent sight this must have been! The rays of the westering sun illumined the distant mountains with their purple glory, and glittered with dazzling sheen upon the surface of the lake close by. All around was the quiet of nature's afternoon, and above a sky of clear and cloudless blue—fit banquet-hall for the feast that was about to be provided. Taking the barley cakes in his hand, the Lord of the feast stepped forth into the midst of the companies, and reverently gave thanks to God for his mercies toward them, then breaking the bread, he gave the portions to his disciples, who, in their turn, subdivided them among the multitudes ; and " they did all eat and were filled." We know not how it was done, for every miracle is incomprehensible save to God by whom it is wrought. We cannot tell at what precise point the process of multiplication came in. There is nothing in the least degree analogous to it in Nature. We know, only, that by these five loaves and two fishes, five thousand men were fed and satisfied—yea, so satisfied, that twelve baskets of fragments were taken up after the meal was finished, for Jesus had said to his disciples, " Gather up the fragments that remain, that nothing be lost."

* Greek Dictionary s. v. πρασιά.

Strangely overawed for a while were these divinely fed multitudes, but ere long, as the truth flashed into their minds, they exclaimed, " This is of a truth that prophet that should come into the world." They remembered Elisha and the man of Baalshalisha, Elijah and the widow's handful of meal and cruise of oil, Moses and the manna; and they placed the Lord Jesus in their company, nay, recognized him as the great " coming one," to whom Moses pointed as one like unto himself, but greater, whom the people were to hear in all things whatsoever he should say unto them. Nor was this all. They regarded this miracle as a proof that he was the Messiah, and as with their mistaken interpretation of Old Testament prophecy they had come to believe that their expected Messiah was to be a great earthly ruler, they were for taking him, there and then, and making him a king. And his own followers would willingly have helped them to attain their purpose. But he had not come to earth to wield a worldly sceptre, or wear a monarch's crown. His kingdom was not of this world, either in its constitution, its principles, or its honors, and therefore, that the people might be kept from doing anything that would have brought them under the penalty of the Roman law, he sent them to their homes; and that his disciples might be withdrawn from the seductive influence of the temptation to which they had been exposed and might meanwhile have their thoughts turned into another direction, he put them into the boat, where, before long, they were sorely bestead in contending with a terrible storm, while he himself ascended the mountain to find the rest he needed, in fellowship with his Father.

The great lesson of this miracle—the spiritual truth of which it furnishes a material symbol—is that which the

Lord himself founded on it, when in the discourse which immediately follows the account of it in John's gospel he said, " I am the bread of life."   To the longings of men's souls, he is what this bread furnished by him was to the multitude.   He meets our spiritual need as these loaves and fishes met their hunger.   Not only so, as that bread was sufficient for all who reclined that day upon the grass at Butaiha, so there is in Christ that which is adequate for the salvation of all.   " In our Father's house there is bread enough and to spare."   O, poor prodigal, whose soul is starving on the husks of this world's provender, dost thou hear that ?   Arise, and go to thy Father's house.   Betake thyself to Christ, for " his flesh is meat indeed, and his blood is drink indeed."

But while this is the great lesson of this wonderful work, there are other, as we may call them, subsidiary and subordinate practical suggestions rising out of the narrative which must not be overlooked.

First of all, we have here contrasted two methods of dealing with a difficulty.   That proposed by the disciples, as related in the first three gospels, is that the multitude should be sent away ; but that suggested by the Lord was " give ye them to eat."   They were for removing out of sight those whose presence caused the emergency; he was for grappling with and overcoming the difficulty with the means at their disposal.   Now, if you care to think it out, you will find that the same contrast exists still alike in the world and in the church, with this difference, that both methods are now tried, whereas here only that of Christ was put to the test.   If a son in the family has caused unusual trouble ; if his deeds have brought some kind of disgrace upon the household ; if the question, how shall we get him to a proper sense of the importance and significance of life ? is constantly coming up before his parents, then is proposed the favorite expedient, " Send him away. Let him go out west, and struggle for himself." But the wiser and more Christian way is to keep him at home ; to give more thought, and prayer, and care to his treatment; to draw him more closely into the household, to let him see more of parental love, and to give him more personal attention. His wayward- ness ought to be to his parents a reason for bringing him nearer them, and not for sending him away from them. You do not solve a difficulty by ignoring it ; you do not help your son by putting him out of your sight, you simply repudiate your own responsibility, and that can end only in disaster. See what comes out of it on a larger scale, with questions which this nation and age have still in some degree to settle. We have the In- dians on our hands, and how often has the cry been raised regarding them, " send them away " ? They have been pushed back and back across the continent. We place them on what we call reservations, but, in reality, there is nothing reserved about them, and ever as white men covet their lands, either for their fertility on the surface, or for their mineral wealth, they have been sent away to make room for the Ahabs who have coveted their territory. Then how did we treat the negroes ? The only plan tried, in the days of slavery, for the miti- gation of their condition was that of African colonization, and men said, " Send them away, back to Africa." But it did not work, and for the selfishness that could devise no more thorough way of grappling with the problem there came the penalty, in the shape of a terrible civil war, which solved it for the time. Now we have the Chinese, who have broken in upon our self-complacency; and the problem presented has been what shall we do with them ? " Send them away," say many, even among the disciples of Christ. " Let them go back to their own land; or, since that would be, perhaps, retaliated, by the sending home of all the Americans in China, let no more Mongolians land upon our shores." Now over against that comes Christ's method of dealing with all such questions : " They need not depart, give ye them to eat." My brethren, how far-reaching is the principle beneath this contrast! And how it rebukes the ostrich-method of meeting all social problems, by shutting them out of our sight, and going on as if they were not in existence. We have the means of meeting them, aye, and of solving them, too, by evangelizing the people as a whole, and though there be many among us who say, like Andrew, " What is that among so many ? " Christ will hold us to our responsibility, and pointing us to cases in the history of the past, in which that very gospel was more than sufficient to meet the need, will send upon us, in some terrible form, a Nemesis, for our neglect to use it for the purpose. It is never necessary to send men away from him, but it is the bringing of men to him which alone can fit them, no matter what their color or their nationality, for becoming good, useful, peaceable citizens on earth, and for entering upon the freedom of the New Jerusalem on high.

But here, in the second place, comes in a lesson of faith. Whenever in the history of the church anything great or noble was to be done, Andrew has been there with his question, " what are they among so many ? " It was so in the days when Zerubbabel was rebuilding the Temple, and Nehemiah the walls of Jerusalem. It was so in the beginning of the gospel, when the fishermen went forth to preach it unto all nations. It was so when Luther started out in his Reformation work. It was so when Carey commenced his crusade for foreign missions, a hundred years ago. It is natural, it is common to "despise the day of small things," but if these small things are put into the hands of Christ, and blessed by him, he will make them great. So let no one be discouraged because he cannot do much, or allow himself to be laughed out of his efforts with the little that he has, but let each of us do his utmost, and, whether that be great or small, let us put it into the hands of Christ, for he will multiply it for the meeting of the emergency.

Finally, we have here an example of frugality. The Lord said, "Gather up the fragments that remain that nothing be lost." Jesus will not work a miracle and let the bread be wasted. The fragments were more than the original feast, for benevolence gains more than it gives. But it could not do that if it were not accompanied by frugality. These two graces—for frugality in its right place is a grace—ought always to go together. We should be frugal that we may be able to be liberal in our benevolence. There is no need of parsimony, and avarice is abominable in the sight alike of God and man. The miser answers to the meaning of his name, and is one of the most wretched of human beings. But the waster, get what he may, never sees the time when he can afford to give ; while he who gathers up the fragments has always something which he can lay upon God's altar. I have been in a room in a bookbindery, where the gold dust extracted from the sweepings of the floor, amounted to some thousands of dollars annually, and the saving of these enabled the principals of the establishment, to give more to the cause of Christ than otherwise would have been the case. Nay, more, even from such giving as we see here, there is a large return. We must not give to get that kind of return—but when we give from the right motive, there will be a recompense, if we will only be careful enough to gather it up; and when we do so, we shall have more than ever to give for God's glory in the welfare of our fellowmen. " There is that scattereth and yet increaseth; there is that withholdeth more than is meet, and it tendeth to poverty."

XX.

CHRIST WALKING UPON THE WATERS.

Matt. xiv. 22-33.   Mark vi. 45-53.   John vi. 15-21.

THE circumstances immediately preceding the miracle
of the walking on the waters have been sufficiently set
forth in the preceding discourse, and need not be re-
counted here.   The feeding of the multitudes had roused
them to such a pitch of enthusiasm that they were for
taking Jesus by force and making him a king.   But in
seeking to act on this impulse they were adopting a
thoroughly false idea of the royalty of the Messiah.
They thought that the deliverer of whom their prophets
had spoken was to be a temporal potentate, and that,
gathering earthly followers around him, he would break
the yoke of the Roman oppression, set up his throne in
Jerusalem, and distribute among his adherents the re-
wards of place and preferment.   But of a kingdom
founded upon truth and love, or of a royalty over the
hearts, and consciences, and lives of men, they had not
even the faintest conception.   In seeking, therefore, to
make Christ a king after their pattern, so far from con-
ferring honor upon him, they were doing their best to
wreck the cause of which he was the head.   They were
repeating, only in their own way, and in a sense, too,
with a desire to advance his cause, the temptation which
282

Satan had set before him on the mountain, when he offered him the crown without the cross ; therefore, for his own sake, as well as for theirs, " he sent the multitudes away."

But the disciples, just at this stage in their development, were more in sympathy with the crowd than with their Master in this matter. They also longed to see him a king, as the request of James and John, presented through their mother, and the question put by them to their Lord, just before his ascension, fully prove. It was dangerous, therefore, to let them remain in the company of the multitudes while this frenzy was upon them, and something had to be done with them also, to take their minds entirely from the proposal of the people. Accordingly, the Lord " constrained them to get into a boat, and go before him unto the other side." They were unwilling to go, as, in the circumstances just explained, was perfectly natural, and he had to use a kind of force to get them to depart. And as soon as he had prevailed on them to go, and had dismissed the crowd whom he had so recently fed, he went up alone to the mountain, to find rest and solace for himself in fellowship with his Father.

While he was thus engaged one of those sudden and furious storms to which the Lake of Tiberias, as we have before seen, is liable, came down upon them, so that even strong rowers, as the fishermen apostles were, had to strain themselves to the utmost, and even after nine hours' toil they had made no more than five and twenty or thirty furlongs. At length, as the dawn was approaching, in the fourth watch of the night, they beheld one moving majestically toward them, " walking on the sea." The sight, however, only aggravated their misery, for, with the superstition of their times strong within

them, they supposed it was a phantom rrom the
spirit world, and cried out for fear, saying, " It is a
ghost." But immediately the mysterious One, who had
up till this moment seemed as if he was going past them,
and who was indeed their Lord himself, spoke to them,
and said, " Be of good cheer, it is I, be not afraid."
Upon this the ardent and impulsive Peter made response,
" Lord, if it be thou, bid me come unto thee on the
water." Nor were these words of doubt, as if he hesitated whether, after all, it was the Master himself.
Rather they were an utterance of impulsive faith, as if
he had said, " Since it is indeed thyself, let me be
sharer with thee in the calm self-poise which can move
thus, unaffected by the storm around thee, and unsub-
merged by the waves beneath thee." He spoke not in
forwardness, merely, as some would have us believe, but
in faith, quickened by affection, though deficient in depth,
and therefore the Lord said unto him, " Come." And
" when Peter was come out of the boat, he walked on
the water to go to Jesus." So, for a time all was well.
But, by-and-by, seeing the boisterousness of the wind,
he began to be afraid, and as he feared he began to sink,
and cried, " Lord, save me ! " And the appeal was not
in vain, for immediately Jesus stretched forth his hand
and caught him, and said unto him, " O thou of little
faith, wherefore didst thou doubt." Then when this
singular episode was over, Jesus went into the boat with
his fellowers ; the wind ceased, they reached the land
immediately, and they that had been in the boat came
and worshipped the Lord, saying, " Of a truth thou art
the Son of God."

Such is the marvellous story told with utmost simplicity in the gospel narratives. But as considerable difficulty has been felt by many in reconciling the accounts

given by the three Evangelists of the directions, given, or supposed to be given, by our Lord, and in making the entire narratives accord with the topography of the region, I may quote here the explanation made by Dr. Wm. M. Thomson : "According to John (vi. 17) the disciples went over the lake toward Capernaum; while Mark says that Jesus constrained them to go to the other side before unto Bethsaida. Looking back from this point at the southeastern end of Butaiha, I see no difficulty in these statements. The case was this, I suppose : As the evening was coming on, Jesus commanded the disciples to return home to Capernaum, while he sent the people away. They were reluctant to go, and leave him alone in that desert place, probably remonstrated against his exposing himself to the coming storm, and the cold night air, and reminded him that he would have many miles to walk round the head of the lake, and must cross the Jordan at Bethsaida, before he could reach home. To quiet their minds, he may have told them to go on before toward Bethsaida, while he dismissed the crowd, promising to join them in the night, which he intended to do, and actually did, though in a manner different from what they expected. Still they were reluctant to leave him, and had to be constrained to set sail. In this state of anxiety they endeavored to keep near the shore, between this and Bethsaida, hoping, no doubt, to take in their beloved Master, at some point along the coast. But a violent wind beat off the boat, so that they were not able to make Bethsaida, nor even Capernaum, but were driven past both, and when near the plain of Gennesaret, at the northwest corner of the lake, Jesus came unto them walking upon the sea. All this is topographically natural, and easy to be understood on the supposition that the miracle took place on this spot, that Bethsaida was at the mouth of the Jordan, and Capernaum at Tell Hûm. Nor is there need of the marginal rendering in our Bible, ' over against Bethsaida.' The disciples would naturally sail toward Bethsaida to reach Tell Hûm. Neither is there any thing inconsistent with the statement of John,* that ' the people took ship the next day, and came to Capernaum, seeking for Jesus.' They came from the southeast, where the miracle had been wrought, and would naturally seek him in Capernaum, for that was his home, but it seems they did not find him there, for John immediately adds, ' When they had found him, *on the other side of the sea.*' A very singular mode of expression if they found him in Capernaum itself, but perfectly natural on the supposition that they had *to go on* to the plain of Gennesaret, where he landed. They would probably find him somewhere about Ain-et-Tîny, near which, I presume, the party reached the shore from their wonderful sail. But if it should appear to any one more probable that the people actually found Jesus in Capernaum, this might easily be, for Capernaum was not more than an hour's walk from the corner of Gennesaret, and he could easily have returned home, for they reached the shore very early in the morning. I, however, have very little doubt, but that the people had to pass on from Tell Hûm to Ain-et-Tîny to find him whom they sought." He adds, " It follows, of course, from this explanation, that Capernaum was itself *not in Gennesaret,* and I must add, that neither Matthew, Mark, Luke nor John locates it in that plain, nor does Josephus, nor any other ancient author. It is carried thither and anchored there by a modern theory which, I think, is a mistake."

* John vi. 24.
† "The Land and the Book," English edition, pp. 372-373.

But passing from all such topics, let us endeavor now to find some of the spiritual lessons which this narrative was designed to teach. And foremost among these I place the fact that God may send trials upon us simply to take us out of the way of temptation. Our afflictions are not merely chastisements to mark the divine displeasure at sins of which we have been guilty, or restoratives to bring us back to the life from which we have partially strayed, but they are frequently also preventives, and come to occupy our attention and engage our energies so that some temptation which we were courting or coquetting with may be neutralized and counteracted. Christ sent these disciples into the boat to contend with the storm, just to keep them from being carried away by the foolish project of the multitude. So when we are bent on something which will endanger our spirituality, God may send upon us a serious affliction simply to take us out of harm's way. Can we not look back on many occasions in our own history when it was so with us? The world was too much with us; we were becoming enamored of its pleasures and pursuits; we were just on the outer rim of the vortex, and were beginning to feel the fatal in-draught of the whirlpool, wherein many have been engulfed, when lo! a beloved child was stricken with dangerous illness, or our business became dreadfully involved, or we were made the target at which the unscrupulous and the vicious shot the arrows of their scorn, and by the pressure of the terrible calamity we were delivered from the spell by which we were so nearly beguiled. Let us be thankful, brethren, that the ordering of our lives is in the hand of One who sees the end from the beginning, and who makes our very buffeting with the billows of trial the means of holding us back from folly, and of delivering us from the influence of evil.

But, as a second lesson here, we may learn that God may use affliction to prepare us for higher service in the future. Look again at these disciples. Up till this time they had been in visible companionship with the Lord, from the hour when they had been called to follow him, with but the exception of that preaching tour from which they had so recently returned. But he was not to be with them thus all through their lives. The day was coming when he would be crucified, and though, after his crucifixion and burial, he would rise from the dead, yet that was to be followed by his ascension into glory, after which he would no more be with them in the body. It was needful, therefore, that before that time arrived, they should have some experience of what it was to be absent from him, and in this night upon the deep, when " it was now dark and Jesus was not with them," they had what I may call a rehearsal, in symbol of some of the difficulties with which they would have to contend, after he was taken up into heaven. He withdrew to the mountain to give them a foretaste of what should come after he had ascended into glory; and I have a firm conviction that much of that persistence in the face of opposition, which so strongly impresses us in them as we read the early chapters of the Acts of the Apostles, had its root in their remembrance of what they had learned in this night's contendings with contrary wind on the Galilean lake. If the child is never allowed to be off its mother's lap, it will never learn to walk, and so, the mother, while lovingly keeping watch over it, sets it frequently down, and leaves it to itself. This was one of the first experiments made by the disciples in walking alone, and the remembrance of it helped to steady them afterwards.

Now it is quite similar with many believers yet. Our

encounters with early difficulties fit us for later service.
Take such a case as that of Thomas Guthrie, and you will
see that those five years of waiting between the obtaining
of his license to preach the gospel and his securing of a
parish, which seemed to him at the time to indicate that
he had mistaken his profession, were, as he afterwards
declared, among the most useful to him of all his early life ;
for, during the first, he " walked the hospitals " in Paris,
and so fitted himself for work in the dens of the Edinburgh cowgate, and during the rest, he conducted a bank
in his native town, and so familiarized himself with business, that he could speak intelligently and wisely to men
of every occupation and of all ranks. And the same is
true of many other men. The very necessity of rowing
against the wind develops new strength, and brings latent
resources into play. It is questionable if John Kitto would
ever have been an author had it not been for his deafness ;
and so much have difficulties to do with the development
of character and the attainment of a sphere of exalted
usefulness in the church or the world that we may assert
the truth of the apparent paradox, that the greatest of
all misfortunes which can befall a youth is to have nothing but good fortune. It may help to nerve us against
despondency, therefore, to know that under God's wise
and loving Providence our present trials, if rightly borne,
are the prophecies of future eminence.

But, in the third place, we may learn that during all
our trials the Lord is closely watching us and earnestly
praying for us. Mark informs us that from his station
on the mountain, Jesus saw his followers " toiling in rowing." If they had known that, it would have put new
heart into them, for they would have felt sure that no
real harm would be suffered to come to them beneath his
eye, and they would have been convinced that whenever

he saw it to be necessary, he would come to their relief.
But precisely that this narrative teaches us. It tells us
that though Jesus is unseen by us, he is still looking
down with interest upon us; that he is making intercession for us within the veil, and that in some way, and at
the right time, he will come to succor us. The Church
of Christ, as a whole, has often been like that little boat
on the stormy Lake of Gennesaret; but her Lord's
prayers for her in the heavenly temple have prevailed
on her behalf. And for individual martyrs, confessors,
reformers, and less known believers, his intercession has
had such power that amid the fiercest antagonism of un-
godly men, they have been enabled to possess their souls
in patience. I fear that we, in these days, make all too
little of the intercession of Christ on our behalf. Have
we not too largely forgotten the assurance that "he ever
liveth to make intercession for us"? We are apt to
imagine that, as on earth, the man who would intercede
for a multitude must make his petitions so general that
they do not descend to the individual wants of each,—so
it must be also with the intercession of our great High
Priest. But that is a mistake, for the omniscience of
his Deity makes him acquainted with our deepest necessities, and the sympathy of his humanity disposes him to
plead on our behalf. Is any among you afflicted?
Then let him remember that "we have an advocate with
the Father, Jesus Christ, the righteous," and let the
consciousness that he is interceding for him fill his heart
with that peace "which passeth all understanding."

In the fourth place, let us learn from this narrative
that in his own good time Christ will give us deliverance
out of our trials. Mark how he brought them all safely
to land here, and learn thereby some of the features of
his loving kindness. He did not come so soon as the

storm burst upon them. But he let the night wear on until the fourth watch before he went to their relief. So our rescue has not always come at the moment when the peril appeared. The Lord has left us to ourselves, that we may test our strength and discover our weakness. He has waited till the object of his discipline has been accomplished in us and then he approached us with his help.

Again the Lord came to these disciples over the very waves which constituted their trial. So he often makes the very affliction by which we are distressed his pathway into our hearts. No one else can do that. For in every one of our trials there are elements which we must keep concealed from our fellowmen. But these are altogether well known to Christ, and it is most especially through these secret, and, as one might call them, underground passages, that he enters into our souls and brings with him his comfort and support. What comfort there is for us in the knowledge of this fact! The Lord makes our trial his avenue into our hearts. It is rough to us, but it is smooth to him, and we may well put up with the roughness, if he makes it subservient to our good.

Still farther, the disciples did not know Christ when he came, and aggravated their distress for themselves by supposing that it was an " apparition." * But let us not laugh at their superstition. Have we never mistaken Christ for a ghost? or even for something worse? We have been in trouble, and matters, as we think, have come to a crisis, when something happens which, at first, we judge, will surely consummate our ruin, and we cry out for fear: " We are undone! The Lord hath forsaken us! we are utterly overwhelmed!" But we wait a little; and, wonderful to tell, we come to see that what at first

* Revised_Version.

seemed our undoing has actually become our salvation. Such an experience, I am sure, is not unknown to you. And as you heard the Master's voice saying to you, "It is I, be not afraid," have you not had your fears put to shame, and reproved by his favor? Brethren, this night scene on the Galilean lake is the similitude of much that is happening every day to the people of God; and if we studied it more closely we should know more than we have ever done of the ways of providence. "Whoso is wise and will observe these things, even they shall understand the loving kindness of the Lord."

Once more, when Christ comes and is recognized, he brings relief. The very recognition of him is a relief; for there is no real distress, and no formidable danger to the Christian while his Lord is near. His presence may not immediately still the tempest, but it will enable us to walk upon the waves, for he who sees Jesus in his troubles, always keeps them under him. It is when the Christian fails to keep his eye upon the Lord, that he begins to sink under them. Yet even then there is help at hand, if he will but call for it, as Peter did, when he exclaimed, " Lord, save me, I perish." O thou afflicted and tossed with tempest, but not comforted, take to thy heart this word of comfort. He who " stilled the rolling waves of Galilee," can hush into peace the storm that is howling around thee. Make thy prayer then to him, for he has said, " Call upon me in the day of trouble. I will deliver thee, and thou shalt glorify me."

I have said nothing thus far of the episode in which Peter played so conspicuous a part, because I wished to set clearly and uninterruptedly before you the lessons to be learned from the main narrative, and because the appended story belongs rather to the life of Peter, than to a series of discourses on the miracles of our Lord. But

I cannot conclude without asking you to observe how thoroughly in keeping the conduct of the Apostle in this instance was with all that, we know of his character from other sources. He was impulsive, sometimes even rash, always the foremost. He never took time to count the cost before entering upon any course of action. The consequence was that while he was frequently ahead of all the others in his protestations of faith in Christ and attachment unto him, these occasions were often followed by great reactions, in which he fell as far below his brethren, as before he had risen above them. Thus, after his noble confession of faith in the Messiahship of Jesus, which was so heartily commended by the Lord, he almost immediately drew down upon himself the rebuke, " Get thee behind me, Satan, for thou savorest not the things that be of God, but the things that be of men." And again, at the washing of the disciples' feet, he went from the one extreme of emotion that exclaimed, "Lord, thou shalt never wash my feet, " to the very opposite, which cried out, "Not my feet only, but my hands and my head." This was in fact, at this time, the leading feature of his character, and I cannot but think that when he asked the Saviour to bid him come to him on the water, his request was granted in order that he might have a revelation of himself made to him, if haply he might be put upon his guard against the disposition which so nearly caused his utter undoing when he denied his Lord. His request here corresponds to his profession then, " Though all men shall be offended because of thee, yet will I never be offended." His beginning to sink into the waters here corresponds to his denial then. And the help here given him by the Lord is analogous to the loving look which then the Saviour turned upon him, and to his formal restoration on the afternoon of the first Easter day, and his full and final reinstatement on the shore of the Sea of Galilee.

Thus this experience was a warning to him, if he had but heeded it, of the dangers that lurked in his impulsiveness and self-confidence, while at the same time it assured him that if he would but cry to Jesus in his time of peril, the Lord would not suffer him to sink into perdition.   He who, even at the bidding, or by the permission, of Christ essays to walk upon the waters, has need of strong faith in him, and constant contemplation of him; and it is better to remain in humble self-distrust in the boat, than, without these, to seek permission to walk upon the waves and sink.   Let us all take this warning to ourselves ; and if at this moment, in consequence of our rashness, we are sinking in some troubled sea, let us cry out in earnestness, " Lord, save me, I perish, " in the sure confidence that he will give deliverance.

XXI.

THE SYRO-PHŒNICIAN WOMAN.

Matt. xv. 21-28.   Mark vii. 24-30.

THIS miracle, in the order of time, came shortly after the feeding of the five thousand on the shore of the Lake of Tiberias, and it was wrought by our Saviour while he was in the region which bordered on the territory of Tyre and Sidon, to which he had retired for a season.

Matters had come to a critical point in his Galilean ministry. Herod, the murderer of John the Baptist, had heard of him, and was beginning to inquire after him, presumably with no good intention.* The great mass of the people, dazzled by the splendor of his miracles, and hoping for the restoration of Israel, by his instrumentality, to its ancient independence among the nations, were for taking him by force and making him a king; † and even his own disciples had shown that they were not proof against the influence of that seductive delusion. The Pharisees and Scribes, writhing under his withering exposure of the hypocritical casuistry by which they explained away the plainest precepts of the word of God, were seeking an occasion for his destruction. For these reasons, therefore, as well as that he might secure some

* Matt. xiv. 1-12.   † John vi. 15.

much needed rest, it probably was that he betook himself at this time to the extreme northwestern boundary
of the land, where it touched the edge of Phœnicia.   In
any case, it was plainly his design to seek retirement,
for Mark tells us that "he entered into an house, and would
have no man know it," but even as the sun always reveals
—cannot but reveal, his presence by the light he brings,
—so the Lord Jesus " could not be hid."   There was that
about his character, appearance, and work, which, go
where he would, attracted attention and recognition, and
drew toward him all who were in distress.

Among these was a woman, belonging to the old
Canaanitish race, and living just over the boundary of
the land of promise, who came into the house and made
a very earnest application to him for help.   Her daughter was a victim of demoniacal possession.   As the words
in Matthew may be literally rendered, she was " badly
demonized," and her mother sought a cure for her.   She
had heard the report of his wonderful works of healing,
and, living just over the frontier of the land of Israel,
she had obtained some knowledge of those ancient prophecies on which the Jews founded their faith that a
Messiah was to come; so she addressed him as the Son
of David, stated her case, and besought his mercy.
But she was received with a silence that was apparently
cold and repulsive, for " He answered her not a word."
Nay, as if to finish the colloquy at once, it would seem,
from Matthew's narrative, that he arose, and left the house.
But she was not thus to be shaken off, for she followed
him with her entreaties, which were so loud and earnest
that the disciples were annoyed with her importunity,
and said to him, " Send her away, for she crieth after
us."   To this he replied, " I am not sent but unto the
lost sheep of the house of Israel."   That might have

appeared to her to be the death-blow to her hopes; yet it only increased her earnestness, for now she went and fell at his feet, and worshipped him, saying, "Lord, help me." And then, for the first time, he directly addressed her, but it was in a style entirely unusual with him, and one would have thought excessively discouraging to her, for he said, "Let the children first be filled; for it is not meet to take the children's bread and cast it unto the dogs."

The "children" are, of course, the Jews, and the "dogs" are the Gentiles, whom the chosen people frequently called by that name, just as a Christian in Syria to-day is often by Mohammedans styled contemptuously a "Christian dog." Surely this was a mode of speech well calculated to destroy all hope in the woman's heart. It seemed nothing short of a refusal, given too in somewhat of an offensive way, but she was determined not to be repulsed, and so she made reply, "Truth, Lord, yet the dogs under the table eat of the children's crumbs." This was much as if she had said, "I know that I have not the claims of the children, and I do not ask to sit at the table with them; that which I request, so great is thy power and goodness, is but to thee as a crumb fallen from one of the children's hands as he eats his bread, and even the little dogs beneath the table may eat that unhindered." Thus out of what seemed a rebuff, she drew a plea, and so revealed the strength of her faith as to evoke this eulogy from the lips of Christ, "O woman, great is thy faith; be it unto thee, even as thou wilt, for this saying go thy way: the demon is gone out of thy daughter," and when she reached her home, she found her loved one healed, and lying on the bed, as if at rest after the tumult that had so long raged within her.

It is a touching narrative, yet not without its difficulties,

and among these the most formidable is in the question,
Why did the Lord deal with this woman in this singular
manner ?   Now, of course it is impossible for us to answer that inquiry with any assurance of accuracy, but
it may be profitable for us to suggest one or two reasons
which might perhaps have moved the Saviour to take
the course which he adopted.   Dr. Edersheim, in his very
admirable work entitled " The Life and Times of Jesus
the Messiah, " has adopted the view that our Lord at the
outset, under the conviction that he was not sent but to
the lost sheep of the house of Israel, had not the purpose
of granting the Gentile woman's request, and that this
accounts for his silence on her first application.   He
thinks also that this explains both his answer to the disciples, and his reply to the woman when he said that it
was not becoming to take the children's bread and to cast
it to dogs; and he alleges that it was only when the faith
of the woman proving that she was a spiritual daughter of
Abraham, and already at the table, showed itself, that
he yielded to her entreaty.   But I cannot adopt this hypothesis, not only because, as appears from many other
portions of the gospels, he knew what was in the hearts
of those who came to him,* and also what he was about
to do for them ; but also because on the supposition
that this is the true explanation it is difficult if not impossible to find in it any such analogy to his dealing with
the sinner in the matter of his salvation, as is to be
sought for in the narrative of every one of his miracles.

We must therefore look elsewhere for an answer to the
question which we have just proposed, and we find part
of it, I think, in his desire at once to benefit the woman
herself, and to prepare his disciples for their work in after
days among the Gentiles.   As regards the woman, the

----

* See John ii. 24-25 ; vi. 6.

course adopted by the Lord, was well fitted to test her faith. He would prove whether she were really as earnest as she seemed to be, and so he made as though he would refuse her ; just as when the disciples were in the boat " toiling in rowing, " and he walking on the sea, he made as though he would have passed them by,* and as again at Emmaus, on the day of his resurrection, after his walk with the two disciples, " he made as though he would have gone further." † Had the woman failed to stand this trial, in all probability she would have gone unblessed. The Lord tests his people by his treatment of their prayers. His delays to grant their requests are drops of acid which prove whether or not they are of genuine gold ; and if we more frequently remembered that we would both feel and speak very differently on the subject of delayed answers to our supplications. The spirit that wonders at such delays, or complains about them, is not yet ready to receive the blessings which it has asked, for true faith holds on through the delay and simply renews its plea.

It is but an extension of the principle that underlies these remarks to say that our Lord wished to *strengthen* the faith which he saw this woman already had. It was much that, Gentile as she was, she had come to him as the Son of David, and now that she had come, he would lead her up to something higher. Therefore, he began by treating her with apparent indifference. Do you marvel ? Is it not always the case that resistance is necessary for the development of strength. This is true physically, as every athlete knows, but it is equally true spiritually. Difficulty, in every brave heart only stiffens resolution, and braces the soul for greater effort, and where true faith is, it is, within certain limits indeed, but

* **Mark vi. 48.**   † **Luke xxiv. 28.**

yet it is really strengthened by trial. Abraham would never have been able to offer up Isaac, if it had not been for the long process of education through which God had led him up to the supreme moment of his life. Now seeing the reality of this Syro-Phœnician's faith the Lord took means to make it stronger. You may observe the same thing often still. A man sets his heart upon some object. He prays for it. He labors for it. But he does not obtain it. Yet he does not give up either hope or effort. He works on in faith and patience and perseverance, and meanwhile, through these, he gets a character well-knitted, having as its constituent elements, piety, steadfastness, integrity and humility, and then when it has become safe for him to get what he desired, that also is bestowed upon him. How many there are among us, who have to confess that it has been good for us that the Lord caused us to wait for the blessing for which we asked long ago, because in the interval he gave us, through the discipline of delay, that without which the blessing might have proved to be a curse.

Still farther, the delay to answer this woman's prayer might be intended as an encouragement to others. The Lord, it may be, sought hereby to warn his people generally against putting a false construction on his treatment of them, when he seems to turn their entreaties away from him. At any rate, every reader of the narrative feels that it teaches him " to pray and not to faint." We may have long to wait, but we may be sure that we shall not have to wait in vain. I say not, indeed, that we shall always receive the precise thing which we asked for, so far at least as temporal blessings are concerned. He has given us no unconditional promise to that effect, but the prayer will be answered in some way : by the appearance of the strengthening angel, if not by the removal of the cup; by the reception of grace sufficient for us, if not by the extraction of the thorn. Let us, therefore, not be dismayed, or cast into despair, by delays in answer to our prayers, but let us maintain the firm persuasion that "true prayers never come weeping home," and that we shall always have either that which we have asked, or that which we would have asked, could we have seen, as God saw, what was best for us.

Thus far we have been dealing with the question in its relation to the woman and other believers through her. But there is another side to the subject. Some of Christ's words in this section, while spoken *to* the disciples, were, if I may use the expression, spoken *at* the woman, but I have a strong conviction that the whole colloquy that is here recorded was also meant to be a lesson to the disciples themselves, whereby they might unlearn their pride of race and be prepared for going forth at a later day beyond the boundary of the promised land, and preaching the gospel to Gentiles of every name and nation. It was true that our Lord's personal ministry was formally restricted to the lost sheep of the house of Israel. It had to be localized somewhere, else it never would have gathered sufficient head to be of any service to humanity. But while that was the case, he was careful to let it be known that his ultimate mission was to men as men. In the Synagogue of Nazareth he roused the indignation of his townsmen by giving prominence to the instances in which Elijah and Elisha had been sent to Gentiles. He did not hesitate to preach to the Samaritan woman and the men of her city, and in the present instance he healed the daughter of a Gentile. All these were preludes and anticipations of the blessing which was eventually to come upon the nations generally through his gospel. As yet, however, his disciples were very far

from either apprehending or approving of such a making
of the Gentiles fellow-heirs of the promises with themselves.   They were Jews, and therefore proud of their
own nationality, and jealous of all others.   What the
Pharisees were among the Jews, that the Jews were
themselves at that time among the nations.   They
" trusted in themselves that they were righteous, and despised others."   To be a child of Abraham according
to the flesh was in their estimation of far higher consequence than to be a Roman citizen, and they looked
down upon all other races as if they belonged to a lower
order.   We know how much was needed before Peter
would consent to preach to the household of Cornelius ;
and how the members of the church at Jerusalem were
stirred when they heard that he had actually done so.
We remember too how bitter the circumcision controversy was among the Christians of Antioch and the
churches in the province of Galatia.   That was long subsequent to the ascension of Christ, and the giving of the
commission to preach the gospel among all nations ; and
therefore we can easily understand that at the time to
which the narrative before us belongs, the disciples were
anything but well disposed toward Gentiles.   They
were, in fact, just like other Jews of their day, narrow,
bigoted, race-proud, and contemptuous to all Gentiles.

When, therefore they said to Christ, " Send her away,
for she crieth after us," they were not only seeking to
get rid of her importunity, but also giving expression to
their national antipathy to one who was a woman of Ca-
naan.   Had she been a Jewess, they might perhaps have
been willing to put up with her crying after them, but
as a Syro-Phœnician they had little or no interest in her,
and were eager to be rid of her.   And the Lord in what
he says to her afterwards is speaking *at* them as well as *to*

her. He is giving utterance to the thoughts which at the moment were in their hearts, and that accounts, as I believe, for the unusual harshness of his words. He is holding up a mirror to them, in order that they may see themselves, and so he took her at the estimate of the disciples, and spoke to her as they would have spoken, in order to show them, as he afterwards showed Peter, that "in every nation they that fear God and work righteousness are accepted of him." It was as if he had said, "I know that you think her a ' dog,' but see how much better she is than many of the ' children.' You have witnessed the malice of the rulers and the Pharisees toward me ; yet this Gentile has shown unparalleled faith in me. It is not blood that proves the true Abrahamic lineage, but faith, and, tried by that test, this Syro-Phœnician woman is a spiritual daughter of Abraham. If she is a Gentile in nationality, she is an Israelite in disposition, and as such she has been blessed." Thus, the Lord taught them, and teaches us through them, to put faith above nationality, and gave a reproof, all the more telling because it was incidental and indirect, to that pride of race which was a national sin among the Jews, and which, alas ! is far from being unknown even among Christians in our own day and in our own land.

But, turning from the consideration of the probable reasons for the unusual procedure of our Lord in this case, let us conclude by drawing a few lessons of practical value to ourselves from the whole subject. The first is one of encouragement to take our troubles to the Lord Jesus. This woman acted upon a verbal report which she had heard of the gracious miracles of Christ. We cannot tell from whom she had received it, and it was probably enough somewhat vague, but vague as it was, there was enough in it to stimulate her to earnestness, and to make her resolve, that, if it were possible, she would obtain from him the cure of her daughter. Now *we* know far more about Jesus than she did, and we have far stronger reasons for believing that, than she had for believing the statements regarding him which had come to her ears. We know that he to whom she made supplication then is living still, the " same Jesus " as he was when she applied to him; the same, and yet exalted far above all principalities and powers and every name that is named; for, having become obedient unto death, and having borne the sins of men upon the cross, God hath raised him from the dead, and set him at his own right hand in the heavenly places, where he wields the sceptre of universal dominion. We know that he whom she called " the Son of David " is also David's Lord, the incarnate God, at once the fellow of the Almighty and the brother of our humanity. We know that as man we can go to him in the full assurance that he will in no wise cast us out, and that as God he is not only willing, but also able to give us succor. We know that as man he sympathizes with our sorrows, and that as God he can hear our cry and send us relief. We have thus in him the accessibility of humanity united to the infinitude of Deity, and so the resources of God become in him available for us. He is a man, and therefore we can go to him without dread or terror. He is the God-man, and therefore when we get to him we find that the shield of omnipotence is our defence. To him therefore let every burdened one repair, crying like this suppliant, " Have mercy upon me : Lord, help me ; " or, like the weeping Hezekiah, " O Lord, I am oppressed ; undertake for me," and he will give perfect sympathy and effectual aid

But, in the second place, let us learn that success in prayer comes through the acceptance by us of the place into which Christ puts us. He said to this woman, "It is not meet to take the children's bread and cast it to the dogs." And she did not rebel against his words. She did not say, "I am no dog. I am as good as any Jewess of them all." Far wiser she! Accepting the place into which he put her, she asked for a blessing appropriate to that, saying, "Give me the dog's crumbs, and I am content." Now here we have a most valuable general principle for our own guidance. The first thing to do with any word of Christ is to accept it; but the next thing is to turn it to the best account in our appeal to himself, and patiently to wait the result. No good will come of repudiating, or denying, or rebelling against the statements of God's book. These have to be accepted, and our supplications have to be based on them. When he speaks to us, the first words of our answer to him should always be "Truth, Lord." And then our plea should be founded on the admission of that. I cannot better illustrate this thought than in the following words of Thomas Guthrie : "By the voice of our conscience or of his word does God say you have been a sinner? We reply, 'Truth, Lord.' There is no commandment of mine you have not broken, and no mercy of mine you have not abused. 'Truth, Lord.' You have crucified my Son. 'Truth, Lord.' You have grieved my Spirit. 'Truth, Lord.' You deserve to be cast into hell. 'Truth, Lord.' It is all true; but, God of mercy, so is this, that thou never saidst to any of the sons of men, 'seek ye my face' in vain; that thou art not willing that any man should perish; that thou hast no pleasure in the death of the wicked; that thou didst send thy Son to seek and to save the lost; that the blood of Jesus Christ cleanseth from all sin.   The woman was successful, why should not we?   We will hope in thy mercy, for is it not written, 'The Lord taketh pleasure in them that fear him, in them that hope in his mercy.'"

Finally, let us learn how inconsistent pride of race or the spirit of caste is with the gospel of Christ.   The spirit of the Pharisees lives again in those who treat with injustice and contempt the man who is "guilty of a skin not colored like his own,"—whether it be black like that of the negro, or red like that of the Indian, or brown like that of the Mongolian.   We cannot hope by legislation to secure a social status for these races.   That must be the fruit of their Christian recognition, but we may enforce legislation already in existence, like that which asserts the equality of white and black before the law; we may hope to repeal other legislation founded only on prejudice and self-interest, which prevents the Chinaman from coming among us; and we may be able to secure such a change in our treatment of Indians that we shall not need to blush for shame at every mention of their name.

This, however, will be done only when we acknowledge their manhood, and regard them as redeemed by the precious blood of Christ equally with ourselves.   What he paid such a price for, we must not despise, for all who have been so bought by him are brethren.   And there will be no color line yonder, where all are robed in white.   This is one of the topics of the times, and every one has his own suggestion for the solution of the problem.   But I see no hope of any permanent settlement of it, until these principles are recognized and white skinned Phariseeism is made to retire before the all-embracing love which the gospel of Christ both exemplifies and enjoins.

XXII.

THE FEEDING OF THE FOUR THOUSAND.

Matt. xv. 32-39. Mark viii. 1-10.

THIS miracle, in its general outlines, has so much resemblance to that of the feeding of the five thousand
with five loaves and two fishes, that some have supposed
that the narratives here and in Mark viii. 1–10, are only
echoes of those which we have formerly considered, and
all refer to the same occasion. But to this view there
are many fatal objections. The localities are different,
for the feeding of the five thousand was at the head of
the lake, near the entrance of the Jordan into it, and in
the district of Bethsaida; while the miracle now before
us was performed on the eastern shore of the lake, in the
region of the Decapolis, and at a point presumably opposite to Magdala, or Magadan. Now that has been generally identified with El-Mejdel, which is situated on the
extreme southern edge of the flowery plain of Gennesaret, and, therefore, a position opposite to that would be
on the eastern side of the lake, not far from the outlet of
the Jordan.

Again, the circumstances preceding and following in the
two cases were different. On the former occasion Christ
had crossed the lake for rest, and was followed by the
multitudes, who walked round the head of the lake upon

the shore, while at the end of the day he sent his followers away in a boat, and they encountered a furious
storm, during which he went to them, walking on the
water. On this latter he had come from the region of
Tyre and Sidon, and was already in Decapolis, and after
the miracle he crossed the lake, " entering into the
boat" along with his disciples, and there is no hint of
any storm. On the former occasion the multitudes had
been only one day in his company ; on the latter they
had been with him for three days. On the former occasion they came from the immediate neighborhood, on the
latter " divers of them " had " come from far." On the
former occasion five thousand had been fed with five
loaves and two fishes ; on the latter, four thousand were
fed with seven loaves and a few little fishes. On the
former occasion the multitudes were commanded to sit
down upon the green grass ; on the latter they were
seated " on the ground." On the former occasion there
were twelve baskets filled with fragments that remained ;
on the latter seven. On the former occasion the baskets
were κοφίνοι , the ordinary hand-baskets of the people ;
on the latter they were σφυρίδες, which were much
larger than the others, capable, indeed, of holding a
man, for it was in one of that sort that Paul was let
down over the wall of Damascus.

These considerations are of themselves sufficient to
prove that the miracles were entirely distinct. But all
possible doubt upon the subject is removed when, in
Matthew xvi. 9, 10, we read, " Do ye not yet understand, neither remember the five loaves of the five
thousand, and how many baskets ye took up ? " And in
Mark viii. 19–21, "When I brake the five loaves among
five thousand, how many baskets full of fragments took
ye up ? they say unto him, Twelve. And when the

seven loaves among four thousand, how many baskets full of fragments took ye up? And they said, Seven. And he said unto them, How is it that ye do not understand?" Now, observe here three things; first, that these records are found in the gospels of Matthew and Mark, who alone of the four make mention of and clearly intended to describe two miracles; second, that the speaker is the Lord himself, and he as clearly refers to two separate occasions; and, third, that in the Saviour's questions addressed to his followers there is the same discrimination between the names of the baskets as we find in the separate narratives of the miracles, for in referring to those employed on the first occasion the Saviour uses the term κοφίνοι, while in speaking of those employed on the second occasion he uses the word σφυρίδες. This settles the matter most conclusively, and if it should seem strange to any one that the disciples, when appealed to in the present instance, should seem to have forgotten what their Lord had done in the former, the reply is easy, that such forgetfulness is not unparalleled, since we have the same thing in the case of the Israelites under Moses, and even after the sight of both miracles here, the Lord, as we have seen, upbraids his followers for having forgotten both. For the rest we may fall back on the words of Edersheim, " The strange forgetfulness of Christ's late miracle, on the part of the disciples, and their strange repetition of the self-same question, which had once— and, as it might seem to us, for ever—been answered by wondrous deed, need not surprise us. To them the miraculous on the part of Christ must ever have been the new, or else it would have ceased to be the miraculous. Nor did they ever fully realize it till after his resurrection they understood and worshipped him as God in-

carnate.   And it is only realizing faith of that, which
it was intended gradually to evolve during Christ's ministry on earth, that enables us to apprehend the Divine
Help as, so to speak, incarnate and ever actually present
in Christ.   And yet, even thus, how often do we who
have so believed in him forget the Divine provision
which has come to us so lately, and repeat, though not,
perhaps, with the same doubt, yet with the same want
of certainty, the questions with which we had at first
met the Saviour's challenge of our faith." *

Without hesitation, therefore, we accept these narratives as the records of a miracle quite distinct from that
which we have formerly considered, and proceed to its
more particular consideration.

The Saviour was in the region of the Decapolis,
which was very largely populated by Gentiles, and a
great multitude had followed him into a desert region,
where, attracted by his discourses, they remained with
him at least over two nights, holding what might almost
be called a kind of " camp-meeting."   But on the third
day it became necessary for him to leave, and he, therefore, proposed to send the people to their homes.   This,
however, he would not do, without making provision for
their wants ; for they had been with him so long that
presumably the stock of provisions which they had
brought with them had been exhausted, and as " divers
of them " were a long way from their homes, they needed
something to sustain them on their return journey.   So,
taking his followers into his council, he said, " I have
compassion on the multitude, because they continue with
me now three days, and have nothing to eat; and I will not
send them away fasting, lest they faint in the way."   Upon

* Edersheim's "Life and Times of Jesus the Messiah," vol. ii. p.
p. 66, 67.

this they responded, not, perhaps, from any doubt of his ability to furnish what was needed, but simply to indicate the insufficiency of their own resources, " Whence should *we* have so much bread in the wilderness as to satisfy so great a multitude ? " It might even be that, after all that objectors have said on this point, there was an inarticulate reference in their words to the former occasion, as if they had said, " Lord, thou knowest, that as for us, we have no such supply as would meet the emergency." For he answered, as if entirely ignoring all that they had said, " How many loaves have ye ? " and they replied, " Seven, and a few little fishes." And he commanded the multitude to sit down on the ground. Then, taking first the loaves, he gave thanks, and brake them, and gave to the disciples, and they to the multitude. In the same manner he took the fishes, and blessed and divided them, and when the repast was finished they took up seven baskets full of fragments. Then, having thus supplied their wants, he sent the people to their homes, while he and the twelve crossed the lake to the coasts of Dalmanutha, which were, as is supposed, in the vicinity of the city of Tiberias.

Now the great lesson of this miracle, as of the former, is that which the Lord himself taught when he delivered the discourse in which he said, " I am the bread of life." Men spiritually have nothing which can quicken and support their souls; but Christ offers himself to them as the bread of life, and they are to appropriate him to themselves by believing on him. The symbolism is the same as that in the Lord's supper, which has often in the experience of his people preserved them from fainting in the way. This, as I have said, is the great teaching of the miracle. Other subordinate lessons are very largely the same as we have already illustrated in our treatment of the former narrative, but there are one or two for which there we had no place, and these may fitly enough be introduced here.

First of all, then, we have in this miracle an illustration of the thoughtful kindness of the Saviour. Mark these words, " I will not send them away fasting, lest they faint in the way." How characteristic this was of him ! The perception of a need was with him immediately followed by the prompting to meet that need. Many of them had a long way to go ; they were already exhausted by their attention to his words, and they had nothing to eat. To send them away as they were, therefore, would have been the cause of great suffering among them, and so out of his compassion for them, he miraculously supplied their wants. Now in all this we have an illustration in the material department of his dealing with his followers in spiritual matters. You remember the words of Paul, " Who goeth a warfare upon his own charges ?" When the Lord gives us a work to do, he gives us also everything that is necessary for its performance. When he lays a cross upon us, he furnishes us also with that which is to sustain us under it. When he sends us on a journey, he takes care so to supply us with his grace, that we shall not faint by the way. When Elijah was lying under the juniper tree, the angel of the Lord, twice over, prepared food for him, and let him sleep in the interval between the meals. Then he said, on the second occasion, " Arise and eat ; because the journey is too great for thee ; " so that we are not surprised to read in the next sentence, " And he arose, and did eat and drink, and went in the strength of that meat forty days and forty nights." * Similarly in modern

* I Kings xix. 5-8.

times many of Christ's disciples have gone through weeks of anxiety, or suffering, or sorrow, or privation, without fainting because of the hold which on some previous day of privilege he had given them on himself; or because of some gracious promise of which he had specially reminded them, just before their time of trial came. In his own case the glories attendant on his baptism came just before his conflict with the adversary in the wilderness; and his experiences on the Mount of Transfiguration preceded by but a short time those in Gethsemane and on the cross. And often his followers are carried safely through the darkest chapters of their history, because he had prepared them for the ordeal by special manifestations of his grace. What a kind, considerate, ever-watchful Master the Christian serves! and how perfectly acquainted he is with the circumstances and necessities of each of his people! He knows from what we have come, and into what we are going, and his compassionate heart will prompt his omnipotent hand to give us that which we need either for preparation for exertion, or revival after exhaustion.

But, in the second place, we, have here an illustration of the working of the supernatural in relation to the natural. Ordinarily God works for his people in connection with the use of their own resources by themselves. I say ordinarily, for while there are instances in which we see what may be called a positively creative act, like the new creation in regeneration, his usual way of working for his people is connected with their working for themselves, and this is foreshadowed in many of the Bible miracles. Thus he might as easily have wrought out the deliverance of his people from Egypt without Moses and his rod, as with them. It required divine power in the one case, and it would have needed no more in the other.

In the same way he might have provided for the payment of the widow's debt in Elisha's day, by some direct gift from heaven, but he chose rather to bestow his favor through the multiplication of the oil which she had already in the house. And in the case before us our Saviour, instead of literally creating out of nothing a supply of food for the four thousand, preferred to make a feast for them by using the means which were already at his disposal and multiplying them. So he said unto his followers, " How many loaves have ye ? "

Now in all this, as I cannot but think, there was intended to be an illustration of his spiritual working in and with men for their individual salvation, and for the conversion of their fellowmen in the world. Thus, take it in the case of the salvation of a man, and we find that he is saved by faith in Christ. Now faith, in a very true sense, is God's gift, but in another sense, which is equally true, it is the sinner's own act. He is depraved indeed, and ruined, yet even so he has something left. His natural powers remain, even though he is spiritually impotent. He knows what it is to believe, and through his attempt, impotent as he is, to act upon that knowledge, God gives him that after which he strives. Through the exercise of that which he has, God bestows upon him that which he has not. The paralytic had no power to rise, but he could will to attempt to do so at the bidding of Christ, and through that, he obtained ability from God to rise and walk. The supernatural thus entered into the natural, and lifted it up into a supernatural result. So in the case of the sinner the supernatural enters into his natural effort to believe in the Lord Jesus, and lifts it up to a supernatural result. His act is natural all through, but in that act and along with it God is also working all through, and the result is salvation. He works out his salvation, because God is working in him to will and to do of his good pleasure.

Take it again in the case of the efforts for the welfare of our fellowmen, to the making of which God in his word so earnestly summons us, and you will see how clearly the same thing appears. Jesus might have fed this multitude without the seven loaves, as easily as with them; but he used these loaves in order that he might show us all how, through our employment in his service of the means which are at our disposal, or,—in other words, through the putting of our efforts into his hands,— the mightiest results may be achieved. He commands us to feed the multitude of our perishing fellowmen with the bread of life, and if we wonderingly ask, " Whence should we have so much bread in the wilderness as to fill so great a multitude ? " his only reply is, " How many loaves have ye ? " Moses probably spoke truly when he said, " I am not eloquent, but I am slow of speech and of a slow tongue," for he was not likely in such a presence to say the thing that was not, but he went with that which was in his hand, and through him God spoke with a voice which has come sounding down through forty centuries for freedom, for law, for holiness and truth, and with that rod of his God broke the pride of the Egyptian monarchy. Paul probably had something about him which gave his adversaries ground for their assertion that his bodily presence was weak, and his speech contemptible; but as he was, and with what he had, he set forth on his missionary career, and was per- mitted at length to see his converts in the very palace of the Cæsars. He had a thorough knowledge of the Jew's religion, and through that and with that God wrought to emancipate Christians from the bondage of the law, and introduce them into " the glorious liberty of the children of God." The supernatural influence flowed through the channels of his natural endowments to give to the Church his matchless epistles, and to secure the introduction of the gospel into the great cities of Europe. And what was true of these two men is true also of all God's servants who have been honored to accomplish great things in his cause. They have put what they had into his hands, and he has multiplied it to meet the emergency. They have done what they could, and the result has been such as no mere human power could have accomplished. If, therefore, we wish to be made useful to our fellowmen in the highest and noblest of all senses, we must put what we have into Christ's hands, and let him do the rest. Christ is as mighty as he ever was, and what is needed on our part is that we give ourselves up as the apostles did to become the open channels of his grace. Then we shall see again as signal manifestations of his saving power, as those which gladdened the hearts of the first preachers of the cross. It is the "self" in us that is a non-conductor and arrests the current of his might, which else would flow through us in its full energy. Let us then get rid of self and be willing that Christ should have all the glory of our lives, then putting ourselves into his hands he will work in us, and through us, for the blessing of multitudes.

Finally, let us not fail to note the example which the Saviour here has left us, in the matter of giving thanks. Matthew says that after he had taken the seven loaves and the fishes, he gave thanks; and Mark tells us that first he gave thanks for the bread, and afterwards blessed the fishes. This action of his glorified God, revealed the piety of his own heart, and had its own influence on the performance of the miracle; but it is particularly significant to us as illustrating the manner in

which we should receive the good gifts of God's provi‑
dence. We are too apt to regard them, and to receive
them and partake of them, as things of course, without
feeling any emotion of gratitude for them, or giving
expression in any form to such gratitude as we may feel.

Time was when it was as common for Christians
to give thanks before meat as it was for them to
eat, and in the history of the Scottish covenant‑
ers there is a story of the discovery of a spy which is
very significant in this regard. Two or three of those
hunted men were hiding together in a cave to which day
by day a little girl was sent to them with food from the
nearest farm. A stranger, whom they had never seen
before, joined them, and they were naturally suspicious
of him, but he talked so like one of themselves that all
their misgivings were removed. After a time the little
girl came with their supplies, and with genuine polite‑
ness they helped the stranger first, when to their sur‑
prise he began to eat without giving thanks. That little
thing revealed the true character of the man. It was as
they had at first suspected. He was a spy, and they
had only time to make their escape from the dragoons
with whom he was in league. But, alas! now‑a‑days
multitudes do as he did without occasioning any surprise,
for the giving of thanks has, through our dining in res‑
taurants, hotels, on board ship, and other such places, be‑
come very largely obsolete.

Now among the followers of Christ this ought not
so to be. We ought to imitate our Saviour here, and
give thanks as we sit down to meat. The act may
not multiply our store, but it will make it sweeter,
and it will teach all who are at our table to acknowl‑
edge God in everything, because for everything we are
dependent upon him.

If I were a painter I would like to portray three scenes of Scripture history and put them into one frame. In the centre I should seek to delineate the Last Supper, catching the moment described by the Evangelist in these words, "He took bread and gave thanks," and bringing out the reverent attitude both of the Master and his disciples. Then the picture on the left should be the representation of this scene which has been before us to-night, with the multitude seated on the ground, and the Saviour and his disciples standing in the posture of devotion, while he, with the loaves in his hands, was giving thanks before them all. The picture on the right should be that of Paul on the deck of the ship that was at anchor in the storm, standing in the dim light "while the day was coming on," and at the moment when after making a comforting address to the two hundred and seventy-five people who were about him, and urging them to partake of some food, he took bread "and gave thanks to God in the presence of them all." Then I would hang the work in the dining-room that, every time the family sat down around the table, its members might be reminded of the example of the Saviour and his apostle, and how we ought always to follow it. But, alas! I cannot paint, and yet I hope that this mention of these three scenes may hang the Scripture portrayal of them in the gallery of your memories, where you may often look at them, and always as you do look at them remember the lesson which they teach.

XXIII.

THE DEMONIAC BOY.

Matt. xvii. 14-21   Mark ix. 14-29.   Luke ix. 31-42.

THE arrival of the Saviour on the scene of this miracle was almost dramatic in its timeliness. He and the three " pillar " apostles had been for the whole of the preceding night upon the mountain-top, where he had been transfigured before them, and they had enjoyed the signal privilege of listening to the conversation of Moses and Elijah with him, on " the decease which he was to accomplish at Jerusalem." But the other nine apostles had been, for at least a part of the time of their Master's absence from them, far otherwise engaged. In the early morning, while the Lord and the privileged three were descending from " the holy mount, " a poor distressed father had brought to the others his only child, suffering from a peculiarly aggravated form of demoniacal possession.

The physical symptoms minutely described both by Mark and Luke, were such as these,—severe convulsions, foaming at the mouth, grinding of the teeth, and a general rigidity of the body ; the attacks coming so unexpectedly that often he fell, in consequence of them, into the fire, and often into the water. These were complicated with deafness and dumbness, so that all communication between the sufferer and others was exceedingly difficult.

With the exception of those last mentioned, all these symptoms would describe a case of epilepsy; and no doubt, as Trench has remarked, that " was the ground on which the deeper spiritual evils of this child were superinduced: " but there is just as little doubt that there was more than epilepsy. That seems to me clear, not only from the presence of deafness and dumbness in the patient, but also from the words of the Lord when he performed the cure : " Thou dumb and deaf spirit, I command thee to come out of him." Dr. Abbott, while accepting this view of the case, however, makes a difficulty from the fact specified, that this malady had been on the youth from his childhood, " and therefore, presumptively before his own wilful transgression could have given the demon control over him." * But such an objection takes for granted that demoniacal possession was, in every case, the result of wilful transgression on the part of the person so afflicted; and that it would be difficult, if not impossible, to prove. For the rest, the difficulty which he has suggested is only an aggravated form of the same mystery which confronts us in the diseases, sufferings, and deaths of infants, and is not exclusively connected with such a case as this.

But the disciples were not asked to explain the cause of this boy's affliction—they were entreated rather for a cure ; and when they attempted to comply with the father's request, they found themselves baffled. It was a new experience for them. They were perplexed. They were humiliated. They were put to shame before the multitude that had gathered round them to look on ; and as some Scribes were there, they would most likely jeer

* Commentary, *in loco.*

and ridicule them for their failure in such a way as to put them to still greater confusion. Moreover, these malicious adversaries might even suggest that Master and disciples were alike deceivers, and that all the difference between them was, that he was more adroit in covering up his failures than they. In any case, there was an animated and perhaps not very amicable altercation going on between them, when just at the most opportune moment the Saviour appeared, and turned the attack from his followers to himself by saying, "Why question ye with them ?" that is, "If you have anything to say, say it to me, and I will answer." Thus he at once relieved the anxiety of his followers, and struck dismay into the hearts of their assailants.

But even before he had spoken, his very approach had not been without its effect, for Mark tells us that "straightway all the multitude, when they saw him were greatly amazed." Now some have sought to account for their amazement by alleging that there was probably lingering yet upon his countenance something of the glory which irradiated it when, a few hours before, he had been transfigured. But though this explanation would satisfactorily account for the wonder of the crowd, and though it seems to receive some confirmation from the fact that, after Moses had been forty days with Jehovah in Sinai, "the skin of his face shone when he came down from the Mount," yet I doubt if any outward appearance of that sort was about the Saviour here. If there had been any such thing, I think that it would have been mentioned by one or other of the Evangelists. But a special reason for the absence of any such radiance is, to my mind, furnished by the fact, that as Jesus and the three "were coming down from the mountain, he charged them that they should tell no man what things they had

seen, save when the Son of Man should have risen from
the dead." They were not to say a word to any one
about the transfiguration until after his resurrection.
Now, if there had lingered any traces of the mountain
glory about himself, that would have stimulated all who
saw them, and especially the nine who were not with
him, to inquire what had happened while they were
away, and would have made it harder for Peter, James,
and John to obey his injunction. It is not likely, therefore, that he would have commanded them to silence,
while yet there were tell-tale traces of something unusual about himself.

For that reason I prefer to explain the amazement
of the people, by his sudden arrival at such a critical
moment among them. It was almost like the confront-
ing of Ahab by Elijah, in the vineyard of Naboth,
when the time, the place, and the man combined to make
the meeting a great and disagreeable surprise to the
monarch. For here, the Master came into view in the
very nick of time—just when he was most needed by
his disciples; and when he was least wanted by the
Scribes. The coincidence, therefore, was amazing. If
it had been described in a novel, is would have been
styled improbable; but because it is fact, and not fiction,
we call it dramatic : for life is dramatic, and the surprises
which it brings, in the appearances of those who are
most needed, at the time and in the places where they
are most desired, are often at least as surprising in our
common experience as they are in the literature of ro-
mance.

In response to the question of our Lord, both the
Scribes and the multitude were silent, but the father of
the boy stood forth and told in a very plaintive and pathetic style all the facts which have come out already in

our summary of the story, saying, "Master, I brought unto thee my son, which hath a dumb spirit, and wheresoever it taketh him it dasheth him down, and he foameth and grindeth his teeth and pineth away, and I spake to thy disciples that they should cast it out, and they were not able." Whereupon the Saviour answered, "O faithless and perverse generation, how long shall I be with you? how long shall I bear with you? Bring him unto me." There has been much difference of opinion among expositors as to the question to whom these words were addressed, but I incline to think that they were intended for all who heard them. To the Scribes they were a reproof for their antagonism, to the disciples and the father of the boy they were a lamentation for their lack of faith; while from another point of view they may be regarded as an ejaculation of weariness and oppression on the part of the Saviour at having to bear so long the burden both of the perversity of his enemies, and the faithlessness of his friends. But in the command, "Bring him unto me," there was the promise of a cure. Yet at the first, it seemed as if the attempt to obey that command only produced an aggravation of the boy's affliction. An enemy is always most destructive when he is on the very point of being dislodged, and when an army is compelled to evacuate a city, the soldiers try to leave it in flames. So the demon, finding himself here about to be driven out, did all the mischief he could, for Luke tells us "as he was yet a coming, the spirit tare him," and Mark, with, as usual, more fulness, says, "straightway the spirit tare him grievously," *i. e.* convulsed him terribly, "and he fell on the ground and wallowed foaming."

It was a pitiful spectacle, and to take the poor father's eyes away from it, and help his faith to the

birth, as well as to bring out the dreadful nature of
the case before the people, and in some degree thereby
explain the failure of his disciples, he said, " How long
time is it since this has come unto him ? and he said,
From a child.   And ofttimes it hath cast him both into
fire and into the waters to destroy him; but if thou canst
do anything, have compassion on us and help us."   How
touchingly the parent here identifies himself with the
child, " have compassion on us and help us," and yet
what a great contrast between him and the leper who
said, " If thou wilt, thou canst make me clean " !   Both
were lacking in faith, but the one had no doubt of the
ability of the Saviour, and only besought his willinghood;
while the other apparently was not very sure about either,
and came rather as a peradventure.   Neither was rejected, but while the one received at once the answer,
" I will, be thou clean," the other needed to be led to
greater faith before he could receive that for which most
of all he craved.   So the Saviour said to him, " If thou
canst ! all things are possible to him that believeth."
This is the reading preferred by the Revisers, and though
it leaves the phrase somewhat difficult to interpret, it is
doubtless the correct one.   The Saviour goes back on
the man's words, and turns them upon himself.   Much as
if he had spoken thus: " If thou canst—the *if* does not
lie with me, but with thyself; there is no question about
my ability in the case, the only question is whether thou
hast faith in that ability, for ' all things are possible to
him that believeth.' "

Yet let us not misunderstand this assurance, for,
as Morison most wisely says, " The expression does
not mean in this connection, it is possible for the
believer to *do* all things, but it is possible for the believer to *get* all things.   Omnipotence is in a sense at

his disposal. But the universality of things contemplated by our Lord was *not*, as the nature of the case makes evident, the most absolute conceivable. We must descend in thought to the limited universality of things that would be of benefit to the believer. We must consider the benefit of the believer not absolutely or unconditionally, but relatively to the circumstances of the other beings with whom he is connected. With these limitations, inherent in the nature of the case, all things are possible for him that believeth."*

On receiving this answer the man replied, "Lord, I believe." He had at the moment a glimpse of the ability of Christ to help him, and yet even as he saw that, its light showed him how little his faith was, after all, and in the struggle to overcome every thing that stood in its way, he cried, "Help thou mine unbelief." Then the Lord commanded the evil spirit to come out of the child and enter no more into him, and after tearing him much, the demon left him so exhausted that he lay like one dead. Many of the onlookers, indeed, thought that he was really dead. But the Great Reviver was there; and taking him by the hand the Lord raised him up and delivered him, wholly and permanently cured, to his rejoicing father.

Then, after all was over, and they had him in the privacy of a house, the nine disciples asked him, "Why could not we cast him out ?" and he replied, "This kind can come forth by nothing but by prayer," and Matthew supplements Mark by adding, " Because of your unbelief: for verily I say unto you, If ye have faith as a grain of mustard seed, ye shall say unto this mountain, Remove hence to yonder place ; and it shall remove ; and nothing shall be impossible unto you." The Revised

* Morison on Mark, p. 250.

version omits the words, " and fasting " in both gospels, as deficient in MS. authority ; and so the substance of the Saviour's answer is, that " this kind " of demoniacal possession had in it unusual elements of difficulty ; and that they had attempted to deal with it without sufficient faith ; for even a little faith, if it were real, would enable them to do what to human view seemed as impossible as the removal of a mountain from one place to another. He wished them to understand that the power which wrought miracles, even through their instrumentality, was his power, and that therefore it was equal to every emergency. They were able to work miracles only in so far forth as they were in living union with him ; and as the bond of union between them and him was faith, they could be powerful in his service only when they really believed in him. But when their faith was real, then, though it were little, it would enable them to do what to others was impossible. One with him, they were one with omnipotence, and on that they could always draw for all things that are right and necessary for them to do. Or, as Paul put it afterwards, " they could do all things through Christ which strengthened them."

Now, like all our Saviour's other miracles of healing, this also is a spiritual parable, and, in that aspect of it, we are taught by it such truths as the following, viz. : that the soul of the sinner is in bondage to Satan, deaf to the truth of God, and dumb in the utterance of his praise ; that no mere human power can emancipate it from this terrible condition ; that what is impossible for others to do can be done through Christ ; that deliverance from this bondage to Satan may be received from Christ by any one, through the exercise of faith in him ; and that to have this faith we must pray to Christ himself, that he may help our unbelief, while at the same time we must stir ourselves up to exercise it for ourselves, so that we can say, " Lord, I believe." But, as I have already illustrated and emphasized all these from different points of view, in former discourses, I shall pass on, to draw from the whole narrative some more general lessons.

In the first place, then, we have suggested to us the contrasts of the Christian life. Raphael, in his magnificent cartoon of " The Transfiguration," has violated fact to bring out truth. He represents the conflict of the nine disciples at the foot of the hill, with the demon in the boy, and with the malice of the Scribes, as simultaneous with the glorious experience of the other three disciples on the mountain-top, and so brings both of them into view together. Obviously, this could not have been physically possible, but by taking that course he has succeeded in setting vividly before the spectator the contrast between the two. And a very striking contrast it was. On the mountain-top were the highest harmonies of earth, sublimated and glorified by their alliance for the time with the harmonies of heaven. In the valley were the wildest discords of earth, aggravated, for the time, by the addition to them of the dissonance of hell. On the mount the three were sharing by anticipation in the gladness of Christ's victory over all his enemies; in the valley the nine were suffering under the shame of a defeat. On the mountain-top the three were enjoying most exalted privileges; in the valley the nine were laboring hard in conflict with opposing forces, both earthly and diabolical. Now we have similar contrasts still. For Christian experience is neither all enjoyment nor all conflict, but it is very frequently an alternation between the two. The enjoyment prepares the spirit for the conflict; and then, the conflict over, the enjoyment comes again to restore the soul after its exertions. Peter foolishly desired to rear tabernacles on the mount. that he and his companions might abide there continually, but when he came down and saw the state of things, as between his brethren and the Scribes, it would become at once apparent to him that evil would have resulted had they tarried longer in the place of privilege, It would not be good for us to be always at the communion table, or in the sanctuary, or on the mount. We must leave such ecstasies of devotion, after a brief season, and when we do, let us look out for this demoniac boy, and seek by prayer to cast the evil spirit out of him. Nor need we go far before we meet him, for he is still among us in many forms. You may see him in the poor victim of intemperance, held captive by his appetite; or in the forlorn waif of womanhood who sells herself for bread; or in the mass of human driftwood that gathers at the corners of our streets. All these are possessed by a demon of some sort, and it is your work and mine, as the servants of Christ, to cast these demons out. Privilege such as we now and here enjoy is not meant to chloroform us into inactivity, but rather to spur us to exertion, and to refresh us after work; and if we allow it to detain us from labor, and allure us for its own sake, it will become a curse to us, and not a blessing. Therefore let us never think of building tabernacles on the mount, but, when the time of privilege is past, let us hasten away, that we may bring

"The poor and them that mourn,
The faint and over-borne,
Sin-sick and sorrow-worn—
To Christ for cure."

But, let us learn also that in the prosecution of that

work we must have Christ with us. We cannot do any good in the service of our generation without him. No doubt he is no more on the earth. We cannot have him in visible form, by our sides, as these disciples had. But though withdrawn from us in bodily presence, he may be present with us by his Spirit; and we should never try to work moral miracles on our fellow-men, by their conversion, without that Spirit. If we do, we shall most certainly fail. He who works for Christ, must work with Christ. If he lays one hand on the sinner in pleading love with him, he must keep the other in simple earnest faith in that of Christ, and so he will become the conductor of new life from Christ into him. Therefore, in every enterprise which we set on foot for the salvation of men, let us begin with prayer for the presence and the power of Christ to be manifested among us, by his Holy Spirit. "This kind goeth not out but by prayer," and so to be successful we must be prayerful.

Finally, we may learn that the beginning of deliverance for the sinner, seems often for a time only to aggravate his bondage. When Moses said to Pharaoh, "Let my people go," the first effect was that their burdens were doubled, and the straw withdrawn, so that the people cried out: We are worse than ever. And when Jesus called this boy to him, the evil spirit tare him, and seemed as if he would make an end of him. But let us not be discouraged by all that. The docile slave is petted and pampered; but he that seeks to run away is loaded with a heavier chain. Satan does not for the present very much distress those who are his willing subjects; but when they attempt to rebel, then he makes their bondage bitter. The strength of a habit is not felt when you are yielding to it; but when you try to break it off—then comes the tug of war. So it often happens,

that after a man has come to be awakened to a sense of
his sin and his need of salvation, and really and earnestly tries to turn from it to Christ; he falls back most
grievously for a season, and has perhaps the worst out-
break he has had for long—but that is only the repetition of the experience of this boy. The evil spirit
within him has become conscious of the approach of
Christ to him, and in sheer malice is seeking to undo
him. Let not the poor victim sink into despair. Christ
is stronger than the devil. Put your hand in that of the
Saviour, and there is no power in earth or hell that will
be able to pluck you out of it; for your safety depends,
not so much on your hold of him, as on his hold of you.

XXIV.

THE COIN FOUND IN THE FISH.

Matt. xvii. 24-27.

AFTER the healing of the demoniac boy, at the foot
of the Mount of Transfiguration, our Lord returned from
the neighborhood of Cæsarea Philippi, to his Galilean
home in Capernaum. While there, his disciple, Peter,
being met, as it would seem casually, by the collectors
of the temple dues, was asked, in a way altogether re-
spectful and considerate, whether his Master paid this religious rate, and replied without any hesitation in the
affirmative. I have called this assessment a religious
rate, for such indeed it was, and we shall totally misunderstand the significance, both of the miracle which we
are about to consider, and of the Saviour's conversation
with Peter concerning it, if we fail to keep that in remembrance. It is quite unfortunate, therefore, that
King James' translators here should have rendered the
original word, which is the name of a coin, by the term
tribute, which among us denotes a civil tax imposed by
the government of a nation for purely civil purposes.

The history of the matter is briefly this. At every time
of taking the census among the Jews, each person
enumerated was expected to pay half a shekel, according

to the statute contained in Exodus xxx. 11–16, which reads
as follows: " When thou takest the sum of the children
of Israel, after their number, then shall they give every
man a ransom for his soul unto the Lord, when thou
numberest them, that there be no plague among them,
when thou numberest them. This they shall give, every
one that passeth among them that are numbered, half a
shekel, after the shekel of the sanctuary, [a shekel is
twenty gerahs] a half shekel shall be the offering of the
Lord. Every one that passeth among them that are
numbered, from twenty years old and upward, shall give
an offering unto the Lord. The rich shall not give more,
and the poor shall not give less than half a shekel, when
they give an offering unto the Lord, to make an atonement for your souls. And thou shalt take the atonement
money of the children of Israel, and shall appoint it for
the service of the tabernacle of the congregation, that it
may be a memorial unto the children of Israel before the
Lord to make an atonement for your souls." It was
originally designed to be made only when the people
were numbered, aud was expended in the maintenance
of such sacrifices in the tabernacle, and afterwards, in the
Temple, as were offered in the name of the whole congregation of Israel. In the course of time, however, it
was made an annual impost; that is to say, it was asked
every year, while at the same time it was left optional
with each whether he paid it or not. It thus corresponded with what used to be called in England a voluntary
assessment. If one chose to pay it, he was expected to
give half a shekel; but if he declined to pay it, no legal
measures were resorted to for the purpose of compelling
him to do so.

It was paid, at first, in weighed silver; but after the
Maccabees had coined money in shekels and half-

shekels, these were used by the people. In the days
of our Lord, however, these coins had become scarce, and
the Roman didrachmon, (or double drachma) was regarded
as equivalent to the half-shekel. So the rate itself came
to be distinguished by the name of the coin, the didrachmon. Now that is the word used here by the collectors
in the question addressed by them to Peter, and the Revisers are exactly right when they translate it thus,
" Doth not your Master pay the half-shekel ? " But although the people commonly paid the collectors with the
Roman didrachmon, yet the coin itself, owing to the
symbols and images, deemed to be idolatrous, which were
stamped upon it, could not be received by the Temple
servants, and had to be changed for Jewish money at
Jerusalem. That accounts for the traffic of the money-
changers whom the Lord expelled from the Temple on
his first public visit to its courts. The didrachmon was
equivalent to about thirty cents of our money ; and as it
was a religious rate, those who collected it were not regarded with the hatred and contempt with which the
publicans, who gathered the taxes for the Romans, were
everywhere treated.

Such then was the character of the impost to which
allusion is made in this narrative ; and when Peter answered the question of the collectors, by saying that
his Master did pay it, he spoke somewhat hastily and as
one judging merely from general principles, but apparently
without any personal knowledge of the habit of the Saviour
in the matter. He supposed that as it was for religious
purposes, and as all good and reputable Jews in all parts
of the world cheerfully paid it, his Master would of course
do the same.

But when he went into the house—either his own house,
or that in which his Master statedly resided at that time—

and before he had time to tell what had just occurred between him and the collectors, the Lord anticipated him with this question : " What thinkest thou, Simon ? Of whom do the kings of the earth take custom or trib- ute ? of their own children, or of strangers ? " By " custom or tribute " here—for the word rendered tribute is quite different from that so translated in the preceding verse—is meant a poll tax or a tax levied on a commo- dity ; and the answer of Peter showed how well he under- stood his Lord, for he replied, " Of strangers." Then answered Jesus, " Then the children or sons are free." The monarchs of earth do not tax their own sons, but only their subjects, or those whom they have conquered in war and laid under tribute. Those who dwell in the palace and are members of his family, are exempt from the taxation which is laid on others. But the Saviour adds, " Notwithstanding, lest we should offend them," (or better as the Revisers have it, "lest we cause them to stumble"), " go thou to the sea "—that is, the Lake of Gali- lee—" and cast an hook and take up the fish that first cometh up ; and when thou hast opened his mouth thou shalt find a stater,"—a coin of which the value was four drachmas, or just equivalent to a whole shekel—" that take and give unto them for thee and me." This assessment, as if the Lord Jesus had said, " is for the Temple of Jeho- vah. But I am the Son of God, and that Temple is my Father's house (see John ii. 16) ; therefore, on the prin- ciples on which earthly monarchs exact custom or trib- ute, I should go free. Still, if I were to insist on what is my undoubted right as the Son of God, I might cause some to stumble, by giving them a wrong impression re- garding the meaning and purpose of my ministry. They might imagine that I was of opinion that no one ought to pay the Temple dues, and so be led either to reject me on that ground, or to refuse to pay these dues themselves, although they have not my right to exemption ; and in either case they would be stumbling, and I should have been in some degree the cause of their stumbling. Therefore go and find a shekel in the mouth of the fish that you shall first bring out of the lake ; then take that and give it to the collectors for you and for me."

Let it be observed that the Saviour makes a clear distinction in this last direction between Peter and himself. Peter had no right to claim exemption, but Christ had. Peter, though a child of God, was so by God's gracious adoption, even as all Christians are, and all spiritually-minded Jews who were circumcised in heart were ; but Christ was the Son of God in a sense peculiarly and inalienably his own. He was the "fellow" of the Almighty, of the same nature as God—the only begotten of the Father, equally divine, and to be equally worshipped and glorified as such. Peter, however, was only a renewed man, at an infinite distance in nature from Christ, and therefore could claim no exemption from the payment of the half-shekel on any such ground as that which his Master had advanced.

But why did Christ resort to miracle, for the means of paying this assessment ? Some have answered, because of his poverty. But if that were so, this would have been the working of a miracle for his own advantage, and that, as we know, was contrary to the great principle of his public life. He refused to make bread for himself out of the stones lying around him in the wilderness ; he would not call upon his Father for twelve legions of angels in the Garden of Gethsemane ; and he declined to come down from the cross at the bidding of those who stood by. All these things he might have done, with infinite ease ; but he deliberately, and all through his public ministry refrained from using his supernatural power for personal ends. We cannot, therefore, suppose that he departed from that principle here ; and so we adopt the view of those who suppose that, while waiving the assertion of his right to exemption from this Temple tax, he paid it by miracle in order to keep still before the minds of his followers the great fact, as true to-day as it was then,—that he was, and is, the Son of God. He did not stand upon his prerogative as the Son of God, when he decided to pay the half-shekel ; but that he might prove that he was still the Son of God, he paid it in such a way as to show that he had supreme dominion over the whole creation, which had come at first from his hand.

But did Peter get the fish, with the stater, or shekel, in its mouth ? Curiously enough we are not told whether he did or not. Yet from the whole tenor of the narrative, no reader has any doubt that he did so, and that we have here the record of another miracle. For the rest, we may say with Dr. Kitto : * " Fish are easily caught in this mode in the same lake at this day ; and it is not unusual for travellers at Tiberias to order a dinner of fish, and presently to see a man returning from the lake with an ample supply, which he has taken, by hook and line, from the shore. It is also the nature of most fish to catch at anything bright ; and hence there are numerous anecdotes of articles in precious metal being found in fishes. The wonder is not there, but in the fact that, as foretold by his Lord, the first fish that came to Peter's hook contained the precise sum that had been indicated. It was not merely our Lord's fore-knowledge of the fact, though he did foreknow it; but it was the purpose of his will— of that will to which all creation was obedient—that im-

* " Daily Bible Illustrations," Vol. vii. p. 389.

pelled the fish containing this coin, and that one only out of the myriads in the lake, to the hook of Peter."

But now, having made clear not only the nature of the miracle, but also the meaning of the Lord's words to Peter by which it was preceded, let us draw a few inferences from the whole subject bearing both on doctrine and on life.

And, first, let us see in this narrative a proof of the greatness and glory of Christ as divine. When Peter came into the house, he was made to feel that Jesus knew all about his conversation with the collectors. The Lord had been a real witness of all that had passed between them; and yet he had all the while been in the house. What is this but a proof of omniscience? and what is omniscience but an attribute of God? Have we thoroughly realized, that wherever we have been, and whatever we have said or done, everything about us is already well known unto him? Will he not do with each of us, on the day of judgment, as he did here with Peter; and before we can even speak to him, will he not anticipate us, with such questioning as shall make it clear to us that he is "acquainted with all our ways"? Now, let us test ourselves by asking how we are affected by this truth? Do we think of his omniscience and omnipresence, as we do of the dogging detective who tracks the steps of the criminal, that he may bring him to justice? or as of the loving tenderness of a faithful friend and guardian, who keeps his ward in sight, that he may assist him in every emergency, and defend him from all evil? Let us answer these questions to ourselves faithfully, honestly, unshrinkingly, and that will reveal whether Christ, in our view, is really our Saviour, or simply and only our Judge.

But, in this narrative we have still another proof of the deity of Christ,—in the miracle itself. He makes a fish bring money to pay his Temple dues. Here, therefore, we have a fulfilment of the prophecy contained in the eighth Psalm: "Thou madest him to have dominion over the works of thine hands; thou hast put all things under his feet; the fowl of the air, and the fish of the sea, and whatsoever passeth through the paths of the sea." What manner of man is this, that even the lower creation comes obedient at his call, to do his will? The wild beasts minister to him in the wilderness of temptation. The winds and the sea are still at his bidding. The fish of the lake are where he wills them to be; and out of all those who people its depths, that one which he summons appeareth at his call. There is in Christ, therefore, that which is to be found in no other man,—that which differentiates him, not as one man is differentiated from another man, but from the race as a whole, and lifts him above humanity at large. He is deity in humanity. God manifest in the flesh. Mysterious as the incarnation is, that is the only key that will unlock the mystery of his person, or explain the majesty of his works. Let us, therefore, bow down before him in lowly adoration, and give to him the tribute of our trust and service.

But, in the second place, as an inference from this narrative, we may see that Jesus himself laid claim to the possession of deity. His conversation with Peter has no meaning at all, if it does not mean that, as the Son of God, he had a right to be exempted from the assessment for the maintenance of the house of God. And the fact that all this fell out in the hands of Peter, gives confirmation, if any confirmation were needed, that this is the correct view of the case. For it was Peter who, first of the twelve, declared, "Thou art the Christ, the Son of the

living God;" and he knew, therefore, in what sense he was
God's Son. Moreover, the Saviour called the Temple,
" His Father's House." He affirmed that " He and the
Father are one." When the Jews took up stones to stone
him, " because he made himself equal with God, calling
himself the Son of God," he took no means to rectify
their mistake—if it was a mistake ; or to vindicate himself from blasphemy—for blasphemy it was, if he were
not really divine. He asserted that he who had seen
him, had seen the Father ; that he had been with the
Father before the world was ; and when he was put upon
his oath, at last, whether he were the Son of God, he said
unto the high-priest : " Thou hast said; nevertheless I
say unto you, Hereafter shall ye see the Son of Man sitting on the right hand of power, and coming in the clouds
of heaven." Now, either these claims were true or false.
If they were true, then he is both really human and actually divine ; but if they were false, then he was neither
God incarnate, nor even a truthful man. It has been
alleged by many, in our days, that Jesus Christ is the
highest type of manhood; that his moral character is the
noblest of which we have any account in history ; and
that he may fairly be held up as a pattern of perfection,
for us to follow ;—while yet they deny that he is God.
But the passages which I have quoted (and there are
others to the same effect), make it evident, either that such
writers should go much farther, or should not have gone
so far. For if his morality was the highest known to
men, then truthfulness must have characterized his
words, and we must assent to his claims, when he asserted that he was, in a sense distinctive of, and peculiar to, himself, " the Son of God." But, if in making
such assertions, he was stating what was false, then he
cannot be regarded as a perfect man. The truth is, that

he must either be accepted as the God-man, or rejected as a dealer in falsehood—aye, and a dealer in falsehood in regard to matters which are most intimately associated with the most sacred interests of humanity. He cannot be consistently regarded as a model of perfection, while yet we reject his deity. We must either reject both his human perfection and his divine dignity, or we must accept both. They stand or fall together. But the instinct of humanity is right in regarding him as a model of perfection, and that draws us on irresistibly to the acceptance of his deity, as " God manifest in the flesh."

Finally, we may learn from this narrative that it is sometimes well not to insist upon that which is our right. As the Son of God, the Saviour had a right to claim exemption from the dues which were collected for the house of God ; but he chose to waive that right in the present case, and he did so for the sake of others, lest he should cause them to stumble. Thus he acted on the principle which was afterwards so repeatedly enforced by his servant Paul, " It is not good to do anything whereby a brother is made to stumble," and in so doing he left us an example that we should follow his steps. We must distinguish between the having of a right and the exercise of a right. We may have a perfect right to do a certain thing, which yet, owing to other considerations, we ought not to do. For the exercise of a right, with the Christian, must be conditioned by love ; and if, in any case, it will grieve a brother, or cause him to stumble, then it is our privilege—and that is a higher thing than duty—to waive the right, that our brother may be kept either from suffering or from sin. Of course that principle has its limits ; and I should put these at the point where conscience comes into operation. If I am compelled—or let me rather say, impelled—by constraint of

conscience to assert my right, if I feel, under the guidance of conscience enlightened by the prayerful study of
God's word, that unless I assert my right I shall be committing sin, then there is nothing for it but to obey conscience. But short of such constraint as that, if the assertion of my right is to imperil another, or give him
occasion to commit sin, then I am to waive my right for
his sake, remembering that in such a case " even Christ
pleased not himself," or we may put it more simply in
the words of Bishop Ryle, " God's rights undoubtedly
we must never give up ; but we may sometimes safely
give up our own."*

Now see how that would work in the family! It
would promote peace. It would remove friction. It
would minister to holiness. When a member of a household insists upon an undoubted right, even though he
knows that his doing so will provoke another to sin, or
be the cause of much suffering and sorrow, then he is
sacrificing love to self, and the conduct of the Saviour
here may be profitably commended to his study and imi-
tation.

Then again, see how it would work in the Church!
How many controversies and quarrels might have been
prevented if Christ's example in this matter had been
understood and followed! Our rights as individual
Church members may be unquestionable ; but the exercise of them may be in certain circumstances both un-
seasonable and inexpedient, and before we think of
insisting on them, we ought to consider " the profit of
others, that they may be saved."

Mark again how it bears on the question of amusements. Abstractly, I may have a perfect right as between myself and Christ to amuse myself in a certain

* Ryle on Matthew, p. 217.

way ; but if my acting on that right shall be so construed by others, however ignorantly or illogically, as to encourage them to do things positively sinful, or to seem to them to be a giving countenance by me to evil, then it is better for me to pay the Temple tribute, and waive my right, than to work mischief by insisting on the exercise of my right.

Here then is the principle : when the exercise of an undoubted right would cause another to stumble, then, unless I am led by earnest study and prayer to feel that I should be committing sin if I did not exercise that right, I should forego it ; and so follow the example of my Saviour given in this narrative. Take that principle with you wherever you go, and you will find that it will solve many questions of casuistry, over which you might otherwise spend anxious thought, and in regard to which you might otherwise come to conclusions fraught with danger not only to others, but also to yourselves.

XXV.

THE TEN LEPERS.

Luke xvii. 11-19.

On his way from Galilee to Jerusalem to be present at the last passover of his earthly life, our Lord, instead of taking the direct road down through Samaria to Judæa, went by the route on the east side of the Jordan. To reach that river, however, it was needful that he should pass eastward along the boundary line which divided Galilee from Samaria, and it was while he was moving on "between" (the Revised Version, margin,) these districts, that he was met, just outside of a village, by ten men that were lepers. We cannot tell whether their presence at that place and time was accidental, or whether they purposely intercepted him; but, in any case, so soon as they saw him, they lifted up their voices and said, "Jesus, Master, have mercy on us." Their cry was loud—for in accordance with the Mosaic law they stood afar off; and it was united—for misery had drawn them together, and given them such an interest in each other, that they made common cause with each other.

The response of the Saviour to them, was given in the form of a command which implied that they would speedily be healed; and so it was an appeal to their faith. He said to them, "Go show yourselves unto the priests."

For this, as Edersheim tells us,* it was not necessary to repair to Jerusalem, inasmuch as any priest might declare " unclean " or " clean," provided the applicants came singly and not in company, for his inspection, and so in the plural form of the injunction, " show yourselves to the *priests*," we have a minute accuracy, which is, according to the same author, " another point of undesigned evidence of the authenticity of the narrative." But no matter what distance they had to go in order to obey the Saviour's command, that command at once tested them, honored the law which he had come not to destroy but to fulfil, and secured that the declaration of the reality of their cure should be authoritatively made by those whose proper business it was to pronounce on all such cases. But as they were going on their way to do as he had bidden them, they discovered for themselves that they had been cured. The healthy color had returned to their flesh ; the dry, scaly appearance had disappeared from their skin; and a consciousness of thorough physical regeneration was pulsing through their veins. That which each felt in himself, he observed in all the rest; and so the malady by which they had been afflicted—one knows not for how long—passed away almost as in a moment, for "as they went, they were cleansed."

Thus far, their experience and histories run parallel; but now there is a divergence. Nine of them go straight on to the priests, desiring perhaps that the separation between them and their fellowmen might be terminated as soon as possible; but one of them, and he a Samaritan, has somehow discovered that " love is the fufilling of the law," and he returned and " with a loud voice glorified God, and fell at Jesus' feet, giving him thanks." The Saviour was delighted with *his* gratitude; but sad-

* Vol. ii. p. 329.

dened by the absence of the others, he exclaimed, "Were not the ten cleansed? but where are the nine? Were there none found that returned to give glory to God save this stranger." And he said to him, "Arise, and go thy way; thy faith hath saved thee"—for so the words are in the margin of the Revised version. Now this expression, "thy faith hath saved thee," cannot refer to the cure of his leprosy. That was effected before his return to give thanks, for it called out this new blessing from the lips of Christ. Moreover, the nine were healed as well as the Samaritan, and it is clear that the Lord designed to give to him something more than they had received. He had shown a faith which they had not manifested, and he was to get a salvation nobler than the cure which they had obtained. They were healed of their leprosy; he was saved, not from that only, but also from his sin.

It is a simple narrative, yet it suggests some profitable thoughts. Thus, for one thing, we are reminded by it that we often get most where least might have been expected. He who returned to give thanks was a Samaritan. He belonged to an alien race—for, though he received the books of Moses, the Samaritan was the descendant of Gentiles. He had not enjoyed either the privileges or the opportunities of the peculiar people; for in a very important sense it was true that "salvation" *was* "of the Jews." He was acquainted only with the Pentateuch, and so knew nothing of those deeply spiritual utterances with which Isaiah and the other prophets sought to prepare the way for the advent of the Messiah. Therefore, it was not a little remarkable that he should have been so forward to glorify God in giving thanks to the Lord Jesus, and should have postponed his visit to his priest until he had attended to that which he recognized as a higher duty.   Let such a fact teach us not to be too positive in pronouncing, on purely *a priori* grounds, against the character of a man from the place in which we find him, or the race to which he belongs.   Knowing that the Roman army was such as historians have described, we should not have gone to it for specimens of humility, candor, faith and moral decision; and yet all the centurions spoken of in the New Testament were remarkable for these very qualities; and in modern times the most apparently unpromising fields have sometimes been those which have most abundantly rewarded the home missionary's toil.   In the Saviour's own day, the publicans and harlots pressed into the kingdom before the Pharisees and Scribes; and it would be well for some of our dignified and decorous churches, if there were in them as much of earnest enthusiasm, and whole-hearted consecration, as we often meet with among those who have been reclaimed from the streets and lanes of the cities.   Let no one, therefore, be kept from entering upon some particular work because of the uninviting character of those among whom it is to be prosecuted. We must never despair even of the most ignorant, or the most antagonistic.   The one recovered leper, who returned to give thanks to God and glorify Christ, was a Samaritan, and what a marvel that was needs not to be explained to those who know how bitter was the feud between his nation and the Jews.

But, turning this thought round, and looking at it from the other side, we are reminded by this narrative that we often get least where we might have looked for most. The nine after whom the Saviour asked were *Jews*.   We are not told that in so many words, indeed, but it is evidently implied in the description of the exceptional one, as an alien, or stranger. Now the Jews had been highly privileged. Theirs were the oracles of God. Not only had they received the law, but they had the books of the prophets read in their synagogues every Sabbath day, and the duty of gratitude to God was everywhere suggested to them, and exemplified for them, in the book of Psalms. It might have been thought, therefore, that they would have been forward to give glory to God for all his mercies. But just here these nine failed, and therein they were, I fear, only specimens of the average of their kinsmen according to the flesh. For that which these did, after having received their cure, was precisely that which the people of their nation did after having received their special blessings. They forgot God; they took their good things as matters of course; and even when their Messiah came they would have none of him. What a warning that is to us! Blessings statedly enjoyed cease to be appreciated; and the longer people possess the gospel, the more are they in danger of "making light of it." In the case of the Jews, to use the figure of the prophet, God had planted a vineyard, and hedged it round, and done everything for it that was necessary to secure its fruitfulness; but, alas! at the vintage-time only wild grapes were found upon its vines, and then it was laid waste. The expected fruit was not forthcoming. Brethren, let it not be so with us. Let us not trust in our position, or our privileges, as if by merely having these we are secure; but let us show that we have improved them, by manifesting the graces of the Christian life.

A third thing suggested by this narrative is, that gratitude for one blessing secures the reception of another, and a greater. This Samaritan came to thank Jesus for the cure of his leprosy, and received from him the salva-

tion of his soul. So much, as we have seen, is evident
from the words addressed to him by the Saviour, " Thy
faith hath saved thee "—which must refer, not to the
cleansing of his body, but to the regeneration of his
soul.   He who acknowledges God in that which is
little, will receive still greater benefits from his hands.
The grateful heart is in itself a blessing, but it is also
the prophecy of something more.   I say not, indeed,
that we should manifest gratitude with a view to such a
result.   That would be to act in accordance with the
definition of the clerical wit, to the effect that " gratitude
is a lively sense of favors to come," and such a selfish
spirit always, before God, outwits itself.   But I do say,
as a matter of fact, that wherever gratitude is sincerely
and intelligently manifested, it is the precursor of the
reception of still larger blessings.   When a man has
come the length of believingly acknowledging God for
temporal things, he is not " far from the kingdom of
heaven "; and not unfrequently, as in the case of this
Samaritan, the giving thanks to the Lord for recovery
from bodily disease has been the forerunner of the
reception of spiritual salvation.

But, if all this be so, the question presses, why gratitude to God for the benefits he has bestowed on us is so
rare?   The words, " Where are the nine?" keep recurring to our minds.   For, indeed, the spirit of this
Samaritan is far from common among men.   Those who
receive favors, even from a fellowman, are seldom really
grateful for them.   This is so true, that the frequency of
ingratitude has passed into a proverb, and every one
who has had much experience of the world will laugh at
the simplicity of him who expects to receive any real
and abiding return for his kindness.   It has, indeed,
almost come to this, that one is surprised when he is

thanked, in any sincere fashion, for anything which he has done for his fellows. There are, of course, many exceptions ; but, speaking broadly, the facts are undeniably as I have stated them. And, if gratitude from man to man is so rare, then we may conclude that gratitude from man to God is rarer still ; for here we may bring in the principle that underlies the apostle's words, and say, " If a man is not grateful to his benefactor, whom he has seen, how shall he be thankful to God, whom he has not seen ? " Now, how shall we account for this state of things ?

I answer, in the first place, that much of it is owing to the prevalence of pride among men. Thankfulness is the expression of a sense of indebtedness to some giver, for benefits, which we have received from him, and to which we had no claim either of merit or of right. We are not grateful for justice. That we demand as a right, and if it be denied, we feel that a wrong has been inflicted on us. We do not give thanks for wages. These we have earned, and we claim them as our own. But we are grateful for favors. When one, out of his kindness, gives us benefits to which we have no inherent title, and for which we are beholden to his generosity alone, then we feel under obligation to him ; and we seek to make expression of that obligation both in earnest words and loving deeds. Gratitude to God, therefore, springs not only from the reception of blessing at his hand, but also from our own sense of our unworthiness to receive these blessings. But it goes against the grain of our nature to acknowledge that we have no right or title to the favors which he has bestowed on us. The great stumbling block to many, in the way of their reception of salvation through the gospel, is just this, that they must accept it as of grace, and not as the reward of works ; and precisely the same disposition prevents men generally from cherishing the emotion of gratitude to God, either for common or for special mercies. They have to admit that they do not deserve his goodness; that they have not earned his blessings, and that they owe everything to his free, unmerited love. Now that is a hard thing for human nature to do. It involves the dethronement of pride, the repudiation of self-conceit, and the acknowledgment of entire dependence on him in whom " we live and move and have our being," and so we may very largely account for the rarity of gratitude to God among us, by the general prevalence of self-deification. To be thankful, we must be humble; but humility is one of those graces that flower latest in the Christian life, and therefore it is that the thankful heart is so rare in the world.

But we may find some explanation of this rarity also, in the subtle influence over men, of some prevalent forms of philosophy. We cannot be thankful to a " perhaps "; therefore he who calls himself an agnostic cannot be grateful for anything. His creed is, that nothing can be known but that which is apprehended through the bodily senses. He does not say in so many words that there is no God; but he alleges that we cannot certainly know whether there is or not, and so there can be no definiteness or reality about his gratitude. And yet, how irrational such a creed is! For it takes no note whatever of the nature that is within the man himself. It forgets that unless there be something in us for which bodily sensation cannot account, it would be impossible for us to take note even of those things which we perceive through the senses. It ignores the phenomena of conscience, which, by furnishing us with the terms " ought " and " ought not," clearly points to One above us to whom we are individually responsible; and it stifles those universal intuitions, which among men of all nations and all ages have disposed them to worship some supreme ruler of the universe. Still, false as it is, in the proportion in which this creed prevails, gratitude to God drops out, cannot but drop out, of the heart and life.

Again, we cannot be thankful to a machine; and therefore, if it be, as some have alleged, that the universe is nothing else than a piece of mechanism, grinding on blindly in unceasing motion, and that its operations are the result not of intelligent design, and beneficent purpose, but of spontaneous development, then gratitude becomes absurd, and there is no place for worship. For we can be grateful only to a *person*. Now I think it is undeniable that such a view of the universe has been accepted by many in these days. Very irrational the view is, no doubt. For a machine implies a mechanist; and evolution, even if all be true that is claimed for it, is only a method, not a force; but still, in the subtle influence upon men generally of such notions as these, even if they do not themselves believe them, we may find some explanation of the rarity of gratitude to God, among men.

But there is another and a kindred reason for prevalent ingratitude to God, in the fact that the blessings of God come to us, not in the way of direct and abrupt interposition on his part, but through the ordinary operations of his providence. Taking the narrative before us, it is conceivable that some of the nine might have said within themselves: " We do not know whether our cure came from Jesus or not. No doubt we *are* cured; of so much as that we are conscious. But then he did nothing to us. He did not touch us with his hand, or speak any words of power over us. He simply said, ' Go, show yourselves to the priests.' There was no moment in our experience in which we could say that we felt anything out of the common; or that any influence coming out of him, and working within us, was operating upon us. We have only recovered, and he was the first to perceive that our recovery had begun. That is all. Why then should we be grateful to him ? "

Whether any of them spoke after this manner or not, we cannot tell ; but it is in this way that multitudes among ourselves feel, concerning our common and daily blessings. If these had come to them through unusual channels, then they would have been thankful to him for them ; but, because they come in the ordinary course of nature, as they phrase it, they take them as things of course. Now, all that is utterly irrational. A miracle is unusual divine action. The course of nature is usual divine action. That is the whole difference between the two, so far as causation is concerned, for in both alike the power is that of God. If, therefore, one is prepared to admit that God is in a miracle, he ought, also, in consistency, to grant that God is working constantly in the operations of nature. Then, when that is granted, we can easily rise to the conviction that the blessings which come to us through the regular operations of nature, come to us from the heart of God, and should be gratefully acknowledged by us. While, on the other hand, it is equally plain that unless we receive common and ordinary blessings as the gifts of God's providence, even though they come to us through natural channels, we can never be moved to thank him really, not to say intelligently, for anything.

But, finally here, we may account for the prevalence of ingratitude toward God, by the lack of faith in Christ, which is, unhappily, so common among men. I can conceive of some one saying within himself, just at this point, " What you have advanced, about all things coming to us from the hand of God, even when they come through natural channels, may be perfectly true ; but no blessings have come to me. Things with me have always been at the ebb. I have had nothing but a succession of trials. Now it has been bad health, and again it has been pecuniary loss ; now it has been bereavement, and again it has been bitter alienation of friends—worse than any bereavement. How can I maintain a sincerely grateful spirit under such experiences ? " Now to all that the answer must be, that unless a man have something better and more enduring than any of these blessings, whose absence he deplores, gratitude is for him impossible.

But it is precisely here that the revelation of God through our Lord Jesus Christ comes with its steadying influence and divine compensation. For, so soon as we see that, in giving his life a ransom for us, he is the Interpreter—or rather the Revealer—of God unto us, we can be grateful to him for his love, even though we may be in affliction. When we know that he " spared not his own Son, but delivered him up for us all," we can conclude that, after having made that amazing sacrifice on our behalf, he must mean love, and only love, to us in everything that comes upon us. He is Jehovah. He changes not. Therefore, in and through everything, he loves us as much as he did, and means our good as much as he did, when he gave his Son to death on our behalf. Thus the belief in the reality of our redemption through Christ will enable us to say, not only " Thy will be done," in resignation, but also, " Blessed be the name of the Lord," in thanksgiving, even when things are apparently darkest with us. He who does not believe in God's providence, cannot be thankful to God even for blessings ; but he who is a partaker of God's redemption in Christ, and knows him as his Father, can be thankful even in trial, and sometimes—more wonderful still—*for* trial. The love of the cross, in the experience of the Christian, flows into every cup of affliction, and turns it into a cup of blessing. But, where there is no acceptance of redemption through the blood of Christ, there can be nothing but despondency under the discipline of affliction. The atheist cannot be grateful to God for anything. The mere theist may be grateful to God for blessings. But the Christian alone is able to comply with the injunction of the apostle, " In everything give thanks, for this is the will of God, in Christ Jesus, concerning you."

" Where are the nine ? " Are there any of them here ? Have *you* received God's mercies, and given him no thanks ? Have *you* had deliverances from sickness, and pain, and poverty, and yet rendered no glory to him, or shown him no regard, or offered him no service ? Then you are one of them. Let the service of this evening quicken you into gratitude ; and, as you are offering that, God will give you a new blessing, even the blessing of a new heart, which will impel you to offer yourself to him, and so

" Make life, death, and that vast forever,
One grand deep song."

XVI.

THE OPENING OF THE EYES OF A MAN BORN BLIND.

John ix. 1-7.

IT is a peculiarity of the gospel by John that the few miracles which it records—few, that is, in comparison with the other three—are introduced, not so much for their own sake, as on account of the discourses which were delivered by our Lord in connection with them. We have a remarkable instance of this in the miracle of the healing of the impotent man at the pool of Bethesda, which gave rise to the profound address on the relation subsisting between the Father and the Son, involving in it an assertion of the deity of the Son. Another is furnished by the account of the feeding of the multitude with five loaves and two fishes, which is immediately followed by the sermon on the Bread of Life. And we have a third here, in the opening of the eyes of the man who was born blind, which is brought in as a parabolic illustration of the discourse, of which the words, " I am the Light of the world ; he that followeth me shall not walk in darkness, but shall have the light of life," may be said to be the text.

For there is no doubt in my mind that the eighth and ninth chapters of this wonderful gospel constitute one unbroken narrative, and that the works

and words which they record all belong to that great
day of the Feast of Tabernacles, which was signalized by the grand popular ceremony of the drawing of the waters.   It is true, indeed, that just at the
close of the eighth chapter we read that the Jews, exasperated at the statements made by our Lord, and count-
ing him guilty of blasphemy, because he made himself
equal with God, took up stones to cast at him, and that
he hid himself, or " was hidden," and went out of the
Temple.   It is true, also, that some have counted it utterly improbable that, in a moment of excitement, such
as they suppose that must have been, the Lord should
have paused at the gate, or, at least, in the immediate
vicinity of the Temple, to work a miracle like that which
is here described.   And, if the Saviour had been only an
ordinary man, we might be willing to concede so much ;
but there was the unbroken calmness of deity in his
breast.   Even amid the fury of the crowd he was entirely self-possessed, and the incident here recorded may
have been introduced by the Evangelist for this, among
other reasons, that he might bring out, by the force of
the contrast that is here suggested between the excited
violence of a multitude and the calmness of Christ, the
vast, nay, infinite, superiority of Jesus to all other men.
He was not excited.   On the contrary, he was so composed that he took note of the misery and need of the
poor blind beggar, who was sitting by the wayside as he
passed, and stayed to heal him.   " As he passed by, he
saw a man blind from his birth."   He did not wait to be
appealed to by the sufferer ; the sight of his wretchedness
was enough to move his heart.   The beginning of all
good to the sinner is when Jesus sees him thus ; even as
it was his perception of the ruined state of man, at first,
that moved him to become the Redeemer of the race.

When his disciples observed that he was interested in the man, and began perhaps, to anticipate that he was about to heal him, they proposed to him this question : " Rabbi, who did sin, this man or his parents, that he was born blind." They had been accustomed to believe, erroneously, as their Master pointed out on more than one occasion, that special suffering was the consequence of special sin which had been committed by the sufferer. But here was a case which had in it peculiar elements of difficulty, and which could not be accounted for on their ordinary hypothesis, for this man was *born* blind. What were they to think about it ? Whose was the guilt of which this blindness was the punishment ? Was it the man's own ? or, was it that of his parents ? But what could they mean by asking whether it was that of the man himself ? Some have answered, that the Jews had a belief in some kind of transmigration of souls, and that the disciples meant to ask : " Did this man so sin in some former state of existence, as to come into this world blind ? " But although that doctrine was accepted by some among the Jews at a much later date, I cannot find any trace of its being held by any in the Saviour's time, and therefore I cannot accept this explanation. Equally unsatisfactory is the suggestion that they referred to sins which God foresaw that the man would commit, and which he thus punished, as it were by anticipation,—a notion which one would think is as unlikely to occur to a rational mind, as it is dishonoring to God.

It is difficult, perhaps impossible for us now, to formulate the precise idea that was in the minds of the disciples when they asked this question, but the explanation of Stier is as likely to be correct as any, when he fills up their inquiry thus : " Rabbi, who did sin ? This man ? or—since that is impossible—his parents ? that he was born blind ? "

We have less perplexity about the inquiry whether it was caused by the sin of his parents ; for we know as a matter of fact, that certain diseases are entailed upon children by the iniquity of the parents : and in the second commandment God speaks of himself as " visiting the iniquities of the fathers upon the children." The view, that special suffering is the result of special sin, is as old as the days of Job's three friends. And like many other errors, it is the exaggeration of a truth. For suffering is the result of sin. That is a general law under the government of God. But when we go on to affirm that special suffering is always the result of special sin committed by the sufferer, we are presuming to speak of matters which lie beyond our ken. This man belonged to a sinful race, and so he came into the world with this great privation, just as we all come into the world mortal. That is all we know upon the subject; and even that throws us back upon the insoluble mystery of the existence of sin under the administration of a holy, righteous, and benevolent God—a mystery which, like a horizon, surrounds all our thinking on moral subjects, but which must be accepted as a fact, make of it what we will.

Yet dark as it is, this mystery is not entirely unrelieved. For the Saviour, after replying to the question of the disciples negatively, that this man's blindness was not the result of any special sin, either on his own part or on that of his parents—mark, I said *special* sin, for the Saviour's words do not imply that either he or they were absolutely sinless—proceeds to affirm that he was born blind in order that " the works of God should be made manifest in him." By the works of God, here, are

meant works which God alone could perform; and the
sentiment expressed by the Lord is the same as that
which he uttered when, in reference to the illness of Lazarus, he said : " This sickness is for the glory of God,
that the Son of God may be glorified thereby."

This man was born blind, in order that by the power of
God his eyes might be opened, and his soul might be
saved. He was born blind in order that by the grace of
God he might be made in the highest sense to see ; or, to
put it more simply, he was born blind for the sake of his
own spiritual good, that he might be led to the perception and acceptance of Jesus Christ as the Son of God,
the Saviour of men ; and for the sake of others, that
through his case, the tenderness, the compassion, the
grace, and the power of God might be made manifest to
men.

Now here we have a great general law pervading the
Providence of God. It does not explain the origin of
evil, but it shows how God brings good out of evil, and
therefore helps to reconcile us to its existence. Sin is
undoubtedly the cause of all the suffering existing in the
world. Yet, in the wise administration of God, that suffering is so distributed as best to make manifest the works
of God, in the promotion of the highest welfare of the
individual sufferers and of the race at large. This is the
truth taught in these words, and it is applicable not only
to the case of this blind man, but also to all suffering.
And when we are in trouble it becomes us so to conduct
ourselves under it, as to secure that these beneficent re.
sults shall be attained.

The Saviour adds, as if to explain the promptitude of
his action at this time : " We must work the works of
him that sent me while it is day: the night cometh when
no man can work. When I am in the world, I am the

light of the world." There is no time for speculation regarding things which we never can settle. Let us, therefore, leave the question, "Who did sin, this man, or his parents, that he was born blind?" in the hands of God. He will take care of his own honor, but we must do the work of the present moment—for if we neglect that in its appointed time, we shall find that we cannot do it at all. Thus we interpret the meaning and purpose of these oft-quoted words.

The common opinion indeed, is, that "day" here stands for the period of our earthly life, and "night" for the death by which that is ended; and that view seems at first sight to be confirmed by the clause immediately following, " as long as," or, as the Revisers have it, "When I am in the world, I am the light of the world." But Jesus did not cease to be the light of the world when he died; nay, rather by his death, resurrection, and ascension into glory, he became more than ever "the light and life of men." Others, therefore, have preferred to take the day here as designating the time appropriate for labor, and the night as that proper for rest. But that view is open to the same objection as the former, for Jesus has not rested since his ascension. His work before his death, as the language of the Book of the Acts of the Apostles indicates, was only the beginning of his doing and teaching; and the record in the Acts is the history of the continuance of these.* It is better, therefore, to take the day here in the general sense of the season of opportunity, and the night as designating the limit of that opportunity. For every work there is a time, when it can and ought to be done, and that in relation thereto is the day. For every work there is a limit beyond which it cannot be performed, and that in relation thereto is

* Acts i. 1.

the night. This seems to me to be the simplest and clearest exposition of the terms, and it is perfectly in harmony with the Saviour's customary mode of speech on this subject. The works which he was commissioned by him that sent him, to perform, were all arranged and laid out before him, each having its own place and time ; so that if any one was neglected he could not go back to repair the omission. This consideration seems never to have been lost sight of by him, for he spoke of his hour as not having come, and of his hour as having come, with special reference to this very thing.

And it fits perfectly into and explains the urgency of the Saviour in the present instance. He had but just escaped from the violence of the Jews ; his disciples had broached a curious and difficult question as to the administration of the providential government of God ; it was, besides, the Sabbath day, and the performance of a cure thereon might rouse anew the bitterness of those who, in their zeal for the letter of the law, had lost sight of the love that is its spirit. But none of these things moved him. The hour for the healing of this blind man had struck, and it was now or never. Therefore, true to the principle in which from first to last he lived on earth, he said : " We must work the work of him that sent me, while it is day; the night cometh when no man can work. When I am in the world, I am the light of the world," and proceeded at once to give sight to him who had never seen before.

The details of the miracle are few. We read that " he spat on the ground, and made clay of the spittle, and anointed the eyes of the blind man with the clay, and said unto him, ' Go wash in the pool of Siloam.' He went his way, therefore, and washed and came seeing."

Now we are told that at that time a great virtue, especially in diseases of the eye, was believed to belong to the fasting spittle; but every one must admit, that there was nothing in the external application here mentioned, nor in the washing in the pool of Siloam, that could account for the opening of this man's eyes, for the first time in his life, to the perception of outward objects. The anointing of the eyes with clay formed in the manner here described, was better calculated to make a seeing man blind, than to make a blind man see. Why, then, was such an application made? Perhaps to help the faith of the man who was to be cured. It gave him something to build upon. It raised his hope—nay, it led him to expect a cure; and that helps to account for the promptitude of his obedience. Perhaps, also, it was meant to illustrate that which is a fact in the spiritual experience of many, namely, that when Christ began to deal with them in order to their conversion, he made their own condition seem to them darker and more hopeless than ever. Conviction comes before conversion; and while conviction lasts, the soul is more miserable than it was before it began, even as this man's eyes, while the clay was upon them, were more impervious to the light than ever.

Then the command, " Go, wash in Siloam," suggests that in spiritual operations God has his work, and we have ours. The opening of this man's eyes was all of Christ; and yet if the blind man had not done as Jesus had commanded, he would not have been cured. So salvation—understanding by that, not only deliverance from guilt, but the regeneration and sanctification of the soul—is all of God; and yet it becomes ours, through our belief in Jesus Christ, which is a work of our own. You remember the words of Paul, " Work out your own salvation with fear and trembling; for it is God which work-

eth in you, both to will and to do, of his good pleasure."
Here, as one has said, " not only is God's work set forth
as coincident with our work in the matter of salvation,
but it is assigned as a reason, and an encouragement, for
the strenuous and faithful performance of what it falls to
us to do in this matter." *

Now let us observe two things in this brief account of
a great miracle. The first is, the promptitude of the
man's obedience. " He went away, therefore, and
washed." Without any delay ; without any reluctance ;
probably, also, without any misgiving—he went and did
what he was told. He had been so long accustomed to
go through the streets of Jerusalem, that he needed no
guide ; and, waiting for no fuller directions, he set out
at once. So it ought to be with the sinner. When
Jesus says to him, " This is the work of God,"—that is,
the work given you to do by God—" that ye believe in
him whom he hath sent," he should at once respond, not
in a mere formal fashion, but as the sincere utterance of
his soul, " Lord, I believe ; help thou mine unbelief."
You cannot be saved without faith ; and it is you that
must believe. That, you must do for yourself, even as
this man had to go to Siloam and wash.

Then observe also the perfection of the cure, " He
came seeing." Seeing is a thing which, in all ordinary
cases, needs to be learned. If you watch a very young
infant, you will be amused at the mistakes which it
makes in regard to external things. To seize an object,
it will push its hand out much farther than is necessary ;
or it will try to grasp at mere empty space either on the
right or left of the true position of that which it is aiming at ; for the perceptions of the shapes and distances

* W. L. Alexander, D.D., LL.D., "Christian Thought and Work,"
pp. 185–186.

of objects through the eye are what philosophers have called "acquired perceptions of sight." They mean by that, that we do not see these things at first. All that sight gives us in the beginning, is color; but we learn, through touch, and as the result of an experience which comes too early to be remembered by us, to associate with color both form and distance. If you would verify this for yourselves, put on a pair of spectacles having lenses of such focus as you are not accustomed to, and attempt to walk with them; then you will find that you miscalculate at almost every movement, and that when you think you are stepping over a puddle, you step right into it. But in the case before us, this man saw perfectly at once: "He came seeing." What Jesus did for him, he did perfectly; and when he opens the soul's eyes, they see clearly and correctly "wonderful things out of God's law."

Here the account of the miracle, properly speaking, ends, and I shall not attempt to do more than give the briefest summary of the investigation that was made, first by the man's own neighbors, and ultimately by the Jewish officials into the facts of the case.

He was questioned first of all by his neighbors, who, observing the change of expression in his countenance, caused by the opening of his eyes, were puzzled as to his identity. Some of them were quite sure it was he; others more cautiously alleged that he was like him who sat and begged; but he himself set all doubt at rest by saying, "I am he." Then they asked him how his eyes were opened, and he very tersely answered, "The man that is called Jesus, made clay and anointed mine eyes, and said unto me, Go to Siloam and wash; so I went away and washed, and I received sight." But when they inquired where Jesus was, he replied: "I know not." Upon this, his questioners,—from what motive does not appear, but probably with no good will to the Saviour—took him to the Jewish officials that they might take the case in hand. But he told them precisely the same story that he had told his neighbors; and the result was, that some of them declared that Jesus could not be from God, because he wrought the cure upon the Sabbath; while others timidly suggested that he who did such signs could not be other than a messenger from heaven. But curiously enough, they both agreed to refer it to the man himself who had been cured. What do you say about him? What impression has the whole experience produced on you?—these were now the inquiries which they addressed to him; and without the least hesitation, he answered: "He is a prophet."

This somewhat disconcerted them, and so they took refuge in the idea that perhaps the man never had been blind at all, and that the whole affair was the result of collusion between him and Christ. Therefore they sent for his parents, and cross-questioned them. "Is this your son, who ye say was born blind? How then doth he now see?" But the shrewd mother-wit of these common people was too much for them; for they knew enough, apparently, to answer only so far as they themselves had knowledge at first hand, and they said, "We know that this is our son, and that he was born blind; but how he now seeth, we know not, or who opened his eyes we know not; ask him; he is of age; he shall speak for himself." This caution of theirs was due to the facts, that they had not themselves witnessed the cure of their son; that the rulers had determined to put out of the synagogue any man who should confess Jesus to be the Christ; and that they had no desire to put themselves in the way of suffering for his sake.

Finding, however, that they could not prove that the man never had been blind, the officials recalled him for further examination, and said to him : " Give glory to God"—that is, as the words of Joshua * to Achan make plain, " make a frank confession ; tell us the whole truth to the glory of God,"—" We know that this man is a sinner." Whereupon he answered, " Whether he be a sinner, I know not ; but one thing I do know, that whereas I was blind, now I see." Then they asked him to tell them again, how the miracle was wrought; hoping perhaps that he might now say something inconsistent with what he had said before ; but they only provoked him, thereby, to be sarcastic, for he said, " I told you before and you would not hear; why do you want me to tell you again ? Would ye also become his disciples ? " This so exasperated his examiners that they replied with some temper : " Thou art his disciple, but we are Moses' disciples. We know that God spoke by Moses, but as for this man, we know not whence he is." Then, stirred into argument by their perversity, he very cogently said, " Well, this is the marvel—that he hath opened mine eyes, and yet you know not whence he is. Since the world began it was never heard that any one opened the eyes of a man born blind !" That is a work which can be performed only by God ; or if by a man, then by a man who represents God, and is thereby authenticated as his messenger. "If this man were not of God he could do nothing " of that kind. That was unanswerable ; and so, taunting him with having come into the world with the brand of sin upon his eyes, they cried, " Thou wast altogether born in sin, and dost thou teach

* Joshua vii. 19.

us ? and they cast him out of the synagogue "—a penalty with consequences almost as serious as those which followed excommunication from the Roman Catholic Church " with bell, book, and candle," in the middle ages.

When Jesus heard all this, he sought the man out, and, revealing himself to him, drew his faith toward himself, thereby strengthening him to suffer for his sake. While, to the Pharisees who had persecuted him, he said, " For judgment came I into the world, that they which see not might see, and that they which see might become blind," and when they said to him, " Are we blind also ? " he made reply, " If ye *were* blind, ye would have no sin ; but now ye say we see, therefore your sin remaineth."

The opponents of the supernatural have frequently said, that no one of the wonderful works performed by Jesus was ever thoroughly investigated ; but in view of the narrative which we have just outlined, that statement cannot be substantiated. This man was questioned, and cross-questioned, as to whether he had really been born blind, and how he came to see ; but no influence could make him waver, or shake a single statement which he made. His parents also testified to the fact of his blindness, and we may be sure that if any other means could have been used to discredit the miracle, they would have been employed by the Pharisees. But the more they were convinced in their own hearts that a miracle had really been wrought, the more bitter became their antagonism to him who wrought it.

The truth is, as we have formerly said, that the effect of a miracle depends on the intellectual prepossessions and moral proclivities of the spectator. If intellectually he has adopted the philosophy which declares that miracles are impossible, he will not believe one, though it should be wrought before his own eyes; and, if morally he is antagonistic to the Christ, the sight of a miracle will only aggravate that antagonism. So the miracles were as really tests of those who witnessed them, as proofs of the divine commission of him who performed them; and those who reject them now, as they read of them in these Scriptures, would not have been convinced by them if they had seen them performed. We need not be surprised, therefore, at the conflicts that are waged over them in these days.

I have time now for only two practical lessons and to get them we shall go back to the very beginning of this remarkable chapter. The first is, that the maintenance of a calm and untroubled spirit is essential both to the perception and performance of the works which our Father has given us to do. We were struck with the fact, that just at a time when the Lord was emerging from the Temple, within the precincts of which his adversaries had taken up stones to cast at him, he saw this blind man, and determined to heal him. The Lord Jesus, to use a familiar expression, was never " put out " by any thing. He never lost his mental or spiritual equipoise; and that helps very largely, speaking after the manner of men, to account for his constant activity in the service of humanity. His unbroken peace of spirit was an important element of power in his life. They who are in constant anxiety about themselves do not see the necessities of others, and have little prompting to assist them. As Miss Waring's hymn reminds us, we need " a heart at leisure from itself," if we would be able " to soothe " and " sympathize " with others. Peace of spirit is essential if we would keep ourselves abreast of our opportunities and do each work at its own hour. Let us try to imitate the Saviour here; and to this end let us cultivate entire confidence in God, for trust in him is peace. And when we have that as a constant possession we shall both clearly see the work that is awaiting us, and have the will to perform it. The man who is flurried, never knows what to do first, and always takes hold of things by the wrong end, but the calm, self-poised—rather let me say God-poised—man is never in haste, and gets through the work of each day in its own day. This is true in ordinary business life, but it is equally so in the department of Christian beneficence.

The second practical lesson is, that the raising of questions in the domain of mere speculation interferes with the performance of the pressing duties of practical life. The disciples, in this case, brought up a very difficult subject when they asked concerning the origin of the blind man's privation; and they would have been greatly pleased, so at least it seems to me, to have had a long conversation with their Master upon it. But he passes it with the briefest possible remark, and then proceeds to the work before him, saying, " We must work the work of him that sent me, while it is day." It is very much as if he had said, " You and I have nothing to do with such questions as these. They belong to God. We are not responsible for their solution, and we need spend no time upon them. We have other and better work to do. Not the speculative, but the practical, demands our care."

Now this procedure of the Master here, is in perfect keeping with the course which he followed on other occasions. Thus, when his followers asked him, "Are there few that be saved ? " his answer was, " Strive ye to enter in at the strait gate; " and when Peter, after having been informed of the manner of the death by which he was to glorify God, inquired how it should be with John, he was met with the reply, " What is that to thee ? Fol·low thou me." Thus we are taught that if we would keep ourselves in the best possible condition for doing the work of the present, we must restrain ourselves from indulging in matters of curious speculation, which we have no means of settling, or which if settled have no bearing on the work to the doing of which we are called. " Secret things belong unto the Lord our God; but those things which are revealed belong unto us and to our children for ever, that we may do all the words of this law." *

There is a world to be converted. We have a work to do in its conversion, and our time for labor is rapidly hastening to its close. Why then should we waste our energies, and let slip our opportunities, in discussing matters the solution of which is not within our power. Curious speculation is fatal to earnest activity. Therefore, let us always and everywhere avoid it, and let us redeem every opportunity which God gives us to labor in his cause. " The night cometh." Let it not over·take us before our work is done.

* Deut. xxix. 29.

XXVII.

THE RAISING OF LAZARUS FROM THE DEAD.

John xi. 1-46.

ON the eastern slope of the Mount of Olives, and about two miles southeast from Jerusalem, there is a little village, now called El-Lazarieh, which must ever be dear to the Christian heart. It was formerly known as Bethany—the House of Dates—perhaps because of the number of palm-trees in its immediate neighborhood—and in it was the home of Mary, and her sister, and Lazarus. Of Lazarus, the brother, the story of whose illness, death, and resurrection to life is told in this chapter, we know too little to enable us to speak with any precision of his personal qualities. But the characteristics of the two sisters stand out before us, with peculiar distinctness, in the narratives both of Luke and John. Martha was the active housewife intent on looking after the material comfort of her guests. She was not by any means destitute of religious susceptibilities, and had a faith which was clear and firm, so far as it went. But with the management of domestic affairs upon her hands, she was " careful and troubled about many things," and was apt, when friends were under her roof, to be "cumbered about much serving." These, it must be allowed, were blemishes in her; but she was not the worldly-minded and in-

tensely material woman that she has too often been portrayed by indiscriminating critics.   And if it be true
that Mary shows to better advantage than she, when the
Saviour was to be entertained in her house, as described
by Luke, it is no less so that Martha bears away the
palm when sorrow reigned in the home, as recorded here
by John.

Hers was an active, bustling, somewhat anxious and
restless temperament, and her regard for the Lord Jesus
showed itself in a manner which corresponded with that
temperament; but it was no less sincere than Mary's,
though it was less deep in its root, and less keen in its
insight.   For Mary was of a contemplative cast.   She
was of the sort, that, in these days, would be called peculiar—taking comparatively little interest in household
matters, and more concerned with listening to the Saviour's words, than with ministering to his necessities.
And when she did set about anything that might be
called practical, the things which she did were so unusual
and out of the way as to provoke the astonishment, and
sometimes the ridicule or condemnation, of spectators.
Martha was more like Peter, Mary more like John ; and
perhaps the ideal woman would be one who should combine in proper proportion the distinctive excellences of
each.

But different as these sisters were from each other,
they were both devoted to the Saviour.   They delighted
to have him in their house, and their home was one of
the few in the neighborhood of Jerusalem,—perhaps the
only one in that region—into which he was received with
affection and regard.   We cannot wonder, therefore, that
he was often there, or that, after a day of labor and conflict, and fatigue in the city, he sought rest and refresh-
ment by retiring in the evening to this village retreat.

" Jesus loved Martha, and her sister, and Lazarus."
Their abode was to him like an "oasis" in the wilderness, where he might and did find shade and relief,
kindness without any alloy, and affection without any
drawback.

One would have thought that such a home, so long at
least as Jesus was upon the earth and needed just what
it afforded, would have been exempted from all affliction.
But that is not always God's way. His highest honor is
sometimes conferred through and in connection with trial,
and this was the case in the present instance. For Lazarus was prostrated by severe illness, which was speedily
seen to be very serious in its nature ; and the moment
that fact was recognized, the first thought of the sisters
was for Jesus. But, alas ! he was not in the neighborhood ; yet, knowing where he was, they sent a messenger to say to him, " Lord, behold he whom thou
lovest is sick." They did not ask him to come to them ;
but they simply told their need, and left it to himself to
decide how he was to help them.

If the best harmonists are right, Jesus was at this
time in Peræa, on the eastern side of the Jordan, quite a
day's journey from Bethany ; and, after hearing the message of the sisters, he sent the bearer of it back to them,
with this assurance : " This sickness is not unto death,
but for the glory of God, that the Son of God might be
glorified thereby," and deliberately remained where he
was for two days, before going to his friends. Now,
with the full narrative in our hands, and knowing, in
this case, the end from the beginning, we can understand
this enigmatical statement. We see at once that the
Lord meant to assure the sisters that, whatever might be
the case meanwhile, the ultimate issue of the sickness
of Lazarus was not to be death, but was to be such as

should be for the glory of God, and very specially for the glory of the Son of God. By the restoration of Lazarus from the grave, God should be glorified; and by the death and resurrection of Christ, to which, in a very wonderful way, the raising of Lazarus from the dead should very directly lead, the Son of God would be glorified.

We can see and understand that *now ;* but what a perplexing puzzle would it be to the sisters at the moment when it was received by them? For then, if we have reckoned rightly, either Lazarus must have been already dead, or must, at least, have been rapidly sinking into death. What could it mean? Lazarus was dying, if not dead, and yet "this sickness is not unto death." Was Jesus no true prophet after all? Yet "this sickness is for the glory of God, that the Son of God might be glorified thereby." Was there not something of promise for them under these words, and, if so, what precisely was the hope set before them? They could not tell. The waters had gone over them, but they were not thoroughly overwhelmed; and here was given them a life-buoy, by which they might uphold themselves until full deliverance should come. Vague as it was, this message had that in it to which they might cling.

But why these two days' delay? Was it to secure that, when he did arrive, it might be seen that no mere human power could give the help he was about to render? or was it merely that he might finish the work in which he was engaged where he was? We cannot tell. But at the end of these two days, he said to his disciples, "Let us go into Judæa again." The proposal, however, was very disagreeable to them. He had narrowly escaped from being stoned, when he was last there, and they could not understand why he should desire to return. But he sought to calm their fears after this fashion : " Are there not twelve hours in the day ? If any man walk in the day, he stumbleth not, because he seeth the light of this world. But if a man walk in the night, he stumbleth, because there is no light in him." Much as if he had said : " I have a certain work given me to do ; and I have a day in which to do it. So long as that day lasts, and that work is unfinished, I need fear no danger ; for I am walking in the daylight ; and if you walk with me, you are as safe as I am, the while, for you are walking in the light when you are walking with me. But if one should go any whither 'without the light of the divine purpose illuming,' for him, 'the path of duty,' he will stumble, for he is walking in the darkness, which though spiritual and subjective, will be as black as that of night is in the absence of the sun."

This announcement of his determination to return to Judæa, prepared the way for the communication to them of the fact that Lazarus was dead. But observe how gently he broke the sad tidings to them. He began by saying to them, " Our friend Lazarus sleepeth ; but I go that I may awake him out of sleep." Thinking only of his first words, they interpreted them literally. They imagined that he spoke only of such sleep as often marks the crisis of a fever, when the patient gets what Scotch people so expressively call " the turn." They said, " If he sleep, he shall do well." It was a good symptom, as we might say ; but then, if they had only paused long enough to take in the rest of the sentence, they might have seen that they had made a mistake ; for to awake a patient out of such a sleep, might be exceedingly dangerous ; and if it were merely a sleep, why should it be necessary for Christ to take such a journey in order to awake him out of it ? Could not another have done that just as easily as he ?

But apparently they had not heard, or, if they had heard, they did not heed, the latter part of his statement; and so, having gradually led them up to the point, he said to them plainly, " Lazarus is dead," and then added, " and I am glad for your sakes, that I was not there, to the intent ye may believe; nevertheless, let us go unto him."

What a startling statement that is, at least in one aspect of it, " Lazarus is dead, and I am glad "! Yet when we hear it out, we are not so perplexed. There were lessons to be taught to his followers, which could not otherwise have been impressed upon them; and so, for their sakes, he was glad that he had not been at Bethany during the sickness of Lazarus; for if he had been there —such at least seems to me to be the implication of the words—he could not have refused the request of the sisters to heal him. But now that he was dead, there would be opportunity for showing Martha and Mary a richer mercy, and teaching the disciples a nobler lesson, than his cure would have supplied.

" For your sakes "—so Lazarus suffered and died for the sake of others, just as really, though not precisely in the same full sense, as Jesus himself did; and thus a great flood of light is cast on the problem of suffering in the world.

But Thomas, who was ever prone to look on the dark side of things, was not enamored of the prospect that their return to Judæa opened up. In spite of all that the Lord had said about the hours of the day, he felt that his death would be the result of his going back; yet he would not let the Saviour go alone because of that. He loved him too well to desert him, even in what seemed to him to be a rash and dangerous enterprise; and, therefore, he said to his fellows : " Let us also go, that we may die with him." Little faith is sometimes, as here, allied with strong affection. The danger in such a case is, that the smallness of the faith may chill the ardor of the affection; but the hope is that, as in Thomas himself, the warmth of the affection may stimulate the faith.

So they set out for Bethany, and arrived there to find that the remains of Lazarus had been buried for four days. But the mourners, who on such occasions among the Jews, were accustomed to crowd the houses of the bereaved, were still numerous in the home of the sisters; and perhaps to escape them Jesus lingered on the outskirts of the village. Still, " he could not be hid," and his arrival was made known in some way to Martha, who, apparently without saying anything of it to Mary, went out to meet him. As soon as she saw him, she exclaimed, " Lord, if thou hadst been here, my brother had not died "—an exclamation which, as is evident from the fact that Mary subsequently used the very same words, had been the burden of the sisters' cry during the whole time of their sorrow; just as similar " ifs " are wont to be indulged in by mourners still ; and it was followed by an assertion, indicating, on Martha's part, a vague, indefinite hope of something that the Saviour would yet do for them; for she added, " But I know, that even now, whatsoever thou wilt ask of God, God will give it thee."

It is possible that in her heart at that moment there was the expectation that Jesus would restore Lazarus to life, as he had done in the cases of the widow's son at Nain, and of the daughter of Jairus, both of which were probably known to her. If it was, she did not venture to put that expectation into words, and the answer of the Master, "Thy brother shall rise again," was just as general as her remark. So that we catch a tone of disappointment or discouragement in her response, " I know that he shall rise again in the resurrection, at *the last day*," as if she had said, " That is a long way off; and meanwhile we shall have to endure our loneliness and sorrow. It is a glorious hope, but it does not meet my present need."

And it was to that state of mind that the Lord spoke these greatest words of the gospel: " I am the Resurrection and the Life ; he that believeth in me, though he were dead, yet shall he live ; and he that liveth and believeth in me, shall never die." " No, Martha, the Resurrection is not far away. It is here, *in me ;* for the source of that resurrection is in myself; yea, in me, also, is the fountain of life, and that life is imparted by me to every one that believeth. The life which I bestow is spiritual and eternal. It is indestructible by death ; so that the believer, even when dead, lives on, as much a partaker of my life as he was before ; and the living believer, even when he comes to die, does not lose that life which I have bestowed upon him. Believest thou this ?" Such is the import of the words.

But Martha was bewildered by them. She did not understand them. Yet she would not reject them. She only said, with, as we may well believe, a look of perplexity upon her countenance : " Yea, Lord, I believe that thou art the Christ, the Son of God, which should come into the world." " I do not comprehend thy meaning; but I am ready to take anything on thy word; for I have long believed, and I do still believe, that thou art the Christ, the Son of God, that should come into the world."

Then she bethought herself of Mary, who was so skilful in reading the full significance of the words of Jesus ; and at the same moment, apparently, he desired that she should be called out to see him. So, at once to carry out the prompting of her own heart and obey his command, she went into the house and said to her sister: "The Master is come, and calleth for thee." This she did as quietly as possible, in order to secure privacy for the interview; but the friends in the house, on seeing Mary rise up hastily and go out, followed her at once, under the impression that she was going "to the grave to weep there."

When Mary came to Jesus she fell at his feet, and in a paroxysm of emotion, she said to him, with tears, "Lord, if thou hadst been here my brother had not died." And such was the effect produced upon him by the sight of her sorrow, that "He groaned in spirit, and troubled himself." But these last words are very ha d to interpret, for the term rendered "groaned" has it ts usual significance much more of indignation than of grief. Hence it is translated in the margin of the 'te- vised Version, "was moved with indignation in his spirit;" and the question forces itself upon us, at what was he thus indignant? That question is very difficult to answer. Some have supposed that he was indignant at the perception of the temporary triumph of evil, as death—or as personally of the devil, who had brought sin into the world, and death by sin, and of which he was here reminded by circumstances of the deepest pathos. Others have said that his displeasure was di- rected against the Jewish mourners, so many of whom were moved with enmity towards himself. But this latter view can hardly be adopted, inasmuch as the an- tagonism of the Jews had not yet been manifested toward him, as it afterwards was. It is safer, therefore, to rest in the other explanation; but, in any case, the words of Westcott are pertinent, when he says, "Whichever view be taken, it must be remembered that the miracles of the Lord were not wrought by the simple word of power, but that in a mysterious way the element of sympathy entered into them. He took away the sufferings and diseases of men, in some sense, by taking them on himself." * After this wave of emotion had passed over him, he asked where they had buried Lazarus, and as they conducted him to the grave, he " wept."

This was rightly interpreted by some of those around him as an evidence of the depth of his affection for his friend ; but others of them, with perhaps some cynicism in their tone, exclaimed, " Could not this man, which opened the eyes of the blind, have caused that even this man should not have died ? " The only effect of this was to renew for a moment the inner conflict from which he had formerly suffered; and when that subsided, he found that the grave was a cave, against the opening into which a stone had been rolled, and he immediately requested that the stone should be taken away. Thereupon Martha, supposing that he wished to look once more upon the face of his friend, suggested that by this time— the fourth day after interment,—corruption would have set in, and that therefore the remains might better be undisturbed. But the Master answered by reminding her of the message which he had sent her from beyond the Jordan, and so rewaking in her the hope of some great blessing that was to come,—" Said I not unto thee, that if thou wouldest believe, thou shouldest see the glory of God ? "

The bystanders did as they were told, and he, lifting up his eyes to heaven, addressed his Father, not to make a request, but to thank him that his request had been granted, so that, thereby, the fellowship of the Son with the Father, by whose word he quickens

* " Speaker's Commentary," *in loco.*

whom he will, had been manifested to all them who were
about him. Beautifully has Westcott said here, " This
thanksgiving was not for any uncertain or unexpected
gift. It was rather a proclamation of fellowship with
God. The sympathy in work and thought between the
Father and the Son is always perfect and uninterrupted,
and now it was revealed in action. Even in this sorrow
the Son knew the end ; but that which he knew, others
denied, and by the open claim to the co-operation of God,
the Lord made a last solemn appeal to the belief of his
adversaries." *

After this the Saviour " cried with a loud voice, Lazarus, come forth. And he that was dead came forth,
bound hand and foot with grave clothes, and his face was
bound about with a napkin. Jesus saith unto them,
Loose him, and let him go."

The Evangelist, under the guidance of a divine inspiration, makes no attempt to describe the scene of the restoration of the brother to his sisters, but leaves the simple narrative to stand out in its own true sublimity, while
he goes on to tell of the effect produced upon the spectators. This, as on all similar occasions, differed with the
differing pre-possessions of each. Some, with no predetermined hostility to the Lord, believed on him because of what they had seen ; but others, who were before antagonistic to him, were made only more bitter in
their opposition, and went and told the official Jews what
they had seen—with the result that at a formal meeting
of the Sanhedrym it was determined that they should put
him to death. This they did, you observe, not because
the miracle was false, but because they knew that it was
true.

When, therefore, Spinoza said, " that if it were pos-

* " Speaker's Commentary," *in loco.*

sible for him to persuade himself of the resurrection of Lazarus, he would dash his whole system to pieces, and enbrace the faith of ordinary Christians without reluctance," he took only a partial view of the case For these Jews believed in the fact of the restoration of Lazarus to life, and said, " This man doeth many miracles ; " and yet from " that day forth they took counsel together for to put him to death."

Thus a miracle, besides being a sign of spiritual truth to men, is a test of moral character in men. They judge of it according to their nature. Its effect upon them depends upon their pre-accepted opinions, or their underlying philosophy, or their attitude toward him who wrought it. We need not wonder, therefore, at modern adversaries to the gospel. They reject the reality of the miracles, because they reject Christ ; but bad as that is, it is not nearly so inconsistent as was the conduct of these Jews, who admitted the fact of this miracle, and then set themselves to plot for the bringing about of the death of him who wrought it.

Many valuable truths are suggested by this deeply interesting narrative. But as I have already dwelt on the more important of these elsewhere, I shall content myself on this occasion, with giving prominence to one or two, equally obvious and equally natural, which were then passed by, because of the different object which I had in view.

As a spiritual sign, this wondrous work reminds us, that men are dead in trespasses and sins ; that their quickening is the work of Christ, and is the result of his command, "Awake, thou that sleepest, and arise from the dead, and I will give thee light ;" and that, though Christians cannot renew other men, they yet may, and ought, to do many things for the unregenerate in preparation for their regeneration, even as here the by-standers rolled away the stone, and opened the way for Lazarus to come forth at the Saviour's call.

But while that is the spiritual parable taught us in this great miracle, we cannot fail to see, in the accessories that accompanied its performance, a clear proof of the possession by our Lord of the human and divine natures in his one Person. The emotion which came over him on his way to the grave, and his tears as he stood waiting till the stone was rolled away from its mouth, are clear evidences of his humanity. While again the peculiar character of his thanksgiving, and his word of power whereby Lazarus was raised, indicate a special relationship between him and the Father, such as only his participation in the divine nature can satisfactorily account for. His friendship with Lazarus and the sisters was a human fellowship; but his address to the Father was a divine communion. There is a clear difference between the two, which grew out of his possession of the two natures.

Then, again, how can we conceive of a mere man, who was remarkable throughout his life for perfect truthfulness, using such language as this, "I am the Resurrection and the Life; he that believeth on me, though he were dead, yet shall he live; and whosoever liveth and believeth in me shall never die"? That saying is either false, arrogant, and misleading; or it is the saying of One who, though in human nature, was also God. That is the only alternative. But we cannot believe that Jesus could wantonly assert that which is not true; for, if we could, that would be to give up the purity of his moral character; and therefore we believe him to be also God.

As we have often said before, it is impossible to believe that Jesus Christ was even a good man, unless we
believe also that he is God.   We must either believe
more or less about him than that he was a good man.
We must either go farther, or we must not go so far, and
after the review which we have taken of this chapter
we must surely be convinced that it is easier to believe
in his incarnation, than to rest in the idea that he was no
more than a man.

Still farther, we have in this deeply interesting narrative a manifestation of the sympathy of our divine Redeemer.   How tenderly he felt for the sisters in the hour
of their trial! and what tears those were, which he shed,
at the grave!   Truly the church has put these into her
bottle, and they have been in all ages a reminder, to
those who are in sorrow, of the Saviour's fellow-feeling
with them in their grief.   But more than all, this history
shows us that his sympathy is not a blind and merely
impulsive thing, but regulated and directed by a wise
purpose.   The sincerity of his love, as we here discover,
was perfectly consistent with his delay to come with help
when something better was to be secured thereby.   And,
more remarkable still, that sympathy, as it here appears,
was in harmony with his causing of sorrow to some, for
the sake of benefiting others ; for he said to his disciples,
" I am glad, for your sakes, that I was not there."

The remembrance of these things may keep us from
misunderstanding him, or from charging him foolishly
when we are in trouble; while the knowledge that he
wept with the sisters, in their time of sorrow, gives us
assurance that he feels with us in ours.

Finally let us not fail to mark the difference between
the restoration of Lazarus to life and the resurrection
of the Lord himself.   There is an old legend, to the ef-

fect that the first question asked by Lazarus after his
resuscitation, was whether he should be required to die
again, and that on being answered in the affirmative, he
never smiled again. That is only a legend. But we
cannot help remarking on the silence which he maintained regarding the experience through which he had
been brought.

You remember Tennyson's lines :

"" 'Where wert thou, brother, these four days?'"
There lives no record of reply,
 Which, telling what it is to die,
Had surely added praise to praise.

" From every house the neighbors met ;
The streets were filled with joyful sound ;
A solemn gladness even crowned
The purple brow of Olivet.

"Behold a man raised up by Christ !
The rest remaineth unrevealed ;
He told it not, or something sealed
The lips of that evangelist."

But when you come to think it out you will see that
there was no revelation of the future made by the restoration of Lazarus, and that the silence of his lips was
in perfect keeping with that fact. He was brought back
to the old life, with its old relationships to his sisters, his
neighbors and his friends, and he had to die again.
When Christ rose from the grave, however, he did not
come back, but went forward. His resurrection was
not a return, but a going on. He saw his followers, indeed, but it was not after the former fashion. There
was a complete difference between the nature of his intercourse with them after his resurrection, and that of his
fellowship with them before his death. He did not come
back to his former life ; but he went forward to a new

and higher human life, and so his resurrection was also a revelation of the nature of the life beyond. He brought life and immortality to light by it, and he did so because he rose not to die again, but to pass in spiritual and glorified humanity up to the throne of glory. This is what gives its distinctive feature to his resurrection, as contrasted with all mere restorations to life—such as those effected by prophets and apostles, and even by Christ himself. Let us intelligently perceive and firmly grasp that, and we shall begin to realize something of what Paul means by " the power of his resurrection," both for support through life and for comfort in death.

XXVIII.

SABBATH DAY MIRACLES.

Luke xiii. 10-17. Luke xiv. 1-6.

I HAVE taken these two miracles together, because they are peculiar to Luke ; because they are found not far apart from each other in his narrative ; and because both were wrought on the Sabbath day, thereby provoking such a manifestation of feeling on the part of the Pharisees, as to call forth from the Saviour a vindication of himself for what he had done.

The first was performed, as the record says, "in one of the synagogues." We cannot identify either the place in which, or the time at which, it was wrought. Many of the best commentators, however, believe that this whole section of Luke's gospel, extending from chap. ix. 51 to chap. xviii. 14, belongs in its earlier portion to our Lord's final journey from Galilee, and in its latter to the intervals between the Feast of Tabernacles and that of the Dedication in the last year of his ministry, and between the Feast of the Dedication and his last Passover—during both of which he appears to have sojourned in Peræa, on the eastern side of the Jordan, and within the jurisdiction of Herod Antipas. If this view be correct, then the synagogue in which the

387

former of these miracles was performed was in some one of the small towns in that region.

Let it be noted, as we pass, that the Lord *was* in the synagogue on the Sabbath. It was his custom to be there. He went thither to worship, as well as to teach ; for his own benefit, as well as for an example to others ; and so, even though he was on a journey, and merely staying over in the place for the day, he went to the house of prayer. There also was a poor invalid woman, whose case is minutely diagnosed by the Evangelist, whose profession as a physician made him all the more able to describe it, and all the more interested in its details.

She was bent nearly double by a strange malady, which seems to have been partly spiritual and partly physical. She had " a spirit of infirmity,"—a phrase which seems to imply that the disease was first in the spirit ; and that the physical curvature was the consequence of the mental obliquity. Some, indeed, have supposed that it was a case of diabolical possession, because the Saviour speaks of her as one "whom Satan had bound for eighteen years" But when we remember that Paul speaks of his "thorn in the flesh," as a "messenger of Satan to buffet him," and that in the book of Job Satan is set before us as the proximate cause of the patriarch's malady, the inference that this woman had an evil demon seems scarcely to be warranted by the premises from which it is drawn. Perhaps, through some form of insanity, she began to assume the unnatural position in which here we find her, and continued it so long that she became ultimately unable to straighten herself, even if she had been willing to make the attempt, just as there are in India to-day many devotees who have held their arms so long in one position that they are unable now to move them. But, however the rigidity was produced, there she was, "in no wise able to lift up herself."

A pitiable object she must have been to any one ; how much more to the compassionate Christ ! We cannot wonder, therefore, that, altogether unsolicited by her, he sought of his own gracious kindness to cure her of her weakness. With that purpose, he called her, and said to her, " Woman, thou art loosed from thine infirmity,'' and laying his hands upon her, she was thereby encouraged to lift herself up, and immediately became straight, and glorified God.

But that which struck out of her a doxology, only provoked others to anger, for the ruler of the synagogue, to whom the letter of the law was far more important than the spirit of it, immediately accused her benefactor of Sabbath breaking. He was mean enough to be indignant at what was done for the woman, but he was not man enough directly to accuse the Saviour for the doing of it. He spoke *to* the people, but *at* him. He scolded him through them. He blamed them for coming to be healed on the Sabbath, when he really meant to condemn him for healing the afflicted woman on that day. " There are six days," said he, " in which men ought to work ; in them, therefore, come and be healed, and not on the Sabbath." But the Lord replied in language addressed to the whole party to which the ruler belonged, " Ye hypocrites, doth not each one of you on the Sabbath loose his ox or his ass from the stall and lead him away to watering ? And ought not this woman, being a daughter of Abraham, whom Satan hath bound, lo, these eighteen years, to have been loosed from this bond on the Sabbath day ? " As we have seen in a former discourse, the Pharisees had overlaid the Mosaic legislation concerning the Sabbath with a great mass of Rabbinical restric-

tions, which had turned that institution, which was meant
to be a blessing, into a species of slavery; and it was
against these, and not against the Sabbath, when viewed
in the light of its original intention, that the Saviour so
repeatedly protested. The case is presented with singular clearness by Dr. Kitto in the following paragraphs :
" The Sabbath was a divine institution, and as such it
could not be abrogated, nor its prescribed observance
altered or modified, by any authority less than divine.
When our Lord, therefore, claimed absolute power over
the Sabbath day; when he declared that the Son of Man
was " Lord even of the Sabbath day," he claimed no less
than divine anthority, and was understood to do so.   He
might have abrogated it wholly, if he had seen fit, but his
object seems to have been no more than to bring it back
to its primary purpose, as a day of free and blessed rest,
relieving it from the special observances and restrictions
which the law of Moses had imposed, and which, being no
longer needed in the service of the more spiritual nature
which Christ introduced, were to be counted among things
that were old and had passed away.

" Yet it is to be observed, that while Christ claimed
this absolute power, his actual operations, so far as
brought under our notice, did not affect any one of the
Mosaic ordinances, as plainly and literally understood.
We see Jesus again and again accused of Sabbath violation for performing certain acts on the seventh day.
But if we turn to the code of Moses in search of the laws
alleged to be violated, we cannot find them—they are
not there.   The fact is, that in this, as in other matters,
the letter of the law had, in our Lord's time, been overlaid by a mass of traditional explanations, extensions,
and applications, every one of which was regarded as of
equal authority with the letter of the law itself, and every

transgression of which was equally an act of Sabbath-violation, and equally liable to be visited with the penalties of that offence. These traditions only did our Lord's Sabbath acts infringe. But of these traditions he always expressed his utter disregard, and often his reprobation. And his argument, in answer to the charges brought against him in this respect, was, either that the particular act was not a violation of the law of Moses, but was in perfect accordance with its spirit,—or that the power which the Father had given to him was not subject to the limitations of that law." *

The case before us is an illustration of the former class of arguments, and it is presented in the form usually denominated *ad hominem.* The Rabbinical law for physicians was that they might on the Sabbath attend to cases of emergency in which life or death was immediately involved; but not to those of chronic diseases, like that under which this poor woman was suffering; and the intention of the ruler very plainly was to bring the action of the Saviour here under the condemnation of that law. But the vindication made by the Saviour is complete and in fact unanswerable.

The principle that underlies it is the same as that which we shall find in the answer made by him to the lawyers and Pharisees on occasion of his working the second miracle, which is to-night to be under our attention, with this difference, that while the pulling of an ox or a child out of a well is the meeting of an accidental emergency, the watering of an ox or an ass is a daily necessity, and so is a thing that must be done on one day as well as another. The fair deduction, therefore, is that the giving attention by a physician, whether to chronic cases, or to cases of emergency is as justifiable on the Sabbath

* Kitto's " Daily Bible Illustrations," vol. vii. pp. 315, 316.

as on any other day of the week. And we are indebted to Plumtre for reminding us that such a principle must have been specially interesting to the author of this gospel. " We can scarcely fail," he remarks, " to think of the 'beloved physician' as practicing his art for the good of men, his brothers, on the Sabbath as on other days. In doing so he would doubtless be met on the part of Jews and Judaizers with words like those of the ruler of the synagogue : ' There are six days on which men ought to work ; do thy work of healing on them.' For such a one it would be a comfort unspeakable to be able to point to our Lord's words and acts as sanctioning his own practice."*

But let us look at the answer a little more in detail. The Pharisees themselves did not hesitate on the Sabbath to unloose their oxen and asses from the stalls and lead them away to watering; what inconsistency, therefore, was it in them to blame him for unloosing this woman from eighteen years of bondage on that day ? How much was a woman—a daughter of Abraham, too, not only in the mere fleshly sense of being a Jewess, but also in the higher and nobler sense of being a possessor of his faith—better than an ox or an ass ? Surely there was warrant here for his calling them " hypocrites "— who preferred sacrifice to mercy, and condemned others for doing that which without scruple they allowed in themselves. They had no hesitation, when their personal property was at stake, to do what they blamed him for doing, out of love to a sufferer who had been bowed down with weakness for eighteen years. Plainly, therefore, the comfort or value of an ox was more to them than the well-being of an afflicted woman. And in this respect,

* " New Testament Commentary for English Readers," edited by Bishop Ellicott, vol. i. p. 307.

alas! how many are like them even in modern days? We do not wonder that the ruler of the synagogue and his friends were put to shame and silence by this exposure of their hypocrisy. One thinks a little better of them, indeed, for having the grace to be ashamed; but they were evidently in a small minority, and that may have had something to do with their confusion, for " all the multitude rejoiced for all the glorious things that were done by him."

The second of the miracles to which this discourse is devoted was in many respects similar to that which we have just considered, and therefore it need not detain us long. It was wrought in the house of one of the rulers of the Pharisees to which on a Sabbath day Jesus went by invitation to eat bread. There was evidently a party or banquet on the occasion, as we may infer from the verses which immediately follow the account of the miracle. Now it may be rather surprising to some that there should have been such a festive gathering on the Sabbath in the house of a Pharisee, and that Jesus should have been there. But in regard to the former of these, we must remember, that although the Sabbath was hedged round by numberless restrictions in the matter of labor, it was regarded and kept even by the Pharisees as a festival. It was not by any means the gloomy day which is so often sneered at as the Jewish Sabbath. It was a day for social entertainments. There was indeed no work done in the preparation of food. That was all attended to before the Sabbath began; but short of that, festal rejoicing was one of the features of the day. And Jesus, so far as appears from the gospel narratives, did not hesitate, when invited, to take part in such feasts, though it has to be remembered, that on every such occasion he sought to turn the conversation into a profitable channel, and used it as an opportunity for communicating instruction on the things of the kingdom.

We do not know what the motive of this ruler was in asking Jesus to be one of his guests. But, by those who were in his confidence, it was viewed as a favorable time for watching Jesus, if haply they might find in his conduct or in his words some ground for bringing an accusation against him. With that object in view, it would almost seem that they had introduced into the hall of the feast, among the spectators who were at liberty to be present on such occasions, " a certain man which had the dropsy—"calculating on the probability that the Lord would heal him, and would thereby give them some pretext for bringing a formal charge against him. This is not said indeed in so many words in the record. But the fact that the healed man was let go by Jesus immediately after he was cured, and before the Lord began to speak to the guests, while it proves that the sick one was not conscious of the use which had been made of him, does at the same time suggest that the other guests had brought him in to " watch" whether or not the Lord would heal him. Whether we adopt that view or not is, perhaps, not very material. This, at least, is plain, that the presence of this diseased man there raised somehow in the minds of the guests the question whether Christ would cure him, and they waited with some eagerness to see the result. But the Saviour took in the situation in a moment, and checkmated them by asking, " Is it lawful to heal on the Sabbath or not ? "

As he had probably foreseen, however, they would not commit themselves by any reply, and therefore he forthwith proceeded to cure the sufferer. Then when he had

" taken him and healed him and let him go," he made this reply to their unspoken criticism : " Which of you shall have an ass," (or as some very valuable manuscripts read, a son) " or an ox fallen into a pit, (or a well), and will not straightway draw him up on a Sabbath day ? " It was the familiar argument, " How much is a man better than an ox ? " or, if we adopt the rendering son, it was this :—If you would lift your own son out of a well ; why may not I make whole this man, who, in a very real sense, is a son of God, and therefore a son of mine ? But, as in the former instance, they could or would give no reply. And so, the conversation turned into another channel, the diversion being caused by the petty jealousies which he saw in the contentions between the guests for places of priority at the table. But into that discourse we do not enter now. We linger only a few minutes to pick up one or two lessons from the whole subject.

And first of all we are reminded incidentally here of the value of attendance on ordinances. I found that not on the presence of the Saviour in the synagogue on the Sabbath day, although his example in such a matter should never be either lost sight of or forgotten by us. But my reference is to the poor afflicted woman. Many, suffering as she was, would have accounted *that* a sufficient reason for remaining at home. But she was " a daughter of Abraham," spiritually as a believer as well as according to the flesh. She relished the services of the synagogue, and attended them because she valued them. Therefore she was there when Christ came, and then she received a special blessing. So far as the record goes, it does not appear that she came to that place of worship because she expected the Saviour to be there. Had that been the case, she would have made formal application

to him for a cure.   But she was there according to her
custom, for the worship of God.

Now how different all this was from many modern
church-goers, need hardly be pointed out to you.   The
least ache or pain is sufficient to keep them from the
sanctuary.   The rain which would not prevent them from
going to business, or to market, or to a place of amusement, is enough to determine them to stay away from
church.   While again there are many who will go only
when some distinguished preacher is to discourse ; and not
a few who excuse themselves for their remaining in their
homes, by saying that they may study the Scriptures and
other good books there and get in that way as much
good as in the sanctuary.   But there are special blessings promised to those who "forsake not the assem-
bling of themselves together," and the Lord has declared that "where two or three are gathered together
in his name, there he is in the midst of them."   How
much this woman would have missed if she had not been
in the synagogue that day ?   And though it was not the
Sabbath in his case, if Thomas had been with the brethren that evening when the risen Christ appeared to them,
he would have been spared a week of isolation and distress.   How know you, therefore, that the Lord may not
visit the congregation with peculiar blessing on the very
day that you are absent through indifference, and so you
may be passed by while others are benefited ?   Have
regard in your thought of the sanctuary to your meeting
there with Christ, and that will raise it above all earthly
appointments.   Come not to hear a man, but to meet
your Lord, and he will bless you by removing the
weight of care by which the week has bowed you down.
He will set you free to begin anew.   As one has well
said, " No wise defender of public worship ever rested

his case on the ability of the preacher. Many preachers
are men of limited intelligence, and feeble emotions,
much inferior in these respects to some among their
hearers. The interval, however, (between them and him)
to say the least, is not what existed between the teachers
of the synagogue, and Jesus. Men may read at home
sermons far more profound and eloquent than they can
hear in church. Still their true place is in the sanctuary,
for this is still a custom of Christ's, to be where his people are gathered." * The prevalent indifference to the
sanctuary is an evidence of the low state of spiritual life
among us, and indulgence in it will make that condition
lower. Therefore we ought to be on our guard, against
it.

But let us note here, in the second place, that determined antagonism to the truth is only irritated and
stiffened by the presentation of additional evidence. The
deaf man was very shrewd, who in answer to an inquiry
why he took so much pleasure in being present at a discussion, seeing he could not hear a word that was said,
remarked, that he always knew who had the worst of the
argument, by noting which was the first to lose his temper! When no answer to a statement, or to a fact, can
be made, the opponent waxes indignant. This is the
root of all intolerance, and it shows, also, how little is to
be expected from controversy. The Pharisees could not
deny the reality of the Saviour's miracles, but they could
put him to death, and they would not have hesitated to
kill Lazarus, also, if only thereby they could have destroyed all proof of his having been restored to life.
There must be an appropriate moral condition, before
evidence can have its true and proper effect. If a man
does not want to be convinced, you cannot convince

* " The Incarnate Saviour," Rev. W. R. Nicol, p. 172.

him.   This touches a vital principle, and shows how true
it is that man is responsible for his belief.   If the matter,
indeed, were a mathematical demonstration, one might say
that belief is altogether irrespective of volition.   But it
is not so in the moral and spiritual domain.   There one
believes according to his preferences; and the stronger
proof you adduce, to the man who is deliberately antagonistic, the stronger does his opposition become.   This
has been so in all ages.   It is so to-day, and therefore
we may not wonder when we find men intelligent in
other spheres, inflexibly opposed to Christ and Christianity.   They would have been no better than they are
even, if they, like the Pharisees and lawyers here, had
seen Christ working a miracle before their eyes.

Still again, let us remember that the Christian in society is always being watched.   Men are taking knowledge of him all the time.   They take note how he con-
ducts his business; they scrutinize his behavior at the
feast, or in the social circle; they notice how he behaves
himself at the summer hotel, or on board ship, or wherever
he may be.   Would that he could always stand that
ordeal as the Lord himself did in the house of this
Pharisee !

My brethren, when so many are on the watch for our
stumbling, how much need is there for us to take heed to
ourselves ?   Let us seek, by prayerful realization of the
presence of the Lord with us, to be Christians wherever
we are ; and then not only shall we save ourselves, but
we may also be the means of salvation to others.   In
our speech let us be reverent and discreet; in our business let us be unswerving in our integrity ; in our conduct let us be unselfish, and thoughtfully considerate for
others' welfare ; in our general deportment let us be
humble, earnest, holy, and devout; and then men shall

take knowledge of us that we have been with Jesus, and even our enemies " shall not find any occasion against us, except they find it against us concerning the law of our God."

Finally, do not go without remarking anew the constant compassion of Christ for human suffering. But the suffering in these cases is the analogue for moral evil, and all these miracles of healing are just so many illustrations of his cure of sin. So Christ compassionates the sinner, just as here he compassionated the sufferers. Whosoever among you is bowed down beneath a load of guilt, from the burden of which he is unable to lift himself up, let him know that the Lord Jesus is ready to relieve him. He will lift up the stooping one. He will say to him, " Thy sins are forgiven thee." He will give him strength to resist evil, and to walk in holy obedience to God. He will loose him from the bonds in which Satan has held him fast so long, and introduce him into " the glorious liberty of the children of God." O sinner, let him do it now ! Answer promptly to his call, and he will send thee home to-night " glorifying God."

XXIX.

THE OPENING OF THE EYES OF BARTIMÆUS.

Matt. xii. 30-34. Mark x. 46-52. Luke xviii. 35-54.

THE city of Jericho was situated in the territory of
the tribe of Benjamin, about twenty miles northeast of
Jerusalem, and some three or four west of the Jordan.
It was the first place in the promised land to which
Joshua and the tribes came after they had crossed the
river, and the singular manner of its siege and capture
is minutely described in the chronicles of that great captain. At that time he razed it to its foundation, and
pronounced a curse against the man who should dare to
rebuild it. For a time, therefore, it remained in ruins,
but ultimately a town grew up near the ancient site;
and that, in the days of Ahab, was fortified by Hiel the
Bethelite, who, according to Joshua's malediction, laid
the foundation of its walls in his first-born, and set up
the gates thereof in his youngest son.* It was sometimes called the City of Palm trees, and sometimes, also,
the City of Balsams, and it was the scene of some of the
miracles of Elisha. It now consists of " a group of
squalid hovels, inhabited by about sixty families, who
are regarded by the Arabs as a debased race," and are

---

* Josh. vi. 26. I Kings xvi. 34.

400

described by the author of the article Jericho, in Smith's "Dictionary of the Bible," as "probably nothing more or less than veritable gypsies."

From its position it lay directly in the route of those who, coming south on the eastern side of the Jordan, crossed the river, and journeyed thence toward Jerusalem. This was the course followed by the Saviour on his last journey to the Jewish capital, and it was somewhere in the neighborhood of the city during that visit to it, made illustrious by the conversion of Zacchæus, that he performed the miracle which is now to be considered. I say somewhere in its neighborhood; because there is here a rather perplexing diversity between the narratives of the three evangelists, so that we cannot precisely identify the spot, or, indeed, arrange the details. Matthew says that two blind men received their sight, and his language rather indicates that the Lord opened their eyes when he was departing from the city. Mark agrees with Matthew in putting the time of the miracle as the Saviour was going out of Jericho, but speaks only of one blind man, giving his name, as that of one probably well-known in the district, Bartimæus, the son of Timæus. Luke agrees with Mark in specifying only one blind man, but is at variance both with Matthew and with Mark in putting the time of the miracle apparently before the Lord's entrance into the city, for immediately after his account of it he says, "And Jesus entered and passed through Jericho."

Now, as is usual in all such cases, many hypotheses have been devised by the Harmonists, with the view of showing that there is no contradiction involved in the several accounts. But I cannot say that I am satisfied with any one of them. If we were in possession of all the facts as they really occurred, it is quite likely that

we should see at once how all the three accounts are
consistent with truth, and with each other; but as it is,
I prefer to make no attempt at removing the difficulties;
because all such efforts involve an unnatural straining of
the accounts given by the writers; and because the very
existence of such diversities is a proof of the independence of the Evangelists and is absolutely incompatible
with the theory that there was any collusion between
them to palm off a forgery upon their readers. Taking
then the account given by Mark as being probably the
earliest of the three, and availing ourselves of the occa-
sional side-lights given by the other two, let us proceed
with our exposition.

When Jesus entered and passed through Jericho, we
learn from Luke that he was attended by such a multitude, that Zacchæus, wishing to see him, had to climb a
tree in order to gratify his curiosity. We cannot wonder, therefore, that after his sojourn in the house of the
publican, he was accompanied by a similar crowd on his
departure from the city. It may be, also, that many
who were going up to Jerusalem for the feast embraced
the opportunity of doing so in company with the Great
Prophet, in order that they might listen to his teachings,
and look upon his works.

Shortly after he had passed through the gates, he came
upon two blind men, one of whom is particularly mentioned by name, probably because he was well known to
all the dwellers in that neighborhood. They were sitting by the wayside begging; not, we may suppose, because they were unwilling to labor for their own support,
but because their blindness incapacitated them for so doing.
We know not whether, like him who sat at the Temple,
they were blind from their birth, or whether their sad
privation was owing to the same causes which make

ophthalmia so common and so severe in Palestine, even in
the present day. We know only that they were blind ;
and so compelled to cry out of the depth of their darkness and poverty for alms from the passers by.

They heard the approach of the multitude, and with
ears trained to acuteness, by the fact that they had to
depend so much upon them, they perceived that there
was something very unusual about the crowd. So Bartimæus,—speaking for both, and coming into such prominence thereby that the conversation throughout was
with him, and the other drops virtually out of the narrative,—asked the early stragglers, who, on such occasions,
are commonly a few paces ahead of the main body of
the multitude, what was the meaning of it all. They
told him that Jesus of Nazareth was passing by; and
their answer stirred him into unwonted energy and earnestness.

I can imagine him thus soliloquizing in himself : *" Jesus of Nazareth !* That is he of whom I have heard such
wondrous things. They have told me how he has made
the dumb to speak, the deaf to hear, the leper to be
clean, and the dead to live again. I have heard, too,
how he has opened the eyes of the blind, and kind travellers as they dropped their alms into my hand have
said to me again and again that if I could only get to
him, he would be sure to heal me. Often have I prayed
that he might come this way, and now he is here ! This
is the opportunity of my life. Oh ! God that I may use
it well ! "

In a briefer time than I have taken to express them,
thoughts like these must have thrilled through him, and
he cried so loud that his voice rose above the hum of the
crowd : *" Jesus, thou Son of David, have mercy on me !"*
Mark, *" thou son of David !"* Blind as he was, this

poor man, had seen, through his miracles, the Messiahship
of Jesus, and he calls him, therefore, by his royal name.

But the crowd would smother his entreaty, and bade
him hold his peace not, as some have supposed, because
they disapproved of his calling Jesus the son of David,
but rather, as I believe, because they supposed it beneath the dignity of the Saviour to hold parley with such
an one as he was. " Why should he stay to listen to a
beggar ? Why should he be interrupted in his discourse
by the way, by an application from one so insignificant ?
They thought that it would ill beseem the representative
of David's line to speak with *him,* and, therefore, they
told him to be still. But he would not thus be silenced.
His appeal was to Jesus, and he would take no answer
save from him. Therefore, he cried " the more a great
deal, Thou Son of David, have mercy on me." Nor did
he call in vain, for Jesus " stood still and commanded
him to be brought unto him." " To be brought unto
him; " observe, as we pass on, the delicate appropriateness
of the words, as referring to one who was blind. To another Christ might have said, " *Come* unto me," but to
say that now might have painfully reminded Bartimæus
of his privation, for though from long habit he knew the
pathway to his accustomed place beneath the palm tree,
how was he to thread his way through such a crowd?
Therefore, with his usual tenderness, the Lord's command
was that he should " be brought unto him." It was a
case in which the agency of others could be helpful, and
so that was called into operation, not only to rebuke
those who had bidden him hold his peace, but also to remind us, that we may often, like Andrew with Peter, do
lasting good to others, by bringing them to Jesus.

And now, thus reproved, the multitude having discovered that they had made a great mistake in their read-

ing of the Saviour's feelings toward the poor and needy,
are as eager to hasten him forward, as before they had
been to command him to be still, for they say to him,
" Be of good comfort ; rise, he calleth thee." And he
did not need a second bidding, for casting away his upper garment, that it might not impede his movements,
Bartimæus rose at once, and suffered himself to be led
to Jesus. We can imagine the flutter of his emotions at
the moment, and how, though perhaps he had framed
within himself a form of words to be used on such an
occasion, if it should ever come to him, it all went from
him, so that he was at a loss what to say. We can see,
therefore, the tender consideration the Lord had for his
excitement, when, to steady him, and bring back his
calmness of spirit, he quietly said, " *What wilt thou that
I should do unto thee ?* " And now there was no falter-
ing, or trepidation, or suspense. He knew what he
wanted. And with that definiteness which is born of
earnestness, he answered, " *Lord, that I might receive my
sight.*" Then, as Matthew informs us, the Saviour
touched his eyes, and said, " Go thy way, thy faith hath
saved thee," (not simply made thee whole) but "saved
thee," to show him, as Godet has well remarked, that
although his life was in no danger, there lay in this cure
the beginning of his spiritual salvation, if he would only
keep up the bond of faith between him and the Saviour's
person. And again, " *Thy faith* hath saved thee." The
Saviour did not say, " My power hath saved thee "—
though that was true, but " thy faith," to impress on him
the value of that disposition, in view of the still more important spiritual miracle which remained to be wrought
upon him." * " And immediately he received sight ; "
without any such gradual process as there was in the
case of him who at first saw only " men as trees, walk-

* Godet, Commentary on Luke, *in loco.*

ing." "Go thy way,"—so said the Master, leaving it to the choice of Bartimæus what direction he should take. And without hesitation or reluctance he chose to "follow Jesus in the way," and as he went "he glorified God;" nor he alone, for Luke adds, "that all the people, when they saw it, gave praise to God."

Such is the simple story of this gracious miracle, and it is so beautiful that I do not wonder that many have sought to set it to the music of melodious verse. You are all familiar with Longfellow's rendering of the Scripture narrative, and must often have admired the skill with which he has interwoven the very Greek words of the original into his English rhyme. But without disparaging the genius of the poet, whose bust in Westminster Abbey bears witness to his popularity on both sides of the sea, I prefer the more spiritual treatment given to the subject by Dr. H. D. Ganse, formerly of this city, in these beautiful lines :

"Lord, I know thy grace is nigh me,
    Though thyself I cannot see;
Jesus, Master pass not by me ;
    Son of David! pity me.

"While I sit in weary blindness,
    Longing for the blessed light,
Many taste thy loving kindness,
    'Lord, I would receive my sight.'

"I would see thee, and adore thee,
    And thy word the power can give.
Hear the sightless soul implore thee,
    Let me see thy face and live.

"Ah, what touch is this that thrills me?
    What this burst of strange delight?
Lo, the rapturous vision fills me !
    This is Jesus! This is sight!

"Room, ye saints that throng behind him !
    Let me follow in the way.
I will teach the blind to find him
    Who can turn their night to day."

I turn now to consider the lessons taught us by this miracle when viewed, as we have insisted that each miracle of the Lord should be viewed, as spiritual parable. But having already set before you, in another discourse in this series, the analogy between blindness and the sad condition of the sinner, I shall content myself to-night with bringing out a few suggestive thoughts bearing on the opportunities of salvation and the use to be made of them.

And, first, of the opportunities of salvation. When Bartimæus asked why there was such a crowd of people on the road, they told him that Jesus of Nazareth was passing by, and that roused him to exertion. Now what was true then, in a transient sense, is always true under the enjoyment of gospel privileges. Wherever Christ is preached we may make the announcement that the Saviour is passing by. Will you endeavor to realize that, O sinner ? The Bible is put into your hands to tell you that Jesus is passing by. The Lord's Day dawns to repeat the glad announcement. The church-bells ring out upon the sky to renew the declaration. The multitudes hastening along the streets to the house of prayer, if you were to ask them what it all meant, might truthfully answer you in the very words used here by the throng that surrounded Jesus in the way. The sanctuary with its simple service, the preacher with his gracious message, all declare the same thing to you. He who has both the power and the will to pour celestial light upon your inward sight, and to enrich you with the treasures of his grace ; he who can forgive your sins, and renew your souls ; he who can keep you safe from every snare, and every evil work ; he who can give you peace, and happiness, and holiness on earth, and everlasting glory in heaven—is " passing by." O blessed

news! Do not your hearts thrill with rapture at the
thought that now at length you may be saved? If the
soul of Bartimæus was stirred to its depths by the hope
of obtaining natural sight, will not you be moved, by
such an opportunity of obtaining spiritual salvation, to
rise at once to embrace it? Here is the gospel to you
in a phrase : Jesus of Nazareth passeth by,

See how Bartimæus embraced his opportunity. He
cried to Christ for mercy. Cannot you do the same?
Many and keen have been the debates which men who
are fonder of metaphysical subtleties than of giving plain
directions to inquiring sinners, have had over the combination of human agency with that of God in the matter
of salvation. But, without meddling at all with these, it
seems to me that a flood of light upon your present duty,
if you desire salvation at all, is cast by the action of the
blind man here. He cried to Christ for mercy. He did
not wait to have all the questions concerning the mode
of his cure settled, all he wanted was to receive his sight,
and he cried upon the Son of David for that. Now you
can do that. You can if you will. You know that you
can. Do it then, and learn how to do it from this beggar. Do it like him, humbly ; not as if you had a right
to be healed, but as one who looked for it to the mercy
of Christ. Alas! that is the stumbling-block of many.
They want to do something that may entitle them to a
cure. But that is hopeless work. Give over seeking to
work out a righteousness of your own, on the ground of
which, as a meritorious thing, you can claim salvation.
Make your appeal to mercy in the words so familiar to
us all, " God, be merciful to me a sinner."

Do it, again, perseveringly. Let not men silence you
They may tell you that Jesus will not heed your call
Never mind ; cry on. They may try to stifle your con-

victions, and seek to persuade you that you are not so great a sinner after all, and that you do not need salvation. Never mind; cry on. They may attempt to commend you to some other helper, and bid you seek from worldly amusements or earthly pleasures that relief which only he can give. Never mind; cry on. Resolve that you will take no answer save from the lips of Christ himself, and cry on until he shall make reply.

Do it, again, promptly. You have no time to lose. Remember Jesus is *passing* by, and if you let slip this golden opportunity, you may never have another. Bartimæus felt that if he let that opportunity go, another might never come, and therefore he would not delay, and he would not be put down. So let it be with you. I know that, as I have said, Jesus is always passing by in the ordinances and invitations of his gospel; but what security have you that you shall long enjoy these things? He never passes through the place of woe. He performs no cures after death, and you know not when death may overtake you. So this is a real, a golden, a God-given opportunity; but it is a transient one. Therefore I implore you not to lose it, but to call, and call, and call again, if need be, " Jesus, thou Son of David, have mercy on me ; Lord, that I may receive salvation."

> "Pass me not, O gracious Saviour;
> Let me live and cling to thee ;
> O, I'm longing for thy favor;
> Whilst thou'rt calling, O call me."

Still farther here, when Jesus calls you to come to him, let nothing hinder you from complying with his invitation. Behold how Bartimæus, in his eager earnestness to obey the Lord, flung his garment from him, that he might walk unhindered to his side. A poor garment enough it may have been, ragged, torn and as some would say, contemptible, but it was none the less his garment, and he cast it from him that nothing might impede his progress Christ-ward. Do you the same. Whatever that may have been which heretofore you have gathered round you, as the hope or joy of your soul—fling it from you, and seek all from Jesus. Perhaps it has been your righteousness and you have proudly hugged it to you, as a sufficient robe to hide the nakedness of your soul—but now, away with it, for Jesus calls you. Perhaps it has been a sinful habit, cleaving to you—as our very use of the word, in both senses reminds us—like a garment, which, as you fancy, has often kept you from the chill of misery ; if so, fling it from you. Perhaps it has been your money, or your worldly possessions, in which you have been trusting ; much as if Bartimæus might have plumed himself on the contents of his wallet, the proceeds of his begging. If so, away with it, for you are to be no more a beggar. You will not need help from others, for by his spirit dwelling in you, you will be independent, so far as spiritual things are concerned, of every one but himself.

Finally, when Jesus has given you salvation, then follow him in the way, glorifying God. Follow him, by imitating his example, obeying his precepts, and acting on his principles. Go faithfully where these may lead you—accept no guidance but such as comes from him. Follow *him*, not afar off, but closely, even though he should lead you to Jerusalem, to Gethsemane, to the hall of Caiaphas, to the judgment seat of Pilate, yea, to the cross of Calvary itself; follow him, until at last, you find yourself by his side in glory.

And be not silent as you go, but glorify God the while. If he have opened your eyes, do not be ashamed to say so, even if like the poor man of whom John tells us, you should be cast out of the synagogue for your testimony. Tell others what he has done for you, that they may be encouraged to apply to him for themselves. Yea, wherever you go be sure to make known to all around you what a living, great, and gracious Saviour Jesus is. And so by holy deeds, and earnest words, you will become a blessing to the world and be recognized of all as having been with Jesus.

But I cannot conclude without saying a word to those who are apparently the followers of Jesus, as to their treatment of such as are anxious inquirers, or are earnestly calling upon Christ for mercy. I beseech them to beware lest by anything in their conduct, or by anything in their words, they discourage a sinner from calling on the Saviour. If you cannot help, do not hinder. It is a solemn thing to deal with an anxious soul. You had better be silent to such an one than speak foolishly. You had better do nothing in such a case, than do wrong. Do not turn the matter into ridicule. Do not attempt to dissipate convictions that have been produced by the Holy Spirit. Do not criticise and make a laughing stock of the words of the preacher. But rather do everything in your power to work along the line that the Holy Spirit has already taken, and to encourage the inquirer to cry directly on the Lord.

Beware too of seeking to remove anxiety in inquirers by taking them to places of amusement or otherwise engaging them with a view of making them forget their sins. All that is—I cannot use a milder word— "soul murder," and for that, if you are guilty of it, you shall be held responsible. Take the inquirer the shortest way to Christ, and leave him with his Saviour. Be on your guard lest any inconsistency, or levity, or lack

of sympathy on your part should choke the cry, which
but for you, would have come out, " Jesus, thou Son of
David, have mercy on me." It is an awfully solemn
thing to deal with a soul at such a time ; and he who
would direct it wisely, must himself be in constant communion with the Lord. This, at least, is always a safe
rule : Never hinder a sinner from calling on his Saviour.
Bid no one hold his peace who is crying on Jesus of
Nazareth for the salvation of his soul.

XXX.

THE WITHERING OF THE FRUITLESS FIG-TREE.

Matt. xxi. 18-22. Mark xi, 12-14; 20-26.

ON the evening of the day on which he rode in triumph into Jerusalem, our Lord retired to Bethany, where
he spent the night, not unlikely in the house of Mary,
Martha and Lazarus.   The following day, very early,
perhaps not long after sunrise, and certainly before the
hour of the first morning meal, he took his way into the
city, and being hungry, saw in the distance on the side
of the path, a fig-tree in full leaf.   Naturally, therefore,
he expected to find on it some fruit wherewith to satisfy
his craving; for though it was not yet the season of figs,
that particular tree by its ostentatious display of precocious foliage, seemed to indicate that there was fruit
upon its branches, because in the case of that species of
tree, the fruit comes before the leaf.   But when he came
up and examined its branches, he found "nothing but
leaves"; whereupon he solemnly said, "No man eat fruit
of thee hereafter, forever."   His words were heard by
his followers, and on the evening of the following day,
as they were returning from the city, they saw that the
tree was dried up from the root.   This awakened their
surprise, and Peter, almost always the first to speak, said
unto the Lord, "Master, behold the fig-tree which thou

cursedst is withered away," and received for answer these words concerning prayer, " Have faith in God. For verily I say unto you, that whosoever shall say unto this mountain, Be thou removed, and be thou cast into the sea, and shall not doubt in his heart, but shall believe that those things which he saith shall come to pass, he shall have whatsoever he saith. Therefore, I say unto you, what things soever ye desire, when ye pray believe that ye receive " (R. V. that ye have received them) " and ye shall have them. And when ye stand praying, forgive, if ye have aught against any, that your Father also which is in heaven, may forgive you your trespasses. For if ye do not forgive, neither will your Father which is in heaven forgive your trespasses."

Objections, not a few, have been brought against what has been supposed to be the spirit manifested by the Saviour in this miracle, but perhaps the best answer to these will be, to unfold its meaning and set forth the purpose for which it was wrought. To do that, however, we must go somewhat into detail.

The prophets, under the Old Testament dispensation, gave forth their warnings not unfrequently in a symbolic manner. Sometimes they enacted a scene before the eyes of those to whom they were sent, as, when Ezekiel set before the exiles a graphic delineation of the siege of Jerusalem. Sometimes the symbols were expressed in words, as when Isaiah depicted the chosen people as a vineyard, and in a parabolic form sets forth what God had done for them, the ungrateful return which they had made, and the judgment that would come upon them for their sin.*

When the latter method was adopted, the Jewish nation was often spoken of as a tree, as, for example, in

---

* Isaiah v. 1-7.

the eightieth psalm, where it is described as a vine which God had brought up out of Egypt. Now the same course was followed by our Lord and his apostles in the New Testament, as in the Saviour's parables of the wicked husbandmen, and Paul's well-known argument on the rejection and ultimate restoration of the Jews in the eleventh chapter of the Epistle to the Romans. But the nearest parallel to the symbolism of the miracle now under consideration is that which is furnished by the parable of the barren fig-tree, in which, as you may remember, the Jewish nation is represented as a fig-tree planted in 'a vineyard, to which for three successive years the owner came, seeking fruit and finding none, and which was spared from being cut down as cumbering the ground only by the intercession of the vine-dresser, "Let it alone this year also, till I shall dig about it and dung it, and if it bear fruit, well; but if not, then after that, thou shalt cut it down." *

To that parable this miracle of the blighting of the fig-tree, was designed to be an appendix. It is a para-ble, a prophecy, and a miracle, all in one. The year of grace desired by the vine-dresser has ended, the barrenness has continued, the intervention of the vine-dresser is withdrawn, the judgment which he had intercepted falls—and not by the sharp strokes of the axe, but by the withering curse of barrenness it is made henceforth good for nothing but fuel for the fire. Thus the great law of responsibility for privilege, and retribution for failure to improve it, is enforced by emblems drawn from vegetable life after the manner of the author of the Epistle to the Hebrews in the well-known verse: (Heb vi. 7. 8), "For the earth which drinketh in the rain that cometh oft upon it, and bringeth forth herbs meet for them by whom

* Luke xiii. 6-9.

it is dressed, receiveth blessing from God: But that which beareth briers and thorns is rejected, and is nigh unto cursing : whose end is to be burned."

This miracle, then, was a last appeal to the Jewish people, on the very week of the crucifixion. It set before them a symbol of themselves in the fig-tree, whose precocious and showy display of leaves portrayed their self-righteous parading of themselves as better than all others ; whose utter barrenness was a picture of their real character ; and whose withered condition after the word of Christ was a warning and a prophecy of their rejection by God for their refusal to receive the Messiah who had been promised to their fathers.

Now, with this key to the meaning and purpose of the miracle in our hands, it is easy to answer the objections which have been raised in connection with it. It is said, for example, by some, that it was absurd in our Lord to treat the tree as a moral agent, and hold it to a rigid accountability, as if it could be blameworthy for any-thing. But all such criticism falls to the ground when the tree is regarded as an emblem of the Jewish people, who *were* moral agents, and *were* sinners exceedingly, in that with all their pretensions to superior excellence, they knew not the day of their visitation, and failed 'to im-prove the exceptional privileges which had been con-ferred upon them.

It is alleged, again, that the blighting of the tree was a wanton destruction of property, utterly unwarranted and unjustifiable. But when we put the matter in its true light, as in our exposition we have attempted to do, we see that the withering of the fig-tree here takes its place beside the destruction of the swine, which was connected with the cure of the Gadarene demoniac, and is fairly met by the question, " How much is a man bet-

ter than a tree ? " Besides, it is not to be forgotten
that, in the last resort, the tree belonged to him whose
also are " the cattle on a thousand hills ; " and that if, in
the parable, the owner of the vineyard had a right to say
of the barren fig-tree, " Cut it down, why cumbereth it
the ground ? " the Saviour had an equal right to use this
tree as he pleased, in order to give an object-lesson to
his disciples, and through them to the Jewish nation at
large. The withering of the tree was produced by Divine power, and so was the will of him to whom it really
belonged, and who therefore had a right to do as he
pleased with his own.

Once more, it is alleged that the punishment of the
tree, as the objectors call it, was a manifestation of temper on the part of Christ, on a level with the scourging
of the Hellespont by Xerxes, after the submerging of his
fleet in its waters.

But how absolutely ridiculous such an assertion is, in
the light of the solemn warning which is really implied
in the miracle, I need not stay to demonstrate. The objection, as Trench has hinted, comes from those, who are
opposed to anything like punishment at all, and who
have adopted a view of God as Love which eliminates
from the Divine nature anything like justice. Moreover,
in their wilful blindness these objectors fail to see the real
mercy that is apparent to all others in the miracle. For
though we must call it a miracle of judgment, the mercy
that is in it comes not in the fact that the judgment
fell upon a tree, and not yet upon the nation, of which
the tree was the emblem. Besides it was given as a
warning, if haply, even at that eleventh hour, the Jewish
people might be led to repentance, and so be saved from
the guilt of crucifying the Lord, and the doom which
would surely follow such an awful sin. Even in this

work of judgment, therefore, there was love, in that while the tree was withered, the nation which it represented was still spared that it might have space for repentance, and be warned to flee from the wrath to come.

Beautifully as well as truly has Westcott said in reference to another aspect of the case. " As he entered into Jerusalem, parable and miracle were combined in one work of judgment. Elsewhcse he portrayed the growth, the preservation, the support of the church ; but now he bore witness against its barrenness. The fruit-less fig-tree challenged his notice, by its ostentatious show of leaves, and straightway withered at his curse. Yet even here, in the moment of sorrowful disappoint-ment, as he turned to his disciples, the word of judg-ment became a word of promise. Have faith in God ; and whatsoever things ye desire when ye pray, believe that ye received ($\check{\epsilon}\lambda\acute{\alpha}\beta\epsilon\tau\epsilon$) them—received them already at the inspiration of the wish—and ye shall have them."*

The difficulty which has been raised by others as to the reason why the Saviour " came " to the tree, " if haply he might find anything thereon," while yet, if he were omniscient, he must have known already that it bore nothing but leaves, is of quite another sort, and takes us into the mystery of the Incarnation itself. It is of the same class as that involved in the limitations of the Saviour's knowledge, as suggested by the words, " Of that day and that hour knoweth no man, no, not even the angels which are in heaven, neither the Son, but the Father," and the statement made by Luke concerning his childhood, that " he increased in wisdom and stature and in favor with God and man."

We must never forget that just because he was a real man, the divine nature to which that humanity was

---

* " Characteristics of the Gospel Miracles," pp. 24. 25.

united, was, however incomprehensible it may seem to
us to be, conditioned by the humanity, so that to him in
his humiliation some things were contingent, and some
were unknown. His humanity could not have been real,
if this had not been the case. But when we ask how
Deity could be thus conditioned, or when we speculate
regarding the extent of his human knowledge, or inquire
how far his humanity was widened or affected by his
Deity, we are beyond our depth, and have simply to accept in humble faith the statements of the sacred writers.
Such difficulties are inseparable from the very idea of
Incarnation, and if, on other grounds, we are constrained, as I acknowledge myself to be, to accept as a
fact that the Word who was God became flesh, and
dwelt among men, we must accept with it all such statements as that before us, mysterious as they are; for if we
know not fully all the deep things of our own nature,
how can we expect to comprehend that of God, or to
solve all the questions that arise concerning the relations
in every respect between the divine and human natures
in the one person of him who was God manifest in the
flesh ?

But now, turning from these matters, let us consider
the answer of the Saviour to the remark of Peter and the
other disciples, "Master, how soon is the fig-tree withered away." We are told that he said unto them,
"Have faith in God. For verily I say unto you, that
whosoever shall say unto this mountain, be thou removed,
and be thou cast into the sea, and shall not doubt in his
heart, but shall believe that those things which he saith
shall come to pass, he shall have whatsoever he saith,"
etc. Here the interesting question arises, what is the
connection between this strain of exhortation and the
miracle which we have been considering ? And it must

be confessed that it is not easy to answer that inquiry. But perhaps we may find it in two things suggested, rather than expressed by the words. Bear in mind that Peter's surprise is at the immediate effect of the Saviour's malediction, and that Christ answers him by speaking of prayer. This, therefore, seems to imply that the miracle was wrought in answer to prayer. We are here, I admit, on rather dangerous ground, but it would seem, that although some of the Saviour's miracles were performed at his own independent will, and by an inherent supernatural virtue residing in himself, others were wrought by power received from the Father in answer to his prayers.

We saw in our review of the raising of Lazarus from the dead, that before he spoke the words, "Lazarus, come forth!" he lifted up his eyes unto heaven and said, "Father, I thank thee that thou hast heard me, and I knew that thou hearest me always, but because of the people which stand by, I said it, that they may believe that thou hast sent me." *

Now that is not a prayer, but it is a thanksgiving for the answer to a prayer which had been previously offered, implying that the putting forth of power needed for the raising of the dead, was connected with prayer— was, in some sense, an answer to prayer. It would seem, too, that the same thing was true of the power needed for the blighting of the fig-tree ; and if that were so, we can easily understand how, when Peter referred to the speedy withering of the tree from the root, the Saviour answered him as he did.

Then, on the other hand, Peter's words implied that in his heart he was drawing a contrast between the success of the Lord in the working of *his* miracles, and

* John xi. 41-42.

the failures of the disciples in cases such as that of the demoniac boy at the foot of the Mount of Transfigura- tion. And the Lord laid bare the secret both of his suc- cess and of their failure, in this exhortation to faith and prayer. To borrow the words of Neander, " Christ made use of their astonishment for a purpose very im- portant in this last period of his stay with them, namely, to incite them to act themselves by the power of God ; not to be so amazed at what *He* wrought with that power, but to remember that in communion with him *they* would be able to do the same, and even greater things. The sense of his words then would be, " You need not wonder at a result like this ; the result was the least of it ; *you* shall do still greater things by the power of God, if you only possess the great essential faith." *

" The removing of mountains " must be regarded as a hyberbolical figure for " the removing of obstacles," and the large promise here made to faith must be qualified, by the conditions elsewhere laid down, in reference to the answering of prayer. These have respect, first, to the character of the suppliant, who must have faith in God, must abide in Christ, must be of a forgiving spirit, and possess a holy character ; second, to the nature of the things requested, which must be in harmony with the will and wisdom of God ; and, third, to the purpose and prerogative of God himself, who does not exist sim- ply for the hearing of his people's prayers, but is also their Father, to train and discipline them into strength and holiness of character.† Within these limitations, however, the promises here made hold good, and so they give a sure foundation to faith, but no encouragement

* " Life of Christ," pp. 395, 396.
† See this subject more fully treated in the " Parables of our Sa- viour, Expounded and Illustrated," pp. 247–258.

whatever to fanaticism. Even in the twenty-fifth and
twenty-sixth verses of the narrative in Mark, which
contain the promise, there is a restriction of the universal terms in which it is made, to those who as they
" stand praying, forgive, if they have ought to forgive; "
and we must not forget that the Saviour himself, by his
reply to Satan, when he quoted Scripture, has taught us
that one part of the word of God is to be read in the
light of all the rest of that word. Above all, we ought
to remember that the undertone of every true prayer is,
" Nevertheless, not as I will, but as thou wilt." I say
these things not to discourage prayer, but rather to de-
fine it, and to guard against such a misunderstanding of
passages like that now before us, as is responsible for
the utter neglect of means by many in our day and generation.

I conclude with the enforcement of the great practical
lesson of the miracle which we have been considering,
this, namely, that the failure to improve privilege, en-
tails on those who are guilty of it the removal of the
privilege itself. In his discourse on the true vine, Jesus
says, " Every branch in me that beareth not fruit he
taketh away ; " and, again, " If a man abide not in me,
he is cast forth as a branch, and is withered ; and men
gather them, and cast them into the fire, and they are
burned." *

So again in the sermon on the Mount we have these
words, " Every tree that beareth not good fruit is hewn
down and cast into the fire." † The statement is unmistakable, and in the providence of God there have been
many illustrations of its truth. What could be more
marked indeed, in this connection, than the case of the
Jews themselves ? They were the people of God's pos-

* John xv. 2-6.   † Matt. vii. 19.

session, the objects of his peculiar regard. He brought them out of the land of Egypt and planted them in Palestine; he sent unto them his prophets; he trained them by the discipline of his providence; he dwelt among them in the mystic shechinah glory of the holy of holies; "last of all, he sent unto them his Son." If ever any nation might have looked for exemption from the operation of this law, it was surely that of the Jews. But no : they came under its most rigid sweep; and just because they had received so much, they were all the more severely dealt with for their guilty barrenness. Their temple was razed to the foundation; their capital was destroyed; their land was given to others; and they themselves were scattered over the face of the earth, even until this day.

We may see a similar instance in the case of those seven Asiatic Churches, to whom the book of Revelation was addressed. They too had rare privileges and ample warning; but they failed to rise to their responsibility, and the candlestick of each has been removed out of its place, so that the very regions which they occupied have come under the influence of Mohammedanism, and need to be Christianized anew. More modern illustrations may be found in the cases of those lands, which like Spain, Italy, and France, refused to accept the blessings of the reformation when it was in their power to do so, and have been contending with difficulties almost ever since. But in thinking of them we must not forget ourselves, for the law holds of individual churches and individual men, as well as of nations; and if we wish to secure permanent existence and prosperity as a nation, we must remember that we can do so only by maintaining constant fruitfulness in works of faith and labors of love, and holiness of character. When these disappear, bar-

renness has begun, and then there will come the withering sentence, " Let no fruit grow on thee, henceforward
forever."

The history of the past will not compensate for the ster-
ility of the present. We cannot live upon our reputation,
any more than the Jews could save themselves because
they were able to say, "We have Abraham to our Father."
Neither can we secure exemption from the withering blight
of Christ by putting forth the leaves of a showy profession.
That only aggravates the evil, adding hypocrisy to barrenness. Not the leaf, but the fruit it is which makes the tree
valuable ; and if there be no fruit, the leaves are of no account. Let us see to it, therefore, that not only as a
congregation, but as individuals, we so unite ourselves to
Christ and abide in him, that we shall glorify his Father
by bringing forth much fruit ; for barrenness is punished
by barrenness. " To him that hath shall be given, while
from him that hath not shall be taken away even that
which he hath." Remember these suggestive words :
"Abide in me and I in you ; as the branch cannot bear
fruit of itself, except it abide in the vine, no more can
ye, except ye abide in me." And again, " He that
abideth in me and I in him, the same bringeth forth much
fruit." Enter, therefore, into union with Christ, and
then both leaves and fruit will come, for both alike are
required for the rounded completeness of Christian character.

Think not, however, to escape the doom of this
fruit-tree, by putting forth no leaves, or in literal phrase,
by making no public confession of Christ. This tree
was blighted not for having leaves, but for having no
fruit. A confession, where it is not genuinely made, is
hypocrisy ; but to refuse or decline to make a confession,
where there is real faith in Christ, is hurtful to Christian

growth. If it be bad for a fruit-tree to have " nothing but leaves," it is not good for it either to have no leaves. The leaves help the growth and development of the fruit, and so a public confession helps to bring the fruit to ripeness. If, therefore, you have given yourself to Christ, make a confession of him, by giving yourself also to the church, and maintaining a character corresponding to that confession ; then your character will ripen into completeness and you will bring forth your fruit unto holiness and the end thereof will be everlasting life.

XXXI.

THE HEALING OF THE EAR OF MALCHUS.

Matt. xxvi. 51-56. Mark xiv. 46-47. Luke xxii. 50-51. John xviii. 10-11.

THIS incident in the history of our Lord's apprehension is narrated by all the evangelists. But John is the only one of them who tells us that it was Peter who, with a sword, cut off the ear of the servant of the High-priest, and that the servant's name was Malchus. What reason the other three had for suppressing these names must be matter of mere conjecture. Some have supposed that as they probably wrote when all the parties were still alive, they, out of prudence, avoided saying anything that might bring Peter into trouble for what he had done ; but that at the date of the fourth gospel there was no such danger, and so John felt perfectly free to give full particulars. For myself, I am contented to remain in ignorance upon the matter, belonging as it does to a department which is now beyond the reach of our investigation.

But whatever may be said about the omission of the names by Matthew, Mark, and Luke, the insertion of that of Malchus by John, is due, under the influence of the inspiring spirit, to the fact, that as he has himself informed us, "he was known to the High Priest ; " so well known, indeed, to the household of that dignitary, that he needed only to speak to "the damsel that kept the door," in order to secure the admission of Peter. It is quite likely, therefore, that the name of Malchus was well known to him, for as that servant is called especially *the* servant of the High Priest, he was, perhaps, his personal attendant, who would be constantly addressed by his name, by all about the palace. Nothing therefore could be more natural than for John to introduce it here, as he is recalling in his old age the whole scene which had fixed itself so indelibly upon his memory.

But a further comparison of the four narratives with each other reveals the fact that Luke alone mentions the miracle, which was the last performed by our Lord before his crucifixion, and by which the ear of Malchus was restored. Now here again, while it is impossible to account for the silence of the other three, we can see at once how natural it was that it should be mentioned by Luke. For he was a physician, and as such had a special interest in all such cures.

Leaving now the comparison of the four accounts with each other, let us attempt to weave them into one. The Saviour had just come out of the depth of his great agony, and had rejoined his followers, when, after tenderly reproaching the first three of the band, for their inability to watch with him one hour, he directed their attention to the company of Roman soldiers and Jewish officers, and an attendant throng of curious on-lookers, who were approaching, with lanterns, and torches, and weapons, to take him prisoner. As they came forward, he advanced to meet them, and said, "Whom seek ye?" They answered him, "Jesus, the Nazarene," and he replied, "I am he." They were so amazed by the quiet dignity of his demeanor, and perhaps, also, so stricken by an out-flashing of his power, that they went backward, and fell to the ground. Then, as they were rising, he repeated his question, " Whom seek ye ? " and they repeated their answer, " Jesus of Nazareth," whereupon he responded, " I have told you that I am he ; if, therefore, you seek me, let these go their way." But still they hesitated, waiting to be sure that they made no mistake, and at this moment Judas came forward to give them the preconcerted signal, which, sad to say, was a kiss. As he advanced for this purpose, and exclaimed, " Hail, Master ! " the Lord said, " Friend, do that for which thou art come." And then, assured that now he was indeed Jesus, the soldiers laid hands on him, and took him, and proceeded to bind him. Exasperated at the sight, one of his disciples, whose name is not mentioned, exclaimed, " Lord, shall we smite with the sword ? " and Peter, impetuous as ever, without waiting for an answer to the question, smote Malchus with his sword, and cut off his right ear.

But the Saviour was a willing victim, and observing what his ardent but mistaken servant had done, he said to those who were at the moment binding him, " Suffer ye thus far,"—that is, " Give me the use of my arm for a moment longer," and as they yielded to his request, he touched the ear of Malchus and healed him. Then looking round on Peter, he said, " Put up again thy sword into its place ; for they that take the sword shall perish with the sword. Thinkest thou that I cannot now pray to my Father, and he shall presently give me more than twelve legions of angels ? But how then shall the Scriptures be fulfilled that thus it must be. The cup which my Father hath given me, shall I not drink it ? "

Such is the order, in which, as it seems to me, the details given by the four evangelists in this section must be arranged ; and when we take them so, they give to us a very vivid idea of the whole scene.

Now, how shall we explain the act of Peter, which if his aim had been as true as his blow was effective, would have proved fatal to Malchus. It is easy to see that beneath all other motives in his heart, he was actuated by deep and fervent love to his Master, and by a desire to defend him from his enemies. It was in keeping, too, with the rash nature of that Apostle who so often spoke and acted before he reflected—so much so, indeed, that even if we had not been told by John that the act was that of Peter, we "might," as Trench has said, "have guessed" that it was his. If only he had paused a moment to consider, he might have seen how hopeless it was for eleven men with but two swords among them all, to effect a rescue, in opposition to a trained cohort of the Roman army ; and how little such an attempt was in accord with the spirit of his Master, might have been inferred by him from the voluntary surrender of himself, which was involved in the words which he, but now, had used : "I am he; if therefore ye seek me, let these go their way."

Peter, however, was not accustomed to reflect, and the deed was done, almost before he knew,—a deed, too, which if it had not been virtually undone by the miracle which was performed by the half manacled hand of the Lord, would have made it impossible for Christ to have said as he afterwards did to Pilate, "My kingdom is not of this world, else would my servants fight, that I should not be delivered unto thee ; but now is my kingdom not from hence."

But though the love of Peter, coupled with his natural impetuosity of temperament, and his imperfect acquaintance with the nature of Christ's kingdom, will go far to

account for his action, I do not think it will fully explain it.   I am persuaded that it was largely due to a
misunderstanding of the words of the Saviour himself, not
many hours before.   This will be made plain if you read
with me from Luke xxii. 35–38.   Remember, as we read,
that the eleven were still in the upper room, in which
the Lord's Supper had been instituted, and which they
were just preparing to leave in order to go out to Gethsemane.   " He said unto them, when I sent you without
purse, and scrip, and shoes, lacked ye anything ?   And
they said, Nothing.   Then said he unto them : But now
he that hath a purse, let him take it, and likewise his
scrip ; and he that hath no sword, let him sell his garment and buy one,"—or rather, " He that hath no purse,
let him sell his garment and buy a sword,"—" For I say
unto you, that this that is written must yet be accomplished in me : And he was reckoned among the transgressors ; for the things concerning me have an end,"—or
rather, " fulfilment,"—" And they said, Lord, behold here
are two swords.   And he said unto them, it is enough."
    Now, the general purpose of this exhortation seems
very clear.   The Lord is forewarning his followers of the
dangers which they would have to encounter in their
ministry, after his ascension into glory.   It would not be
with them then as it had been when he had formerly sent
them   forth   through   Galilee   without   purse   or   scrip.
Then they were provided for during the days of his popularity without the use of means by themselves.   They
were hospitably received by the people, and had no need
to care for anything.
    It would be far otherwise, however, when they went out
as the disciples of one who had been " numbered with the
transgressors," and   crucified   as   a   malefactor.   Then
they would no longer be able to count on being received

as honored guests; but they must prepare to meet hostility, and be ready to take all proper means both for their support and for their defence. They were to be prepared, if need be, to work with their own hands for their maintenance ; and they were to stand upon their rights as subjects and citizens, if they should be unjustifiably assailed. The sword here, therefore, is used in a symbolical sense as in the phrase elsewhere employed by Christ : "I came not to send peace on earth, but a sword," and must be held as indicating any proper means of defence. But the disciples by their reply, "Lord, here are two swords," showed that they had understood him so literally as to lose altogether the spirit of his words. They said, " Here are two swords," and he dismissed the subject with the reply, " It is enough." But that phrase, " It is enough," must not be supposed to indicate that the Lord is referring to the present necessity. It means virtually this, " Let us say no more ; let us now break up ; events will explain to you my mind, which you do not understand." * Or as Godet, whose interpretation I have just given, suggests as an alternative, it is as if he had said, " Yes, for the use which you shall have to make of arms of that kind, those two swords are enough."

Now, when we take this conversation into consideration, and remember how the disciples by interpreting their Master as they did, had virtually misinterpreted him, it is, I conceive, very easy to account for Peter's act in assailing Malchus with the sword. He thought that he was honoring his Lord, by carrying out his command ; and the only good result of his rashness was, that he drew from Jesus an injunction and an observation, which clearly defined the sense in which he had used the somewhat enigmatical words : " He that hath no purse, let

* Godet, on Luke, *in loco.*

him sell his garment and buy a sword." So that as Alford says : " The saying is both a description to them of
their altered situation with reference to the world without, and a declaration that self-defence and self-provision
would henceforward be necessary." It forms a decisive
testimony from the mouth of the Lord himself against the
views of the Quakers and some other sects on these
points.   Then, on the other hand, the further words addressed to Peter *after* he had wounded Malchus, show
that it is contrary to the express command of Christ to
attempt to enforce the discipline of the church, or to seek
the diffusion of the gospel, by the sword.

But now having seen how Peter came to think of striking Malchus with the sword, let us pause a moment to
see what consequences followed from his doing so; for I
have a firm belief, that this act of his had a very close
connection with his denial of his Lord.   His ardent affection for Jesus, together with his impulsive nature, led
him to follow John to the High Priest's palace, when the
Saviour was under examination.   But when he gained
an entrance, he found himself among those who had
" seen him in the garden," and that immediately recalled
to him the danger in which he stood as having been
guilty of an assault upon Malchus.   Then, there occurred
in him one of those sudden reactions from courage to
fear, which are so common in men of his temperament,
and which were not infrequent in himself.   You know
how, though he set bravely out to walk upon the water,
he very soon became afraid and began to sink ; and how
again, long after, in Antioch, though he received the Gentiles and ate with them at first, he soon resiled from that
position, and withdrew from the Pauline party, after
certain came from Jesusalem.   So here, though his courage took him to the High Priest's house ; the sight of

the servants who taunted him with having met him in
the garden, frightened him, because he knew that he had
compromised himself by his attack on Malchus. Thus,
that which had its origin in the misapprehension of the
Master's words had its culmination in his denial of
the Master himself.

A word or two now regarding the miracle itself. It is
one of the few that were performed by the Lord, without
any formal expression of desire, or exercise of faith, on
the part of him for whom it was wrought. It is exceptional, also, in the feature that it was wrought upon an
enemy, who was at the time among those who were seeking his apprehension. It is to be traced, therefore, to
the tenderness of the Saviour's heart. No doubt it was,
from another point of view, the correction of the mistake
which Peter had made—the repairing of an injury which
that Apostle had inflicted. But still that will not alter our
opinion concerning it; for the question will come back,
why did he wish that no such defence should be made of
him; and when we ask that, we get only this answer:
"The cup which my Father hath given me, shall I not
drink it?" It was his settled principle "when he suffered" to "threaten not," and to take patiently all the
indignities that were put upon him; and so when Peter,
not understanding that, sought to defend him with the
sword, he set himself at once to repair the injury which
his follower had wrought. He laid down his life of himself. He did that for human sinners; and it was his love
for them, that led him thus to heal the wound of Malchus. Love, too, for Malchus himself, if haply, through
the experience of his healing power, he might be led to
the perception of his true character, and Messianic dignity.

Observe, moreover, that there was in it also sub-

mission to his Father's will. Many of the ingredients of
the cup which he was then drinking were injuries inflicted by men who were free agents, working out their
own will, and under no restraint of any sort from God.
Yet the cup in which these ingredients were mingled
was in the Saviour's view given him by his Father.
Just as when Paul's friends found it impossible to change
his determination to go to Jerusalem, they ceased, saying, " The will of the Lord be done. " So here the Lord
accepts, as God's will concerning him, the cruel treatment
of wicked men. Now this is a way of looking at the
deeds of men as affecting us, which is very uncommon.
We recognize Providence in material things, but we are
slow to trace to it the cruelties of men. We say, as I
have heard of one saying, " If it had been a dispensation
of Providence, I could put up with it ; but to be so attacked by wicked and unreasonable men is unendurable."
As if there was no Providence in and over the actions of
men, as well as over other things. I admit that it is
hard to see how God can overrule human actions, without destroying human freedom. But very clearly here
the Saviour believed that he does so ; and the thought
that the cup which men's harsh and unjust treatment
made so bitter came ultimately from God, helped him to
take it calmly amd drink it to the dregs. Let us learn
to look thus on the enmity of men, and that will give us
patience to bear it; while at the same time it will impel
us to do good to them that hate us, as Christ did to Malchus, and to pray for those who despitefully use us, as he
also did, a little later, when in behalf of those who were
in the very act of nailing him to the cross, he said :
" Father, forgive them, for they know not what they do."
He who was so loving to his enemies, will not turn away
those who reverently, and penitently supplicate his

mercy. He who treated his adversaries so generously, must be something wonderful to his friends; and we are his friends, if we do whatsoever he commands us.

That is the great lesson of this miracle; but I cannot conclude without bidding you remark how important it is that we give the true interpretation to the Saviour's words. The expression, "He that hath no purse, let him sell his garment and buy a sword," was so perverted by Peter as to seem to him to be a command to draw the sword in defence of Christ. But in the conversation to which that clause belongs, the Lord did not mean to sanction anything of the kind. He simply wished his disciples to understand that, in the altered circumstances in which they were to be placed after his ascension, the injunctions which he had given for their guidance in their former ministry, would not apply; as a consequence, therefore, they were withdrawn and others substituted for them.

Hence it will not do to quote the instructions given to the seventy, of which this one, "Carry neither purse, nor scrip, nor shoes, and salute no man by the way," is a specimen, as if they were binding now upon us. On this point the words of Bishop Ryle seem to me signally wise, when in commenting on the passage (Luke xxii. 36) he says, "The general purport of the verse appears to be a caution against the indolent and fanatical notion that diligence in the use of means is 'carnal,' and an unlawful dependence on an arm of flesh. To my own mind the whole verse supplies an unanswerable argument against the strange notion maintained by some in the present day, who tell us that making provision for our families is wrong, and insuring our lives is wrong, and collecting money for religious societies is wrong, and studying for the work of the ministry is wrong, and taking part in civil government, is wrong; and supporting police, standing armies, and courts of law is wrong. I respect the couscientiousness of those who maintain these opinions, but I am utterly unable to reconcile them with our Lord's language in this place." *

That is an illustration, on the one side, of misinterpretation of Christ's words; but on the other, they have been equally perverted by those who have maintained that when Christ said, "He that hath no purse, let him sell his garment and buy a sword," he gave his sanction to the use of the sword in propagating and purifying the church. One might have thought that the other words which to-night have been before us: "Put up again thy sword into its place; for all they that take the sword shall perish with the sword," would have been sufficient to prevent that error. The sword has its place. I cannot say that war in every case is sinful. There have been cases in which, on one side at least, the use of the sword was justifiable, and was the only means whereby the right could be vindicated, and liberty preserved. But as far as the Church of Christ is concerned, the weapons of her warfare are not carnal, but spiritual; and it would have been well both for the church and for the world, if this truth had been more constantly remembered and acted upon.

In the hands of a persecuting state, the sword is bad enough; but it is vastly worse in those of an intolerant church. Those who, in the church, would rather perish by the sword, than defend themselves with it, have ever been its noblest ornaments; and Tertullian's words to the effect that "the blood of the martyrs is the seed of the church," have passed into a proverb. But the havoc which has been wrought by intolerant churches using the

* "Notes on the Gospels—Luke," vol. ii. p. 418.

sword for the maintenance of certain forms of doctrine, is attested alike by the Spanish Inquisition, and the fires of Smithfield.

God be thanked that we live in better days than these were ; but only by restricting the sword, and the state which wields it, to its own province, can we prevent their return. Let us see to it, therefore, that even in this free land, we look well to the great principle that is beneath our Saviour's words, for it lies at the foundations of liberty alike in the state and in the church. In the state the sword should never be used for the extension or the repression of any purely religious opinions, and in the church the sword should not be used for any purpose whatsoever, least of all for the repression of what some think to be error, or for the propagation of what others believe to be truth. Within the state, and between one country and another, the sword has its true province; but even in that it should be the last resource, and should never be drawn until every other means have been exhausted. But by the church it ought never to be drawn at all; for it is to prosper as the propagator of peace, and not the votary of war. Mohammedanism conquered by the sword. Christianity saves men, not by the spilling of *their* blood, but by the shedding *of its own.* Once again, here is the principle which we deduce from this evening's Bible study: Christians now must take all proper and constitutional measures for their support and defence ; but they must never think of spreading the gospel by the sword.

XXXII.

THE SECOND MIRACULOUS DRAUGHT OF FISHES.

John xxi. 1-16.

THE twenty-first chapter of the gospel by John, to which we are indebted for the incidents which are now to come under our review, has been commonly regarded as an appendix to the main treatise with which it is incorporated. The gospel, properly so called, seems naturally to close with the last verses of the twentieth chapter; and this other has been added, probably, with the view of authoritatively contradicting the erroneous report which had been circulated among many, to the effect that the beloved disciple, on the assurance of the Lord himself, should live until his second coming.

But, though bearing upon it the mark of having been written at a latter date than the main narrative, it has also unmistakable indications of having come from the hand of the same author. The simplicity of the style, the incidental allusions in the story, the recurrence of certain forms of expression which are frequently found in his other writings, and the personal references in the closing verses—all point to "the disciple whom Jesus loved" as the narrator; and as we pass from the body of the gospel into this epilogue, we are conscious of no such transition as that which we must have felt, had we

been going from the production of one author into that
of another. Like the side chapel in a beautiful cathe-
dral, it has certain features of distinctive excellence; but
it harmonizes so thoroughly with the main edifice as to
convince every candid observer that it is the creation of
the same architect who designed the structure to which
it is an adjunct.

The story belongs to the interval between the resurrection and ascension of our Lord; and the scene of it is
the Lake of Tiberias, with which so many sacred associations are connected. When the angel appeared unto
the women in the early morning of the world's great
Easter Day, Matthew tells us * that he said unto them,
" Go quickly, and tell his disciples that he is risen from
the dead ; and behold, he goeth before you into Galilee ;
there shall ye see him. Lo, I have told you." And when
a little later the Lord himself met them, he repeated the
commission which they had received from the angel, in
these words, " Go tell my brethren that they go into
Galilee, and there shall they see me." †

In obedience to this repeated injunction, the same
Evangelist informs us that " the eleven disciples went
away into Galilee, into a mountain where Jesus had
appointed them." ‡ These statements explain how the
disciples named by John in this chapter came to be in
the neighborhood of the Lake, with the shores of which
they were so well acquainted. There were, in all, seven
of them present on the occasion. These were Peter, James,
John himself, Nathaniel—who is usually identified with
Bartholomew—Thomas, and two others whose names
are not mentioned, and in regard to whom, therefore, all
conjecture is vain.

While they were waiting on the course of events,

* Matt. xxviii. 7.   † Matt. xxviii. 10.   ‡ *Ibid.* xxviii. 16.

Peter, wishing to fill up the time in some kind of occupation, or perhaps desiring to do something for his own support, said, "I go a fishing."

There is assuredly no ground for supposing, as some have done, that he had given up all his Messianic hopes, and was determined to go back permanently to his old employment. His purpose, rather, was to secure some temporary work, by which he might keep himself from unprofitable introspection, or vague and perhaps dangerous speculation as to what might be in the future; and the brethren who were with him immediately volunteered to accompany him. So, finding a boat, they went forth at once, starting, as they usually did on such expeditions, in the evening, because the night was the best time for fishing. But, as on a former occasion, memorable both to Peter and the sons of Zebedee, "they toiled all night and caught nothing." At length, just as the morning was breaking, they saw One, who was apparently unknown to them, standing on the shore, and heard him call to them, "Children"—or, as we might say, "Boys"— "have ye any meat?"—literally, anything to eat with bread. (Much as in these days one, coming on an angler in a stream, might ask, "Have you caught anything?") And they answered, "No." Upon this he called to them again, "Cast the net on the right side of the ship, and ye shall find."

Such a direction could hardly fail to remind them of the former occasion, when, after a night of failure, their Master had given them a similar injunction, their obedience to which had brought them signal success; and there is little doubt that the readiness of their complying with it now was prompted by their remembrance of their experience then. They cast their net, therefore, at once; and they were not able to draw it for the multitude of fishes. In a moment, the keen insight of John having detected the presence of their Master, he whispered to Peter, "It is the Lord." And that Apostle, with his wonted impetuosity, girt about him his upper coat which he had laid aside while he was working, leaped into the lake, and either swam or waded to the shore in his eager haste to be the first to do homage at his feet. With greater deliberation, that they might save all the fish, the others came in the boat, dragging after them the net, which they ultimately pulled on to the shore; and when they landed, they perceived, already provided—how they knew not, and we need not inquire—" a fire of coals, and fish thereon, and bread." In the most natural way possible, the Lord—for it was indeed he—requested them to bring of the fish which they had caught. So Peter went to examine the haul, and found an hundred and fifty-three great fishes, and discovered also that " for all there were so many, the net was not broken." Then at the invitation of the Lord, they partook of a simple repast, the richest feature of which was the presence of their Master, for though they were so filled with reverence and awe at the sight of one who had risen from the dead that they did not dare to question him as to his identity, they knew that it was Jesus. And so, for the third time, Jesus thus showed himself to his disciples as a company, after his resurrection. I say, " showed himself," for nothing seems to be clearer in the glimpses which, through the Evangelists, we get of the risen Christ, in their histories of the forty days between his Resurrection and Ascension, than the fact that his appearances to his disciples were as really the result of his own volition as of their perception.

He is the same Jesus that he was before the crucifixion, and yet a marvellous change has passed upon him, and everything about him seems to be transfigured. His body had still upon it the marks of the spear gash and the nails; he could eat the broiled fish and the honeycomb which the disciples set before him; and one word uttered by him in the familiar voice startled Mary into the recognition of her Master. But then on the other hand, he appeared and disappeared with mysterious suddenness. He came no one could tell whence; he went, no one could tell whither. He entered a room the doors of which were closed and stood in the midst of the apostles, and at last, as if to show that the body of his resurrection was not " subject to the laws of the material order to which his earthly life had been previously conformed," he rose in the air until a cloud received him out of the sight of the spectators. Then we have to mark a similar change in the manner of his fellowship with his disciples. He was no longer with them precisely as he had been before. As Westcott has said,* " The continuity, the intimacy, the simple familiarity of former intercourse is gone. He is seen and recognized only as he wills, and when he wills." His disciples " have, it appears, no longer a natural power of recognizing him. Feeling and thought require to be purified and enlightened in order that he may be known under the conditions of earthly life. There is a mysterious awfulness about his Person which first inspires fear, and then claims adoration. He appointed a place of meeting with his apostles, but he did not accompany them on their journey. He belongs already to another realm, so that the ascension only ratifies and presents in a final form the lessons of the forty days in which it is included."

Now if we bear all this in mind, we shall begin to understand, that his appearances to his disciples, and inter-

* " The Revelation of the Resurrection," p. 8.

views with them during these forty days, were designed
to give them a foretaste of their future life as his servants
on earth during his absence in heaven, and so to prepare
them for that life. It is from this point of view, therefore, that we must look at the miracle which is now before
us.

The former miracle, to which this bears so much
resemblance, was performed at the calling of the first
apostles, and was designed to qualify them for the service of Christ while he should continue with them on the
earth. But that which we are now considering was
wrought on the very threshold of his ascension, and was a
symbolical representation to them of the character of the
work which they were to carry on, and of the experiences through which they were to pass, after he had
gone from them into heaven. This miracle, therefore,
has, like the other signs which Christ gave, a parabolical
significance. In saying that, however, I do not mean to
give any sanction to all the allegorical interpretations
which have been given to its details, but rather to insist
that in its distinctive features it had a symbolical meaning.

To say, as some have done, that there is a mystic
meaning in the number of the fishes, is little better than
trifling with the record; but to affirm with others that
there is here no symbolism whatever, is to run into the
opposite extreme, and miss the purpose of the miracle as
a sign. Now, to get at that in this instance, it may be
well to note the differences between the former miraculous draught of fishes and this of which the fourth Evangelist has given us the record. In the first the disciples
had gone out of their boat, and were washing their nets;
so that he had to ask them to launch out into the deep,
and let down their nets for a draught; in this they were

still in the ship, and presumably also on the fishing-ground ; in that there was a discourse to the people, delivered before the miracle ; in this no discourse or conversation of any extent was entered upon until after the miracle ; in that the command was general, "Launch out into the deep, and let down your nets for a draught" ; in this it was specific, " Cast the net on the right side of the ship, and ye shall find " ; in that there was an appearance of constraint, or at least of overcome reluctance in the answer of Peter, "Master, we have toiled all the night, and have taken nothing ; nevertheless at thy word I will let down the net " ; in this there was unquestioning promptitude in the obedience of the disciples, " They cast, therefore, and were not able to draw it for the multitude of fishes ; " in that the net was breaking with the weight of the haul ; in this, " for all there were so many, yet was not the net broken " ; in that the net with the fishes was lifted into the boat, and so great was the take that two boats were needed to hold it, and even then they began to sink ; in that Peter was so overwhelmed with the perception of the glory of the miracle worker that " he fell down at Jesus' knees, saying, Depart from me, for I am a sinful man, O Lord ; " in this he was so overjoyed at the presence of his Master, that he flung himself into the lake, and hastened to the shore, that he might do homage before him ; after that the Lord said unto his followers, " Fear not, from henceforth I will make you fishers of men ; " after this the Lord prepared a repast for the fishermen, and renewed his commission to Peter, " Feed my sheep."

Now as the general character of the miracles, which in both cases was the getting of a large draught of fishes at the word of Christ, is the same, and the first was undeniably symbolical of their ministry as a catching of

men, we cannot doubt that the second had to do with
the ministry which now under the dispensation of the
Spirit, and in the absence of Christ, they were about to
begin, and if that view be accepted then the differences
in the second from the first must be regarded as indications of those between their experience as apostles after
Christ's ascension, and as disciples during his earthly
life.

And without seeking to find a meaning in every one
of these differences, let me turn attention to one or two
of them which seem to be of special importance. The
first is that now in the dispensation of the ascension, the
presence of Christ with his people is to be known not
by the sight of his visible personality, but by inference
from the effects produced by his workings among them.
As he stood on the shore, they knew not that it was he,
but when John felt the weight of the net with the fishes,
he said, " It is the Lord," a conviction which was immediately shared by Peter, and ultimately also by all the
rest. So now when Christ is with us we know it not by
the sight of the eye, or by the hearing of the ear, but by
inference from the results of his operations in us and
through us. He was as really with them on the day of
Pentecost as he was here by the Lake of Tiberias—they
knew it, they felt it, though they did not see him with
the bodily eye ; and though he was not recognized by any
of the multitude. So we find that in the Book of the Acts
the author represents the things wrought by the apostles
as a continuance of those which before his death Jesus
began both to do and to teach.*

The apostles recognized that their miracles were
wrought not by their own power or holiness,† but by him

* Acts i. 1.   † Acts iii. 13.

whom the Jews had crucified, but whom God had raised up; and when a great multitude believed on Christ as the result of their preaching, they knew that they did so because the Lord was giving testimony to the words of his grace. As Westcott has said of the reasoning of John in the case of the miracle which we have been considering, "Tried by the ordinary process of reasoning, the conclusion was precarious. But there is a logic of the soul which deals with questions of the higher life, and John trusted that he recognized the insight, the power, the love which belonged to one only. And when the truth found utterance, the others acknowledged it. "In the same way we are now to recognize the presence of the Lord Jesus with us. When our hearts burn within us as we study the sacred Scriptures ; when our spirits are soothed, refreshed, inspired, and strengthened as we turn in prayer to God; when the words which we speak in his name are followed by results as astonishing to ourselves as they are to those who behold them,—then we too may say with John, " It is the Lord," and rejoice in the assurance that he is in the midst of us indeed. To borrow again the words of Westcott, " This miracle teaches us to know Christ, both in the history of the church, and in the brief course of our own lives, by the blessings which follow obedience to his word. It appears that even to the last the disciples ' knew the Lord ' only through the interpretation which they put upon their own experience. Not till afterwards, did Christ speak so as to show himself to them in word. The meal, as it seems, was eaten in silence. No thanksgiving was pronounced. The revelation was clear to the seeing heart. Without patient obedience, without cheerful labor, without loving insight, those to whom the Lord came would not have known him. He would have been to them only as one more chance wayfarer who had crossed their path. This is the uniform law. 'The world beholdeth me no more, but ye behold me,' is the final promise to the faithful. At his first miracle Christ manifested his glory and *his disciples*—his disciples and not others—believed on him. Here at his last miracle he *manifested himself*, he *was manifested*, according to his pleasure; and faith apprehended him. It was in vain that his brethren, in a moment of unbelief bade him manifest himself to the world. From the world which has not the will to obey, or the eye to see, the true Christ, the risen Christ, must be always hidden." * If, therefore, we desire the presence of Christ with us, let us obey him, and let us not expect him in visible form; but let us be content to recognize him through the effects which he produces.

A second thing taught us by this miracle is, that the ascended Christ sends us on no unsuccessful errand when he bids us go and preach his gospel to all nations. To the promise, "I will make you fishers of men," is now added the command, "Go into all the world and preach the gospel to every creature," and here, in the draught of great fishes which was drawn up on the shore of the Galilean lake, we have the assurance, the foretoken, and the prophecy, that in obeying that command, we shall not spend our labor in vain. We shall have abundant success ; such success as shall constrain us to say, "It is the Lord,"—fulfilling the promise which in the moment of his ascension, and seemingly so inconsistent with his ascension, he made to his followers : "Lo, I am with you alway, even unto the end of the world."

And has not this symbolic prophecy been gloriously fulfilled ? Read the letters of our modern evangelists and missionaries, and you will see. Wherever they have

* "The Revelation of the Resurrection," pp. 117-118.

gone and proclaimed his truth, he has been with them; and though sometimes they have had times of waiting, like the night which to these apostles preceded the success of the morning, they have been ultimately instrumental in turning multitudes to righteousness, and from the power of Satan unto God. Bear witness Judson among the Karens, Moffat among the Hottentots, Lindley among the Zulus, Scudder among the men of Arcot, and Morrison and Burns, and many more, among the Chinese. No faithful worker who is obedient unto Christ and faithful to his calling, will go without his netful at the last. This word, " Cast the net on the right side of the ship, and ye shall find," stands for all time, and will surely be made good. The success of the missionary enterprise is no mere peradventure. It is as sure as promise and prophecy can make it. The power of the Saviour is not now a thing to be put to the test of experiment; it is a matter of experience. Wherever the net is cast in faith and loyalty to him, the Saviour, though we may not know him at the moment, is standing on the shore, and by his omnipotent grace and spirit he will fill it abundantly. Not therefore to his want of efficacy, but to our own lack of consecration to himself and obedience to his command, must we trace the fact that so large a portion of our race has not yet heard the good news of his salvation. Let us then repent of these things and give ourselves with all Peter's enthusiasm t t. rord whereunto the Lord hath called us.

In the last place, we are reminded here of the reward of those who are obedient to Christ, in laboring for the salvation of men. Not only are they successful in that labor, which itself is a great joy, but Christ prepares for them a feast when their work is done. This repast on the lake shore, is to me a foregleam of heaven. It tells the faithful worker in the furtherance of the gospel, that when he has attained the heavenly land :

> " Christ shall the banquet spread,
> With his own royal hand,
> And raise his faithful servant's head,
> Amid the angelic band,"

And who may attempt to describe the rapture of such an experience ? To hear the " Well done !" of the Lord ; to have our own heaven multiplied for us by that of those whom we have been the means of saving : to enjoy the fellowship of the Blessed Lord, in that special and peculiar sense which is symbolized by the white stone having on it " the new name written which no man knoweth saving he that receiveth it." These things and others like these await all those who have patiently continued here, in obediently working for the Lord, and patiently waiting for his coming. My brethren, let us endeavor to secure that when the morning of eternity dawns upon us, we shall see Christ standing thus on the shore of heaven ready to welcome us, according to his promise in these extraordinary words : " Blessed are those servants whom the Lord when he cometh shall find watching : Verily I say unto you, that he shall gird himself and make them to sit down to meat, and will come forth and serve them."

Printed in the United States
18089LVS00005B/1-30